BARAKAMON

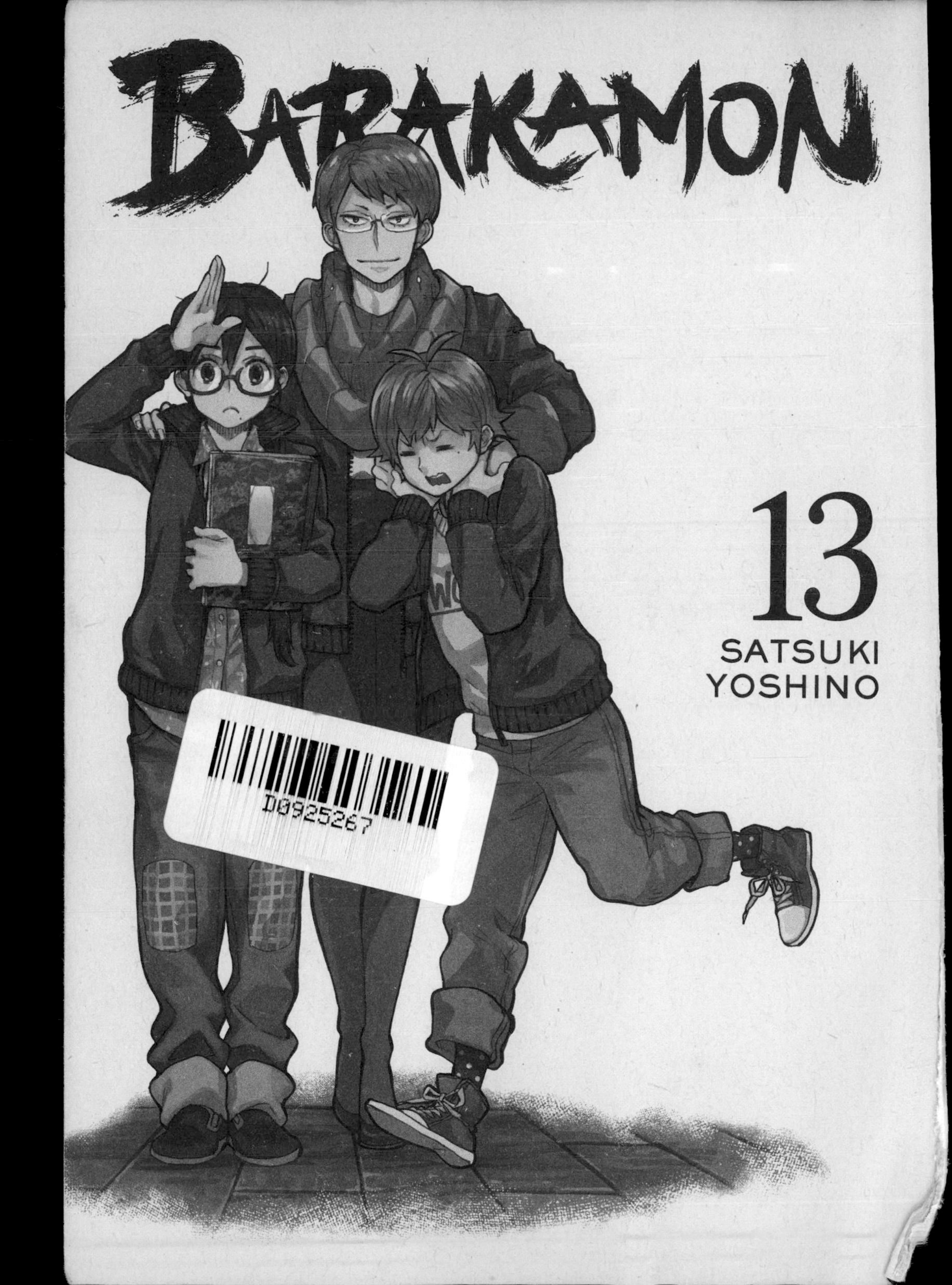

13

SATSUKI YOSHINO

Contents

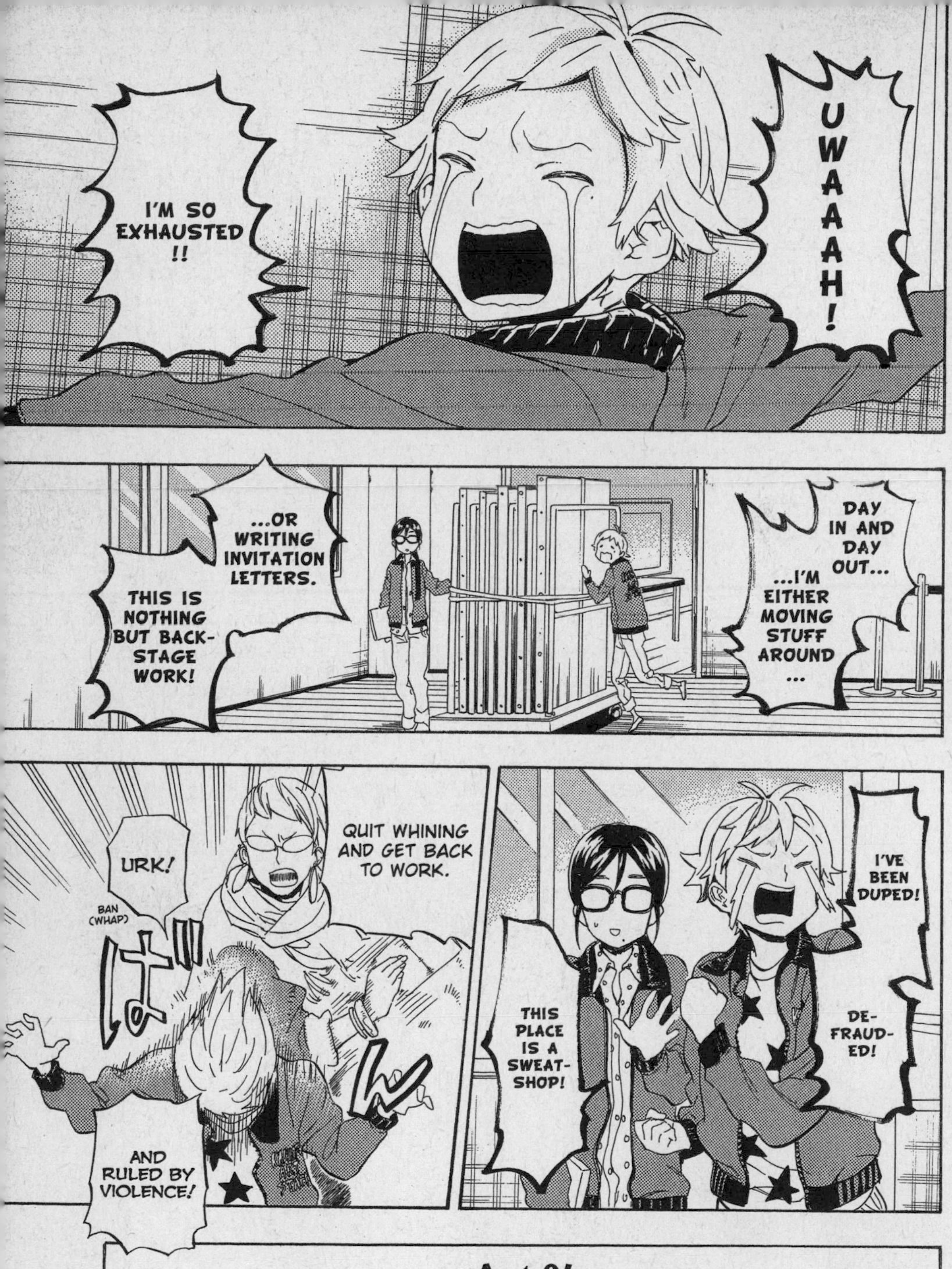
UWAAAAH!
I'M SO EXHAUSTED!!
DAY IN AND DAY OUT...
...I'M EITHER MOVING STUFF AROUND...
...OR WRITING INVITATION LETTERS.
THIS IS NOTHING BUT BACK-STAGE WORK!
I'VE BEEN DUPED!
DE-FRAUD-ED!
THIS PLACE IS A SWEAT-SHOP!
QUIT WHINING AND GET BACK TO WORK.
URK!
BAN (WHAP)
AND RULED BY VIOLENCE!

Act.94

WE'RE GOING TO TOKYO!

[Translation: Tokyo ni Ikken]

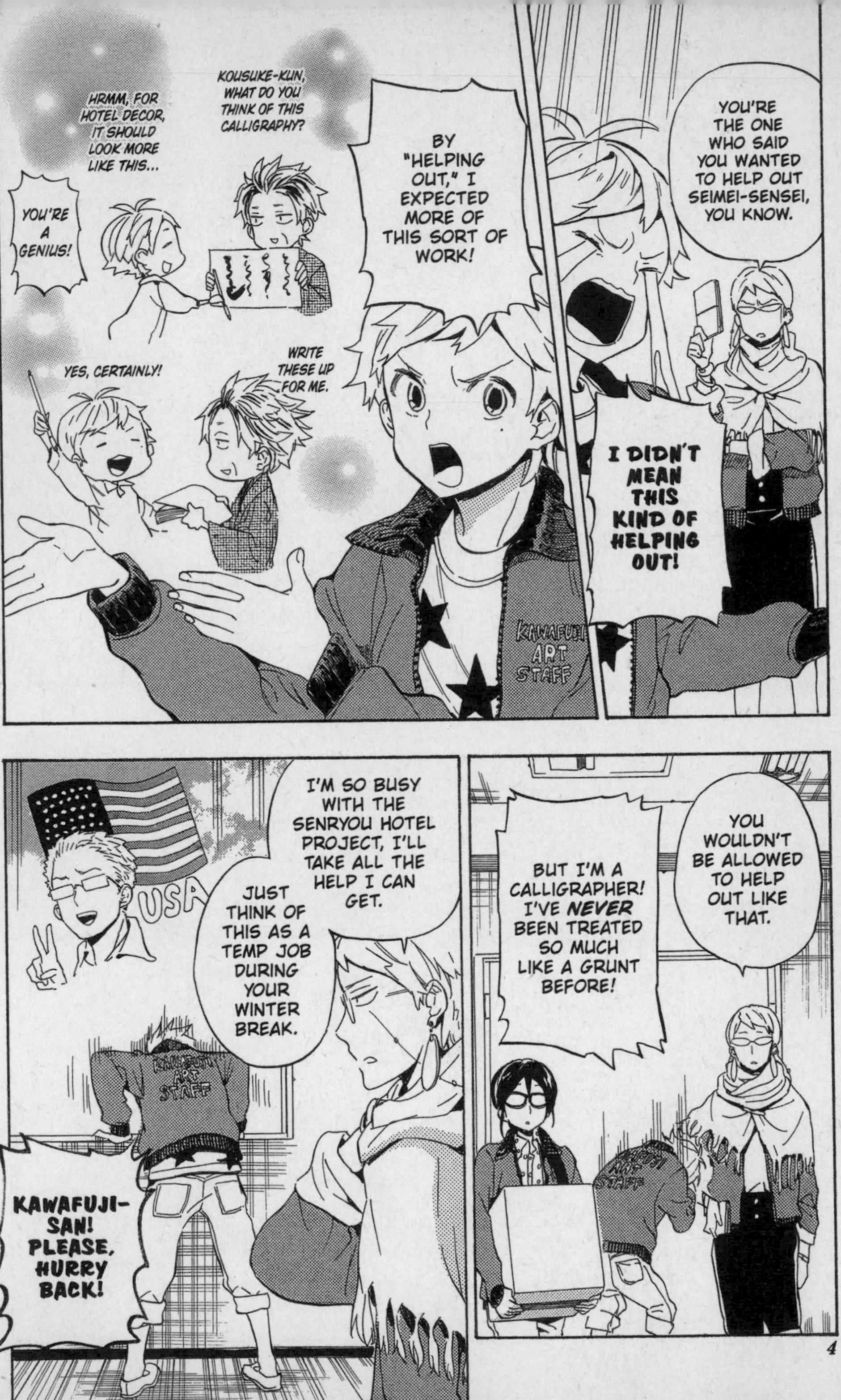
YOU'RE THE ONE WHO SAID YOU WANTED TO HELP OUT SEIMEI-SENSEI, YOU KNOW.
I DIDN'T MEAN THIS KIND OF HELPING OUT!
BY "HELPING OUT," I EXPECTED MORE OF THIS SORT OF WORK!
KOUSUKE-KUN, WHAT DO YOU THINK OF THIS CALLIGRAPHY?
HRMM, FOR HOTEL DECOR, IT SHOULD LOOK MORE LIKE THIS...
YOU'RE A GENIUS!
WRITE THESE UP FOR ME.
YES, CERTAINLY!
KAWAFUJI ART STAFF
YOU WOULDN'T BE ALLOWED TO HELP OUT LIKE THAT.
BUT I'M A CALLIGRAPHER! I'VE *NEVER* BEEN TREATED SO MUCH LIKE A GRUNT BEFORE!
I'M SO BUSY WITH THE SENRYOU HOTEL PROJECT, I'LL TAKE ALL THE HELP I CAN GET.
JUST THINK OF THIS AS A TEMP JOB DURING YOUR WINTER BREAK.
USA
KAWAFUJI ART STAFF
KAWAFUJI-SAN! PLEASE, HURRY BACK!

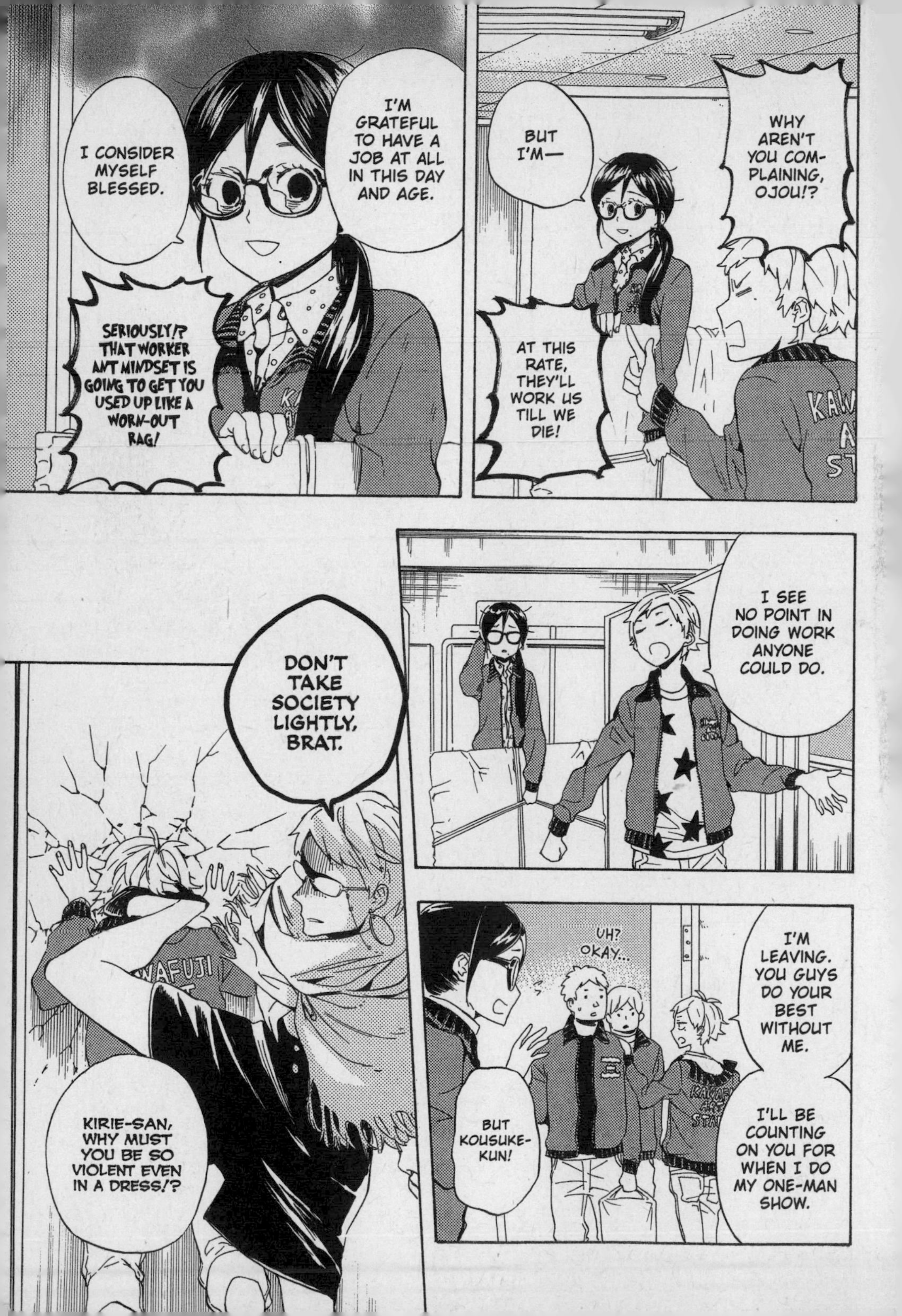
WHY AREN'T YOU COMPLAINING, OJOU!?
BUT I'M—
AT THIS RATE, THEY'LL WORK US TILL WE DIE!
I'M GRATEFUL TO HAVE A JOB AT ALL IN THIS DAY AND AGE.
I CONSIDER MYSELF BLESSED.
SERIOUSLY!? THAT WORKER ANT MINDSET IS GOING TO GET YOU USED UP LIKE A WORN-OUT RAG!
I SEE NO POINT IN DOING WORK ANYONE COULD DO.
I'M LEAVING. YOU GUYS DO YOUR BEST WITHOUT ME.
UH? OKAY...
I'LL BE COUNTING ON YOU FOR WHEN I DO MY ONE-MAN SHOW.
BUT KOUSUKE-KUN!
DON'T TAKE SOCIETY LIGHTLY, BRAT.
KIRIE-SAN, WHY MUST YOU BE SO VIOLENT EVEN IN A DRESS!?

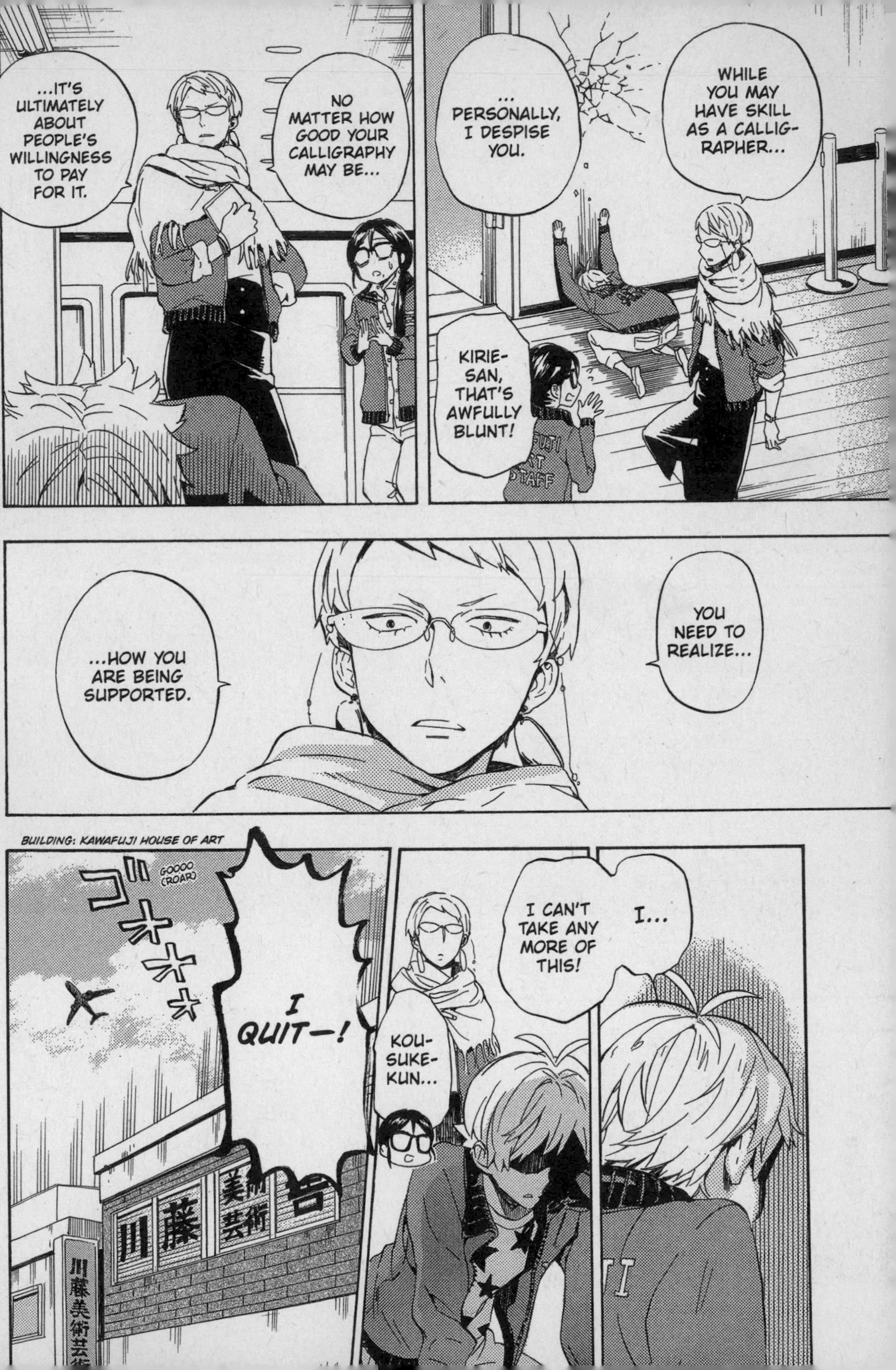
WHILE YOU MAY HAVE SKILL AS A CALLIG-RAPHER...
...PERSONALLY, I DESPISE YOU.
KIRIE-SAN, THAT'S AWFULLY BLUNT!
NO MATTER HOW GOOD YOUR CALLIGRAPHY MAY BE...
...IT'S ULTIMATELY ABOUT PEOPLE'S WILLINGNESS TO PAY FOR IT.
YOU NEED TO REALIZE...
...HOW YOU ARE BEING SUPPORTED.
BUILDING: KAWAFUJI HOUSE OF ART
I...
I CAN'T TAKE ANY MORE OF THIS!
KOU-SUKE-KUN...
I QUIT—!
GOOOO (ROAR)
ゴオオオ
川藤 美術芸術

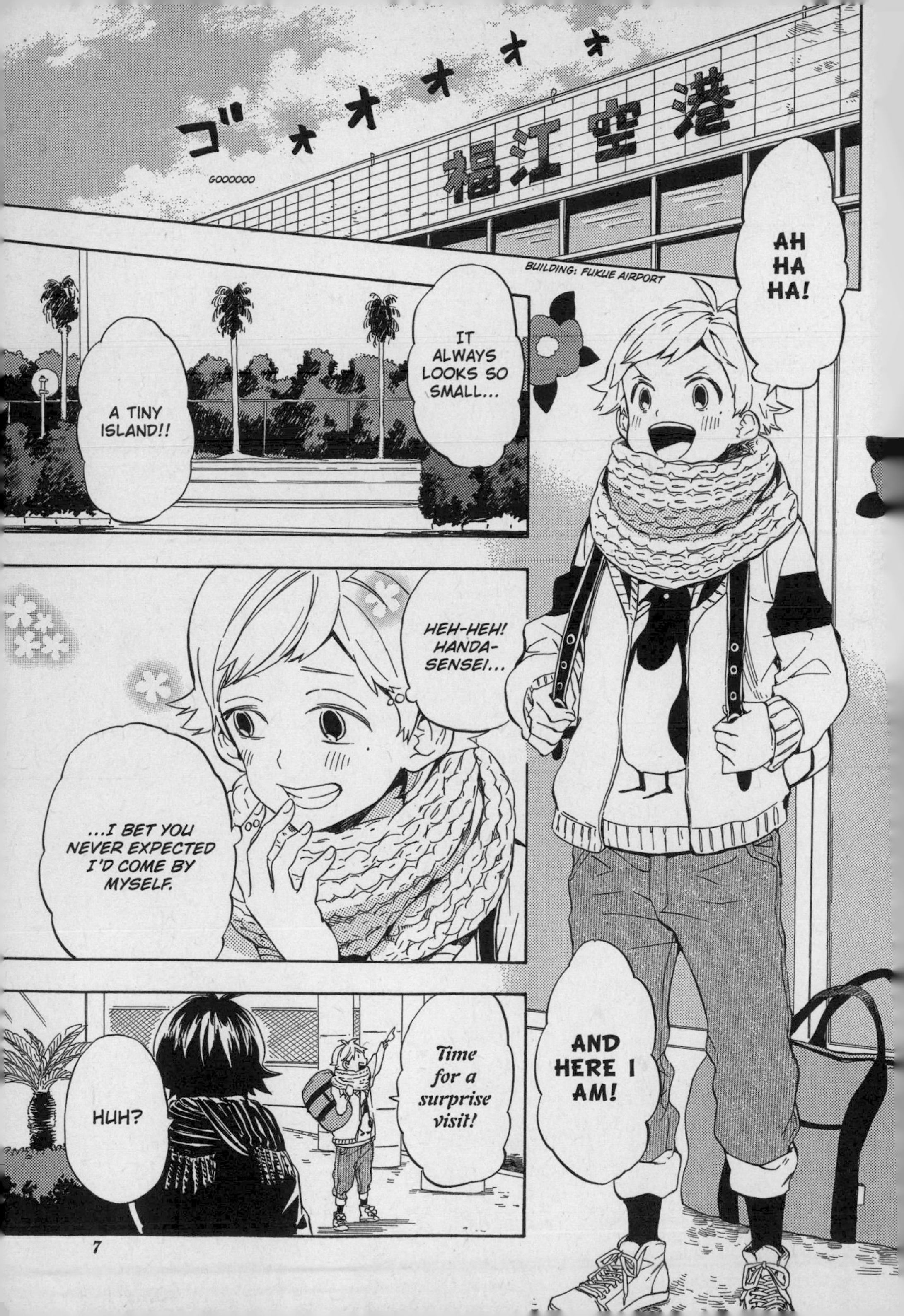
ゴォオオオオ
GOOOOOO
福江空港
BUILDING: FUKUE AIRPORT
AH HA HA!
AND HERE I AM!
IT ALWAYS LOOKS SO SMALL...
A TINY ISLAND!!
HEH-HEH! HANDA-SENSEI...
...I BET YOU NEVER EXPECTED I'D COME BY MYSELF.
Time for a surprise visit!
HUH?

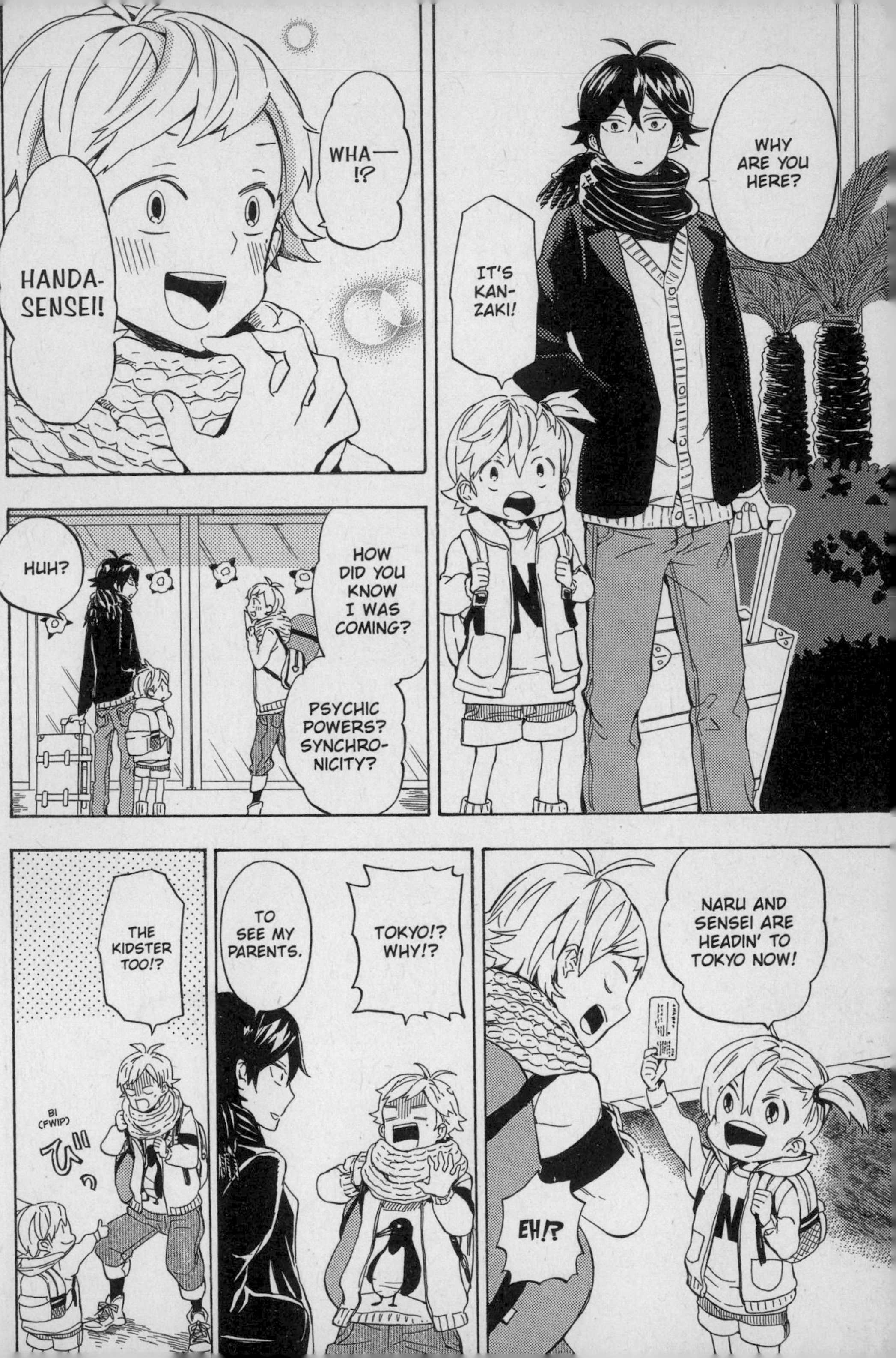
WHY ARE YOU HERE?
IT'S KAN-ZAKI!
WHA—!?
HANDA-SENSEI!
HOW DID YOU KNOW I WAS COMING?
PSYCHIC POWERS? SYNCHRO-NICITY?
HUH?
NARU AND SENSEI ARE HEADIN' TO TOKYO NOW!
EH!?
TOKYO!? WHY!?
TO SEE MY PARENTS.
THE KIDSTER TOO!?
BI (FWIP)

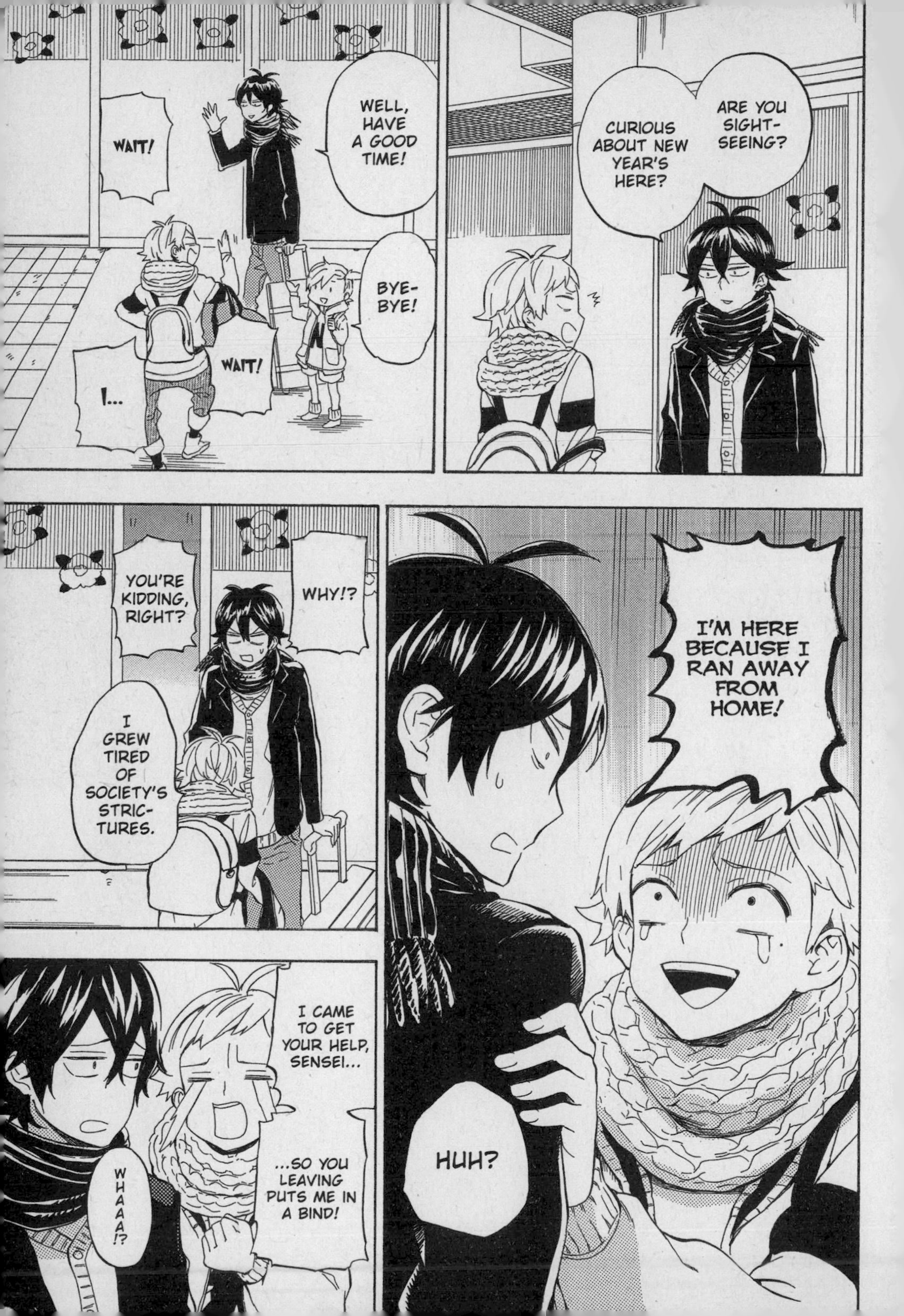
ARE YOU SIGHT-SEEING?
CURIOUS ABOUT NEW YEAR'S HERE?
WELL, HAVE A GOOD TIME!
BYE-BYE!
WAIT!
WAIT!
I...
I'M HERE BECAUSE I RAN AWAY FROM HOME!
HUH?
WHY!?
YOU'RE KIDDING, RIGHT?
I GREW TIRED OF SOCIETY'S STRICTURES.
I CAME TO GET YOUR HELP, SENSEI...
...SO YOU LEAVING PUTS ME IN A BIND!
WHAAAA!?

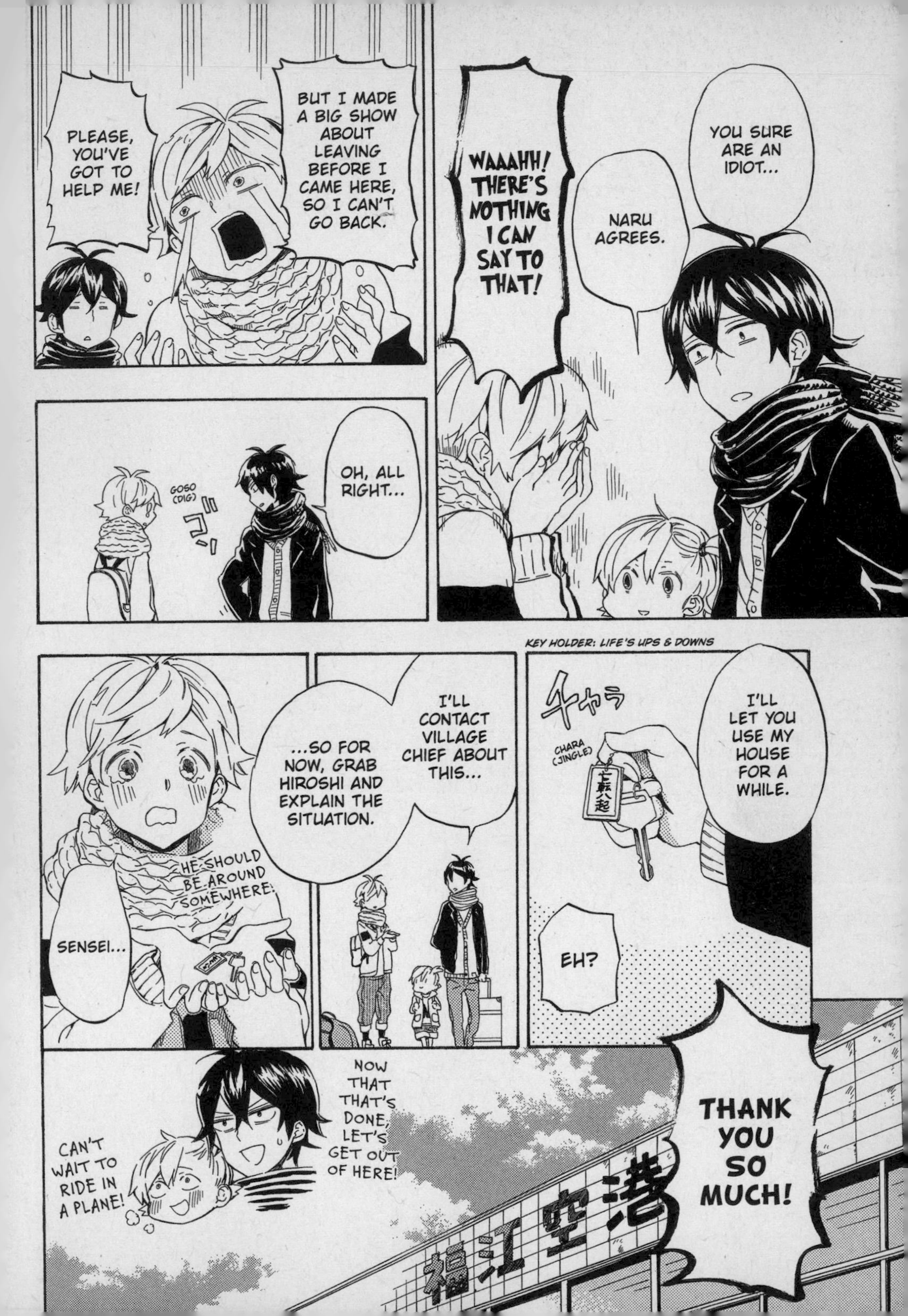
YOU SURE ARE AN IDIOT...
NARU AGREES.
WAAAHH! THERE'S NOTHING I CAN SAY TO THAT!
BUT I MADE A BIG SHOW ABOUT LEAVING BEFORE I CAME HERE, SO I CAN'T GO BACK.
PLEASE, YOU'VE GOT TO HELP ME!
OH, ALL RIGHT...
GOSO (DIG)
ゴソ
KEY HOLDER: LIFE'S UPS & DOWNS
I'LL LET YOU USE MY HOUSE FOR A WHILE.
チャラ
CHARA (JINGLE)
EH?
I'LL CONTACT VILLAGE CHIEF ABOUT THIS...
...SO FOR NOW, GRAB HIROSHI AND EXPLAIN THE SITUATION.
HE SHOULD BE AROUND SOMEWHERE.
SENSEI...
THANK YOU SO MUCH!
福江空港
NOW THAT THAT'S DONE, LET'S GET OUT OF HERE!
CAN'T WAIT TO RIDE IN A PLANE!

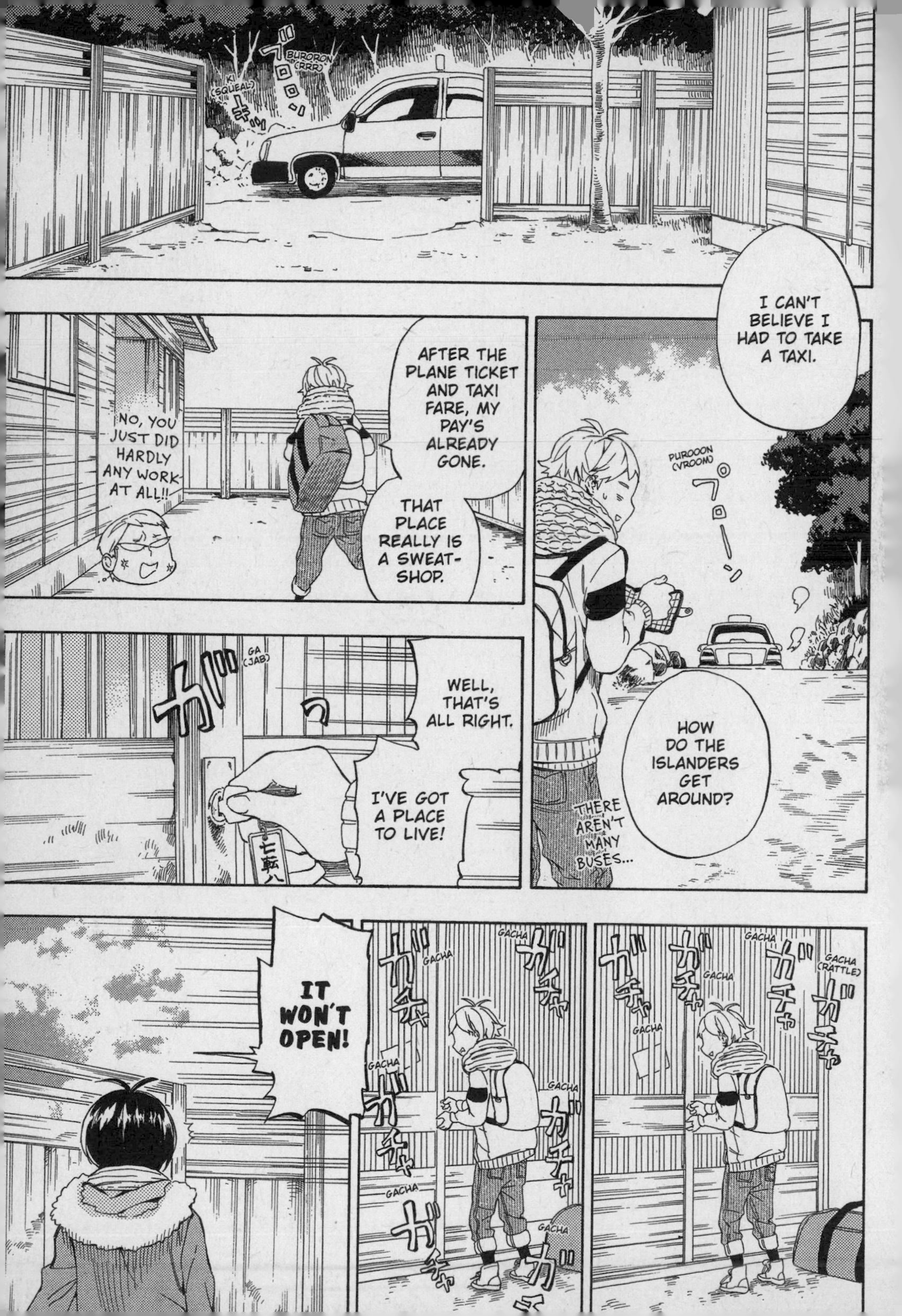
BURORON (RRR)
KI (SQUEAL)
I CAN'T BELIEVE I HAD TO TAKE A TAXI.
PUROOON (VROOM)
HOW DO THE ISLANDERS GET AROUND?
THERE AREN'T MANY BUSES...
AFTER THE PLANE TICKET AND TAXI FARE, MY PAY'S ALREADY GONE.
THAT PLACE REALLY IS A SWEAT-SHOP.
NO, YOU JUST DID HARDLY ANY WORK AT ALL!!
GA (JAB)
WELL, THAT'S ALL RIGHT.
I'VE GOT A PLACE TO LIVE!
七転八
GACHA (RATTLE)
GACHA
GACHA
GACHA
GACHA
GACHA
GACHA
GACHA
GACHA
GACHA
IT WON'T OPEN!

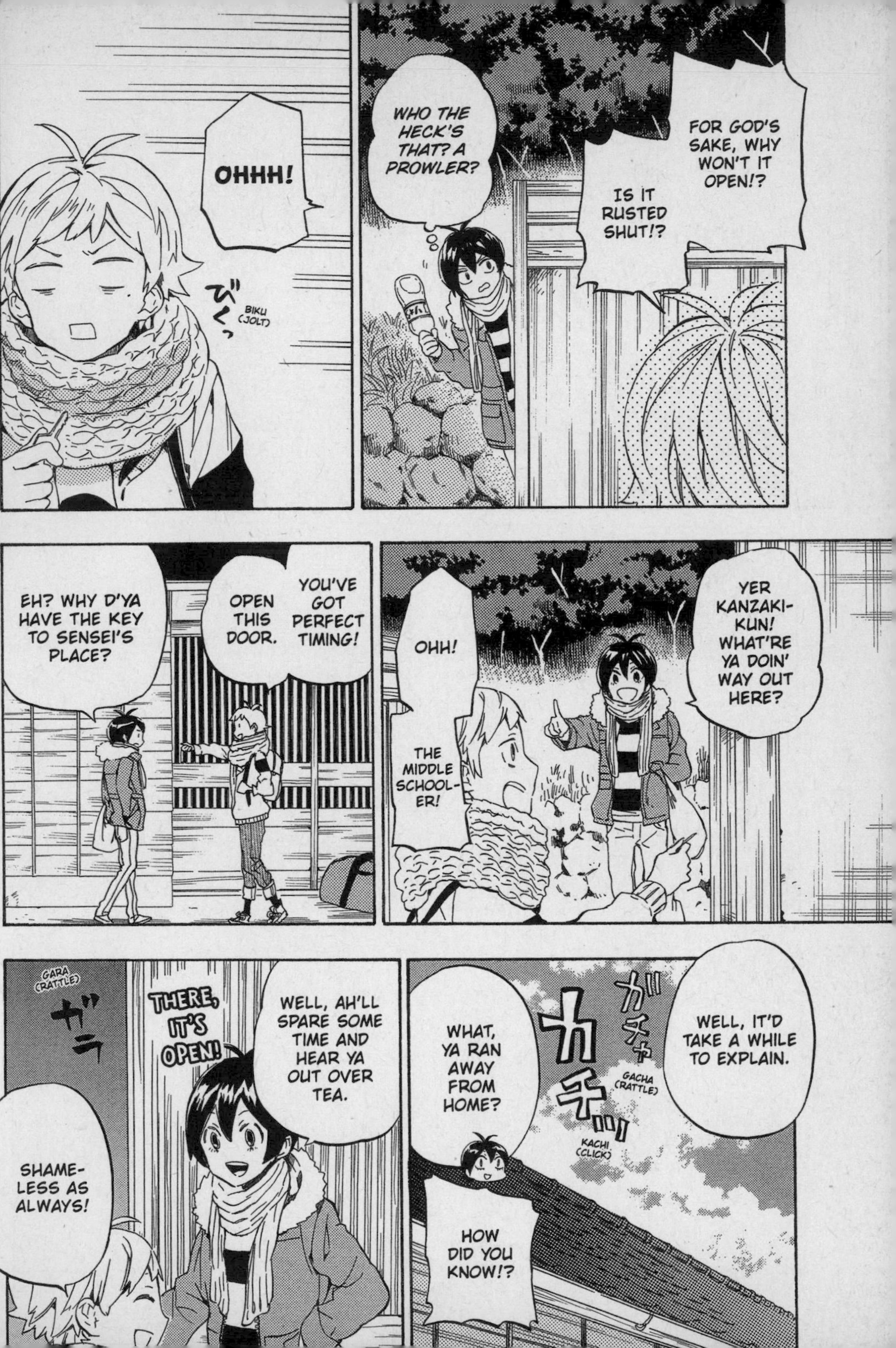
FOR GOD'S SAKE, WHY WON'T IT OPEN!?
IS IT RUSTED SHUT!?
WHO THE HECK'S THAT? A PROWLER?
OHHH!
BIKU (JOLT)
YER KANZAKI-KUN! WHAT'RE YA DOIN' WAY OUT HERE?
OHH!
THE MIDDLE SCHOOL-ER!
YOU'VE GOT PERFECT TIMING!
OPEN THIS DOOR.
EH? WHY D'YA HAVE THE KEY TO SENSEI'S PLACE?
WELL, IT'D TAKE A WHILE TO EXPLAIN.
GACHA (RATTLE)
KACHI (CLICK)
WHAT, YA RAN AWAY FROM HOME?
HOW DID YOU KNOW!?
GARA (RATTLE)
THERE, IT'S OPEN!
WELL, AH'LL SPARE SOME TIME AND HEAR YA OUT OVER TEA.
SHAME-LESS AS ALWAYS!

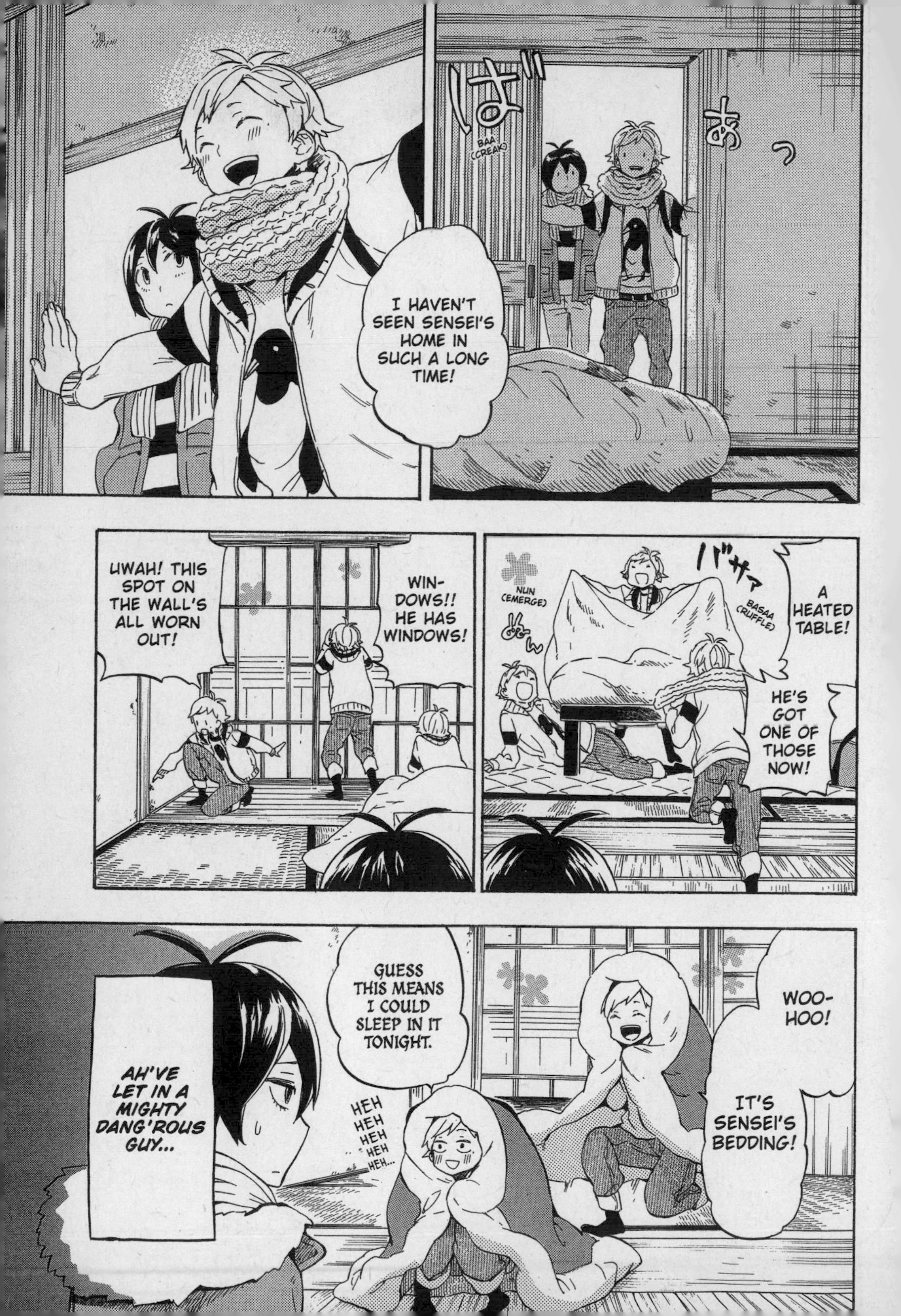
ばあっ
BAA (CREAK)
I HAVEN'T SEEN SENSEI'S HOME IN SUCH A LONG TIME!
バサァ
BASAA (RUFFLE)
A HEATED TABLE!
ぬん
NUN (EMERGE)
HE'S GOT ONE OF THOSE NOW!
WIN-DOWS!! HE HAS WINDOWS!
UWAH! THIS SPOT ON THE WALL'S ALL WORN OUT!
WOO-HOO!
IT'S SENSEI'S BEDDING!
GUESS THIS MEANS I COULD SLEEP IN IT TONIGHT.
HEH HEH HEH HEH HEH...
AH'VE LET IN A MIGHTY DANG'ROUS GUY...

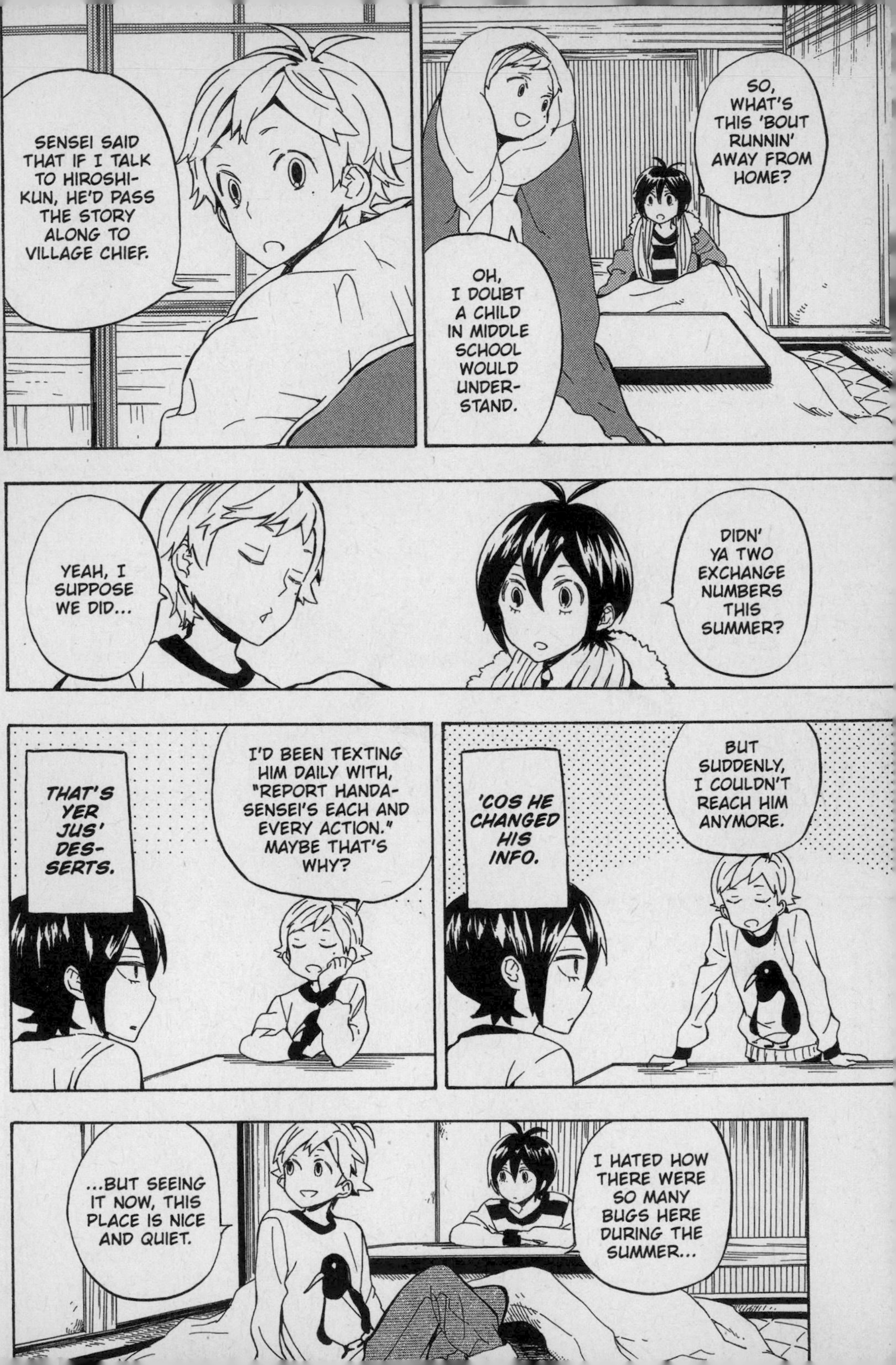
SO, WHAT'S THIS 'BOUT RUNNIN' AWAY FROM HOME?
OH, I DOUBT A CHILD IN MIDDLE SCHOOL WOULD UNDER-STAND.
SENSEI SAID THAT IF I TALK TO HIROSHI-KUN, HE'D PASS THE STORY ALONG TO VILLAGE CHIEF.
DIDN' YA TWO EXCHANGE NUMBERS THIS SUMMER?
YEAH, I SUPPOSE WE DID...
BUT SUDDENLY, I COULDN'T REACH HIM ANYMORE.
'COS HE CHANGED HIS INFO.
I'D BEEN TEXTING HIM DAILY WITH, "REPORT HANDA-SENSEI'S EACH AND EVERY ACTION." MAYBE THAT'S WHY?
THAT'S YER JUS' DES-SERTS.
I HATED HOW THERE WERE SO MANY BUGS HERE DURING THE SUMMER...
...BUT SEEING IT NOW, THIS PLACE IS NICE AND QUIET.

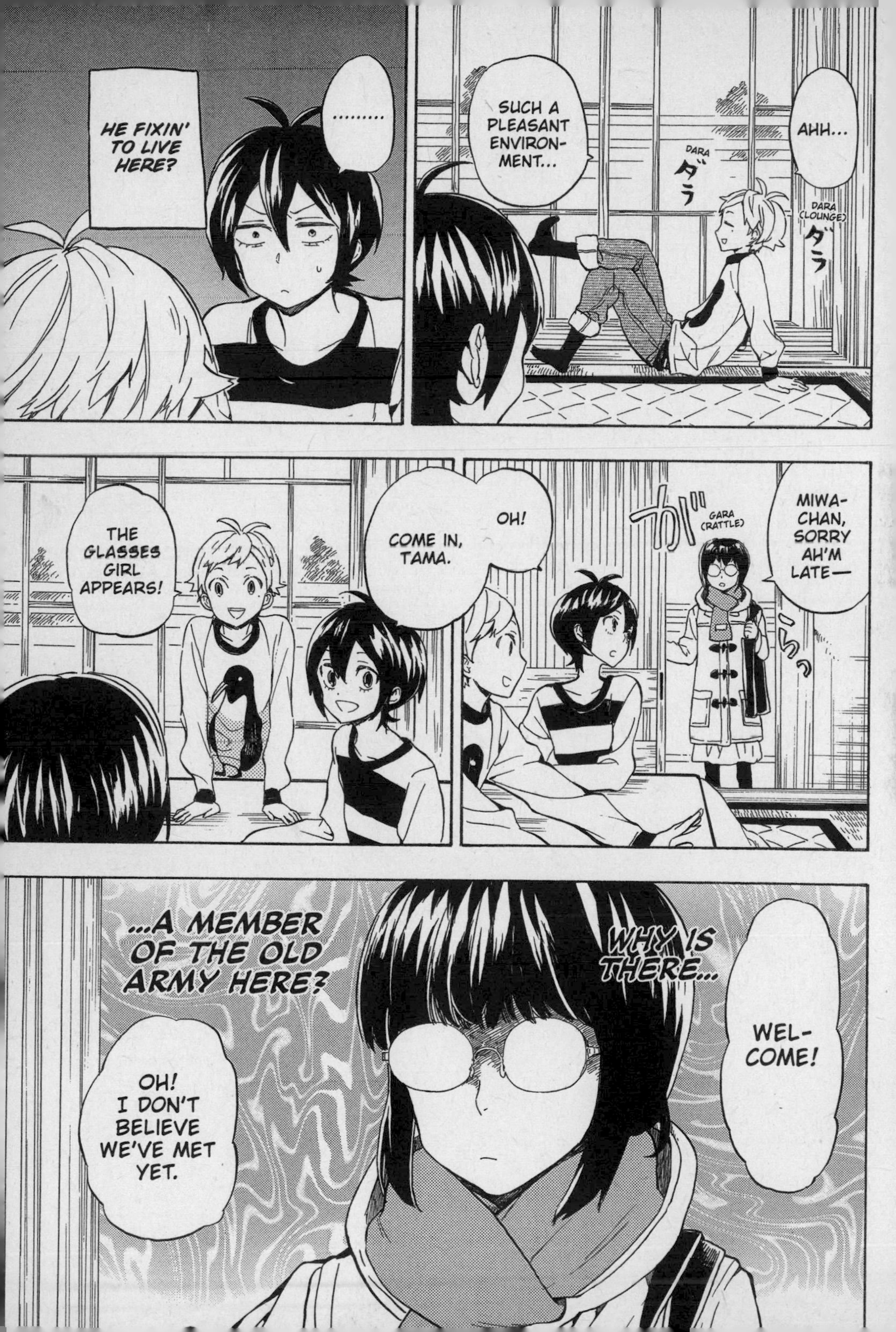
AHH...
DARA
ダラ
DARA (LOUNGE)
ダラ
SUCH A PLEASANT ENVIRON-MENT...
....
HE FIXIN' TO LIVE HERE?
MIWA-CHAN, SORRY AH'M LATE—
GARA (RATTLE)
OH!
COME IN, TAMA.
THE GLASSES GIRL APPEARS!
WEL-COME!
WHY IS THERE...
...A MEMBER OF THE OLD ARMY HERE?
OH! I DON'T BELIEVE WE'VE MET YET.

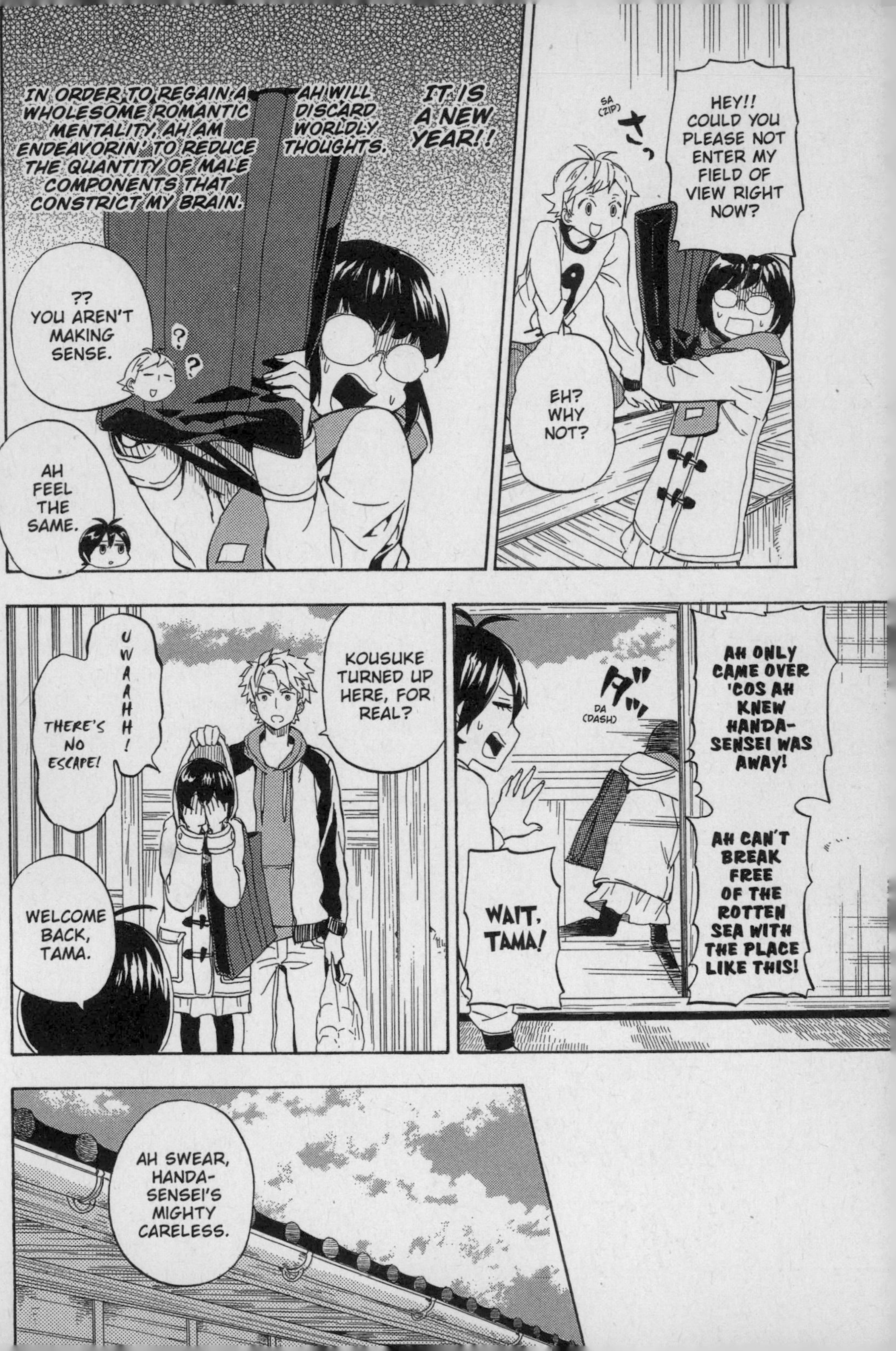
SA (ZIP)
さっ
HEY!! COULD YOU PLEASE NOT ENTER MY FIELD OF VIEW RIGHT NOW?
EH? WHY NOT?
IT IS A NEW YEAR!!
AH WILL DISCARD WORLDLY THOUGHTS.
IN ORDER TO REGAIN A WHOLESOME ROMANTIC MENTALITY, AH AM ENDEAVORIN' TO REDUCE THE QUANTITY OF MALE COMPONENTS THAT CONSTRICT MY BRAIN.
?? YOU AREN'T MAKING SENSE.
? ?
AH FEEL THE SAME.
AH ONLY CAME OVER 'COS AH KNEW HANDA-SENSEI WAS AWAY!
AH CAN'T BREAK FREE OF THE ROTTEN SEA WITH THE PLACE LIKE THIS!
DA (DASH)
ダッ
WAIT, TAMA!
KOUSUKE TURNED UP HERE, FOR REAL?
UWAAHH!
THERE'S NO ESCAPE!
WELCOME BACK, TAMA.
AH SWEAR, HANDA-SENSEI'S MIGHTY CARELESS.

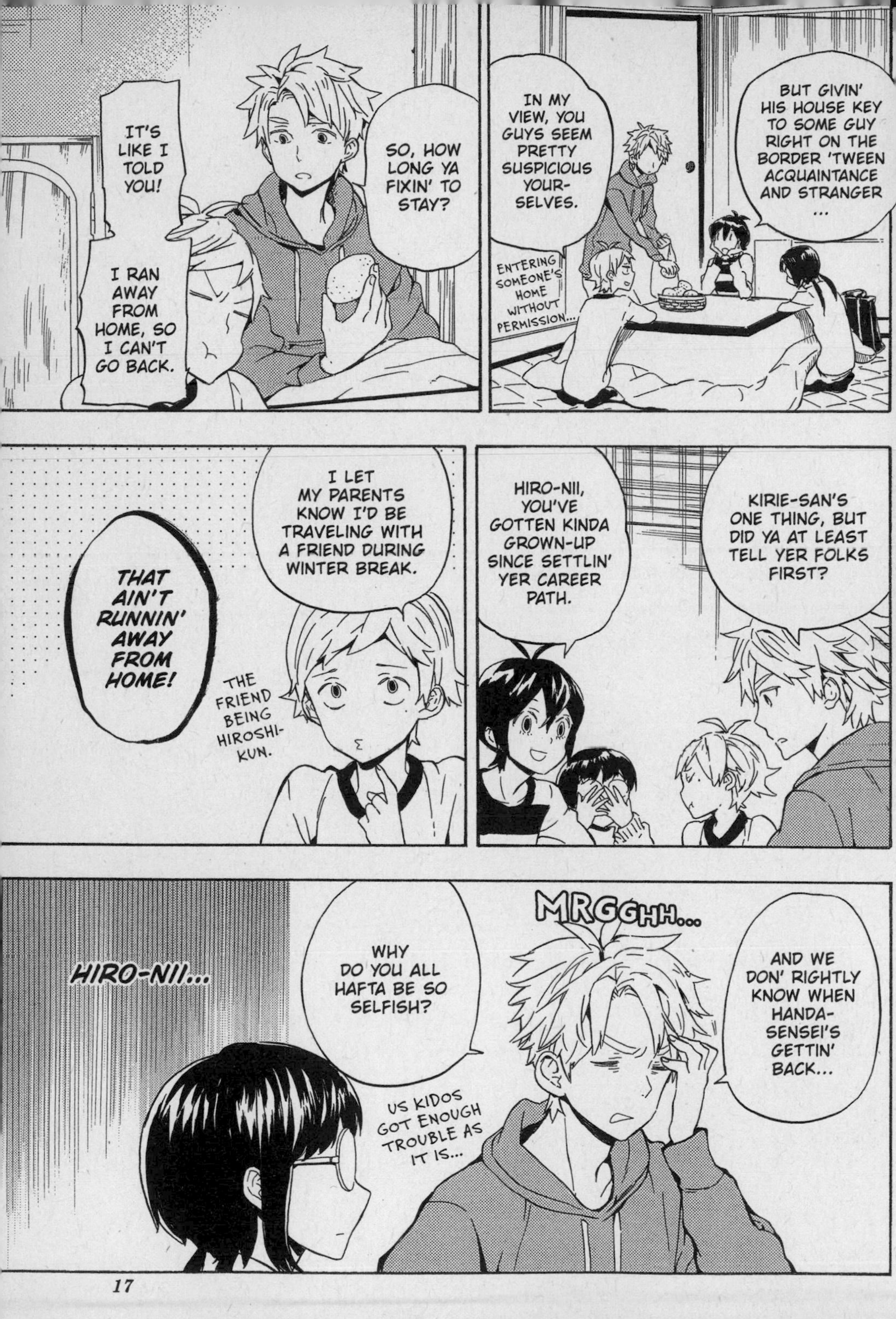
BUT GIVIN' HIS HOUSE KEY TO SOME GUY RIGHT ON THE BORDER 'TWEEN ACQUAINTANCE AND STRANGER ...
IN MY VIEW, YOU GUYS SEEM PRETTY SUSPICIOUS YOUR-SELVES.
ENTERING SOMEONE'S HOME WITHOUT PERMISSION...
SO, HOW LONG YA FIXIN' TO STAY?
IT'S LIKE I TOLD YOU!
I RAN AWAY FROM HOME, SO I CAN'T GO BACK.
KIRIE-SAN'S ONE THING, BUT DID YA AT LEAST TELL YER FOLKS FIRST?
HIRO-NII, YOU'VE GOTTEN KINDA GROWN-UP SINCE SETTLIN' YER CAREER PATH.
I LET MY PARENTS KNOW I'D BE TRAVELING WITH A FRIEND DURING WINTER BREAK.
THAT AIN'T RUNNIN' AWAY FROM HOME!
THE FRIEND BEING HIROSHI-KUN.
MRGGHH...
AND WE DON' RIGHTLY KNOW WHEN HANDA-SENSEI'S GETTIN' BACK...
US KIDOS GOT ENOUGH TROUBLE AS IT IS...
WHY DO YOU ALL HAFTA BE SO SELFISH?
HIRO-NII...

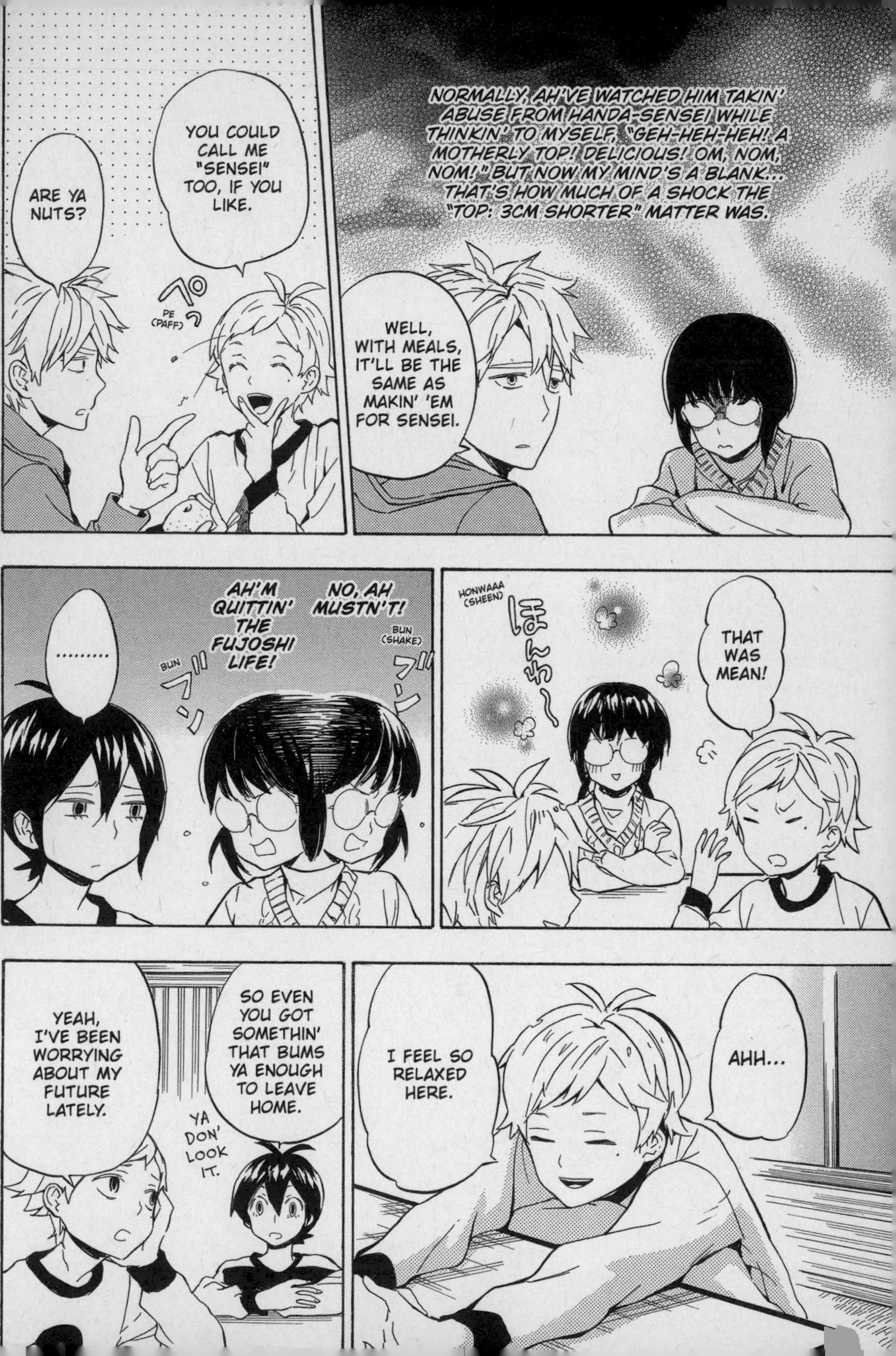

NORMALLY, AH'VE WATCHED HIM TAKIN' ABUSE FROM HANDA-SENSEI WHILE THINKIN' TO MYSELF, "GEH-HEH-HEH! A MOTHERLY TOP! DELICIOUS! OM, NOM, NOM!" BUT NOW MY MIND'S A BLANK... THAT'S HOW MUCH OF A SHOCK THE "TOP: 3CM SHORTER" MATTER WAS.
WELL, WITH MEALS, IT'LL BE THE SAME AS MAKIN' 'EM FOR SENSEI.
YOU COULD CALL ME "SENSEI" TOO, IF YOU LIKE.
PE (PAFF)
ARE YA NUTS?
THAT WAS MEAN!
HONWAAA (SHEEN)
NO, AH MUSTN'T!
BUN (SHAKE)
AH'M QUITTIN' THE FUJOSHI LIFE!
BUN
....
AHH...
I FEEL SO RELAXED HERE.
YEAH, I'VE BEEN WORRYING ABOUT MY FUTURE LATELY.
SO EVEN YOU GOT SOMETHIN' THAT BUMS YA ENOUGH TO LEAVE HOME.
YA DON' LOOK IT.

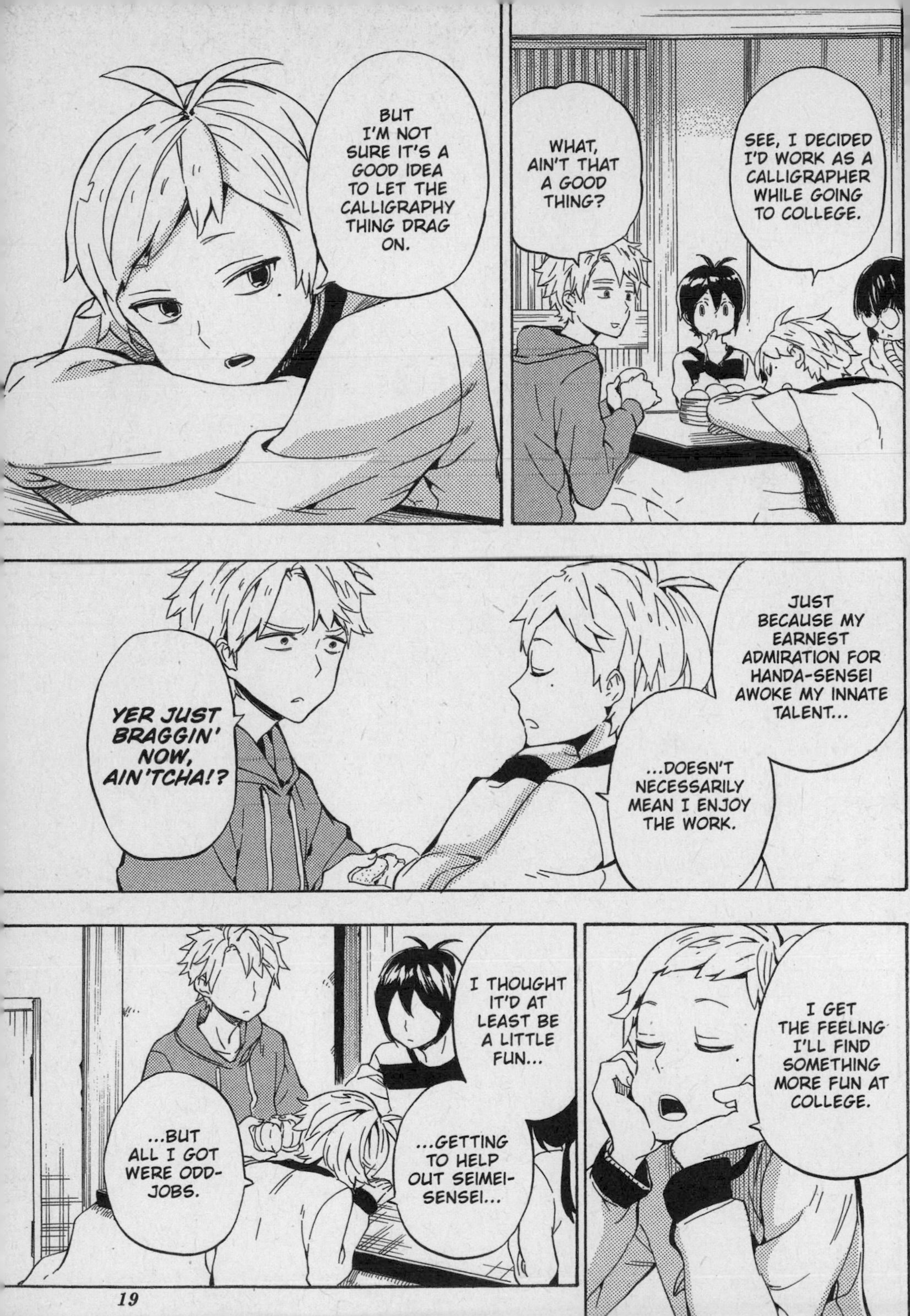
SEE, I DECIDED I'D WORK AS A CALLIGRAPHER WHILE GOING TO COLLEGE.
WHAT, AIN'T THAT A GOOD THING?
BUT I'M NOT SURE IT'S A GOOD IDEA TO LET THE CALLIGRAPHY THING DRAG ON.
JUST BECAUSE MY EARNEST ADMIRATION FOR HANDA-SENSEI AWOKE MY INNATE TALENT...
...DOESN'T NECESSARILY MEAN I ENJOY THE WORK.
YER JUST BRAGGIN' NOW, AIN'TCHA!?
I GET THE FEELING I'LL FIND SOMETHING MORE FUN AT COLLEGE.
I THOUGHT IT'D AT LEAST BE A LITTLE FUN...
...GETTING TO HELP OUT SEIMEI-SENSEI...
...BUT ALL I GOT WERE ODD-JOBS.

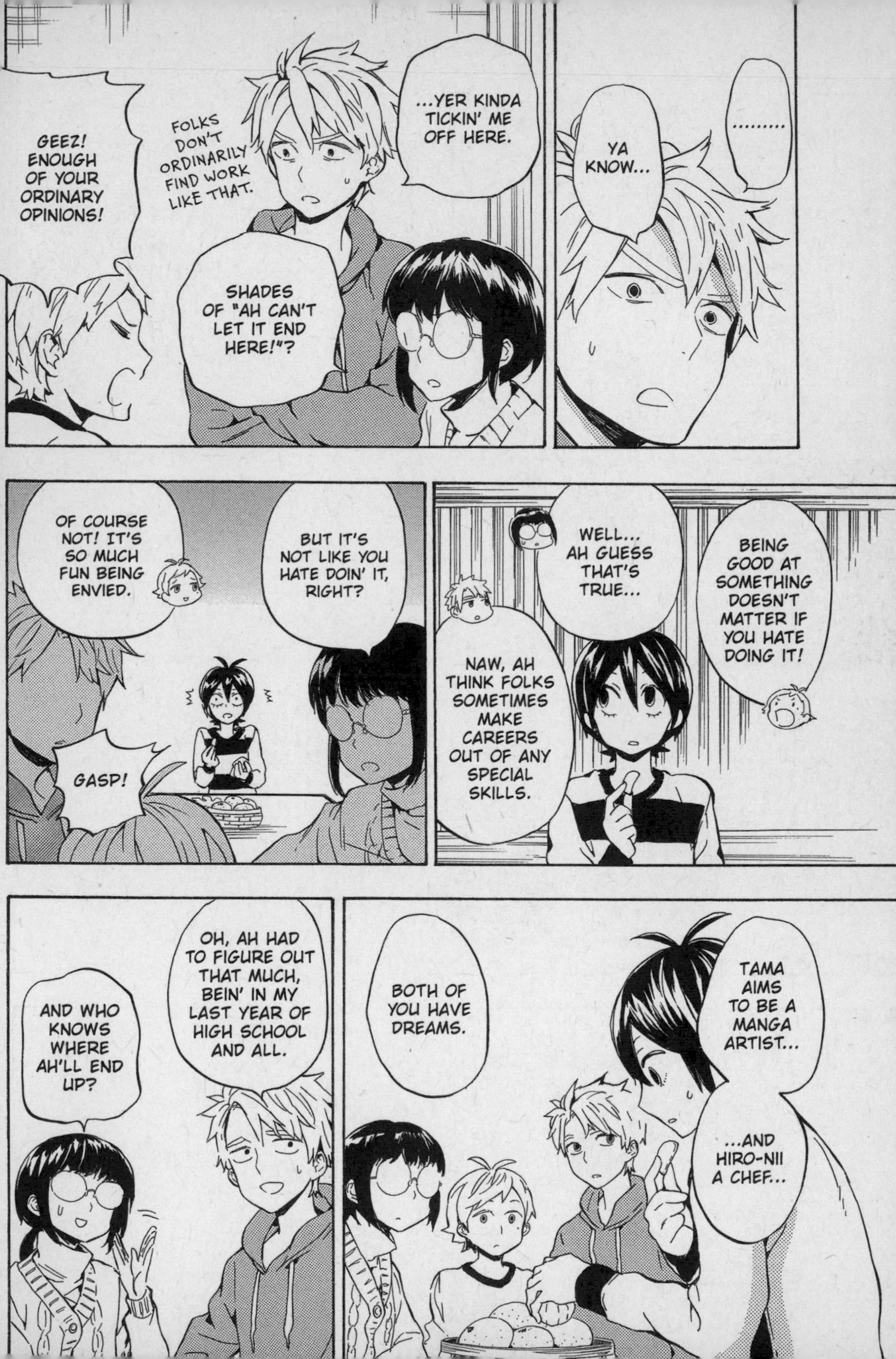
....
YA KNOW...
...YER KINDA TICKIN' ME OFF HERE.
FOLKS DON'T ORDINARILY FIND WORK LIKE THAT.
GEEZ! ENOUGH OF YOUR ORDINARY OPINIONS!
SHADES OF "AH CAN'T LET IT END HERE!"?
BEING GOOD AT SOMETHING DOESN'T MATTER IF YOU HATE DOING IT!
WELL... AH GUESS THAT'S TRUE...
NAW, AH THINK FOLKS SOMETIMES MAKE CAREERS OUT OF ANY SPECIAL SKILLS.
BUT IT'S NOT LIKE YOU HATE DOIN' IT, RIGHT?
OF COURSE NOT! IT'S SO MUCH FUN BEING ENVIED.
GASP!
TAMA AIMS TO BE A MANGA ARTIST...
...AND HIRO-NII A CHEF...
BOTH OF YOU HAVE DREAMS.
OH, AH HAD TO FIGURE OUT THAT MUCH, BEIN' IN MY LAST YEAR OF HIGH SCHOOL AND ALL.
AND WHO KNOWS WHERE AH'LL END UP?

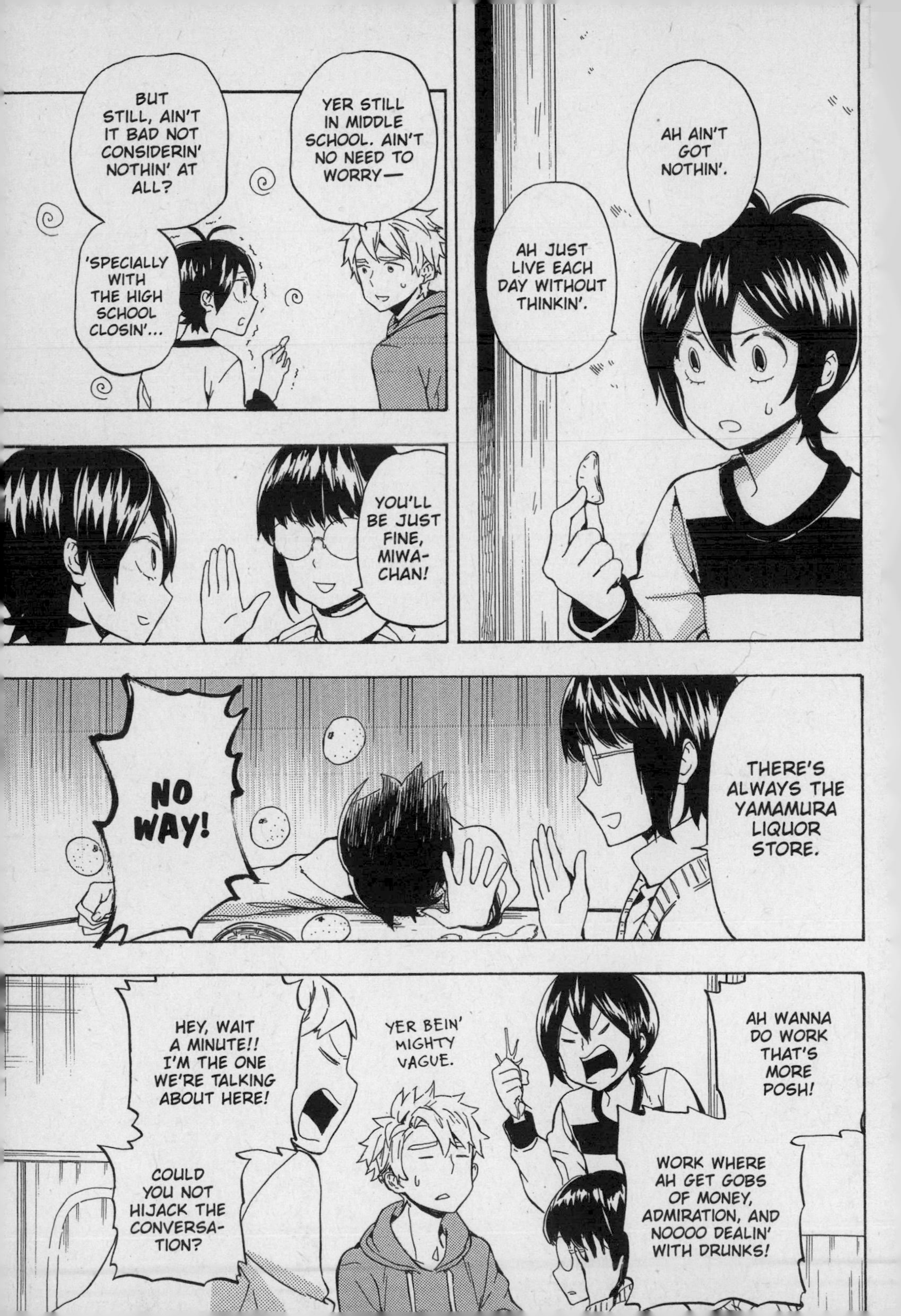
AH AIN'T GOT NOTHIN'.
AH JUST LIVE EACH DAY WITHOUT THINKIN'.
YER STILL IN MIDDLE SCHOOL. AIN'T NO NEED TO WORRY—
BUT STILL, AIN'T IT BAD NOT CONSIDERIN' NOTHIN' AT ALL?
'SPECIALLY WITH THE HIGH SCHOOL CLOSIN'...
YOU'LL BE JUST FINE, MIWA-CHAN!
THERE'S ALWAYS THE YAMAMURA LIQUOR STORE.
NO WAY!
AH WANNA DO WORK THAT'S MORE POSH!
WORK WHERE AH GET GOBS OF MONEY, ADMIRATION, AND NOOOO DEALIN' WITH DRUNKS!
YER BEIN' MIGHTY VAGUE.
HEY, WAIT A MINUTE!! I'M THE ONE WE'RE TALKING ABOUT HERE!
COULD YOU NOT HIJACK THE CONVERSATION?

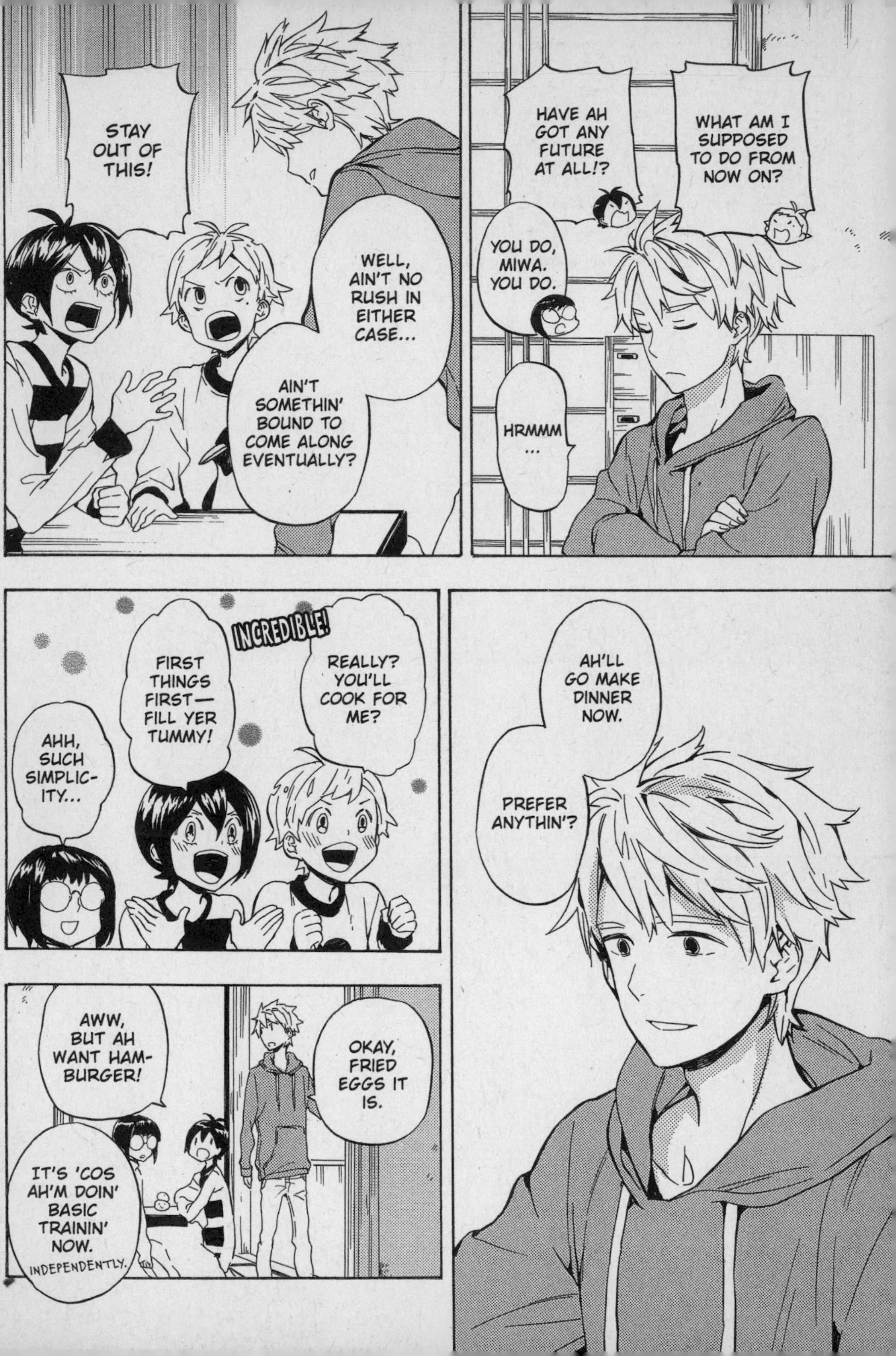
WHAT AM I SUPPOSED TO DO FROM NOW ON?
HAVE AH GOT ANY FUTURE AT ALL!?
YOU DO, MIWA. YOU DO.
HRMMM...
WELL, AIN'T NO RUSH IN EITHER CASE...
AIN'T SOMETHIN' BOUND TO COME ALONG EVENTUALLY?
STAY OUT OF THIS!
AH'LL GO MAKE DINNER NOW.
PREFER ANYTHIN'?
INCREDIBLE!
REALLY? YOU'LL COOK FOR ME?
FIRST THINGS FIRST—FILL YER TUMMY!
AHH, SUCH SIMPLICITY...
OKAY, FRIED EGGS IT IS.
AWW, BUT AH WANT HAMBURGER!
IT'S 'COS AH'M DOIN' BASIC TRAININ' NOW.
INDEPENDENTLY.

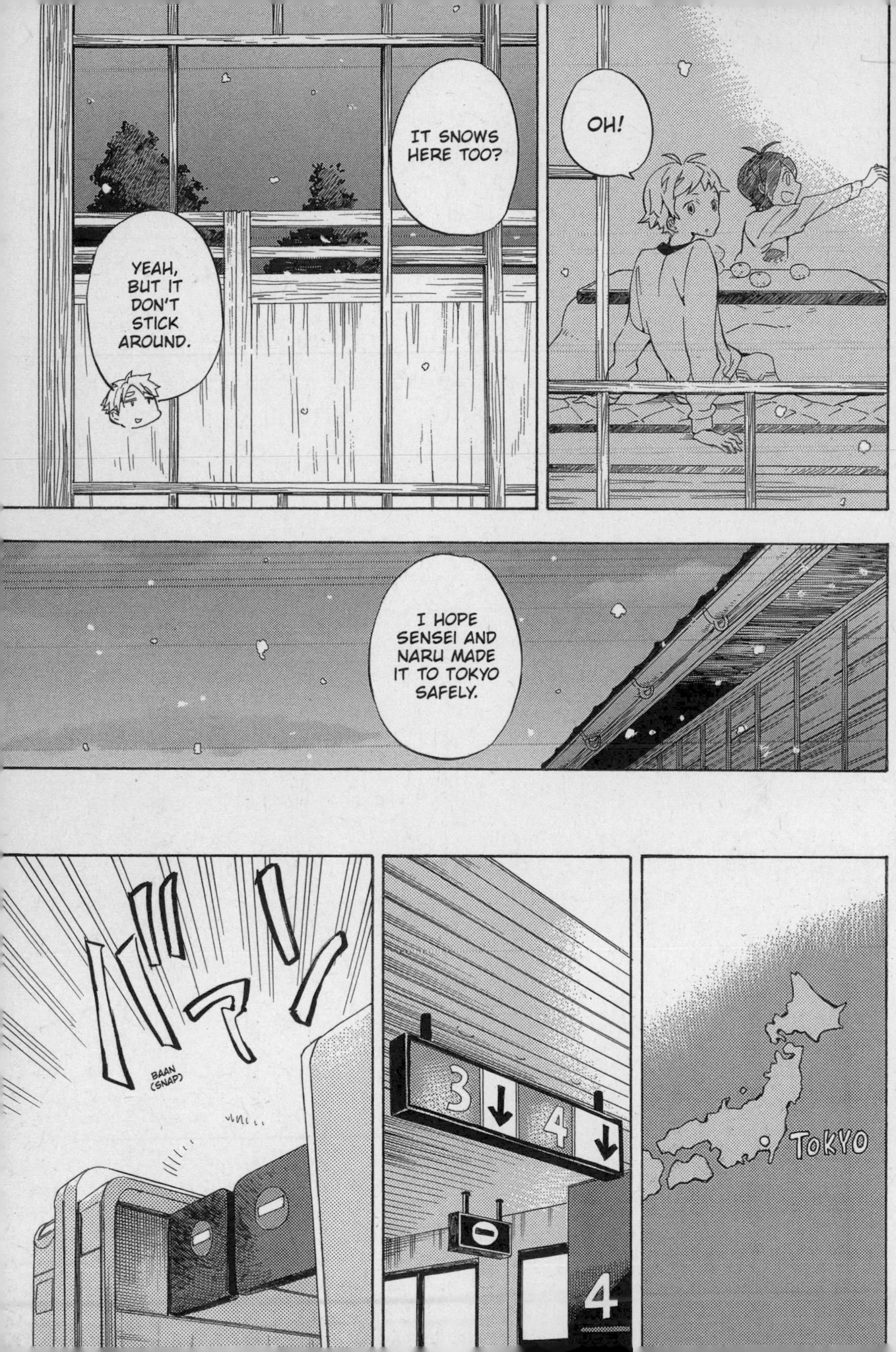
OH!
IT SNOWS HERE TOO?
YEAH, BUT IT DON'T STICK AROUND.
I HOPE SENSEI AND NARU MADE IT TO TOKYO SAFELY.
TOKYO
3
4
4
バァン
BAAN (SNAP)

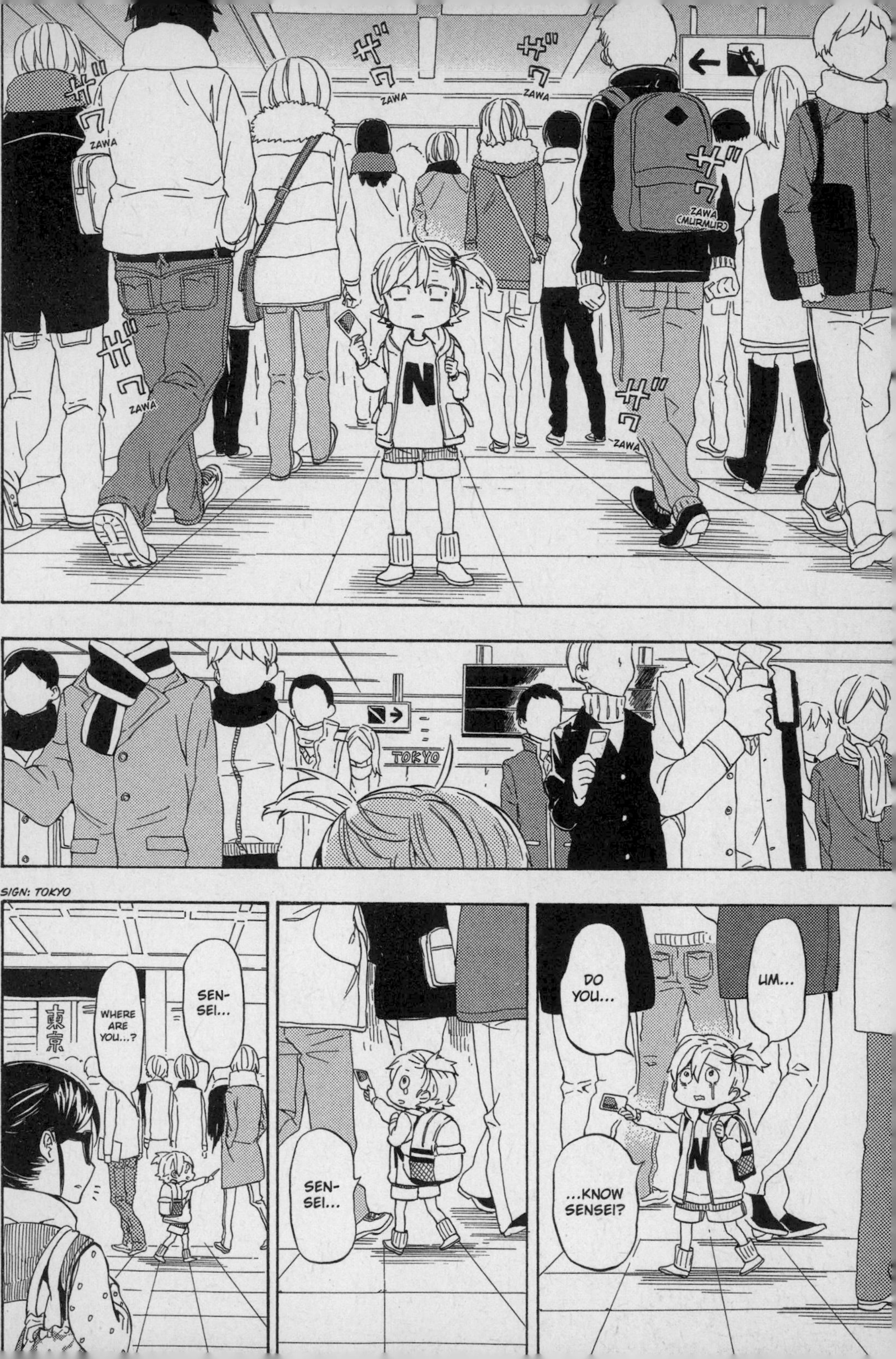
ザワ ZAWA
ザワ ZAWA
ザワ ZAWA (MURMUR)
ザワ ZAWA
ザワ ZAWA
ザワ ZAWA
ザワ ZAWA
TOKYO
SIGN: TOKYO
UM...
DO YOU...
...KNOW SENSEI?
SEN-SEI...
SEN-SEI...
WHERE ARE YOU...?
東京

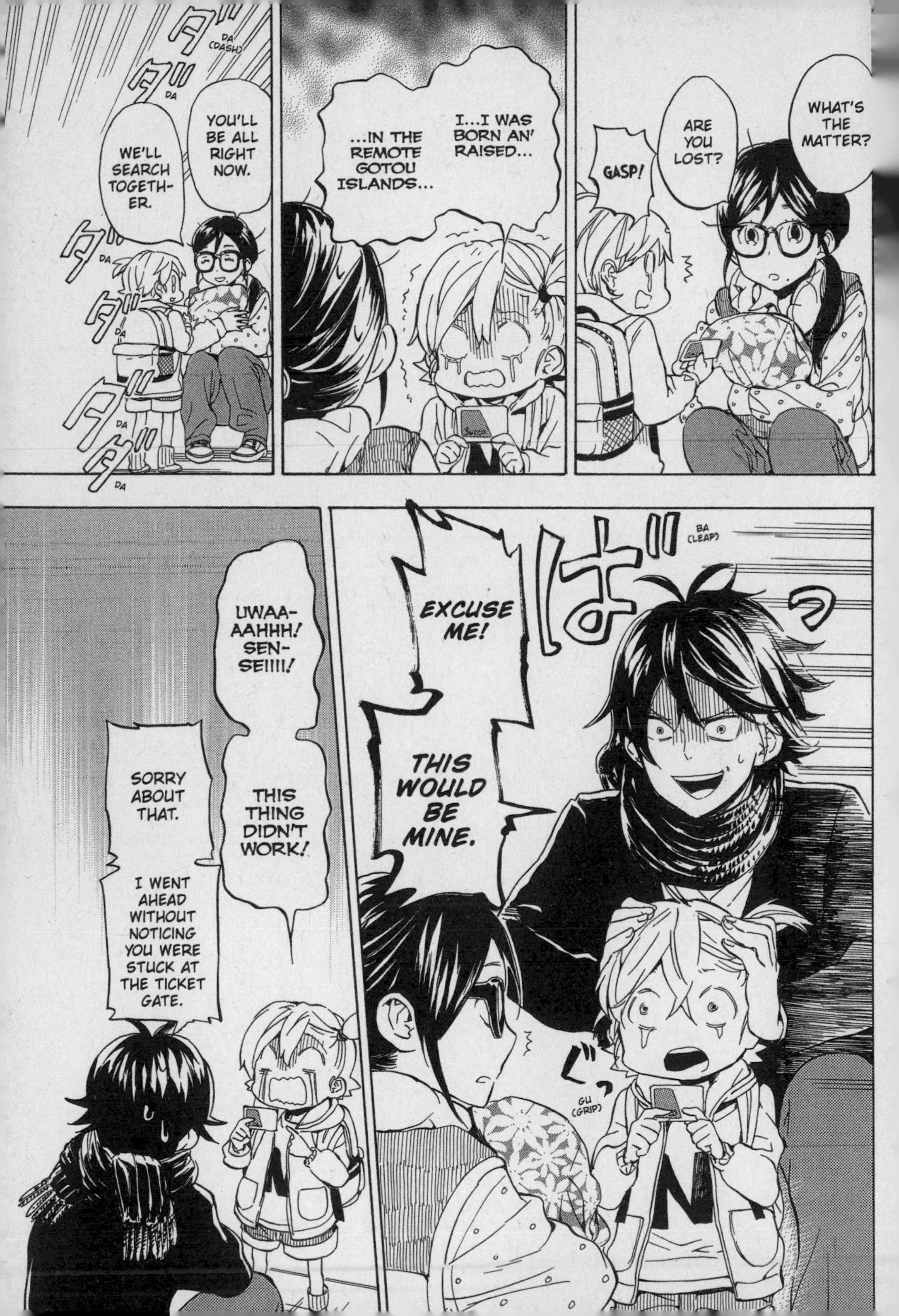
WHAT'S THE MATTER?
ARE YOU LOST?
GASP!
I...I WAS BORN AN' RAISED...
...IN THE REMOTE GOTOU ISLANDS...
DA (DASH)
DA
YOU'LL BE ALL RIGHT NOW.
WE'LL SEARCH TOGETH-ER.
DA
DA
DA
DA
BA (LEAP)
EXCUSE ME!
THIS WOULD BE MINE.
GU (GRIP)
UWAA-AAHHH! SEN-SEIIIII!
THIS THING DIDN'T WORK!
SORRY ABOUT THAT.
I WENT AHEAD WITHOUT NOTICING YOU WERE STUCK AT THE TICKET GATE.

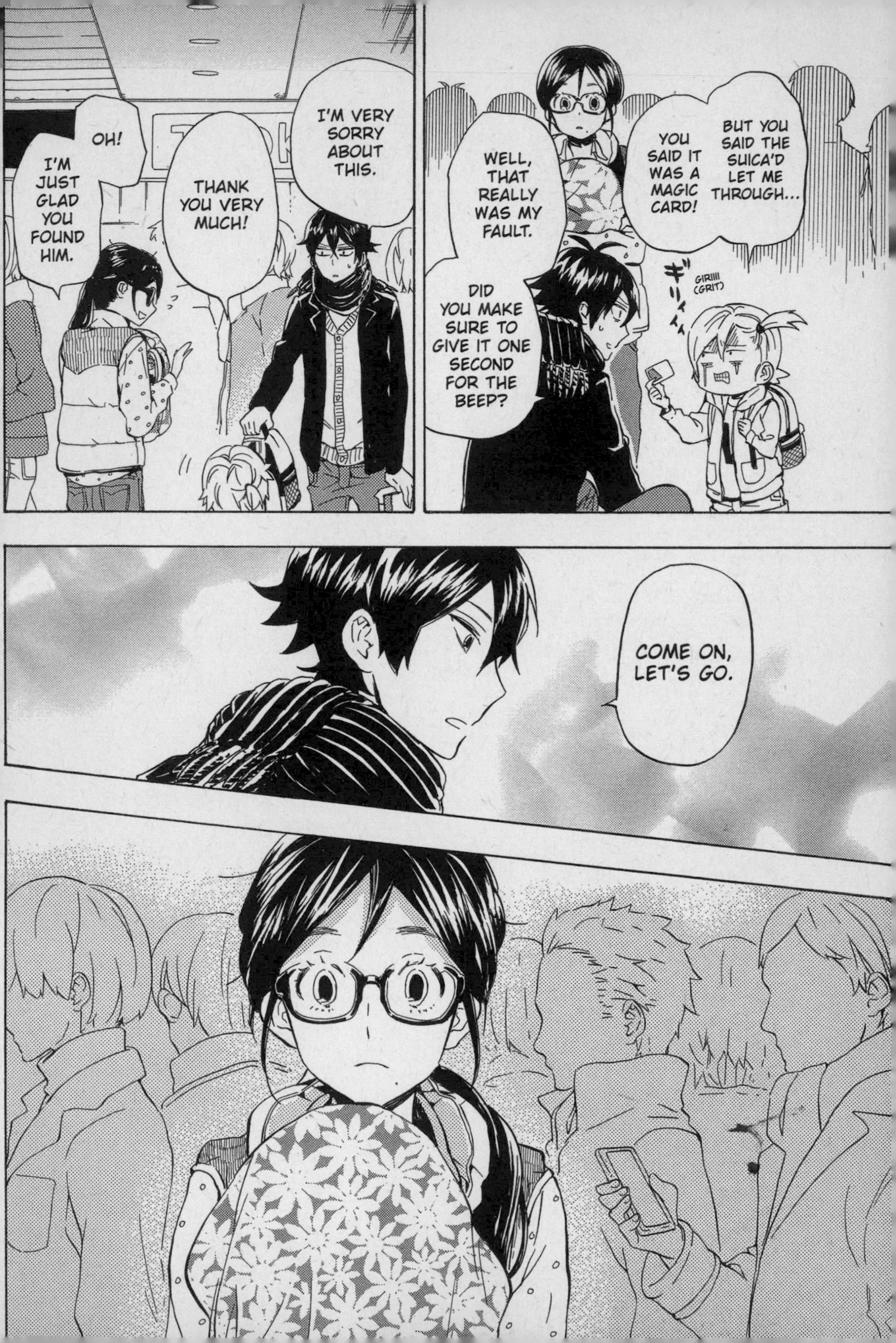
BUT YOU SAID THE SUICA'D LET ME THROUGH...
YOU SAID IT WAS A MAGIC CARD!
GIRIIII (GRIT)
WELL, THAT REALLY WAS MY FAULT.
DID YOU MAKE SURE TO GIVE IT ONE SECOND FOR THE BEEP?
I'M VERY SORRY ABOUT THIS.
THANK YOU VERY MUCH!
OH!
I'M JUST GLAD YOU FOUND HIM.
COME ON, LET'S GO.

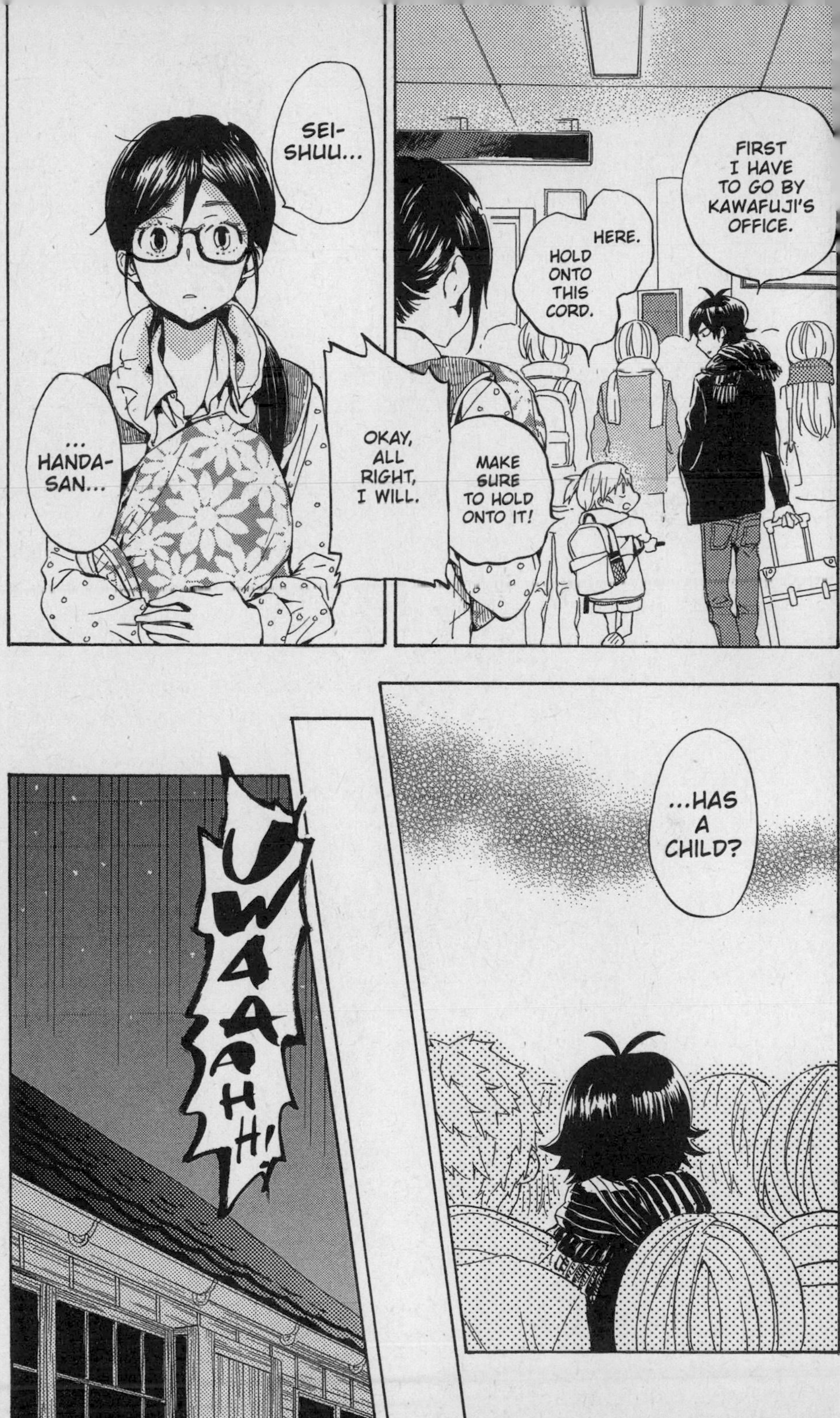
FIRST I HAVE TO GO BY KAWAFUJI'S OFFICE.
HERE. HOLD ONTO THIS CORD.
MAKE SURE TO HOLD ONTO IT!
OKAY, ALL RIGHT, I WILL.
SEI-SHUU...
...HANDA-SAN...
...HAS A CHILD?
UWAAAHH!

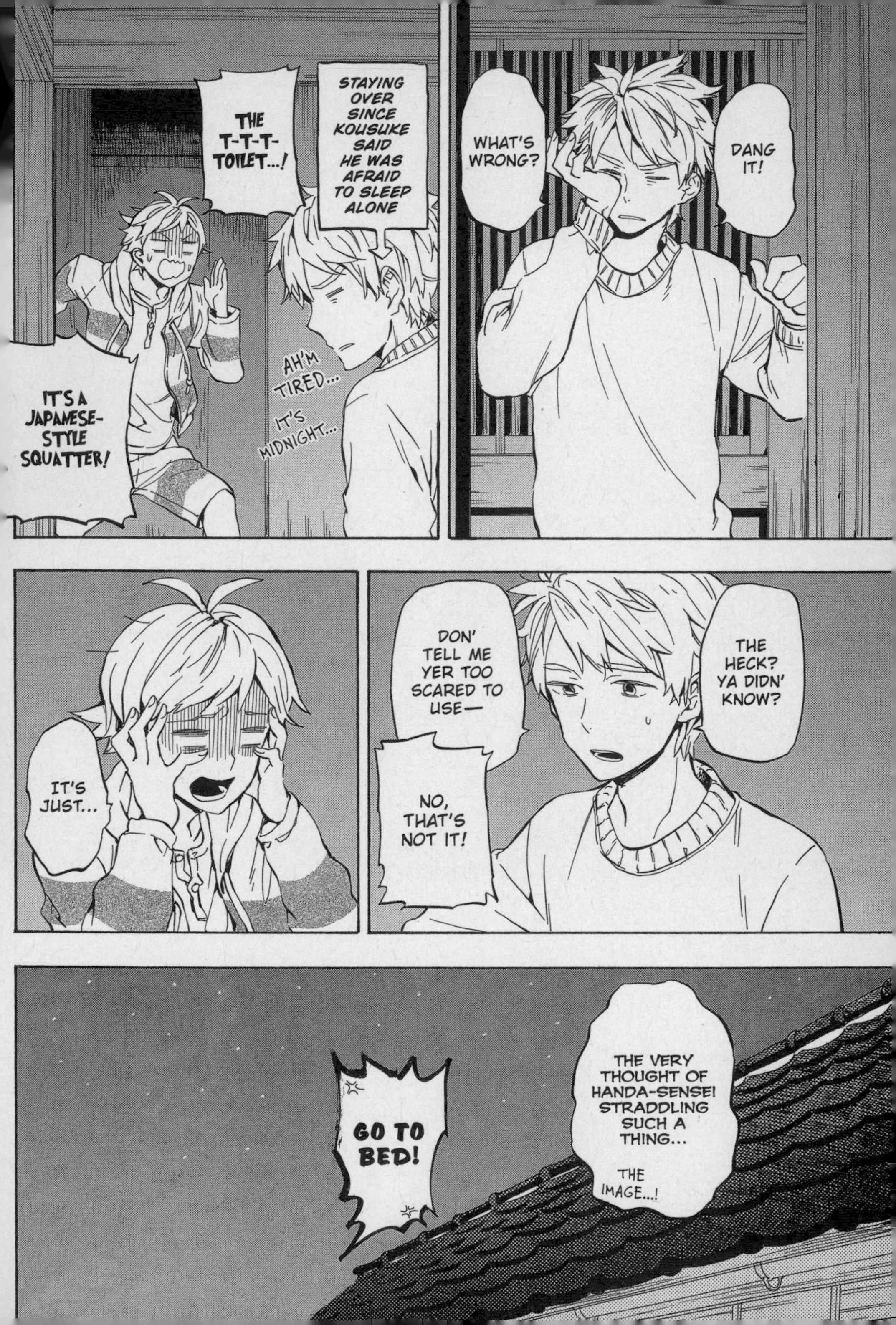
DANG IT!
WHAT'S WRONG?
STAYING OVER SINCE KOUSUKE SAID HE WAS AFRAID TO SLEEP ALONE
THE T-T-T-TOILET...!
AH'M TIRED...
IT'S MIDNIGHT...
IT'S A JAPANESE-STYLE SQUATTER!
THE HECK? YA DIDN' KNOW?
DON' TELL ME YER TOO SCARED TO USE—
NO, THAT'S NOT IT!
IT'S JUST...
THE VERY THOUGHT OF HANDA-SENSEI STRADDLING SUCH A THING...
THE IMAGE...!
GO TO BED!

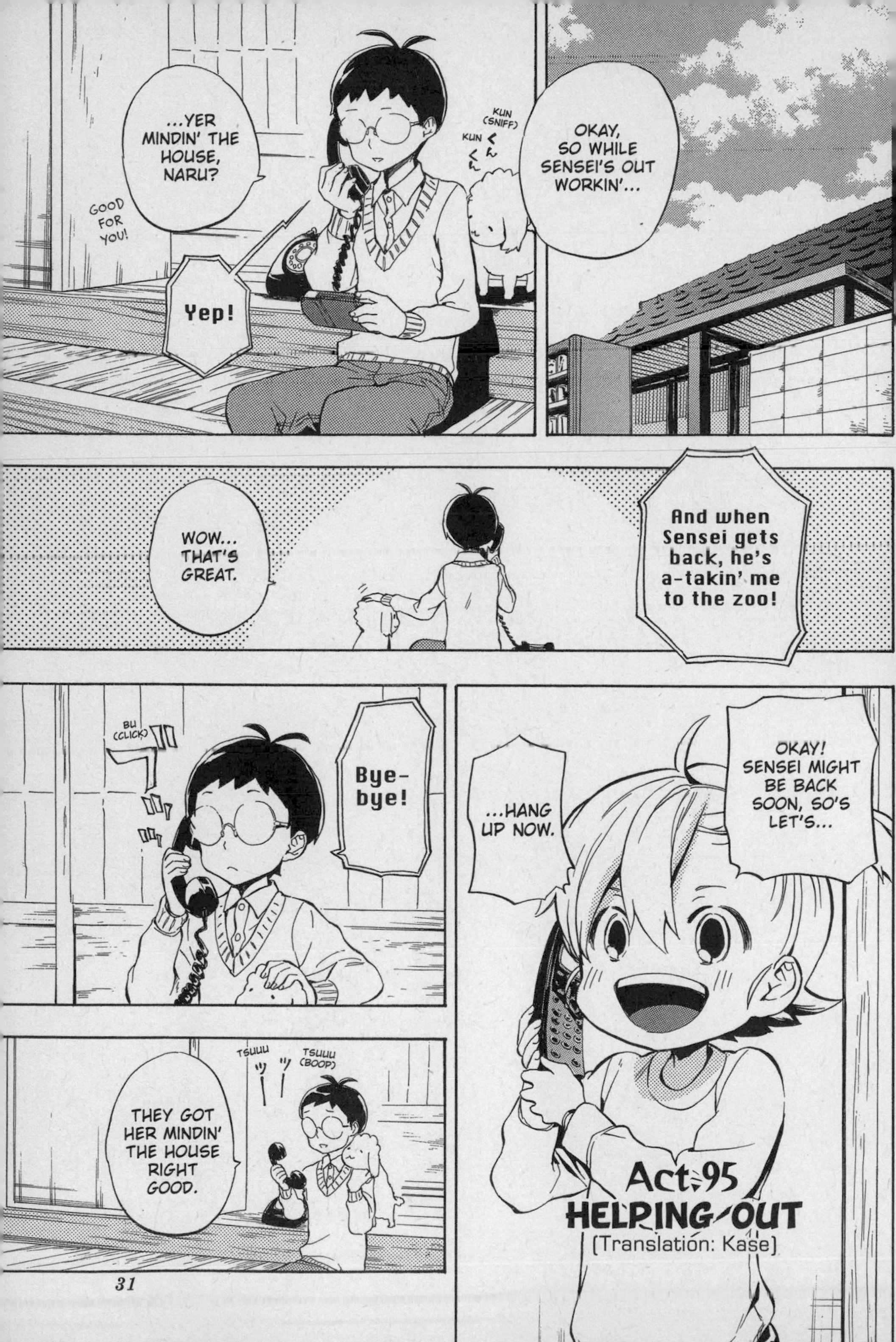
OKAY, SO WHILE SENSEI'S OUT WORKIN'...
KUN (SNIFF) KUN くん くん
...YER MINDIN' THE HOUSE, NARU?
GOOD FOR YOU!
Yep!
And when Sensei gets back, he's a-takin' me to the zoo!
WOW... THAT'S GREAT.
OKAY! SENSEI MIGHT BE BACK SOON, SO'S LET'S...
...HANG UP NOW.
Act 95
HELPING OUT
(Translation: Kase)
Bye-bye!
BU (CLICK)
TSUUU ツ TSUUU ツ (BOOP)
THEY GOT HER MINDIN' THE HOUSE RIGHT GOOD.

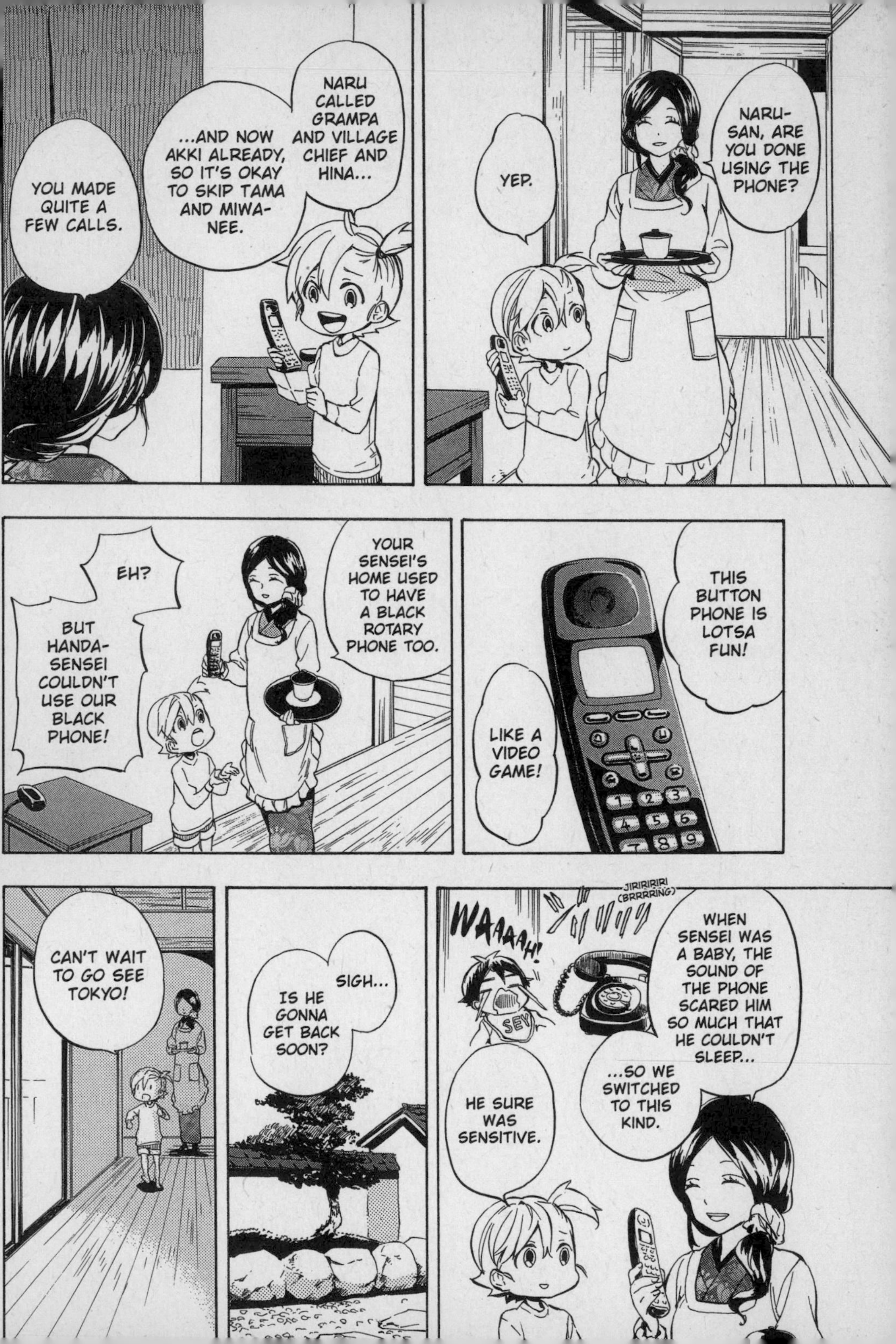
NARU-SAN, ARE YOU DONE USING THE PHONE?
YEP.
NARU CALLED GRAMPA AND VILLAGE CHIEF AND HINA...
...AND NOW AKKI ALREADY, SO IT'S OKAY TO SKIP TAMA AND MIWA-NEE.
YOU MADE QUITE A FEW CALLS.
THIS BUTTON PHONE IS LOTSA FUN!
LIKE A VIDEO GAME!
YOUR SENSEI'S HOME USED TO HAVE A BLACK ROTARY PHONE TOO.
EH?
BUT HANDA-SENSEI COULDN'T USE OUR BLACK PHONE!
JIRIRIRIRI (BRRRRING)
WAAAAH!
SEY
WHEN SENSEI WAS A BABY, THE SOUND OF THE PHONE SCARED HIM SO MUCH THAT HE COULDN'T SLEEP...
...SO WE SWITCHED TO THIS KIND.
HE SURE WAS SENSITIVE.
SIGH...
IS HE GONNA GET BACK SOON?
CAN'T WAIT TO GO SEE TOKYO!

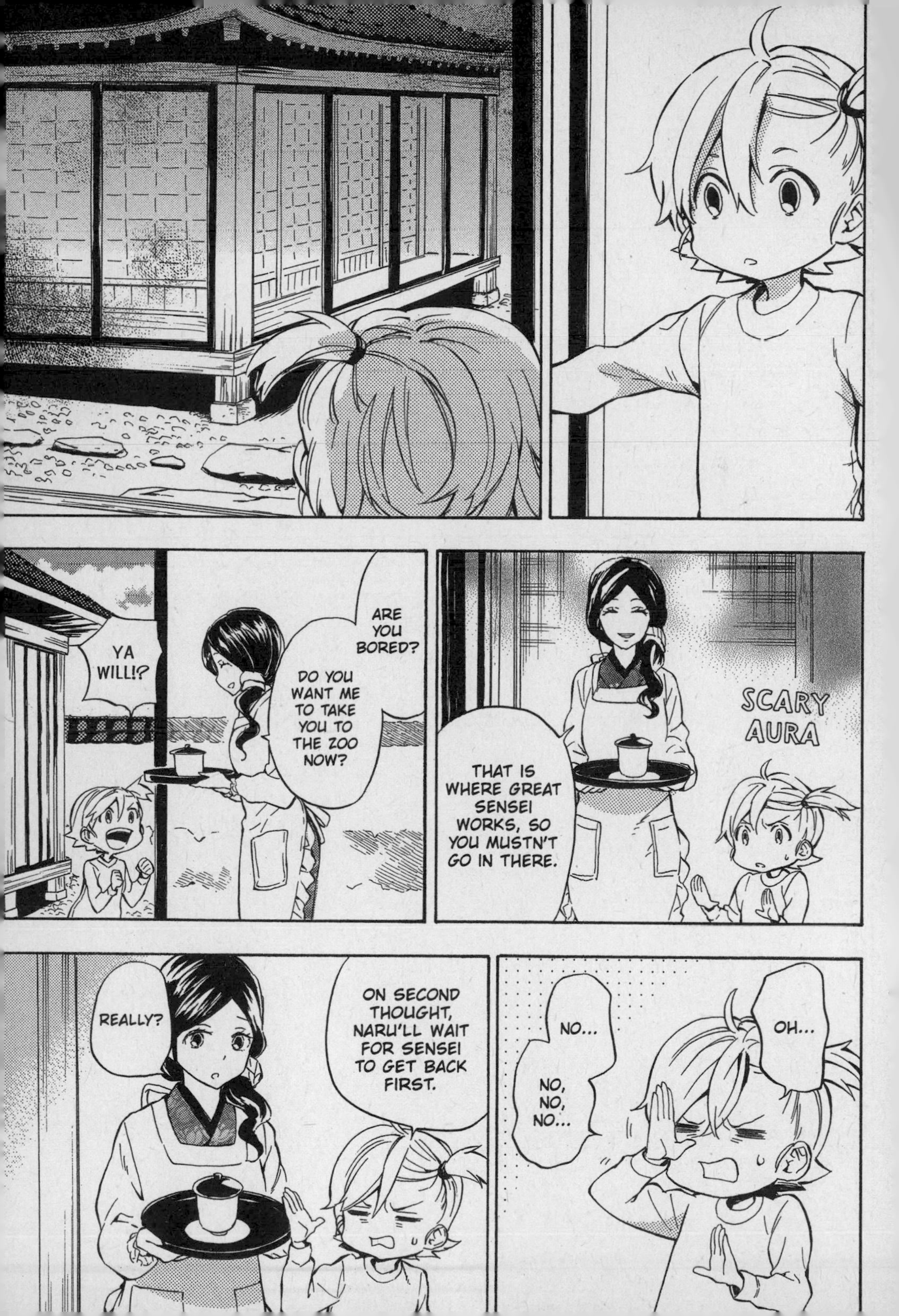
THAT IS WHERE GREAT SENSEI WORKS, SO YOU MUSTN'T GO IN THERE.
SCARY AURA
ARE YOU BORED?
DO YOU WANT ME TO TAKE YOU TO THE ZOO NOW?
YA WILL!?
OH...
NO...
NO, NO, NO...
ON SECOND THOUGHT, NARU'LL WAIT FOR SENSEI TO GET BACK FIRST.
REALLY?

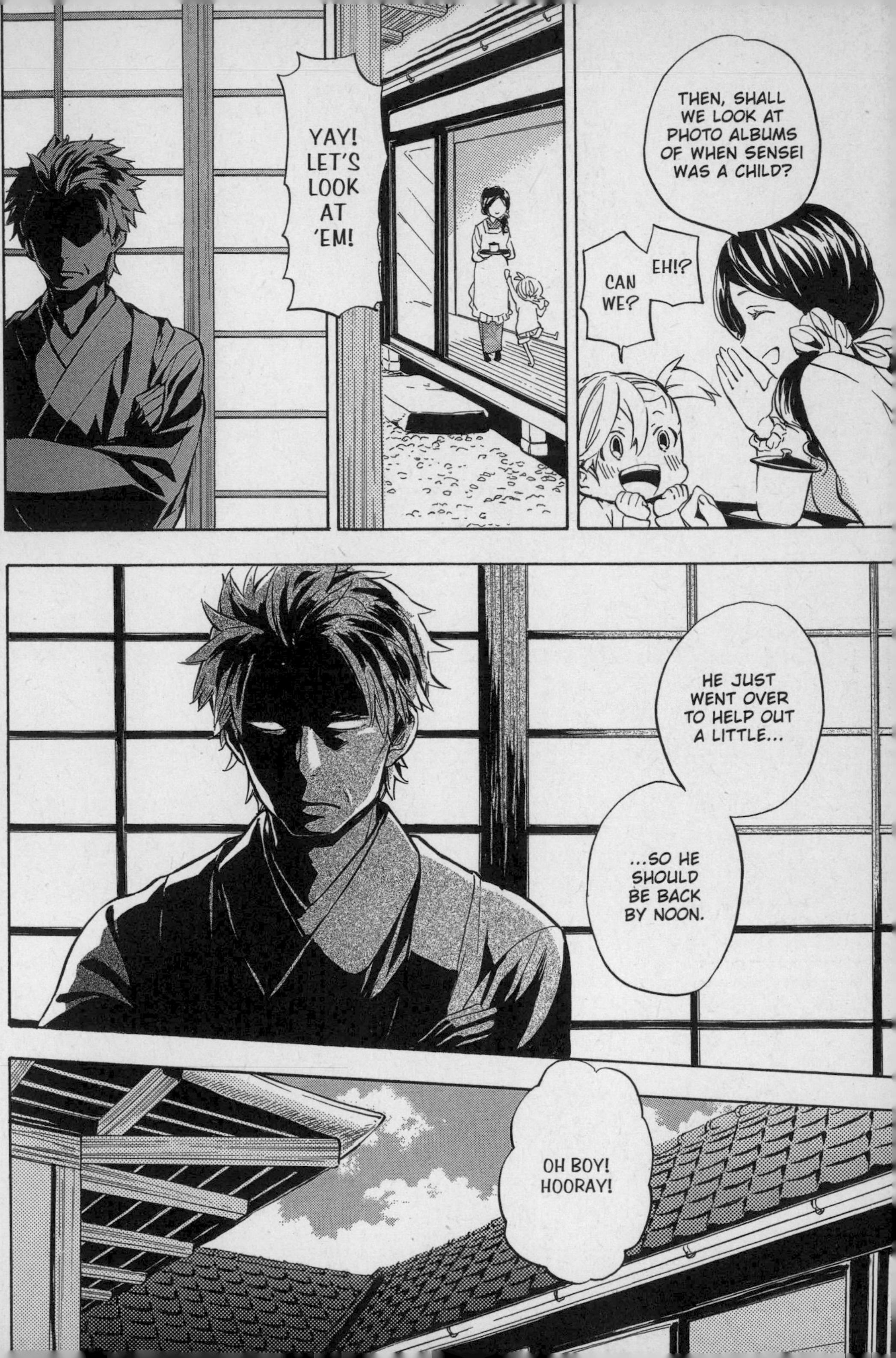
THEN, SHALL WE LOOK AT PHOTO ALBUMS OF WHEN SENSEI WAS A CHILD?
EH!? CAN WE?
YAY! LET'S LOOK AT 'EM!
HE JUST WENT OVER TO HELP OUT A LITTLE...
...SO HE SHOULD BE BACK BY NOON.
OH BOY! HOORAY!

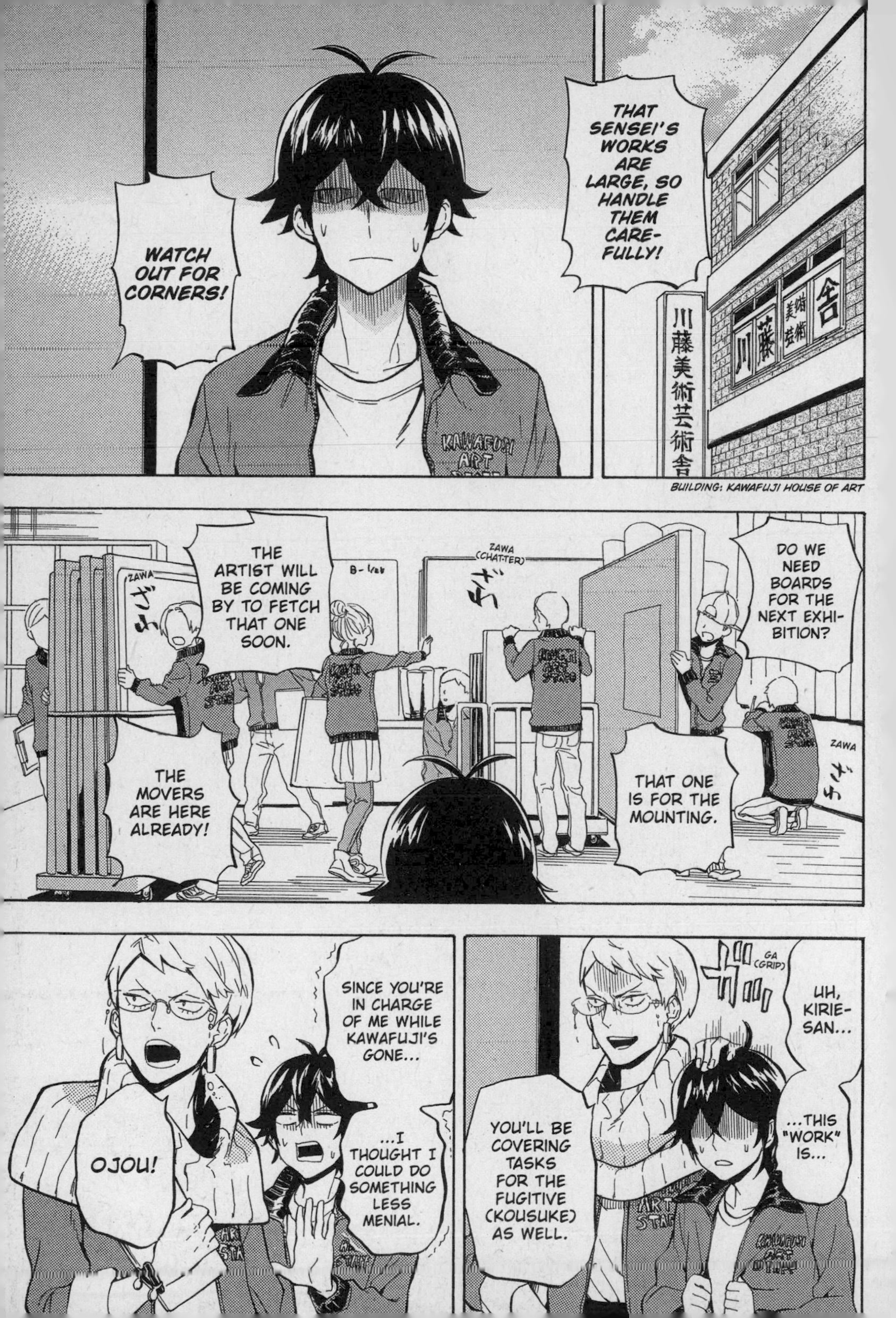
THAT SENSEI'S WORKS ARE LARGE, SO HANDLE THEM CARE-FULLY!
川藤美術芸術舎
BUILDING: KAWAFUJI HOUSE OF ART
WATCH OUT FOR CORNERS!
DO WE NEED BOARDS FOR THE NEXT EXHI-BITION?
ZAWA (CHAT-TER)
ざわ
THAT ONE IS FOR THE MOUNTING.
ZAWA
ざわ
THE ARTIST WILL BE COMING BY TO FETCH THAT ONE SOON.
THE MOVERS ARE HERE ALREADY!
ZAWA
ざわ
GA (GRIP)
UH, KIRIE-SAN...
...THIS "WORK" IS...
YOU'LL BE COVERING TASKS FOR THE FUGITIVE (KOUSUKE) AS WELL.
SINCE YOU'RE IN CHARGE OF ME WHILE KAWAFUJI'S GONE...
...I THOUGHT I COULD DO SOMETHING LESS MENIAL.
OJOU!

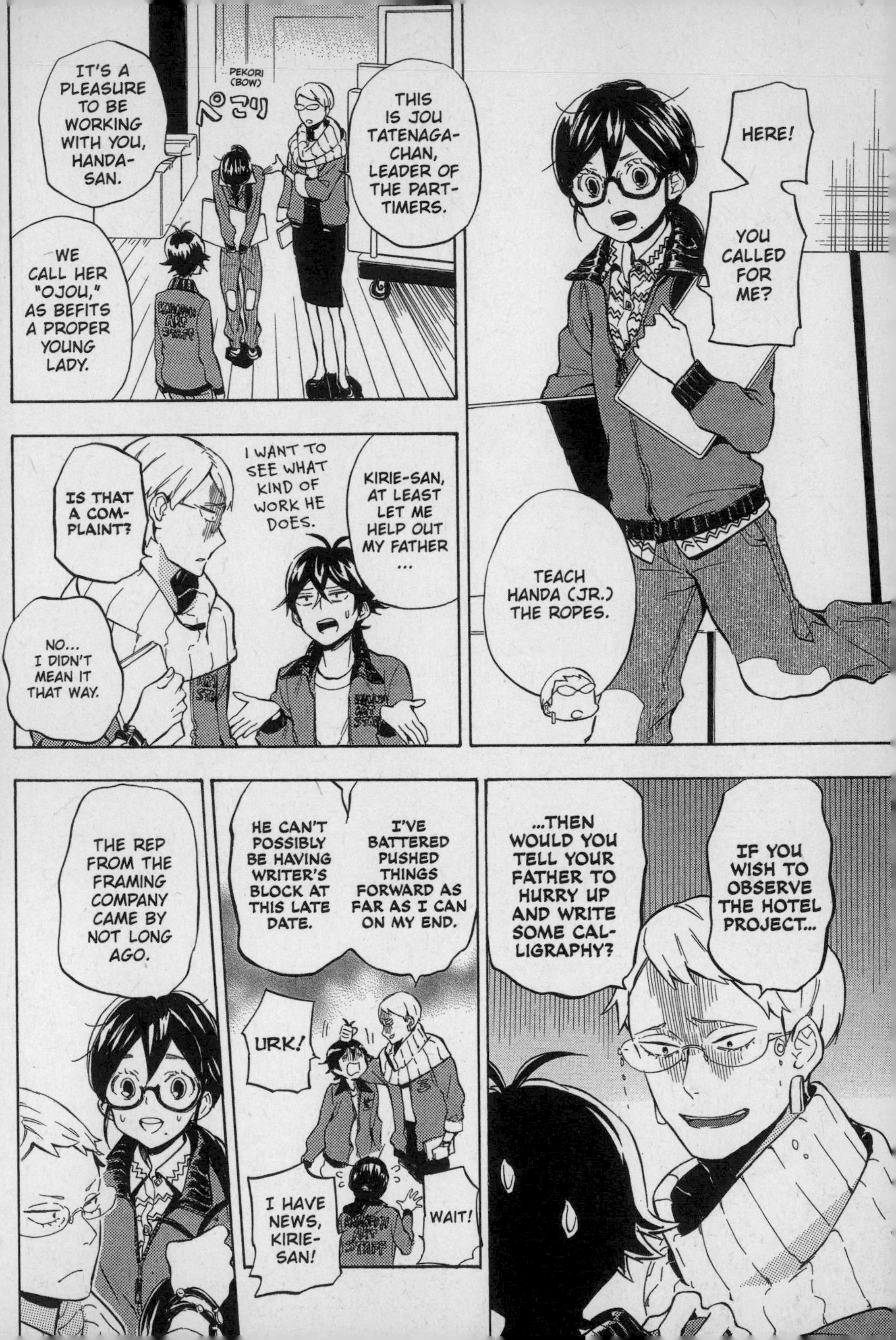
HERE!
YOU CALLED FOR ME?
TEACH HANDA (JR.) THE ROPES.
THIS IS JOU TATENAGA-CHAN, LEADER OF THE PART-TIMERS.
PEKORI (BOW)
IT'S A PLEASURE TO BE WORKING WITH YOU, HANDA-SAN.
WE CALL HER "OJOU," AS BEFITS A PROPER YOUNG LADY.
KIRIE-SAN, AT LEAST LET ME HELP OUT MY FATHER...
I WANT TO SEE WHAT KIND OF WORK HE DOES.
IS THAT A COMPLAINT?
NO... I DIDN'T MEAN IT THAT WAY.
IF YOU WISH TO OBSERVE THE HOTEL PROJECT...
...THEN WOULD YOU TELL YOUR FATHER TO HURRY UP AND WRITE SOME CALLIGRAPHY?
I'VE BATTERED PUSHED THINGS FORWARD AS FAR AS I CAN ON MY END.
HE CAN'T POSSIBLY BE HAVING WRITER'S BLOCK AT THIS LATE DATE.
URK!
WAIT!
I HAVE NEWS, KIRIE-SAN!
THE REP FROM THE FRAMING COMPANY CAME BY NOT LONG AGO.

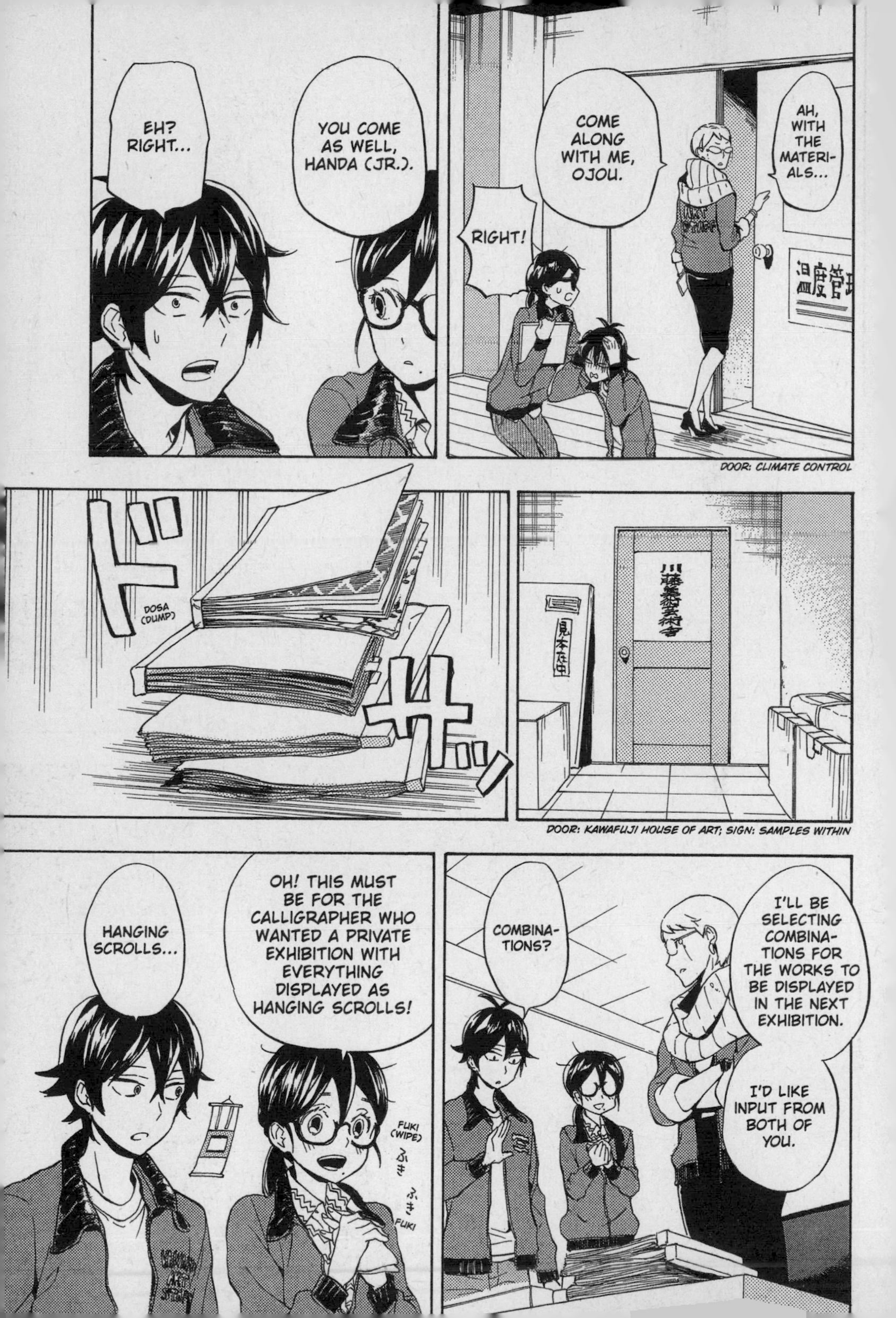
AH, WITH THE MATERI-ALS...
COME ALONG WITH ME, OJOU.
RIGHT!
温度管理
DOOR: CLIMATE CONTROL
YOU COME AS WELL, HANDA (JR.).
EH? RIGHT...
DOOR: KAWAFUJI HOUSE OF ART; SIGN: SAMPLES WITHIN
ドサッ
DOSA (DUMP)
I'LL BE SELECTING COMBINA-TIONS FOR THE WORKS TO BE DISPLAYED IN THE NEXT EXHIBITION.
COMBINA-TIONS?
I'D LIKE INPUT FROM BOTH OF YOU.
OH! THIS MUST BE FOR THE CALLIGRAPHER WHO WANTED A PRIVATE EXHIBITION WITH EVERYTHING DISPLAYED AS HANGING SCROLLS!
HANGING SCROLLS...
FUKI (WIPE)
ふき
ふき
FUKI

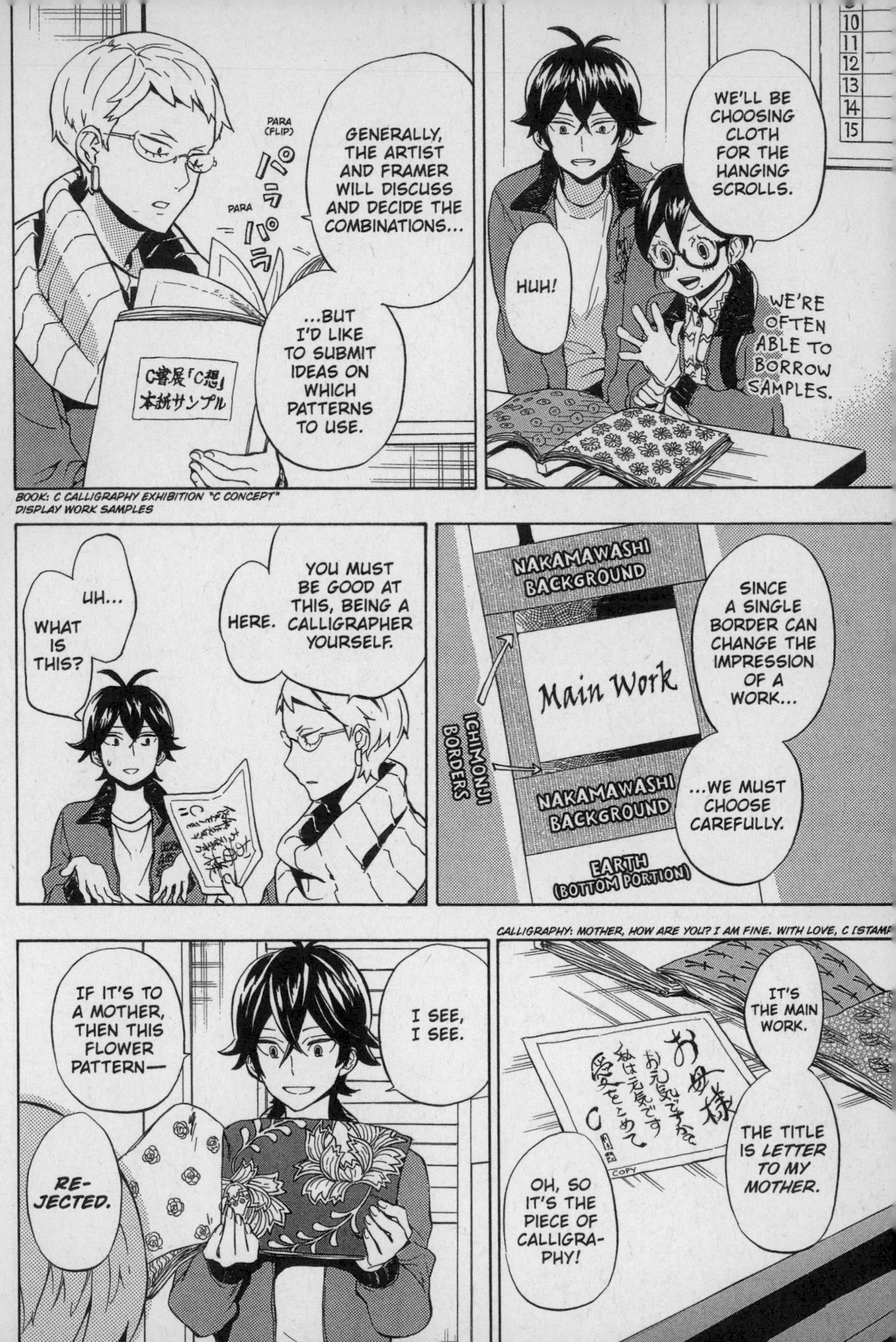
WE'LL BE CHOOSING CLOTH FOR THE HANGING SCROLLS.
HUH!
WE'RE OFTEN ABLE TO BORROW SAMPLES.
GENERALLY, THE ARTIST AND FRAMER WILL DISCUSS AND DECIDE THE COMBINATIONS...
PARA (FLIP)
パラ
PARA
パラ
C書展「C想」本紙サンプル
...BUT I'D LIKE TO SUBMIT IDEAS ON WHICH PATTERNS TO USE.
BOOK: C CALLIGRAPHY EXHIBITION "C CONCEPT" DISPLAY WORK SAMPLES
NAKAMAWASHI BACKGROUND
Main Work
ICHIMONJI BORDERS
NAKAMAWASHI BACKGROUND
EARTH (BOTTOM PORTION)
SINCE A SINGLE BORDER CAN CHANGE THE IMPRESSION OF A WORK...
...WE MUST CHOOSE CAREFULLY.
HERE.
YOU MUST BE GOOD AT THIS, BEING A CALLIGRAPHER YOURSELF.
UH... WHAT IS THIS?
CALLIGRAPHY: MOTHER, HOW ARE YOU? I AM FINE. WITH LOVE, C [STAMP
IT'S THE MAIN WORK.
THE TITLE IS LETTER TO MY MOTHER.
お母様
お元気ですか
私は元気です
愛をこめて
C
COPY
OH, SO IT'S THE PIECE OF CALLIGRAPHY!
I SEE, I SEE.
IF IT'S TO A MOTHER, THEN THIS FLOWER PATTERN—
REJECTED.

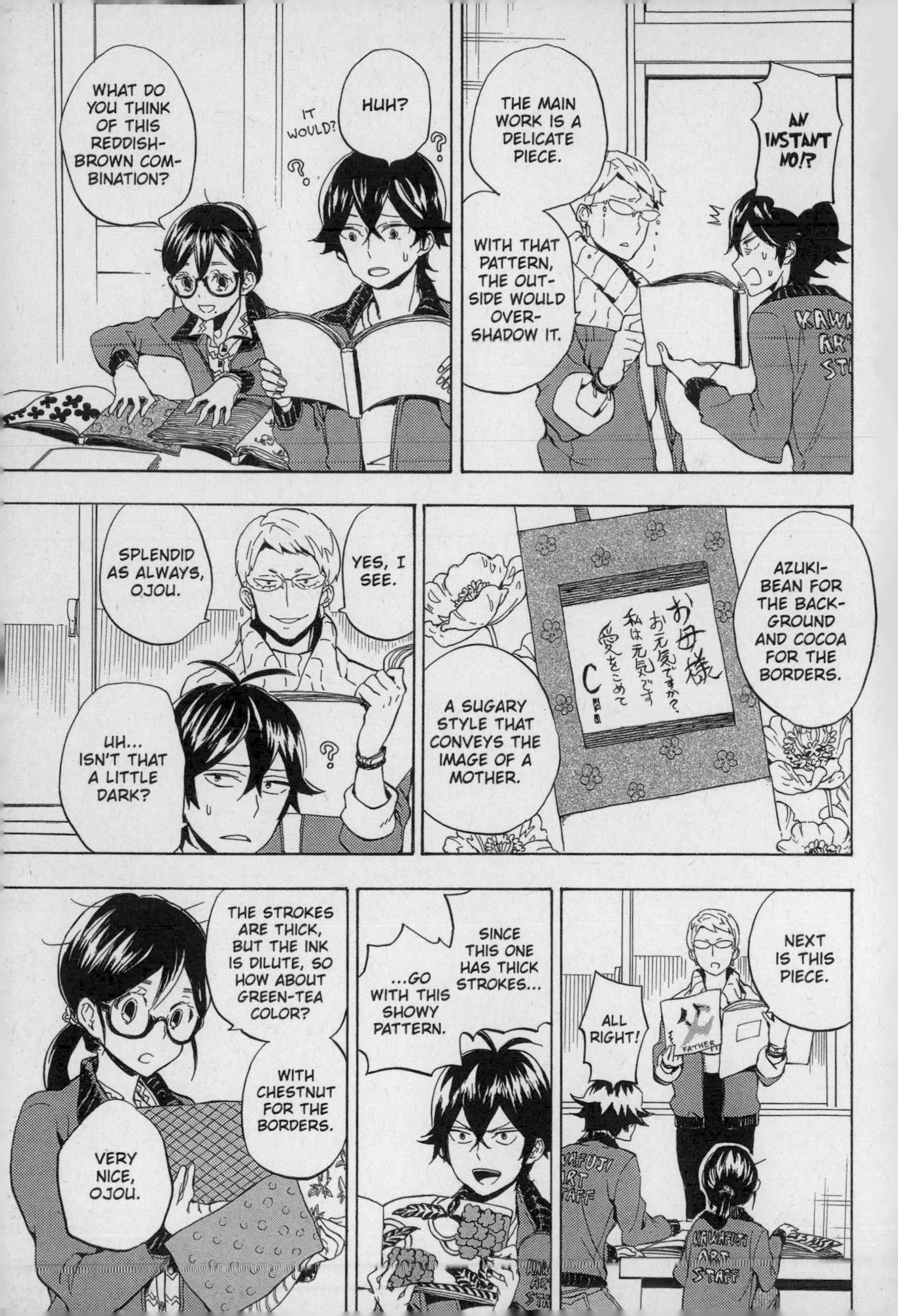
AN INSTANT NO!?
THE MAIN WORK IS A DELICATE PIECE.
WITH THAT PATTERN, THE OUTSIDE WOULD OVERSHADOW IT.
HUH?
IT WOULD?
WHAT DO YOU THINK OF THIS REDDISH-BROWN COMBINATION?
AZUKI-BEAN FOR THE BACKGROUND AND COCOA FOR THE BORDERS.
お母様
お元気ですか？
私は元気です
愛をこめて
C
A SUGARY STYLE THAT CONVEYS THE IMAGE OF A MOTHER.
YES, I SEE.
SPLENDID AS ALWAYS, OJOU.
UH... ISN'T THAT A LITTLE DARK?
NEXT IS THIS PIECE.
父
FATHER
ALL RIGHT!
KAWAFUJI ART STAFF
SINCE THIS ONE HAS THICK STROKES...
...GO WITH THIS SHOWY PATTERN.
THE STROKES ARE THICK, BUT THE INK IS DILUTE, SO HOW ABOUT GREEN-TEA COLOR?
WITH CHESTNUT FOR THE BORDERS.
VERY NICE, OJOU.

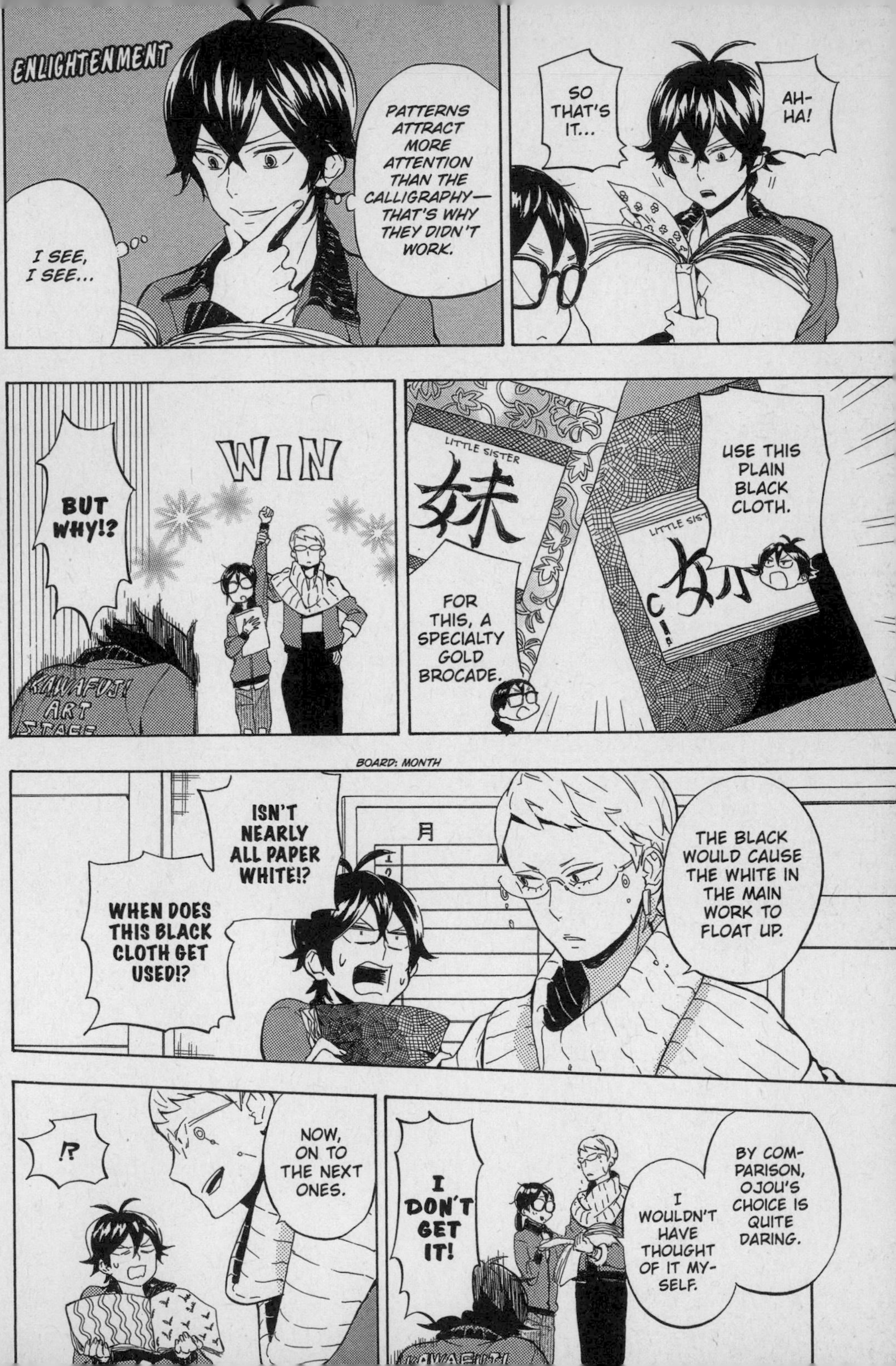
AH-HA!
SO THAT'S IT...
ENLIGHTENMENT
PATTERNS ATTRACT MORE ATTENTION THAN THE CALLIGRAPHY—THAT'S WHY THEY DIDN'T WORK.
I SEE, I SEE...
USE THIS PLAIN BLACK CLOTH.
LITTLE SISTER
LITTLE SIST
妹
FOR THIS, A SPECIALTY GOLD BROCADE.
LITTLE SISTER
妹
WIN
BUT WHY!?
KAWAFUJI ART
BOARD: MONTH
THE BLACK WOULD CAUSE THE WHITE IN THE MAIN WORK TO FLOAT UP.
月
ISN'T NEARLY ALL PAPER WHITE!?
WHEN DOES THIS BLACK CLOTH GET USED!?
BY COMPARISON, OJOU'S CHOICE IS QUITE DARING.
I WOULDN'T HAVE THOUGHT OF IT MYSELF.
I DON'T GET IT!
NOW, ON TO THE NEXT ONES.
!?

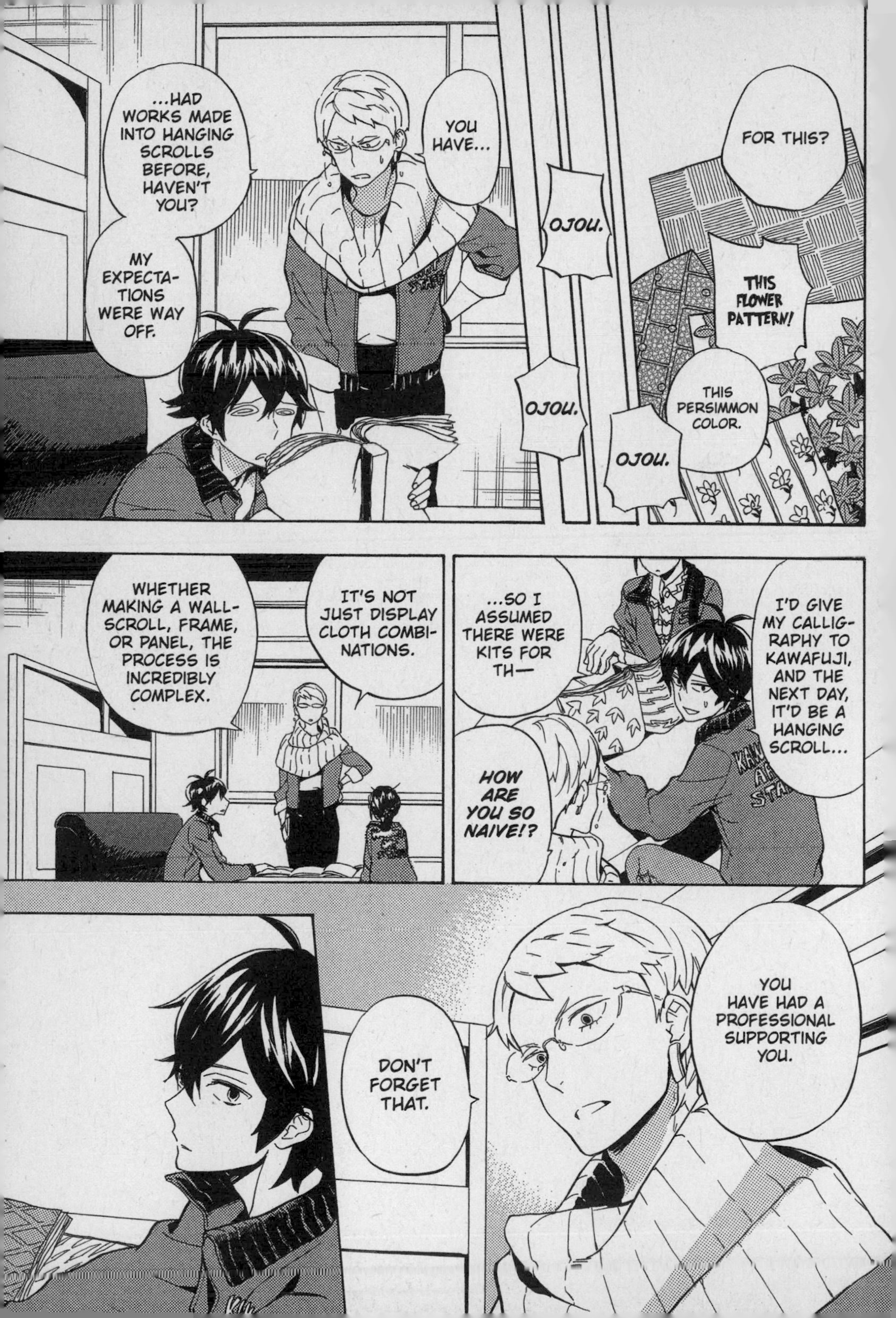
FOR THIS?
THIS FLOWER PATTERN!
THIS PERSIMMON COLOR.
OJOU.
OJOU.
OJOU.
YOU HAVE...
...HAD WORKS MADE INTO HANGING SCROLLS BEFORE, HAVEN'T YOU?
MY EXPECTATIONS WERE WAY OFF.
I'D GIVE MY CALLIGRAPHY TO KAWAFUJI, AND THE NEXT DAY, IT'D BE A HANGING SCROLL...
...SO I ASSUMED THERE WERE KITS FOR TH—
HOW ARE YOU SO NAIVE!?
IT'S NOT JUST DISPLAY CLOTH COMBINATIONS.
WHETHER MAKING A WALL-SCROLL, FRAME, OR PANEL, THE PROCESS IS INCREDIBLY COMPLEX.
YOU HAVE HAD A PROFESSIONAL SUPPORTING YOU.
DON'T FORGET THAT.

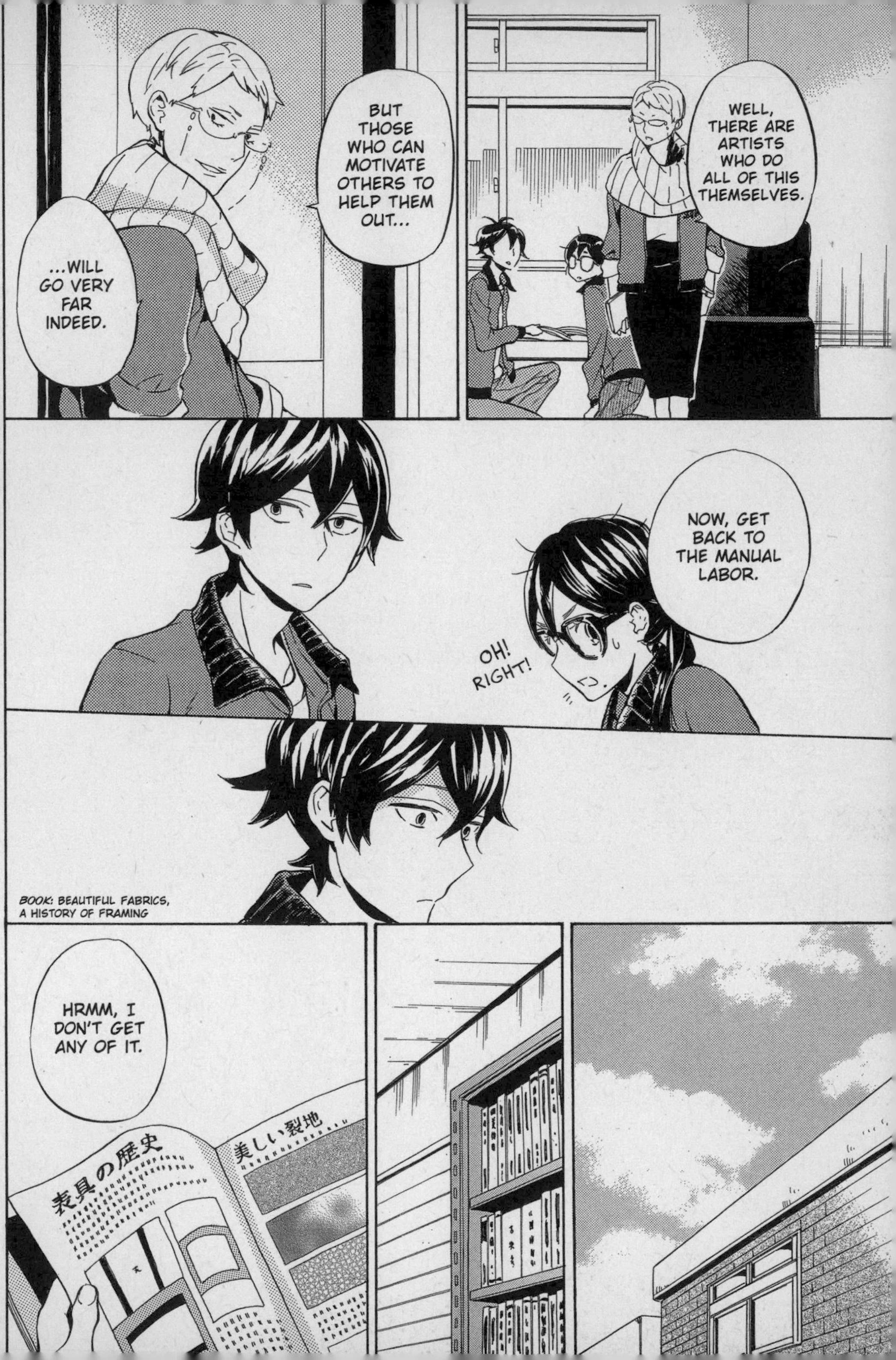
WELL, THERE ARE ARTISTS WHO DO ALL OF THIS THEMSELVES.
BUT THOSE WHO CAN MOTIVATE OTHERS TO HELP THEM OUT...
...WILL GO VERY FAR INDEED.
NOW, GET BACK TO THE MANUAL LABOR.
OH! RIGHT!
BOOK: BEAUTIFUL FABRICS, A HISTORY OF FRAMING
美しい裂地
表具の歴史
HRMM, I DON'T GET ANY OF IT.

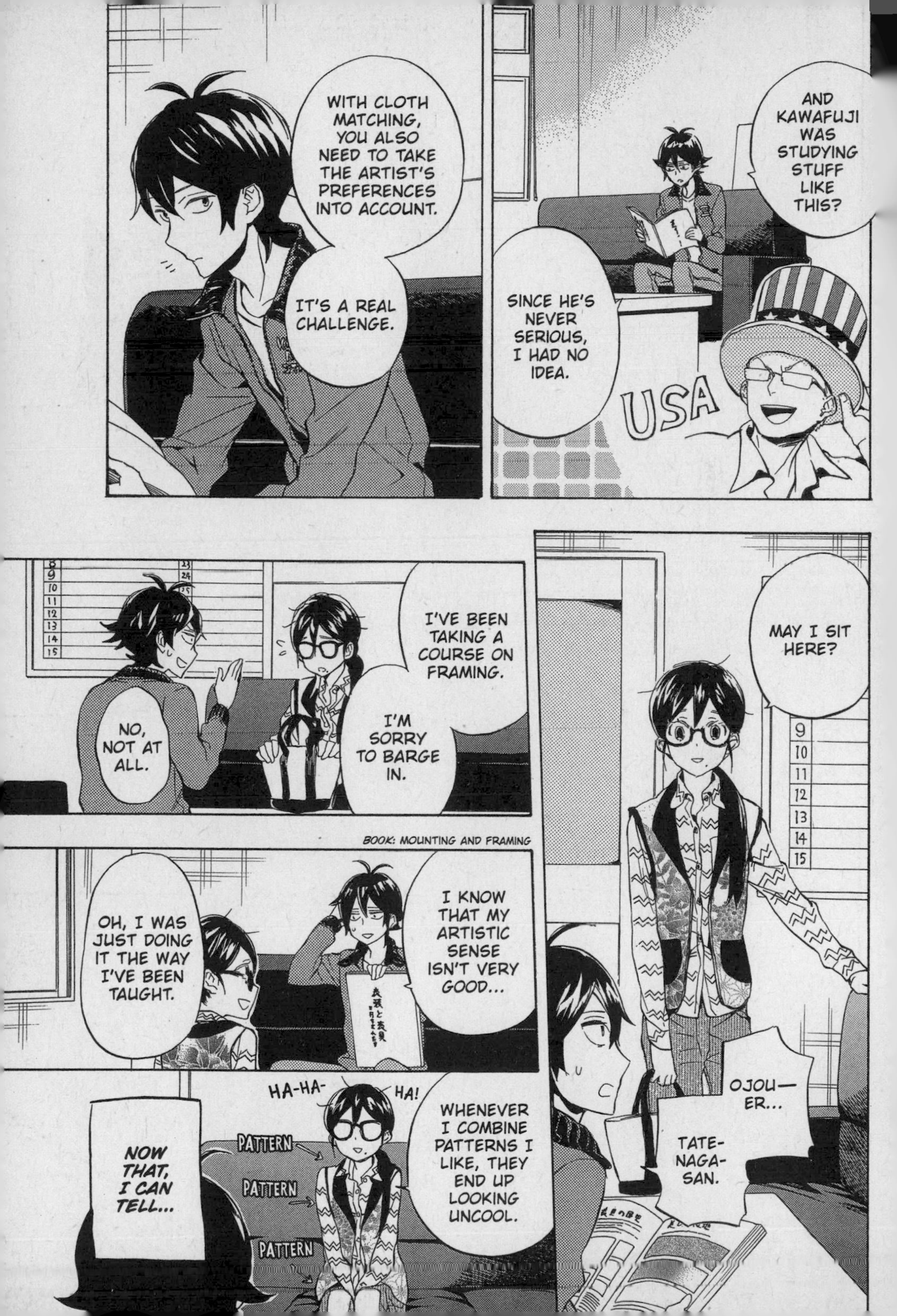
AND KAWAFUJI WAS STUDYING STUFF LIKE THIS?
SINCE HE'S NEVER SERIOUS, I HAD NO IDEA.
USA
WITH CLOTH MATCHING, YOU ALSO NEED TO TAKE THE ARTIST'S PREFERENCES INTO ACCOUNT.
IT'S A REAL CHALLENGE.
MAY I SIT HERE?
OJOU— ER...
TATE-NAGA-SAN.
I'VE BEEN TAKING A COURSE ON FRAMING.
I'M SORRY TO BARGE IN.
NO, NOT AT ALL.
BOOK: MOUNTING AND FRAMING
I KNOW THAT MY ARTISTIC SENSE ISN'T VERY GOOD...
OH, I WAS JUST DOING IT THE WAY I'VE BEEN TAUGHT.
HA-HA-HA!
WHENEVER I COMBINE PATTERNS I LIKE, THEY END UP LOOKING UNCOOL.
PATTERN
PATTERN
PATTERN
NOW THAT, I CAN TELL...

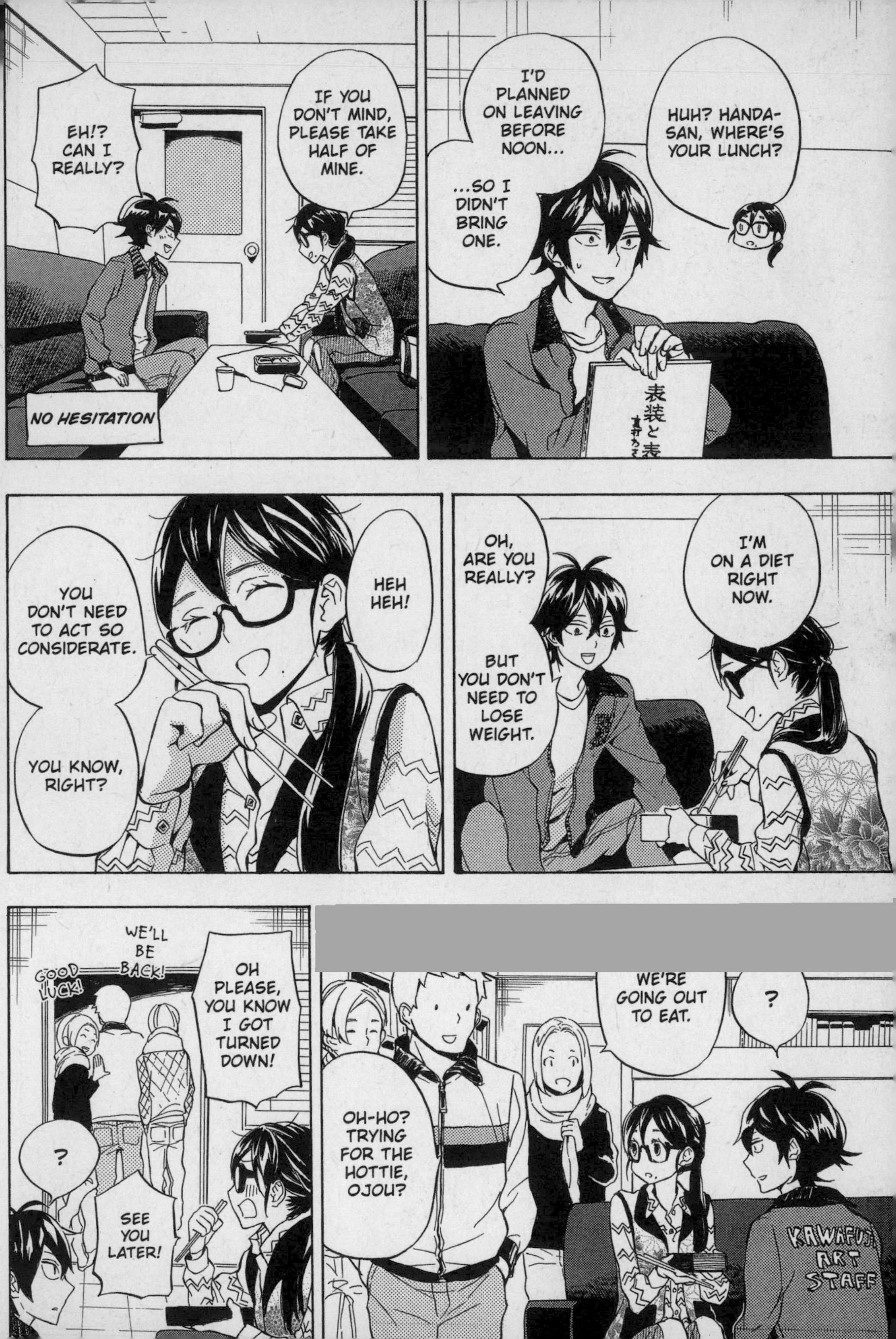
HUH? HANDA-SAN, WHERE'S YOUR LUNCH?
I'D PLANNED ON LEAVING BEFORE NOON...
...SO I DIDN'T BRING ONE.
IF YOU DON'T MIND, PLEASE TAKE HALF OF MINE.
EH!? CAN I REALLY?
NO HESITATION
I'M ON A DIET RIGHT NOW.
OH, ARE YOU REALLY?
BUT YOU DON'T NEED TO LOSE WEIGHT.
HEH HEH!
YOU DON'T NEED TO ACT SO CONSIDERATE.
YOU KNOW, RIGHT?
?
WE'RE GOING OUT TO EAT.
OH-HO? TRYING FOR THE HOTTIE, OJOU?
KAWAFUJI ART STAFF
OH PLEASE, YOU KNOW I GOT TURNED DOWN!
WE'LL BE BACK!
GOOD LUCK!
?
SEE YOU LATER!

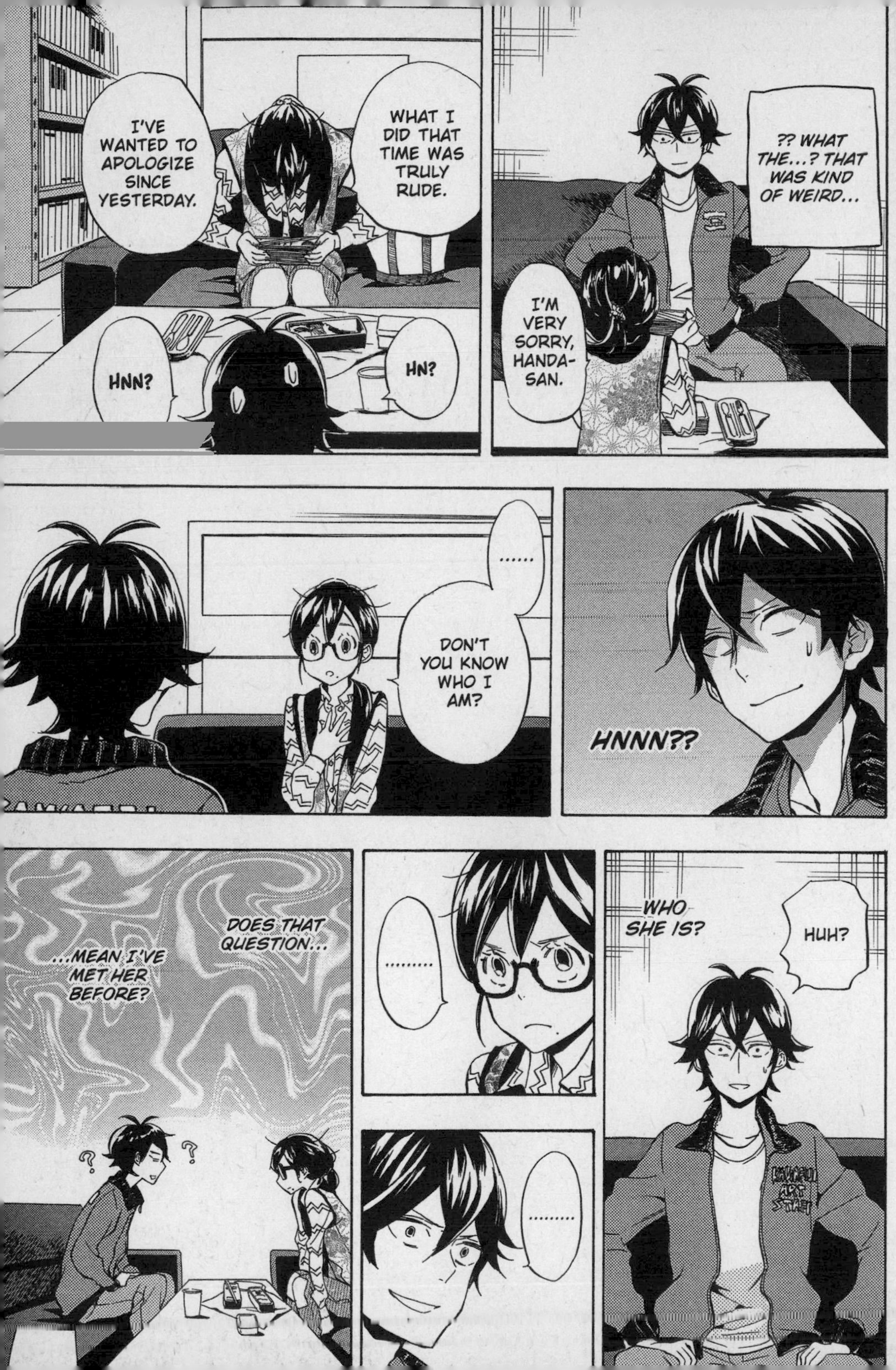
?? WHAT THE...? THAT WAS KIND OF WEIRD...
I'M VERY SORRY, HANDA-SAN.
WHAT I DID THAT TIME WAS TRULY RUDE.
I'VE WANTED TO APOLOGIZE SINCE YESTERDAY.
HN?
HNN?
HNNN??
......
DON'T YOU KNOW WHO I AM?
HUH?
WHO SHE IS?
....
....
DOES THAT QUESTION...
...MEAN I'VE MET HER BEFORE?

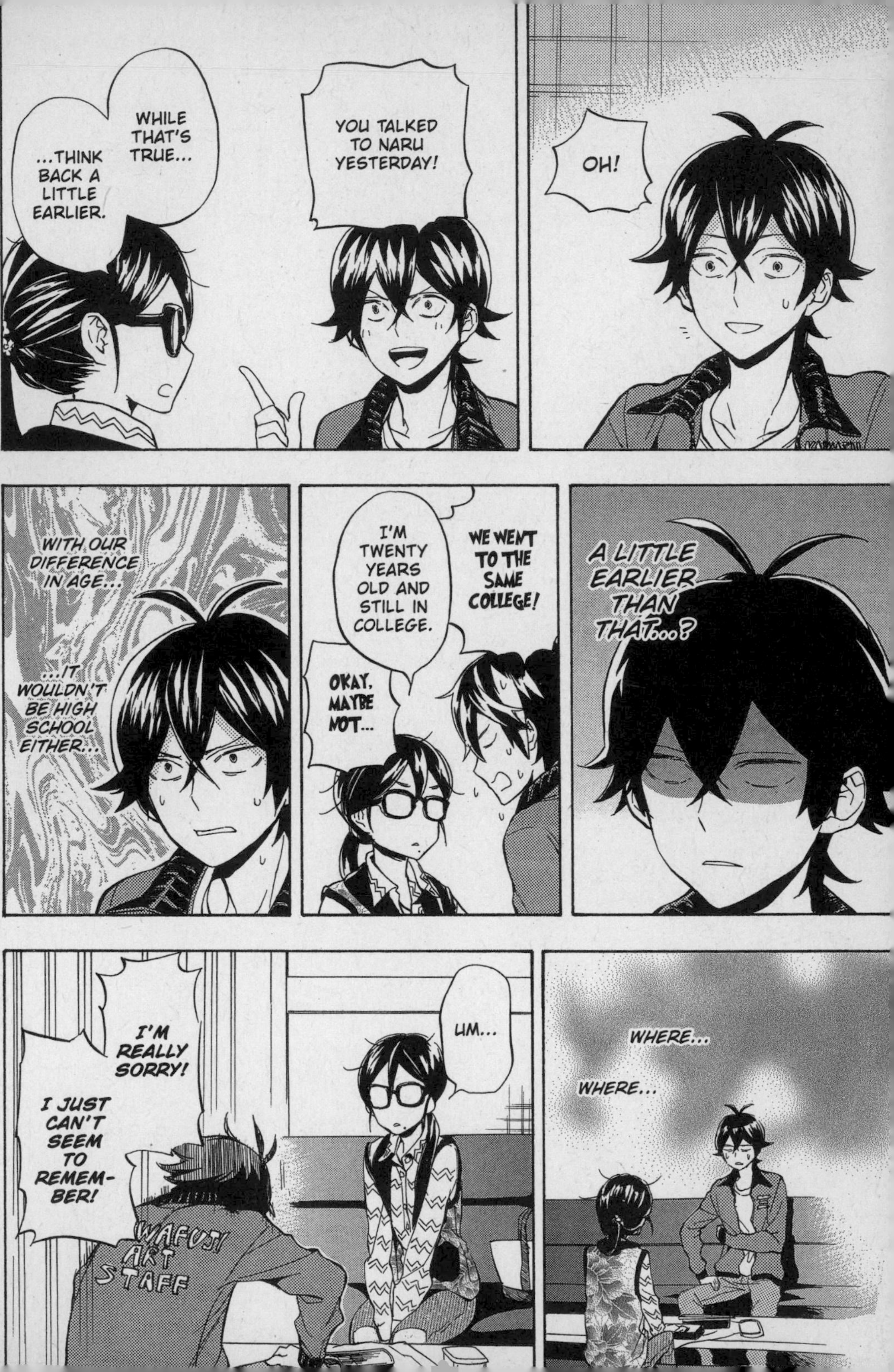
OH!
YOU TALKED TO NARU YESTERDAY!
WHILE THAT'S TRUE...
...THINK BACK A LITTLE EARLIER.
A LITTLE EARLIER THAN THAT...?
WE WENT TO THE SAME COLLEGE!
I'M TWENTY YEARS OLD AND STILL IN COLLEGE.
OKAY, MAYBE NOT...
WITH OUR DIFFERENCE IN AGE...
...IT WOULDN'T BE HIGH SCHOOL EITHER...
WHERE...
WHERE...
UM...
I'M REALLY SORRY!
I JUST CAN'T SEEM TO REMEMBER!
WAFUJI ART STAFF

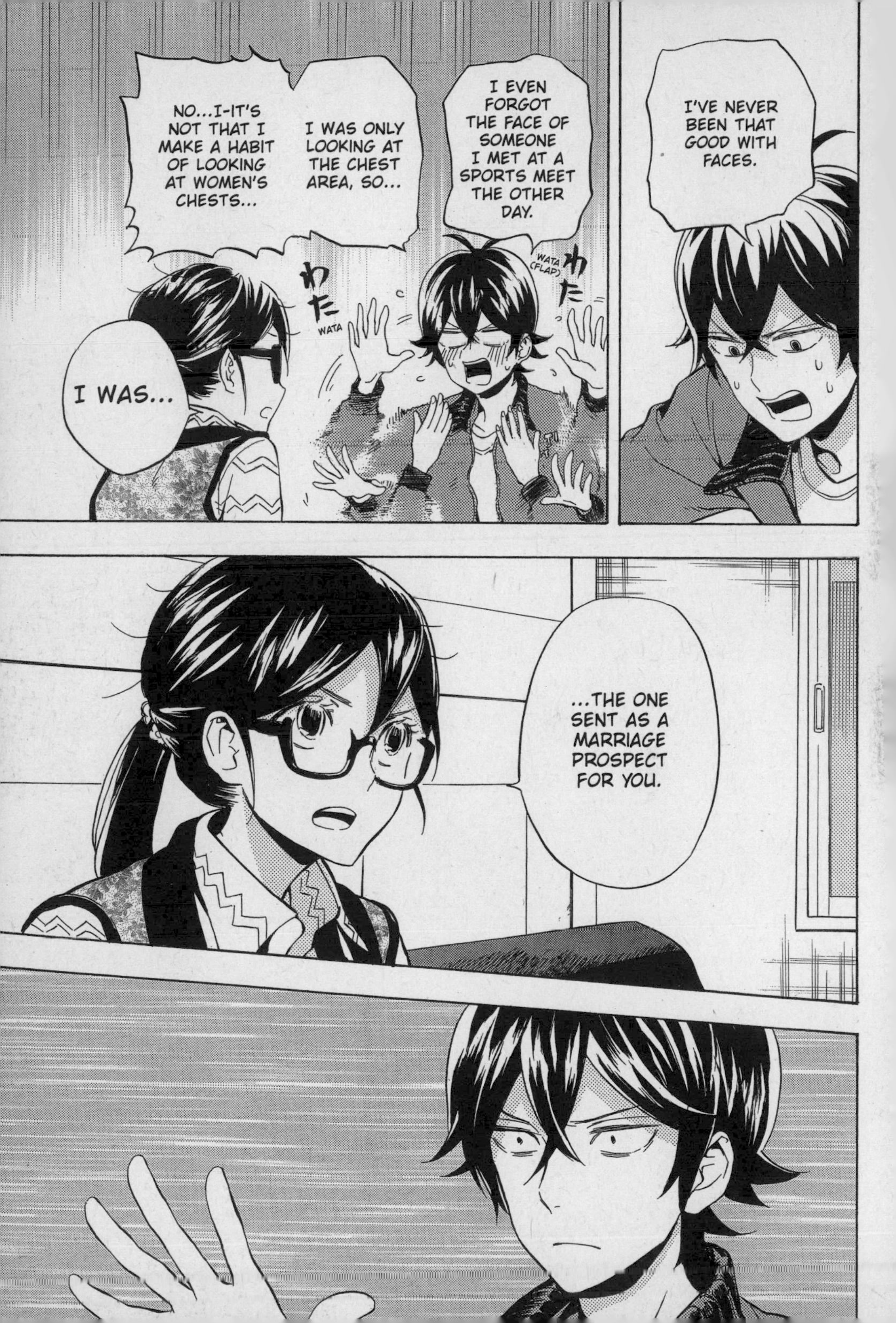
I'VE NEVER BEEN THAT GOOD WITH FACES.
I EVEN FORGOT THE FACE OF SOMEONE I MET AT A SPORTS MEET THE OTHER DAY.
わた WATA (FLAP)
I WAS ONLY LOOKING AT THE CHEST AREA, SO...
NO...I-IT'S NOT THAT I MAKE A HABIT OF LOOKING AT WOMEN'S CHESTS...
わた WATA
I WAS...
...THE ONE SENT AS A MARRIAGE PROSPECT FOR YOU.

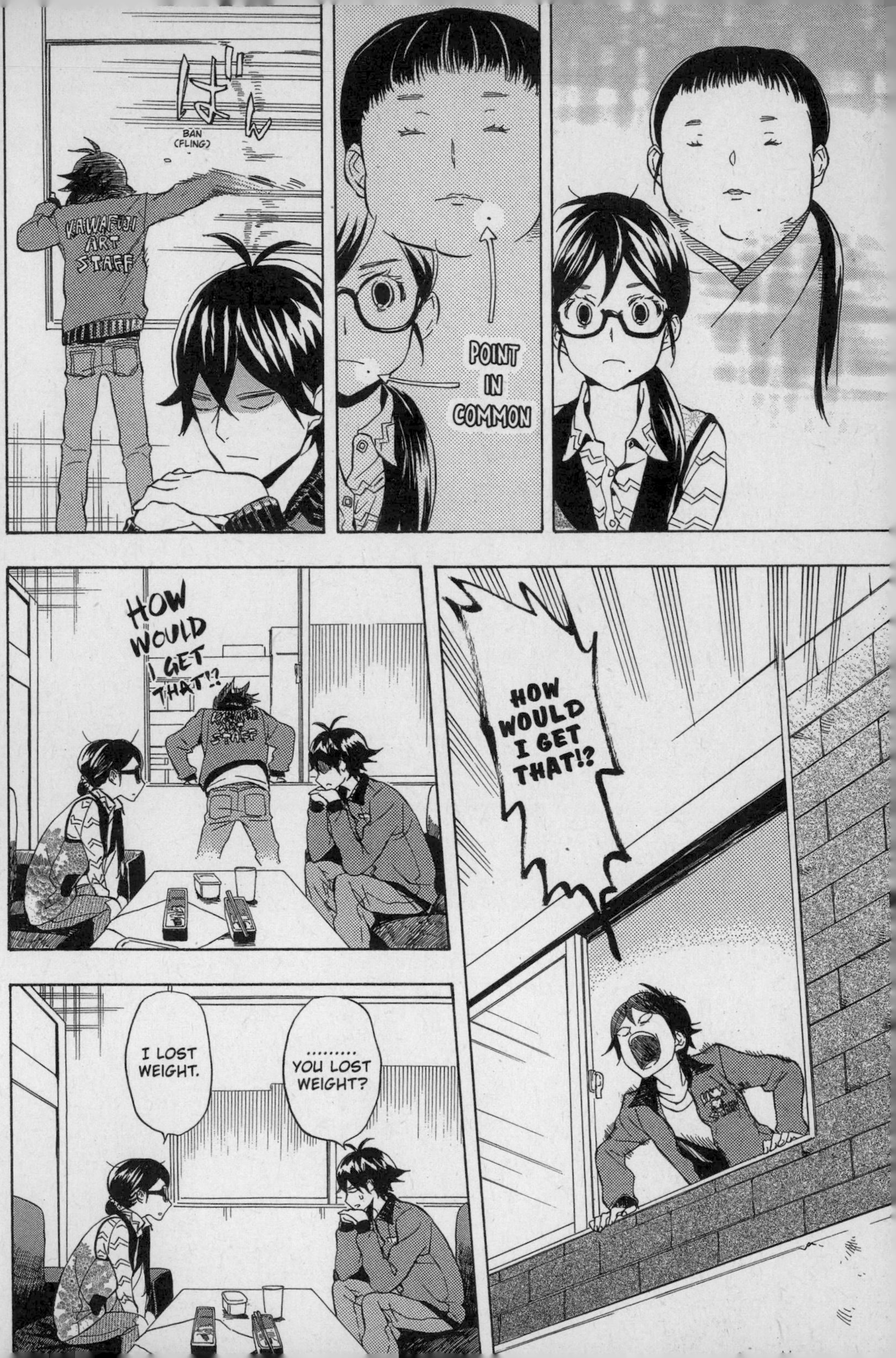
POINT IN COMMON
ばん
BAN (FLING)
HOW WOULD I GET THAT!?
HOW WOULD I GET THAT!?
I LOST WEIGHT.
.... YOU LOST WEIGHT?

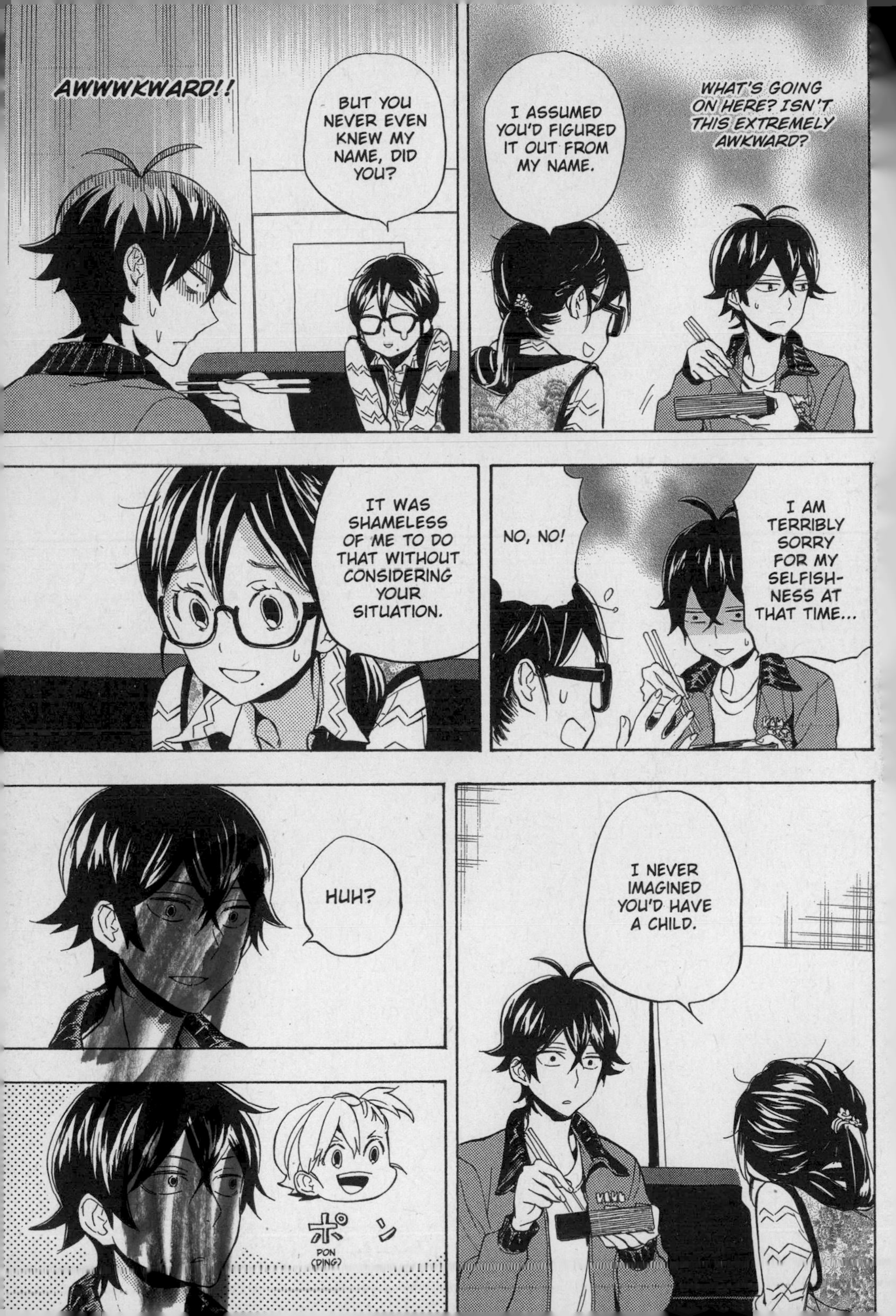
WHAT'S GOING ON HERE? ISN'T THIS EXTREMELY AWKWARD?
I ASSUMED YOU'D FIGURED IT OUT FROM MY NAME.
BUT YOU NEVER EVEN KNEW MY NAME, DID YOU?
AWWWKWARD!!
I AM TERRIBLY SORRY FOR MY SELFISH-NESS AT THAT TIME...
NO, NO!
IT WAS SHAMELESS OF ME TO DO THAT WITHOUT CONSIDERING YOUR SITUATION.
I NEVER IMAGINED YOU'D HAVE A CHILD.
HUH?
ポン
PON (DING)

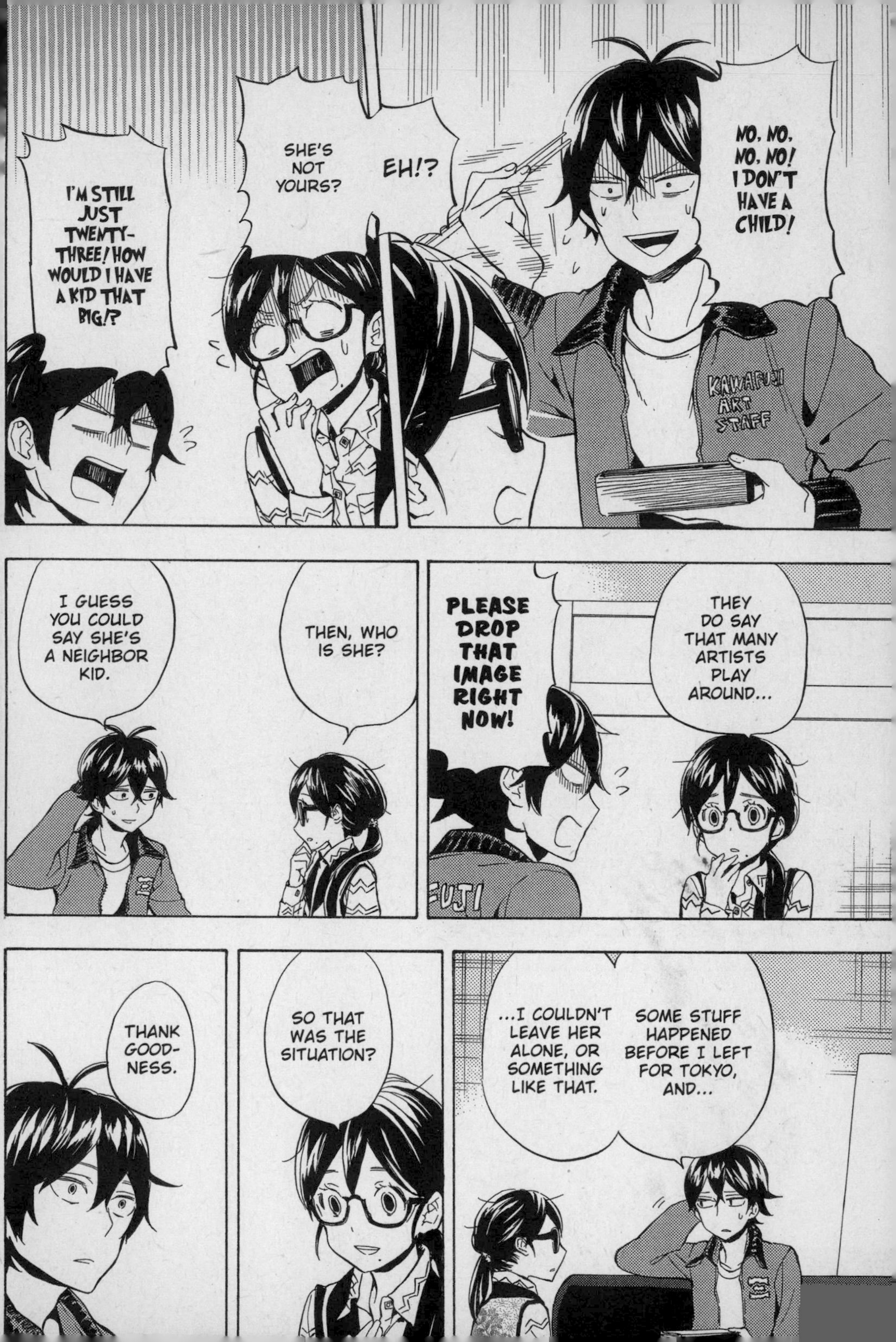
NO, NO, NO, NO! I DON'T HAVE A CHILD!
KAWAFUJI ART STAFF
EH!?
SHE'S NOT YOURS?
I'M STILL JUST TWENTY-THREE! HOW WOULD I HAVE A KID THAT BIG!?
THEY DO SAY THAT MANY ARTISTS PLAY AROUND...
PLEASE DROP THAT IMAGE RIGHT NOW!
THEN, WHO IS SHE?
I GUESS YOU COULD SAY SHE'S A NEIGHBOR KID.
SOME STUFF HAPPENED BEFORE I LEFT FOR TOKYO, AND...
...I COULDN'T LEAVE HER ALONE, OR SOMETHING LIKE THAT.
SO THAT WAS THE SITUATION?
THANK GOODNESS.

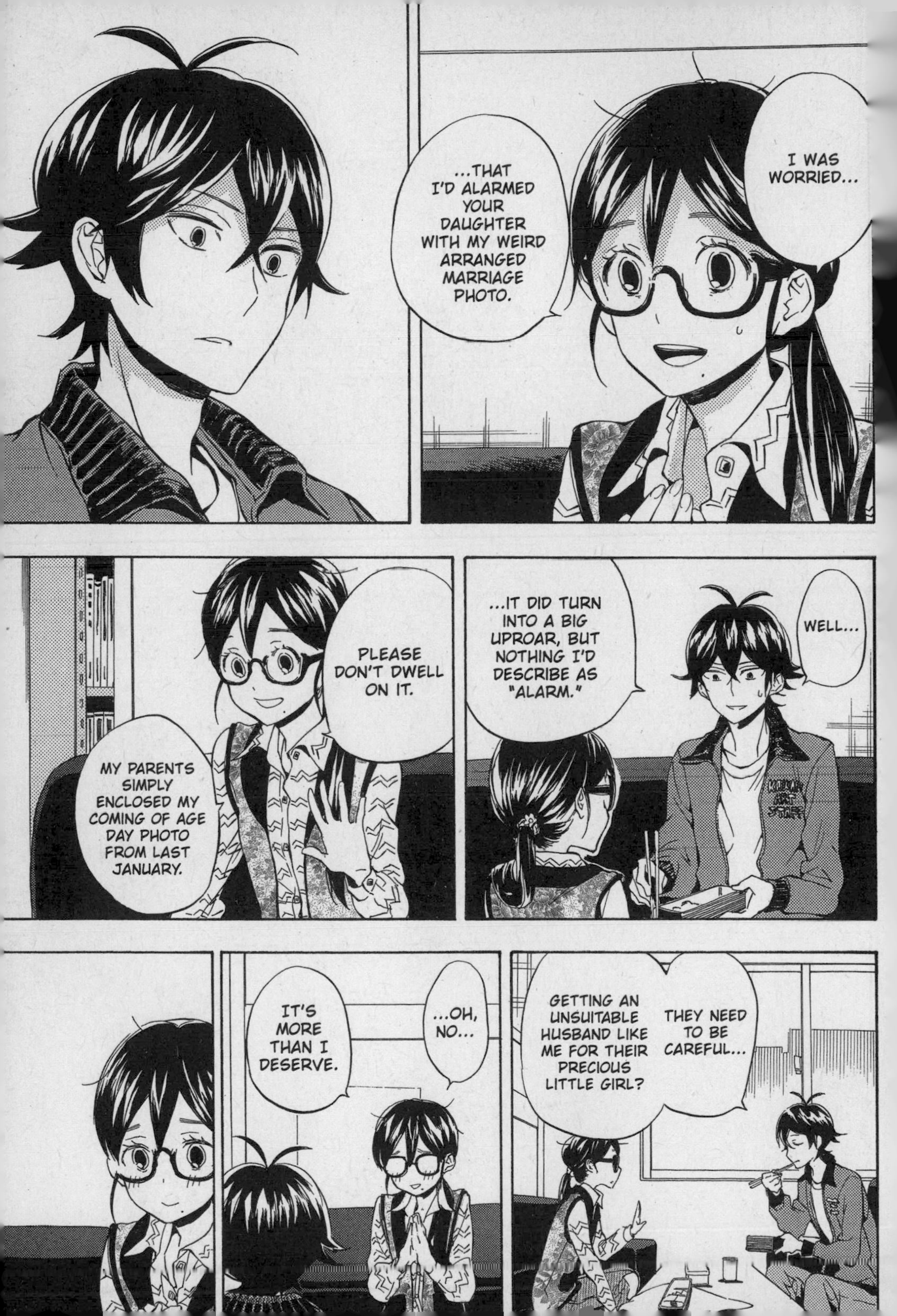
I WAS WORRIED...
...THAT I'D ALARMED YOUR DAUGHTER WITH MY WEIRD ARRANGED MARRIAGE PHOTO.
WELL...
...IT DID TURN INTO A BIG UPROAR, BUT NOTHING I'D DESCRIBE AS "ALARM."
PLEASE DON'T DWELL ON IT.
MY PARENTS SIMPLY ENCLOSED MY COMING OF AGE DAY PHOTO FROM LAST JANUARY.
THEY NEED TO BE CAREFUL...
GETTING AN UNSUITABLE HUSBAND LIKE ME FOR THEIR PRECIOUS LITTLE GIRL?
...OH, NO...
IT'S MORE THAN I DESERVE.

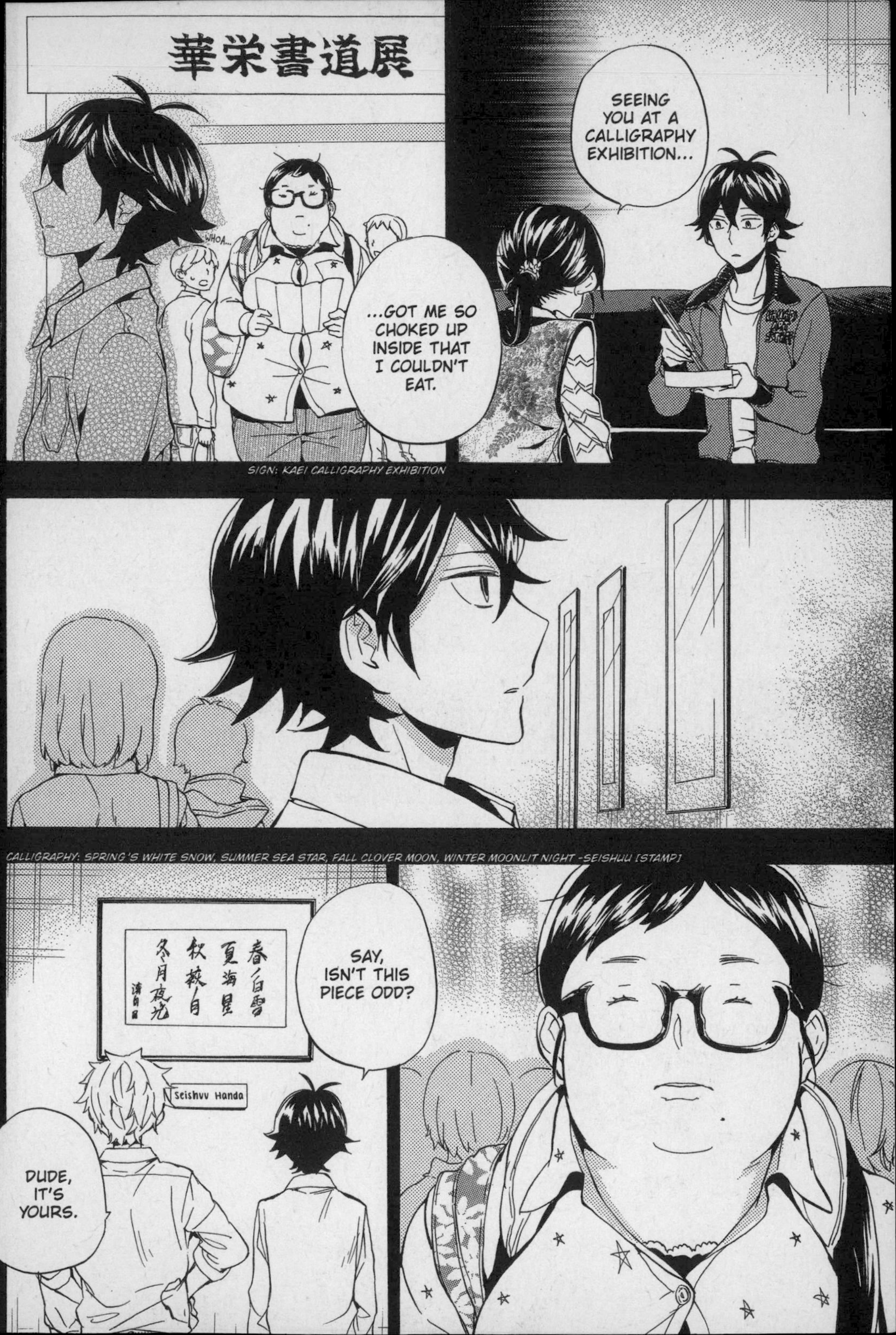
SEEING YOU AT A CALLIGRAPHY EXHIBITION...
華栄書道展
WHOA...
...GOT ME SO CHOKED UP INSIDE THAT I COULDN'T EAT.
SIGN: KAEI CALLIGRAPHY EXHIBITION
CALLIGRAPHY: SPRING'S WHITE SNOW, SUMMER SEA STAR, FALL CLOVER MOON, WINTER MOONLIT NIGHT -SEISHUU [STAMP]
SAY, ISN'T THIS PIECE ODD?
Seishuu Handa
DUDE, IT'S YOURS.

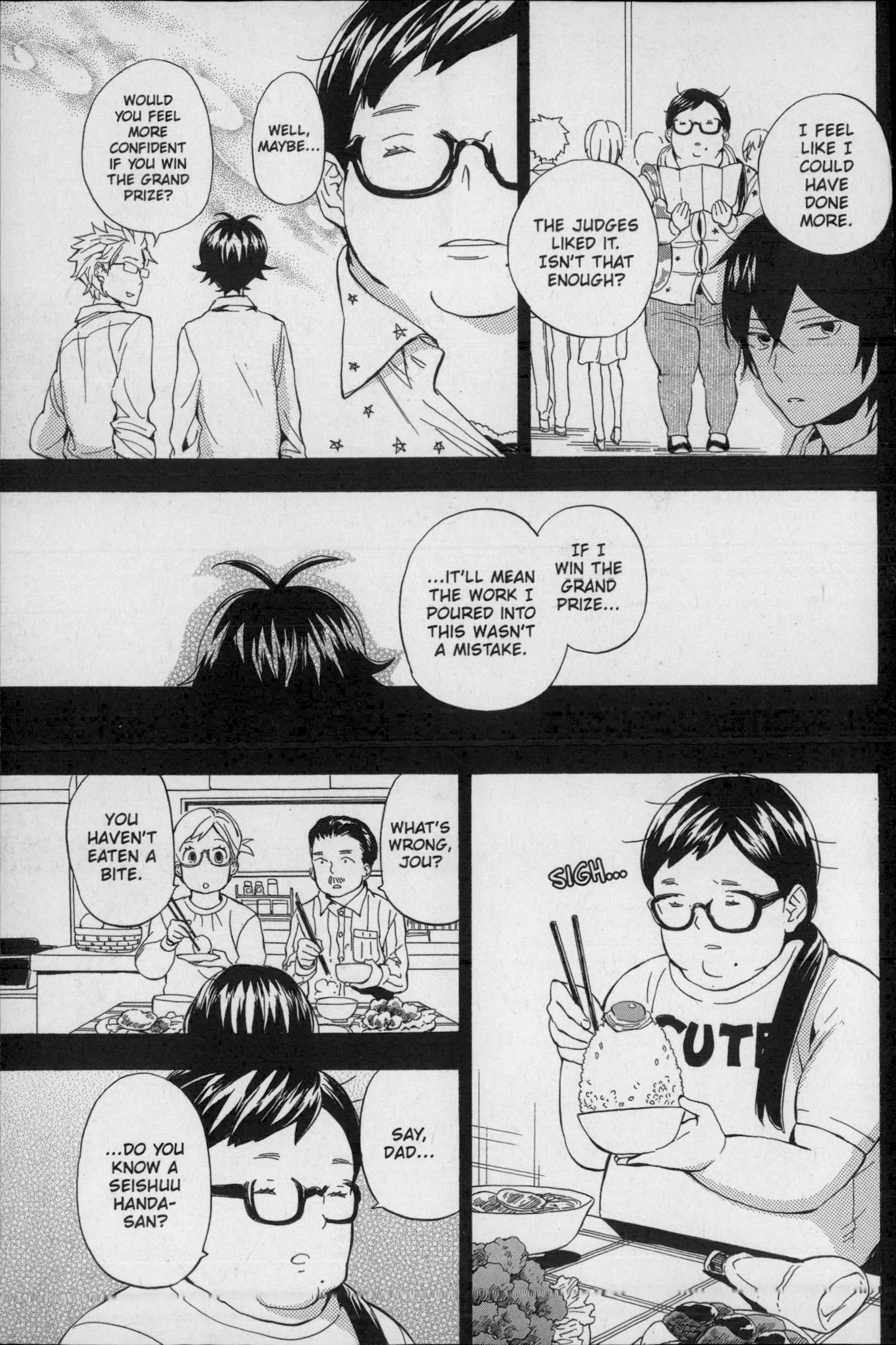
I FEEL LIKE I COULD HAVE DONE MORE.
THE JUDGES LIKED IT. ISN'T THAT ENOUGH?
WOULD YOU FEEL MORE CONFIDENT IF YOU WIN THE GRAND PRIZE?
WELL, MAYBE...
IF I WIN THE GRAND PRIZE...
...IT'LL MEAN THE WORK I POURED INTO THIS WASN'T A MISTAKE.
SIGH...
CUTE
WHAT'S WRONG, JOU?
YOU HAVEN'T EATEN A BITE.
SAY, DAD...
...DO YOU KNOW A SEISHUU HANDA-SAN?

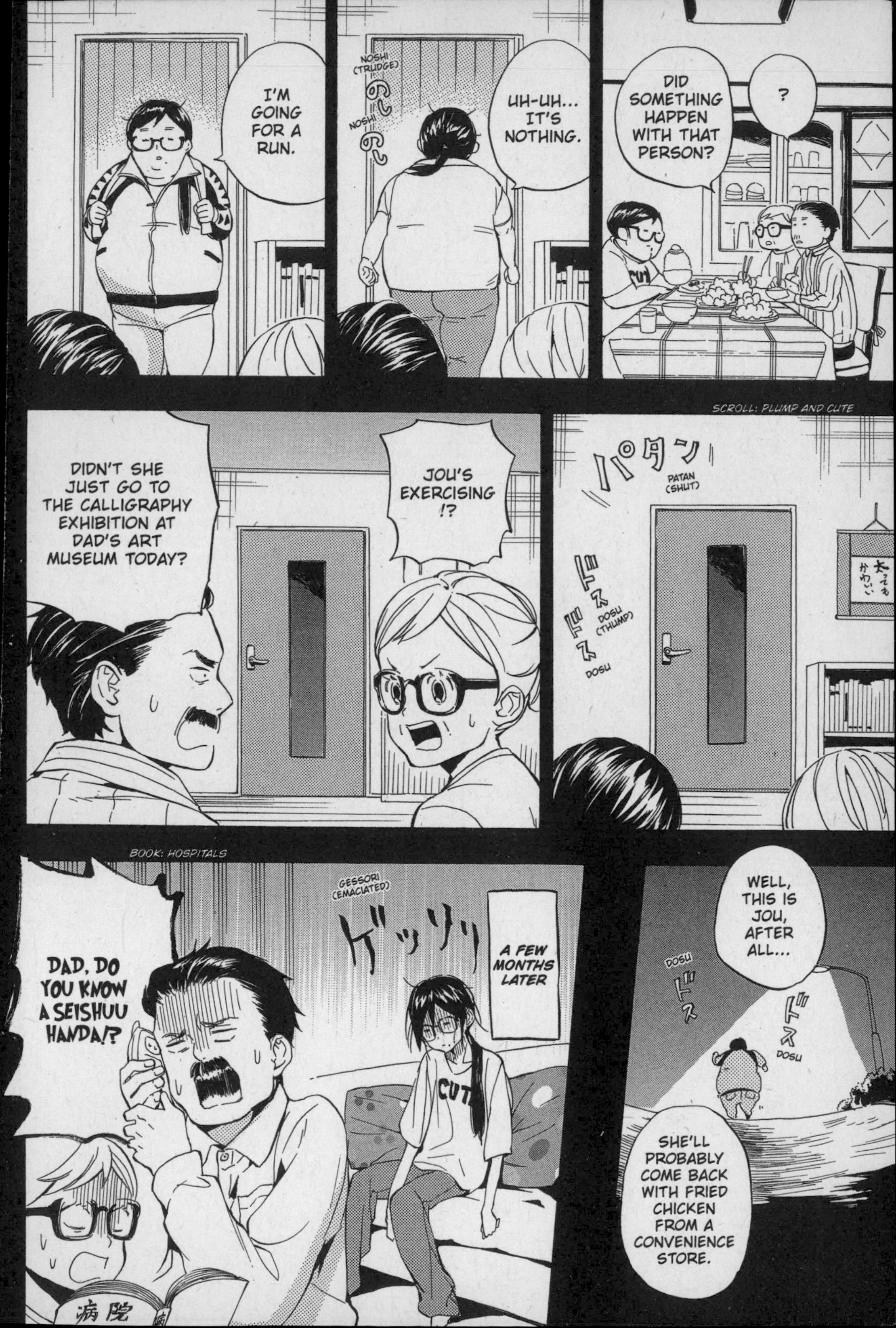
?
DID SOMETHING HAPPEN WITH THAT PERSON?
UH-UH... IT'S NOTHING.
NOSHI (TRUDGE)
NOSHI
I'M GOING FOR A RUN.
SCROLL: PLUMP AND CUTE
パタン
PATAN (SHUT)
ドスドス
DOSU (THUMP)
DOSU
JOU'S EXERCISING!?
DIDN'T SHE JUST GO TO THE CALLIGRAPHY EXHIBITION AT DAD'S ART MUSEUM TODAY?
WELL, THIS IS JOU, AFTER ALL...
ドス
DOSU
ドス
DOSU
SHE'LL PROBABLY COME BACK WITH FRIED CHICKEN FROM A CONVENIENCE STORE.
BOOK: HOSPITALS
GESSORI (EMACIATED)
ゲッソリ
A FEW MONTHS LATER
DAD, DO YOU KNOW A SEISHUU HANDA!?
病院

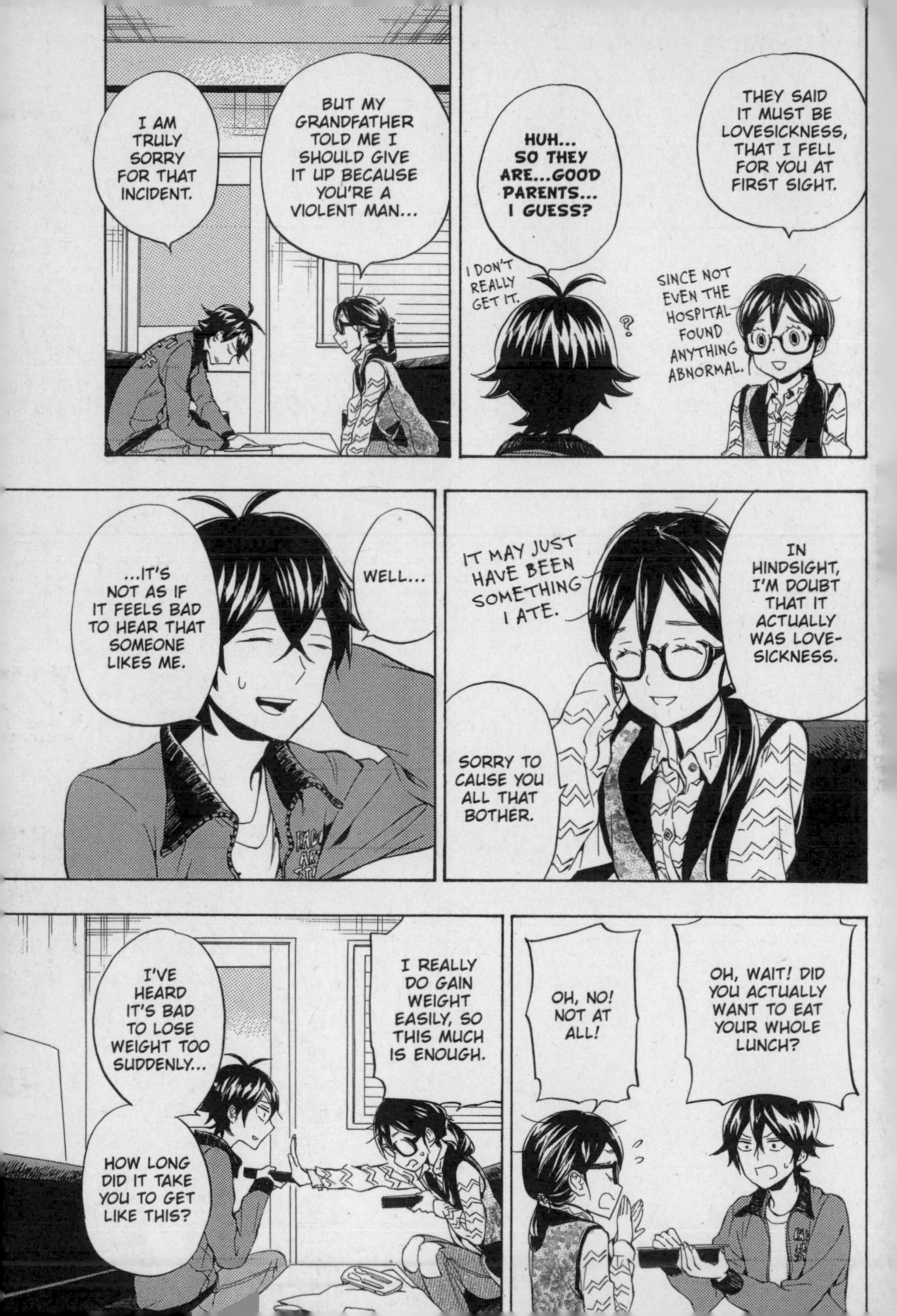
THEY SAID IT MUST BE LOVESICKNESS, THAT I FELL FOR YOU AT FIRST SIGHT.
SINCE NOT EVEN THE HOSPITAL FOUND ANYTHING ABNORMAL.
HUH... SO THEY ARE...GOOD PARENTS... I GUESS?
I DON'T REALLY GET IT.
BUT MY GRANDFATHER TOLD ME I SHOULD GIVE IT UP BECAUSE YOU'RE A VIOLENT MAN...
I AM TRULY SORRY FOR THAT INCIDENT.
IN HINDSIGHT, I'M DOUBT THAT IT ACTUALLY WAS LOVE-SICKNESS.
IT MAY JUST HAVE BEEN SOMETHING I ATE.
SORRY TO CAUSE YOU ALL THAT BOTHER.
WELL...
...IT'S NOT AS IF IT FEELS BAD TO HEAR THAT SOMEONE LIKES ME.
OH, WAIT! DID YOU ACTUALLY WANT TO EAT YOUR WHOLE LUNCH?
OH, NO! NOT AT ALL!
I REALLY DO GAIN WEIGHT EASILY, SO THIS MUCH IS ENOUGH.
I'VE HEARD IT'S BAD TO LOSE WEIGHT TOO SUDDENLY...
HOW LONG DID IT TAKE YOU TO GET LIKE THIS?

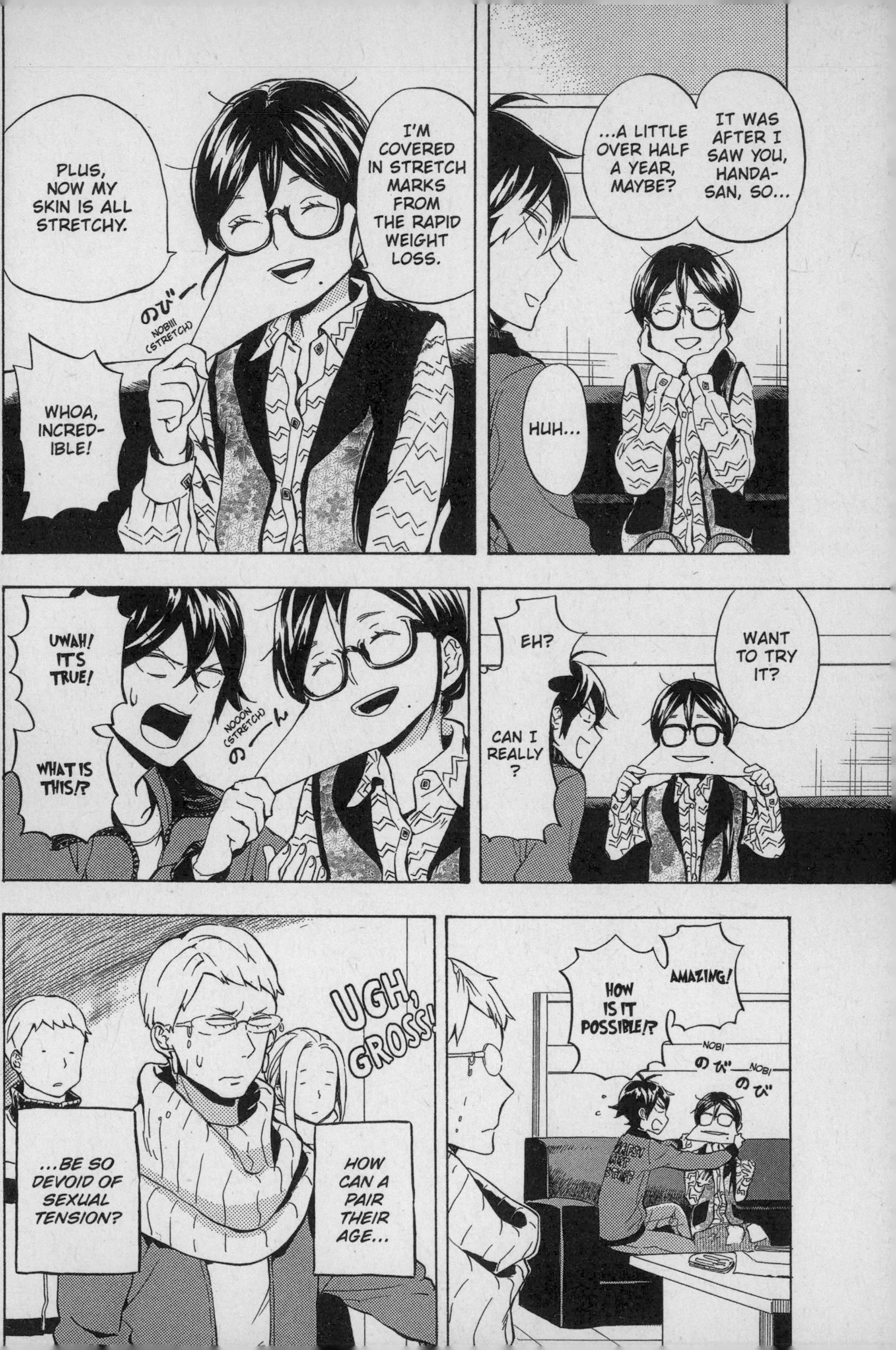
IT WAS AFTER I SAW YOU, HANDA-SAN, SO...
...A LITTLE OVER HALF A YEAR, MAYBE?
HUH...
I'M COVERED IN STRETCH MARKS FROM THE RAPID WEIGHT LOSS.
PLUS, NOW MY SKIN IS ALL STRETCHY.
のびー
NOBIII (STRETCH)
WHOA, INCREDIBLE!
WANT TO TRY IT?
EH?
CAN I REALLY?
UWAH! IT'S TRUE!
のーん
NOOON (STRETCH)
WHAT IS THIS!?
AMAZING!
HOW IS IT POSSIBLE!?
のび NOBI
のび NOBI
UGH, GROSS!
HOW CAN A PAIR THEIR AGE...
...BE SO DEVOID OF SEXUAL TENSION?

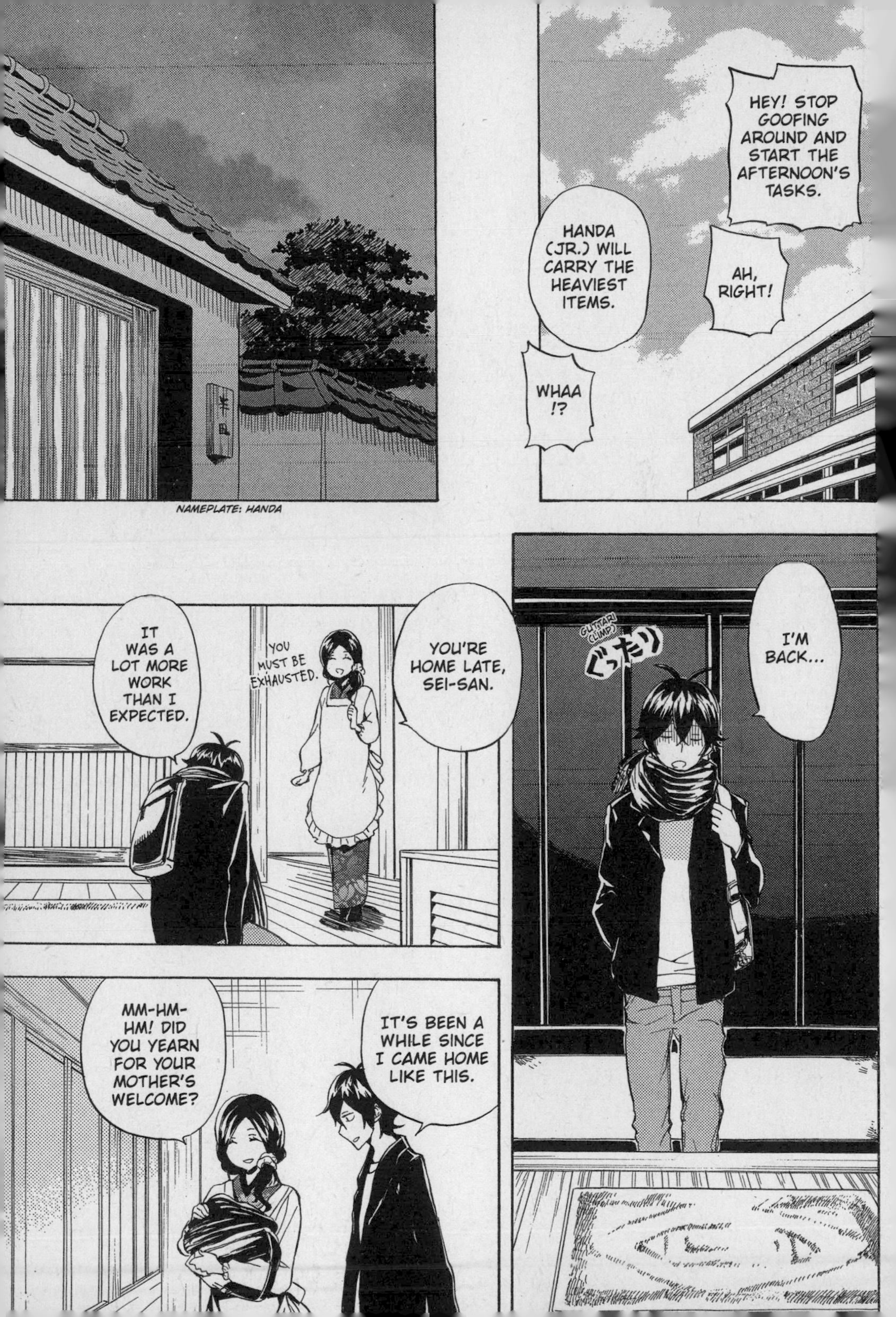
HEY! STOP GOOFING AROUND AND START THE AFTERNOON'S TASKS.
AH, RIGHT!
HANDA (JR.) WILL CARRY THE HEAVIEST ITEMS.
WHAA!?
NAMEPLATE: HANDA
I'M BACK...
ぐったり
GUTTARI (LIMP)
YOU'RE HOME LATE, SEI-SAN.
YOU MUST BE EXHAUSTED.
IT WAS A LOT MORE WORK THAN I EXPECTED.
IT'S BEEN A WHILE SINCE I CAME HOME LIKE THIS.
MM-HM-HM! DID YOU YEARN FOR YOUR MOTHER'S WELCOME?

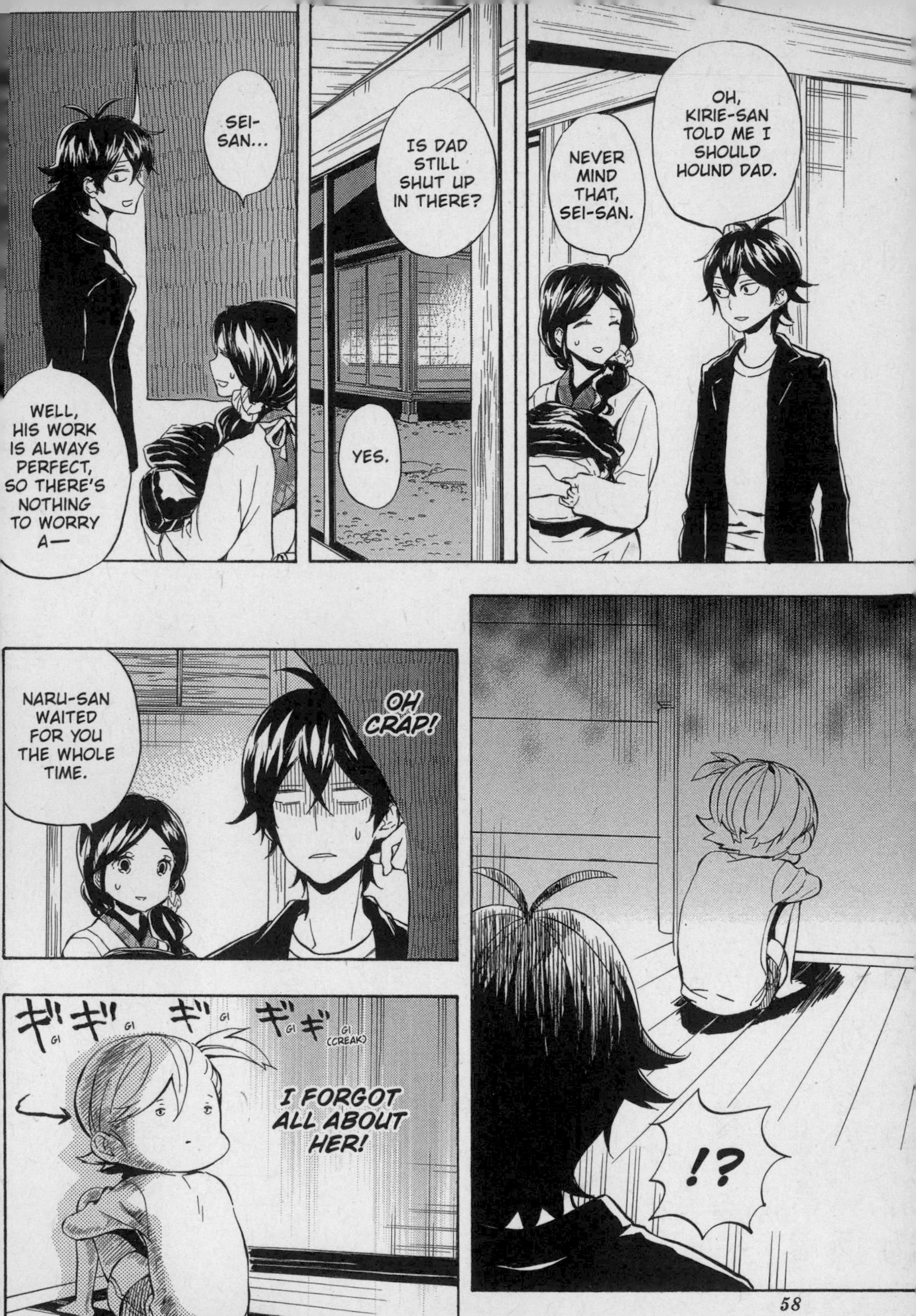
OH, KIRIE-SAN TOLD ME I SHOULD HOUND DAD.
NEVER MIND THAT, SEI-SAN.
IS DAD STILL SHUT UP IN THERE?
YES.
SEI-SAN...
WELL, HIS WORK IS ALWAYS PERFECT, SO THERE'S NOTHING TO WORRY A—
!?
NARU-SAN WAITED FOR YOU THE WHOLE TIME.
OH CRAP!
ギ GI ギ GI ギ GI ギ GI ギ GI (CREAK)
I FORGOT ALL ABOUT HER!

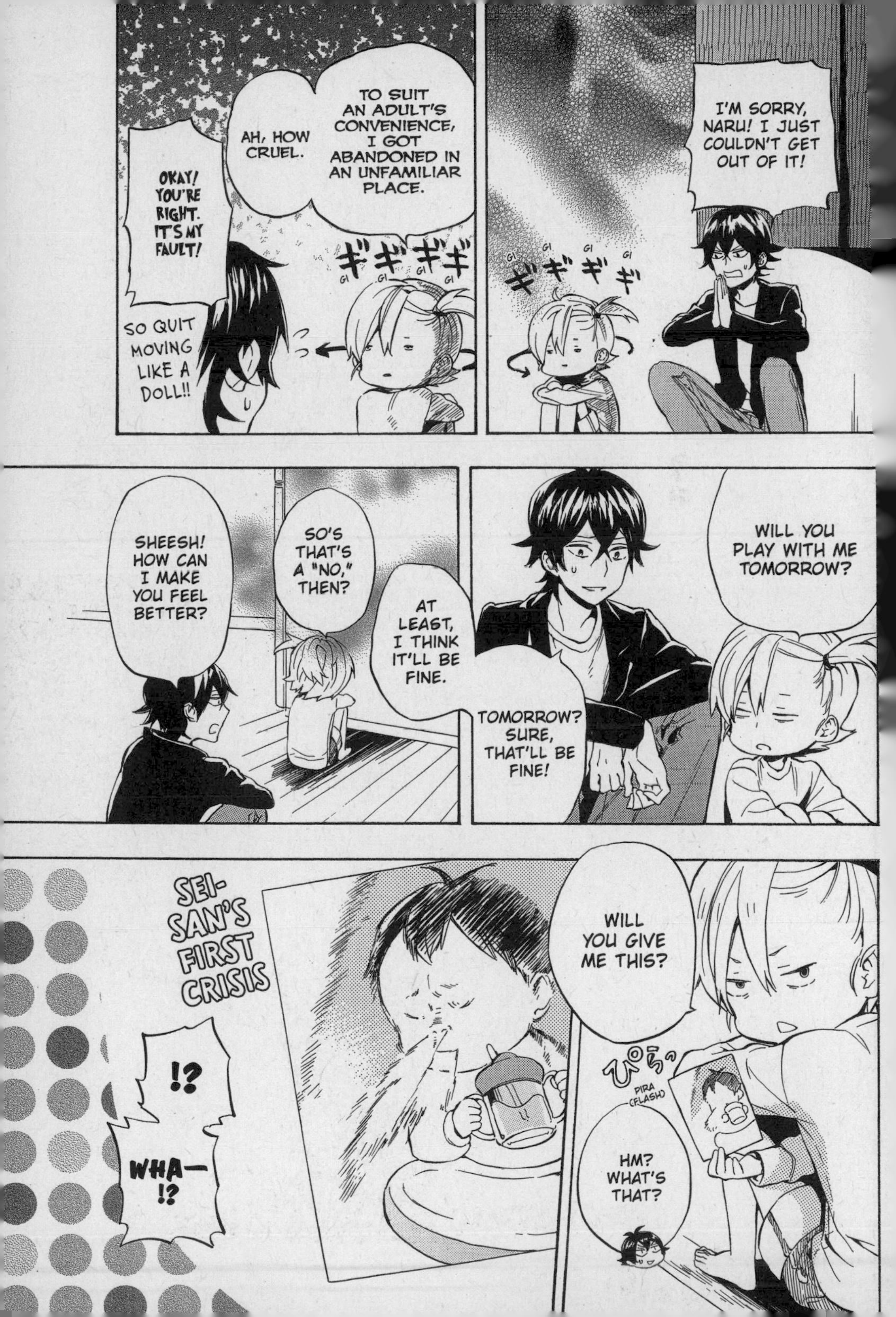
I'M SORRY, NARU! I JUST COULDN'T GET OUT OF IT!
ギギギギ
GI GI GI GI
TO SUIT AN ADULT'S CONVENIENCE, I GOT ABANDONED IN AN UNFAMILIAR PLACE.
AH, HOW CRUEL.
OKAY! YOU'RE RIGHT. IT'S MY FAULT!
ギギギギ
GI GI GI GI
SO QUIT MOVING LIKE A DOLL!!
WILL YOU PLAY WITH ME TOMORROW?
TOMORROW? SURE, THAT'LL BE FINE!
AT LEAST, I THINK IT'LL BE FINE.
SO'S THAT'S A "NO," THEN?
SHEESH! HOW CAN I MAKE YOU FEEL BETTER?
WILL YOU GIVE ME THIS?
ぴらっ
PIRA (FLASH)
HM? WHAT'S THAT?
SEI-SAN'S FIRST CRISIS
!?
WHA— !?

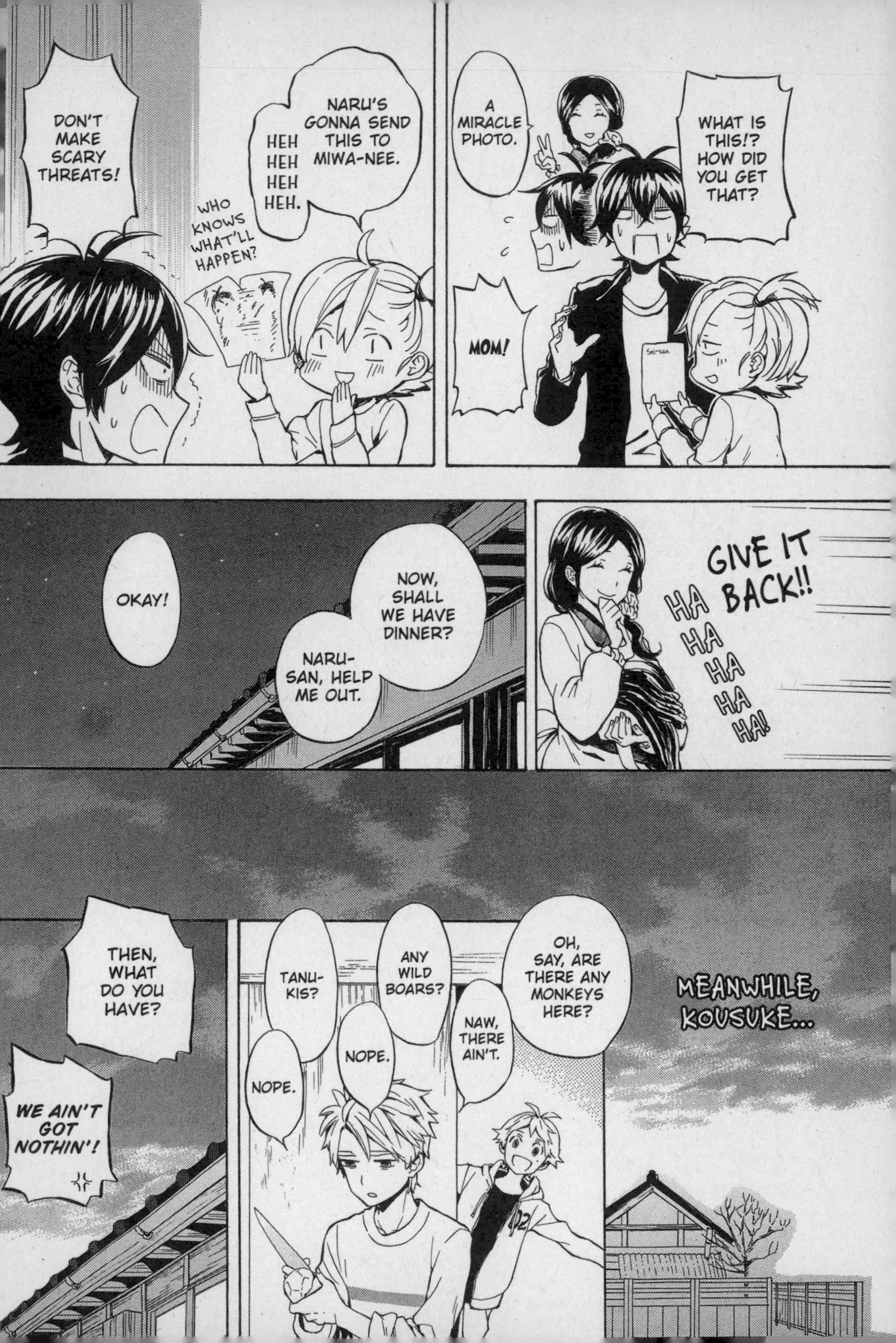
WHAT IS THIS!? HOW DID YOU GET THAT?
A MIRACLE PHOTO.
MOM!
Sei-san
NARU'S GONNA SEND THIS TO MIWA-NEE.
HEH HEH HEH HEH.
WHO KNOWS WHAT'LL HAPPEN?
DON'T MAKE SCARY THREATS!
GIVE IT BACK!!
HA HA HA HA HA!
NOW, SHALL WE HAVE DINNER?
NARU-SAN, HELP ME OUT.
OKAY!
MEANWHILE, KOUSUKE...
OH, SAY, ARE THERE ANY MONKEYS HERE?
NAW, THERE AIN'T.
ANY WILD BOARS?
NOPE.
TANUKIS?
NOPE.
THEN, WHAT DO YOU HAVE?
WE AIN'T GOT NOTHIN'!

THOSE CLOTHES ARE SO CUTE.
NARU USED UP ALL HER NEW YEAR'S MONEY!

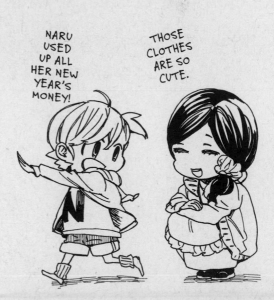

BARAKAMON

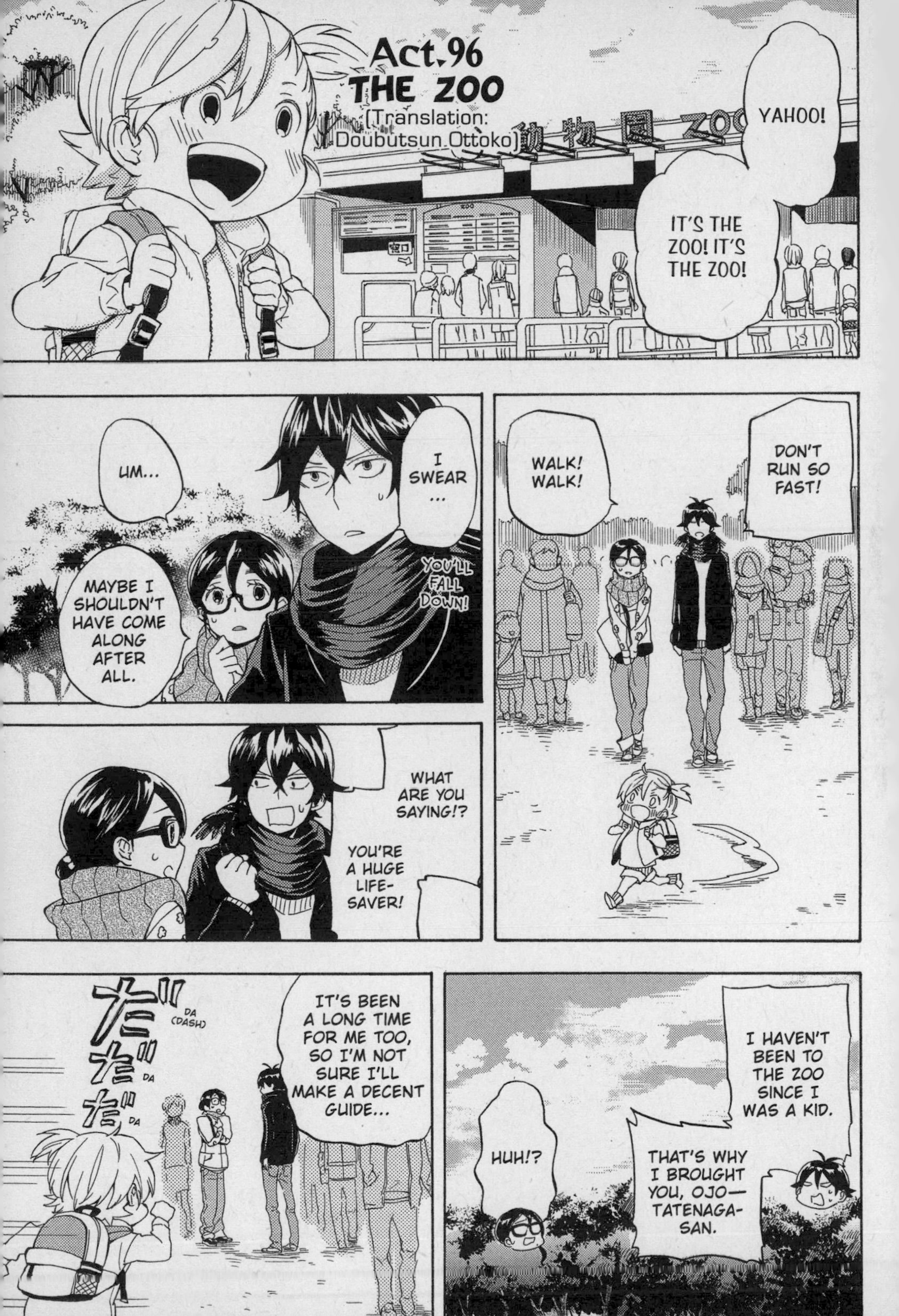
Act.96
THE ZOO
(Translation: Doubutsun Ottoko)
動物園 ZOO
YAHOO!
IT'S THE ZOO! IT'S THE ZOO!
DON'T RUN SO FAST!
WALK! WALK!
I SWEAR ...
UM...
YOU'LL FALL DOWN!
MAYBE I SHOULDN'T HAVE COME ALONG AFTER ALL.
WHAT ARE YOU SAYING!?
YOU'RE A HUGE LIFE-SAVER!
I HAVEN'T BEEN TO THE ZOO SINCE I WAS A KID.
HUH!?
THAT'S WHY I BROUGHT YOU, OJO—TATENAGA-SAN.
ダッ
DA (DASH)
IT'S BEEN A LONG TIME FOR ME TOO, SO I'M NOT SURE I'LL MAKE A DECENT GUIDE...
だっ
DA
だっ
DA

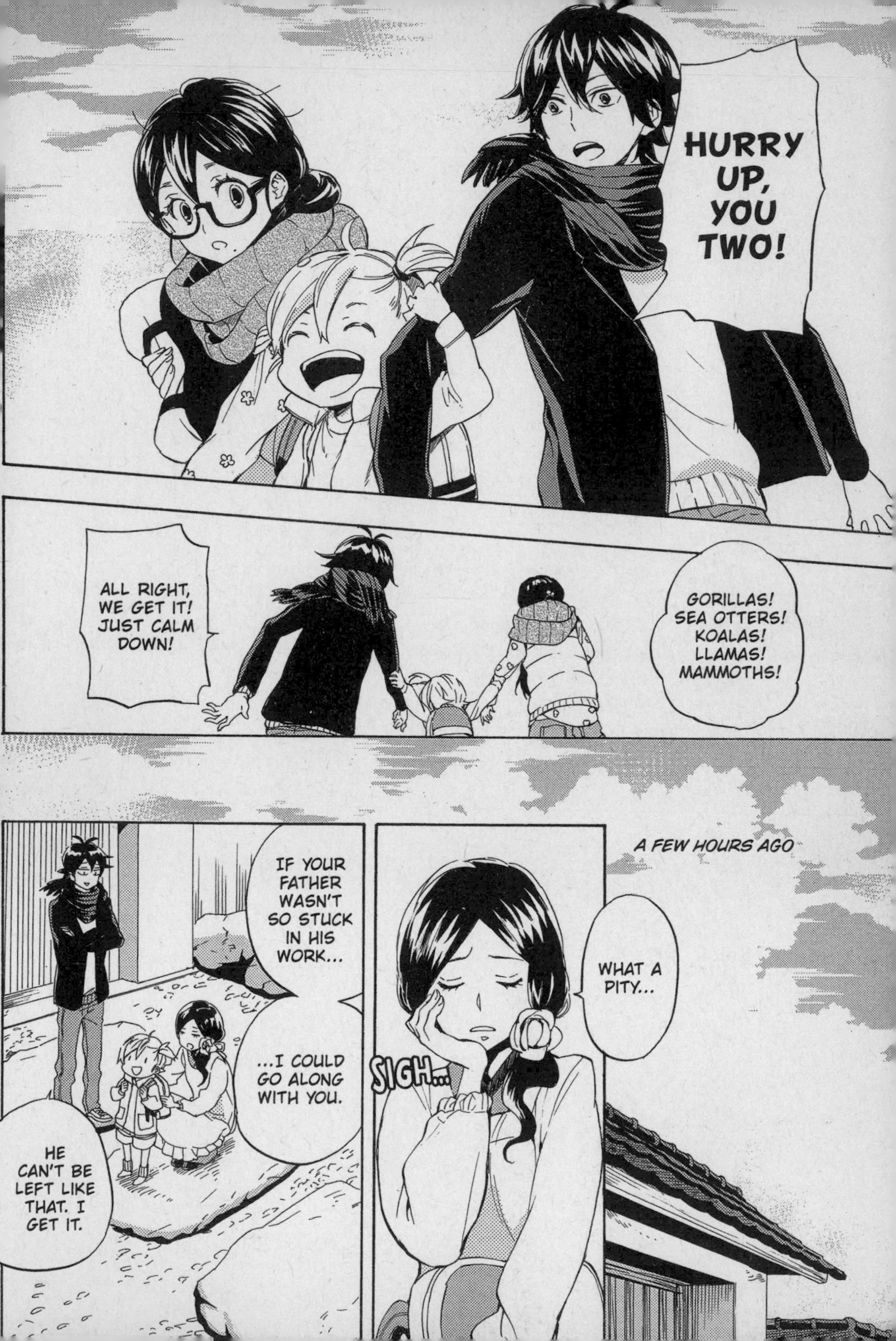
HURRY UP, YOU TWO!
GORILLAS! SEA OTTERS! KOALAS! LLAMAS! MAMMOTHS!
ALL RIGHT, WE GET IT! JUST CALM DOWN!
A FEW HOURS AGO
WHAT A PITY...
SIGH...
IF YOUR FATHER WASN'T SO STUCK IN HIS WORK...
...I COULD GO ALONG WITH YOU.
HE CAN'T BE LEFT LIKE THAT. I GET IT.

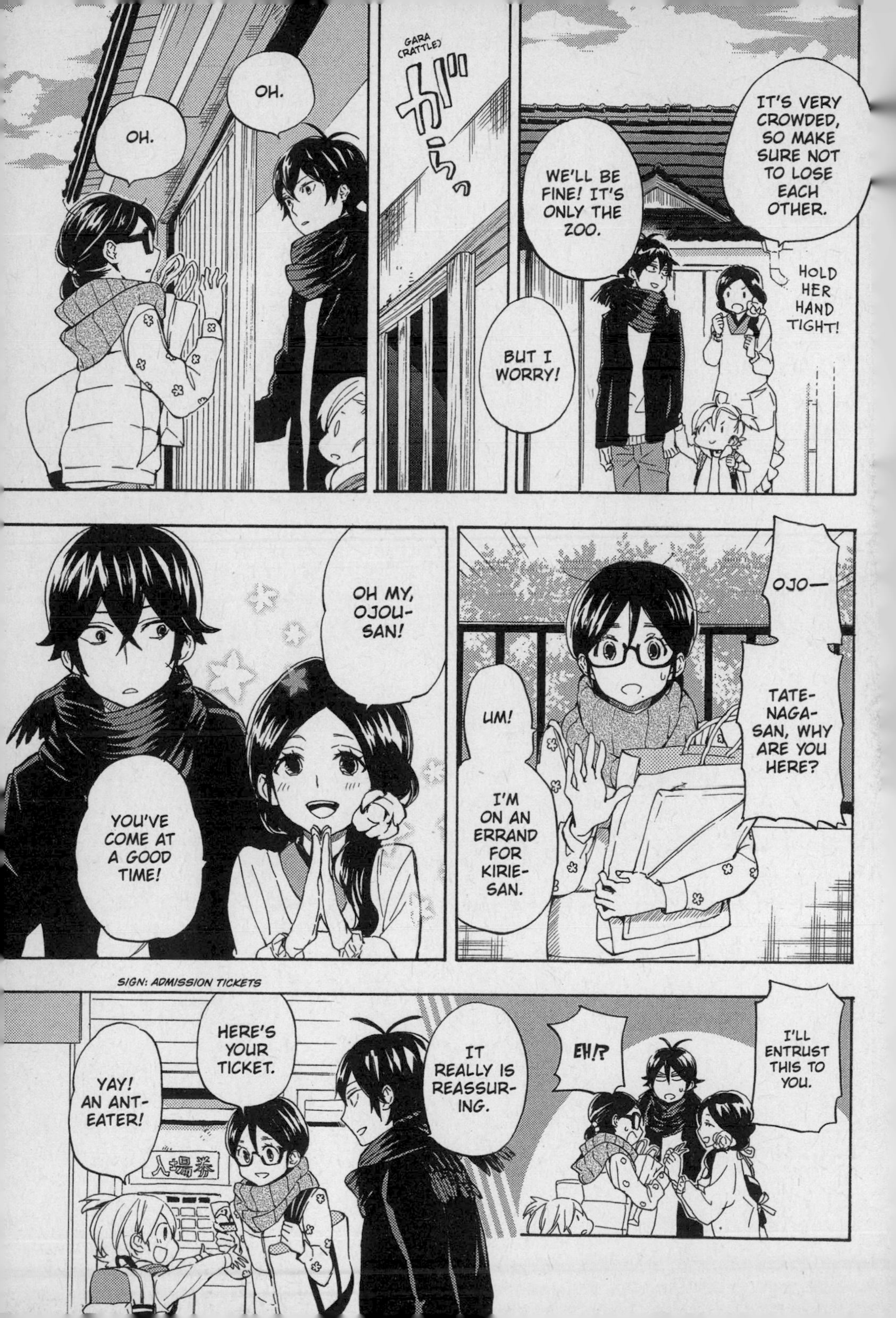
IT'S VERY CROWDED, SO MAKE SURE NOT TO LOSE EACH OTHER.
HOLD HER HAND TIGHT!
WE'LL BE FINE! IT'S ONLY THE ZOO.
BUT I WORRY!
GARA (RATTLE)
がらっ
OH.
OH.
OJO—
TATE-NAGA-SAN, WHY ARE YOU HERE?
UM!
I'M ON AN ERRAND FOR KIRIE-SAN.
OH MY, OJOU-SAN!
YOU'VE COME AT A GOOD TIME!
I'LL ENTRUST THIS TO YOU.
EH!?
SIGN: ADMISSION TICKETS
IT REALLY IS REASSURING.
HERE'S YOUR TICKET.
YAY! AN ANT-EATER!
入場券

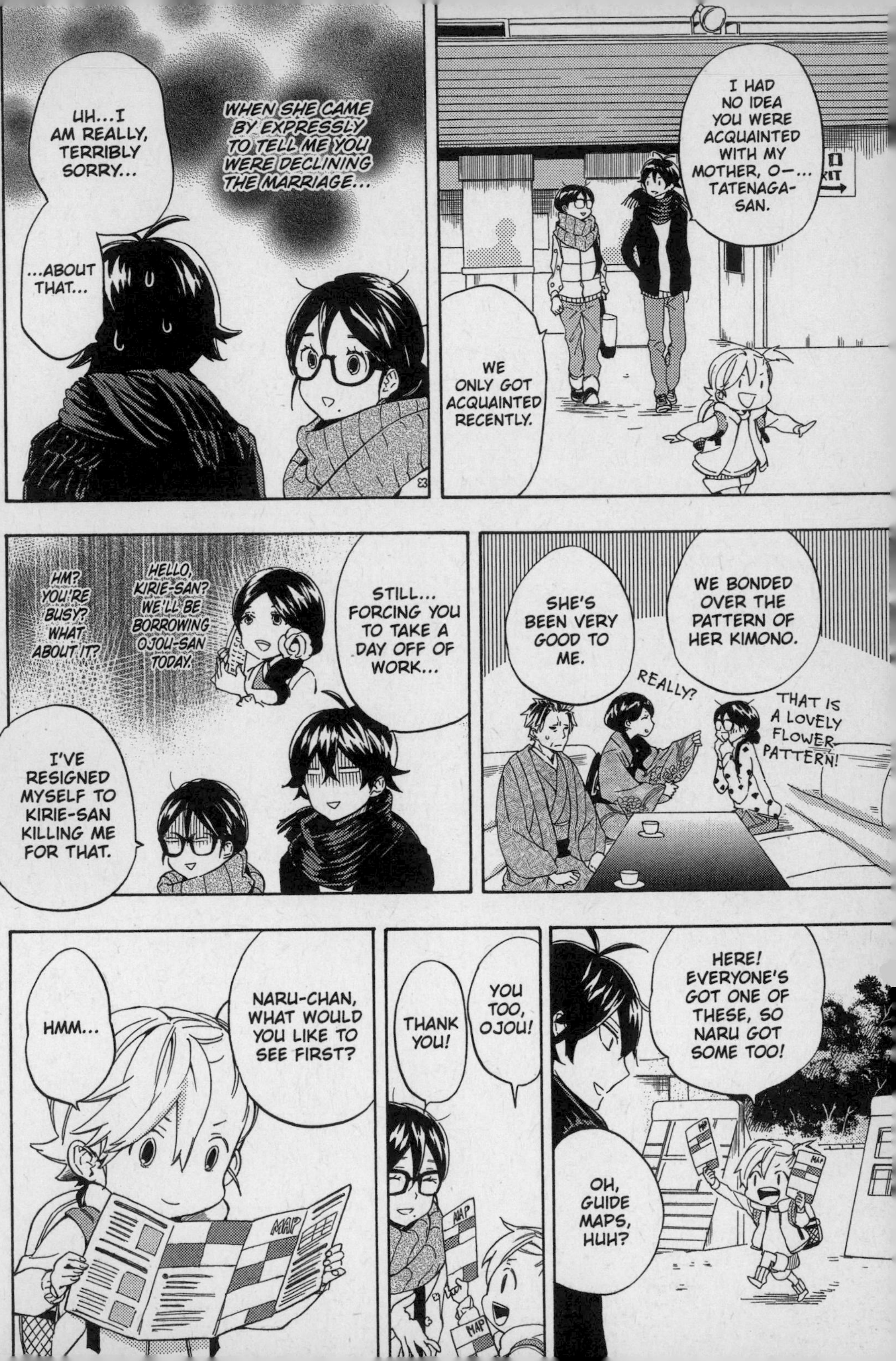
I HAD NO IDEA YOU WERE ACQUAINTED WITH MY MOTHER, O—... TATENAGA-SAN.
WE ONLY GOT ACQUAINTED RECENTLY.
WHEN SHE CAME BY EXPRESSLY TO TELL ME YOU WERE DECLINING THE MARRIAGE...
UH...I AM REALLY, TERRIBLY SORRY...
...ABOUT THAT...
WE BONDED OVER THE PATTERN OF HER KIMONO.
SHE'S BEEN VERY GOOD TO ME.
REALLY?
THAT IS A LOVELY FLOWER PATTERN!
STILL... FORCING YOU TO TAKE A DAY OFF OF WORK...
HELLO, KIRIE-SAN? WE'LL BE BORROWING OJOU-SAN TODAY.
HM? YOU'RE BUSY? WHAT ABOUT IT?
I'VE RESIGNED MYSELF TO KIRIE-SAN KILLING ME FOR THAT.
HERE! EVERYONE'S GOT ONE OF THESE, SO NARU GOT SOME TOO!
OH, GUIDE MAPS, HUH?
YOU TOO, OJOU!
THANK YOU!
NARU-CHAN, WHAT WOULD YOU LIKE TO SEE FIRST?
HMM...

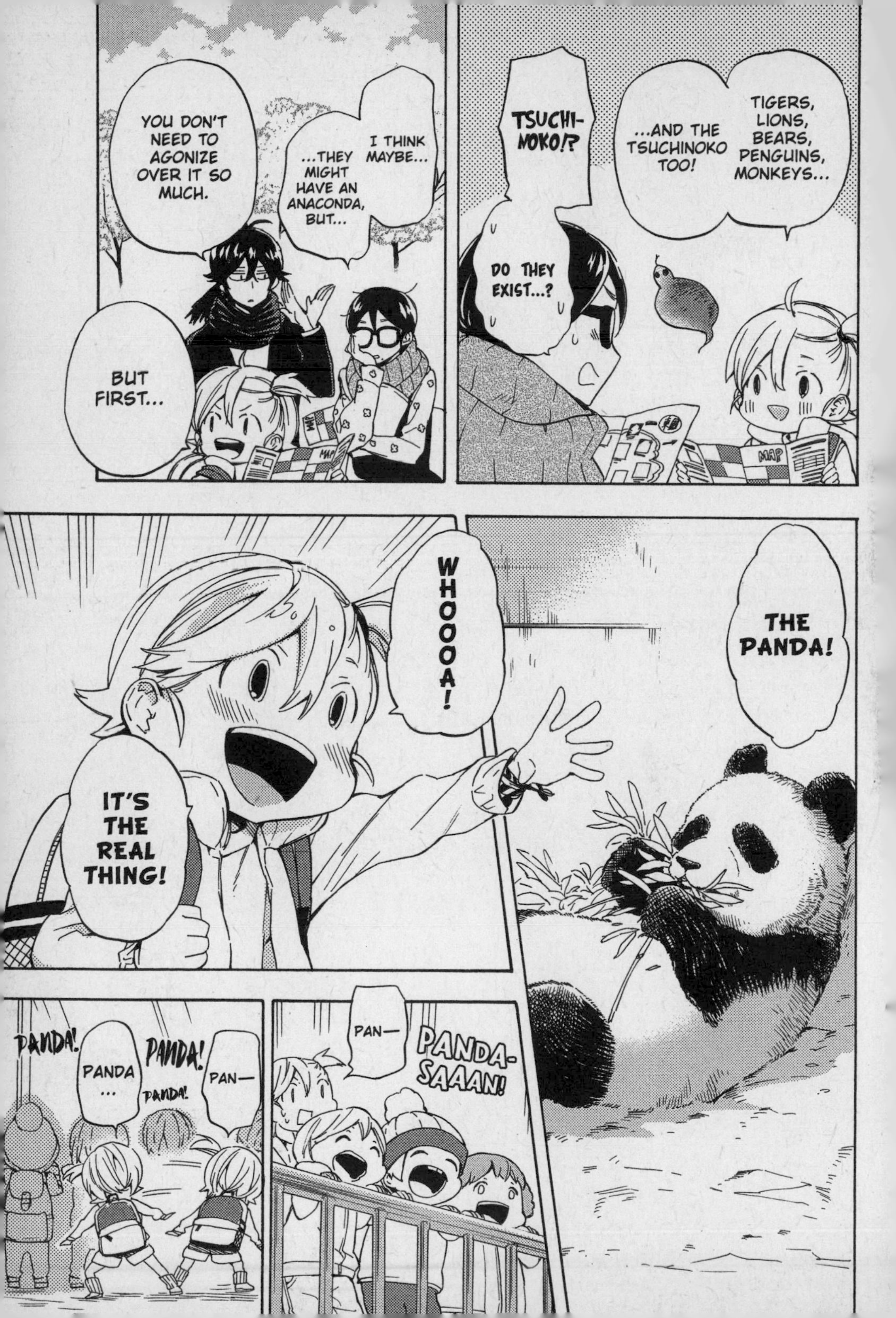
TIGERS, LIONS, BEARS, PENGUINS, MONKEYS...
...AND THE TSUCHINOKO TOO!
TSUCHI-NOKO!?
DO THEY EXIST...?
I THINK MAYBE...
...THEY MIGHT HAVE AN ANACONDA, BUT...
YOU DON'T NEED TO AGONIZE OVER IT SO MUCH.
BUT FIRST...
THE PANDA!
WHOOOOA!
IT'S THE REAL THING!
PAN—
PANDA-SAAAN!
PAN—
PANDA!
PANDA!
PANDA ...
PANDA!

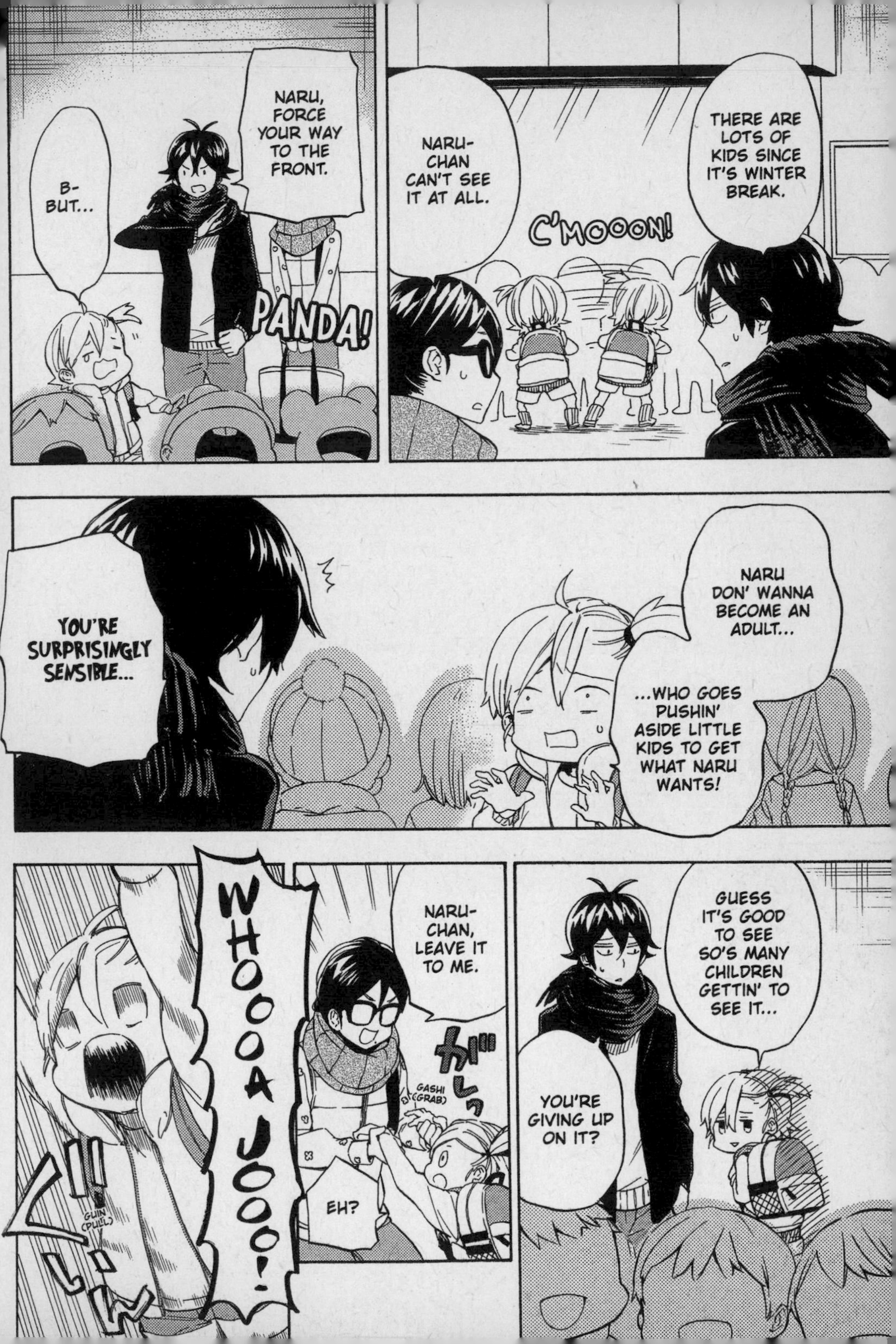
THERE ARE LOTS OF KIDS SINCE IT'S WINTER BREAK.
NARU-CHAN CAN'T SEE IT AT ALL.
C'MOOON!
NARU, FORCE YOUR WAY TO THE FRONT.
B-BUT...
PANDA!
NARU DON' WANNA BECOME AN ADULT...
...WHO GOES PUSHIN' ASIDE LITTLE KIDS TO GET WHAT NARU WANTS!
YOU'RE SURPRISINGLY SENSIBLE...
GUESS IT'S GOOD TO SEE SO'S MANY CHILDREN GETTIN' TO SEE IT...
YOU'RE GIVING UP ON IT?
NARU-CHAN, LEAVE IT TO ME.
がしっ
GASHI (GRAB)
EH?
WHOOOA JOOOO!
GUIN (PULL)

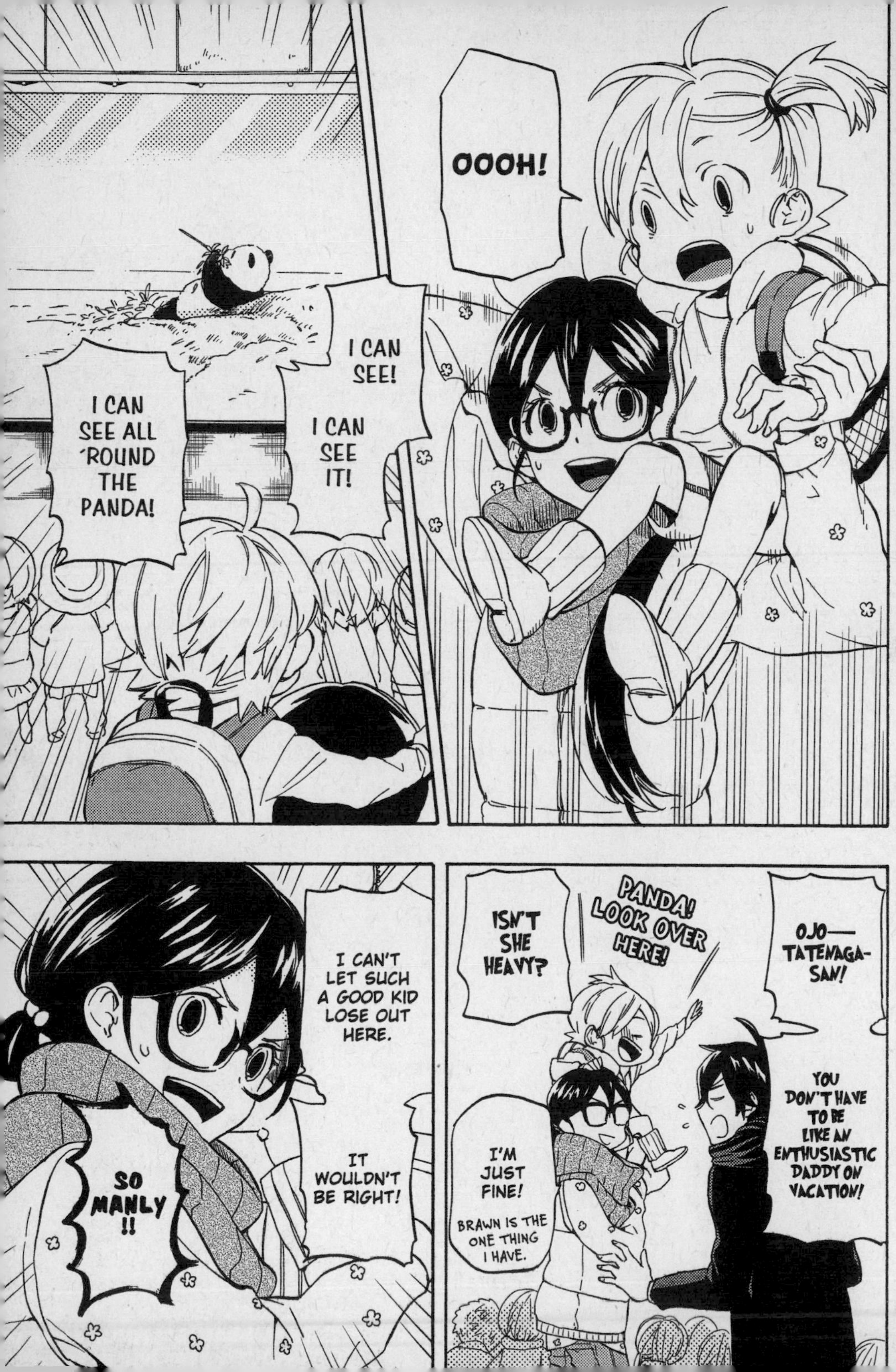
OOOH!
I CAN SEE!
I CAN SEE IT!
I CAN SEE ALL ´ROUND THE PANDA!
OJO—TATENAGA-SAN!
PANDA! LOOK OVER HERE!
ISN'T SHE HEAVY?
YOU DON'T HAVE TO BE LIKE AN ENTHUSIASTIC DADDY ON VACATION!
I'M JUST FINE!
BRAWN IS THE ONE THING I HAVE.
I CAN'T LET SUCH A GOOD KID LOSE OUT HERE.
IT WOULDN'T BE RIGHT!
SO MANLY!!

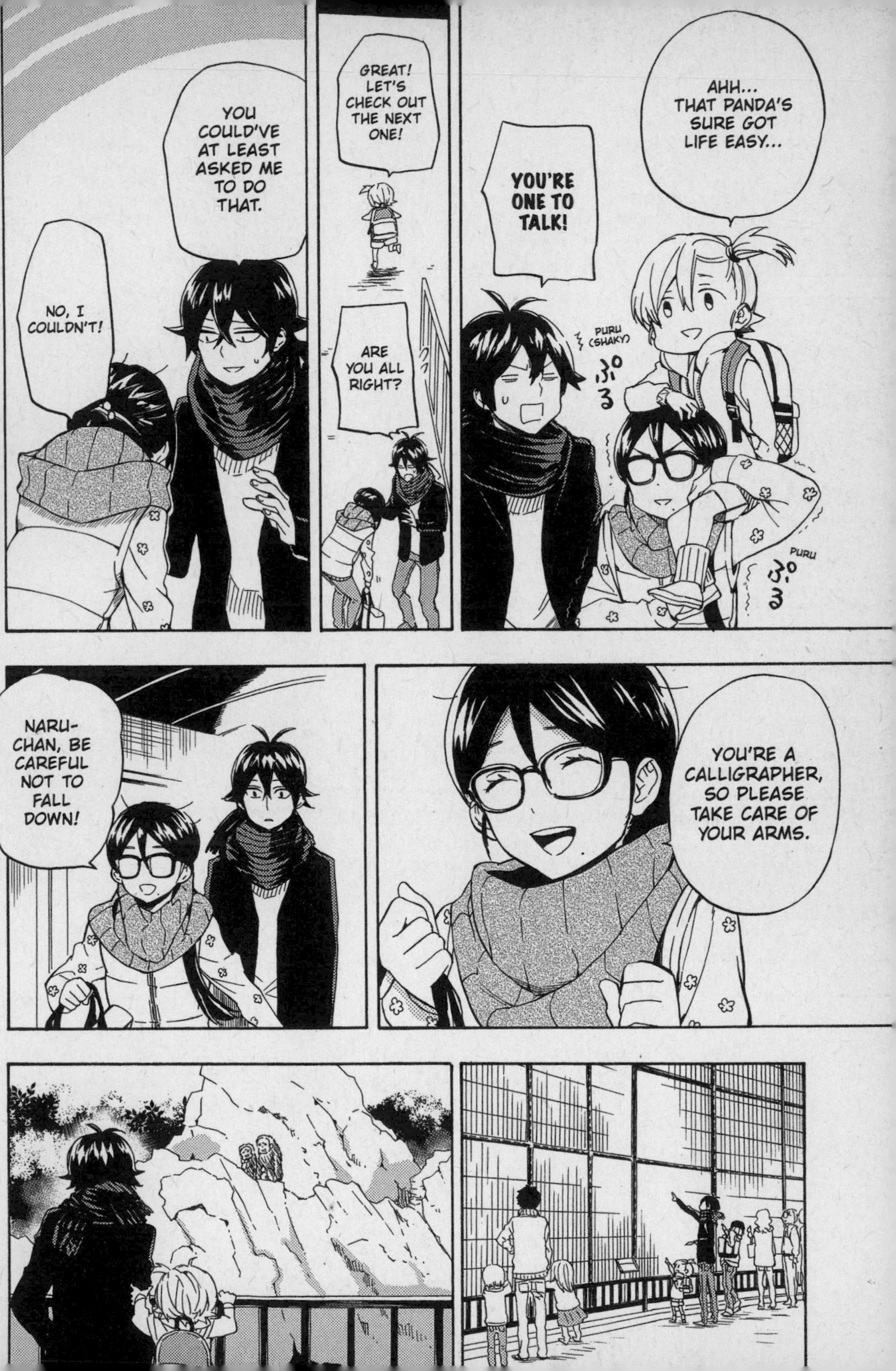
AHH... THAT PANDA'S SURE GOT LIFE EASY...
YOU'RE ONE TO TALK!
PURU (SHAKY)
ぷる
PURU
ぷる
GREAT! LET'S CHECK OUT THE NEXT ONE!
ARE YOU ALL RIGHT?
YOU COULD'VE AT LEAST ASKED ME TO DO THAT.
NO, I COULDN'T!
YOU'RE A CALLIGRAPHER, SO PLEASE TAKE CARE OF YOUR ARMS.
NARU-CHAN, BE CAREFUL NOT TO FALL DOWN!

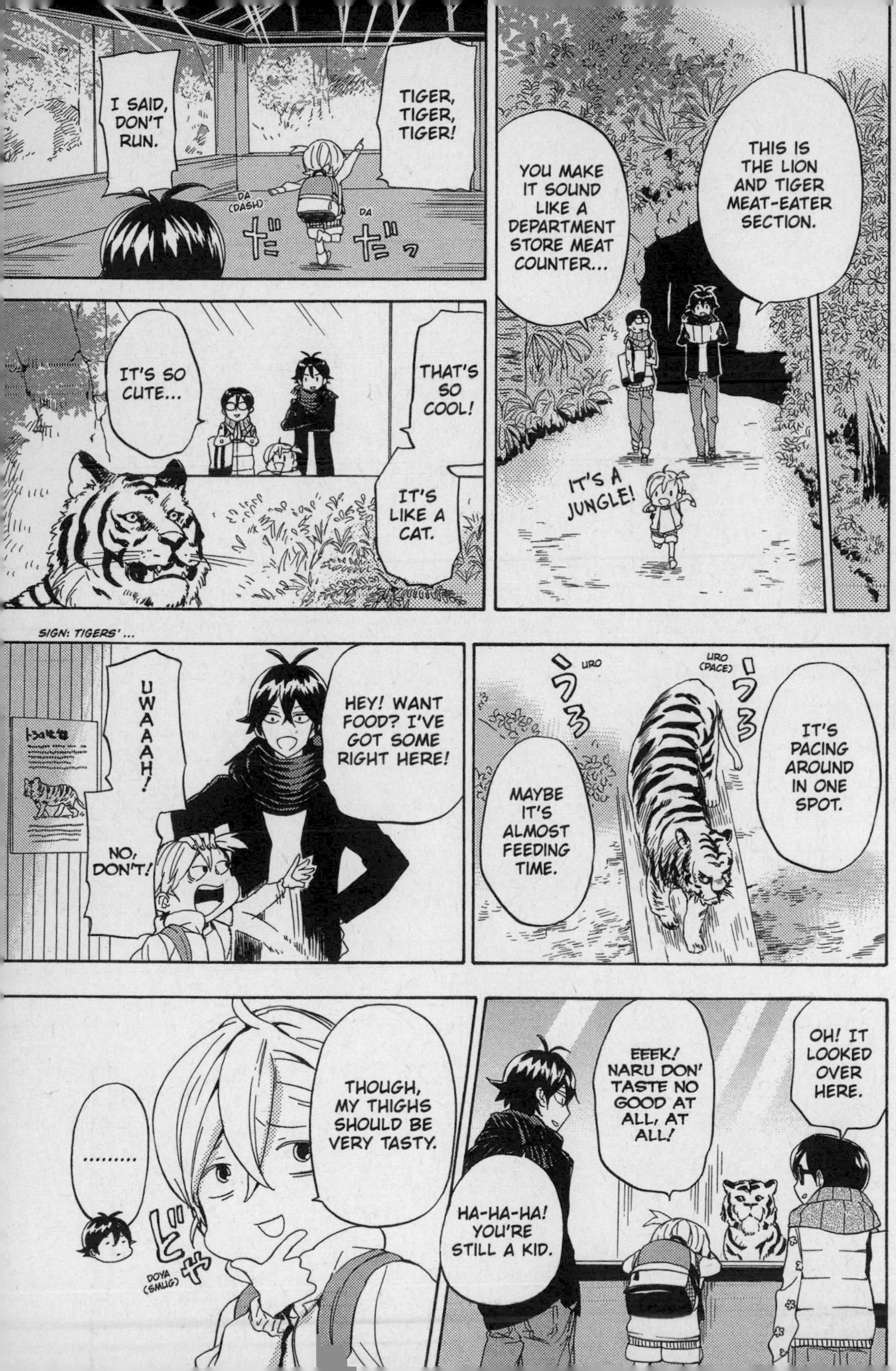
THIS IS THE LION AND TIGER MEAT-EATER SECTION.
YOU MAKE IT SOUND LIKE A DEPARTMENT STORE MEAT COUNTER...
IT'S A JUNGLE!
TIGER, TIGER, TIGER!
I SAID, DON'T RUN.
DA (DASH)
だ
DA
だっ
THAT'S SO COOL!
IT'S LIKE A CAT.
IT'S SO CUTE...
SIGN: TIGERS' ...
URO (PACE)
うろ
URO
うろ
IT'S PACING AROUND IN ONE SPOT.
MAYBE IT'S ALMOST FEEDING TIME.
HEY! WANT FOOD? I'VE GOT SOME RIGHT HERE!
UWAAAAH!
NO, DON'T!
OH! IT LOOKED OVER HERE.
EEEK! NARU DON' TASTE NO GOOD AT ALL, AT ALL!
HA-HA-HA! YOU'RE STILL A KID.
THOUGH, MY THIGHS SHOULD BE VERY TASTY.
....
DOYA (SMUG)
どや

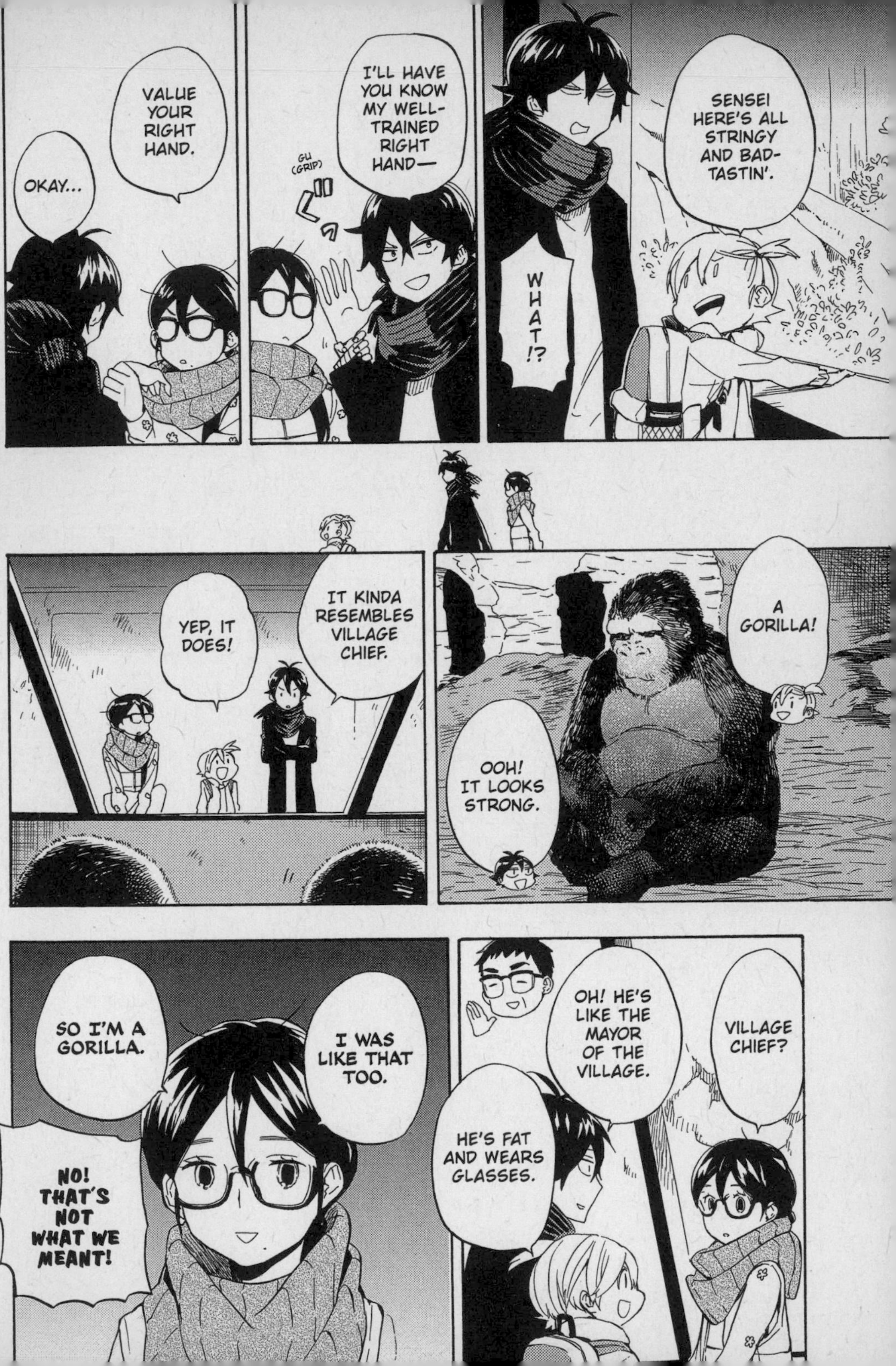
SENSEI HERE'S ALL STRINGY AND BAD-TASTIN'.
WHAT!?
I'LL HAVE YOU KNOW MY WELL-TRAINED RIGHT HAND—
GU (GRIP)
VALUE YOUR RIGHT HAND.
OKAY...
A GORILLA!
OOH! IT LOOKS STRONG.
IT KINDA RESEMBLES VILLAGE CHIEF.
YEP, IT DOES!
VILLAGE CHIEF?
OH! HE'S LIKE THE MAYOR OF THE VILLAGE.
HE'S FAT AND WEARS GLASSES.
I WAS LIKE THAT TOO.
SO I'M A GORILLA.
NO! THAT'S NOT WHAT WE MEANT!

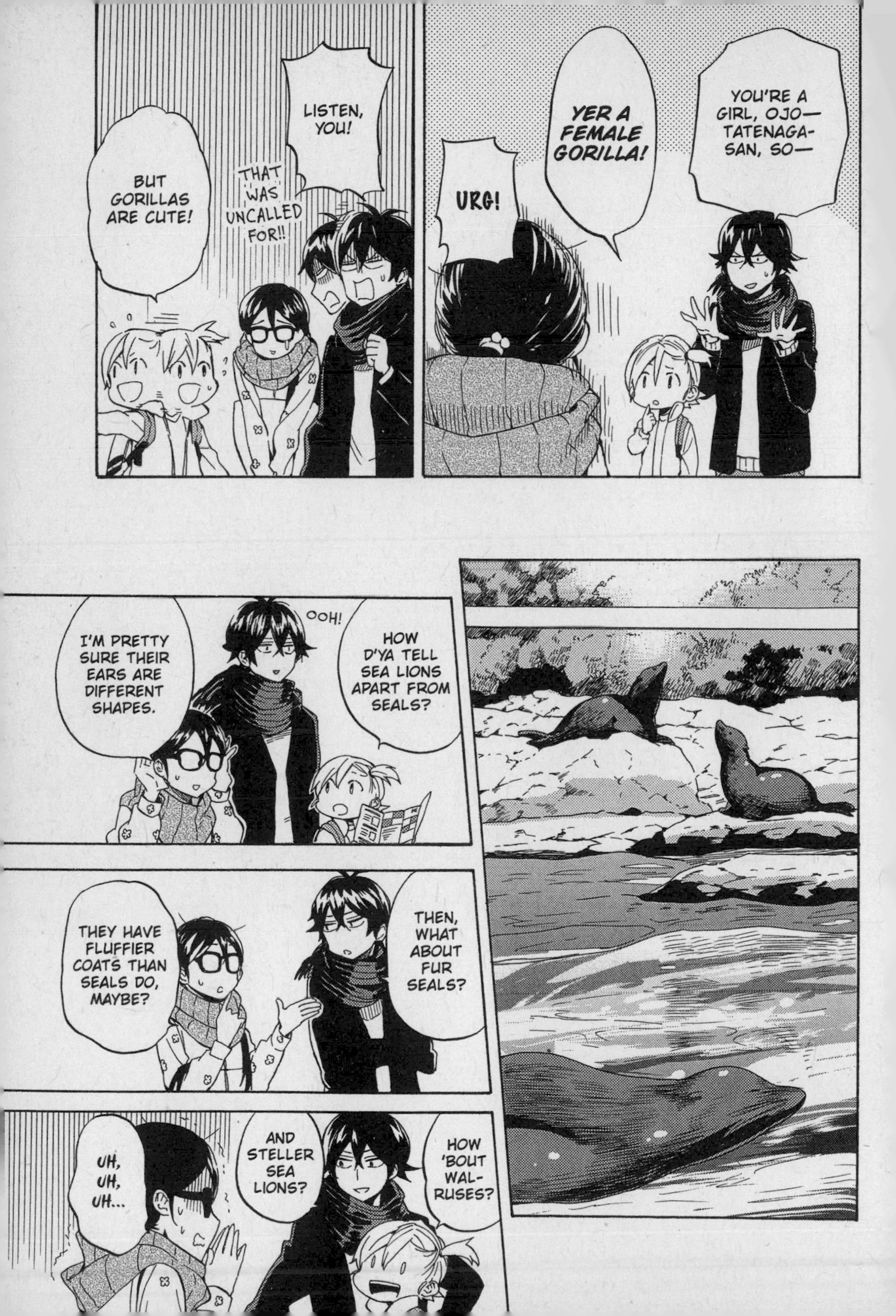
YOU'RE A GIRL, OJO—TATENAGA-SAN, SO—
YER A FEMALE GORILLA!
URG!
LISTEN, YOU!
THAT WAS UNCALLED FOR!!
BUT GORILLAS ARE CUTE!
HOW D'YA TELL SEA LIONS APART FROM SEALS?
OOH!
I'M PRETTY SURE THEIR EARS ARE DIFFERENT SHAPES.
THEN, WHAT ABOUT FUR SEALS?
THEY HAVE FLUFFIER COATS THAN SEALS DO, MAYBE?
HOW 'BOUT WAL-RUSES?
AND STELLER SEA LIONS?
UH, UH, UH...

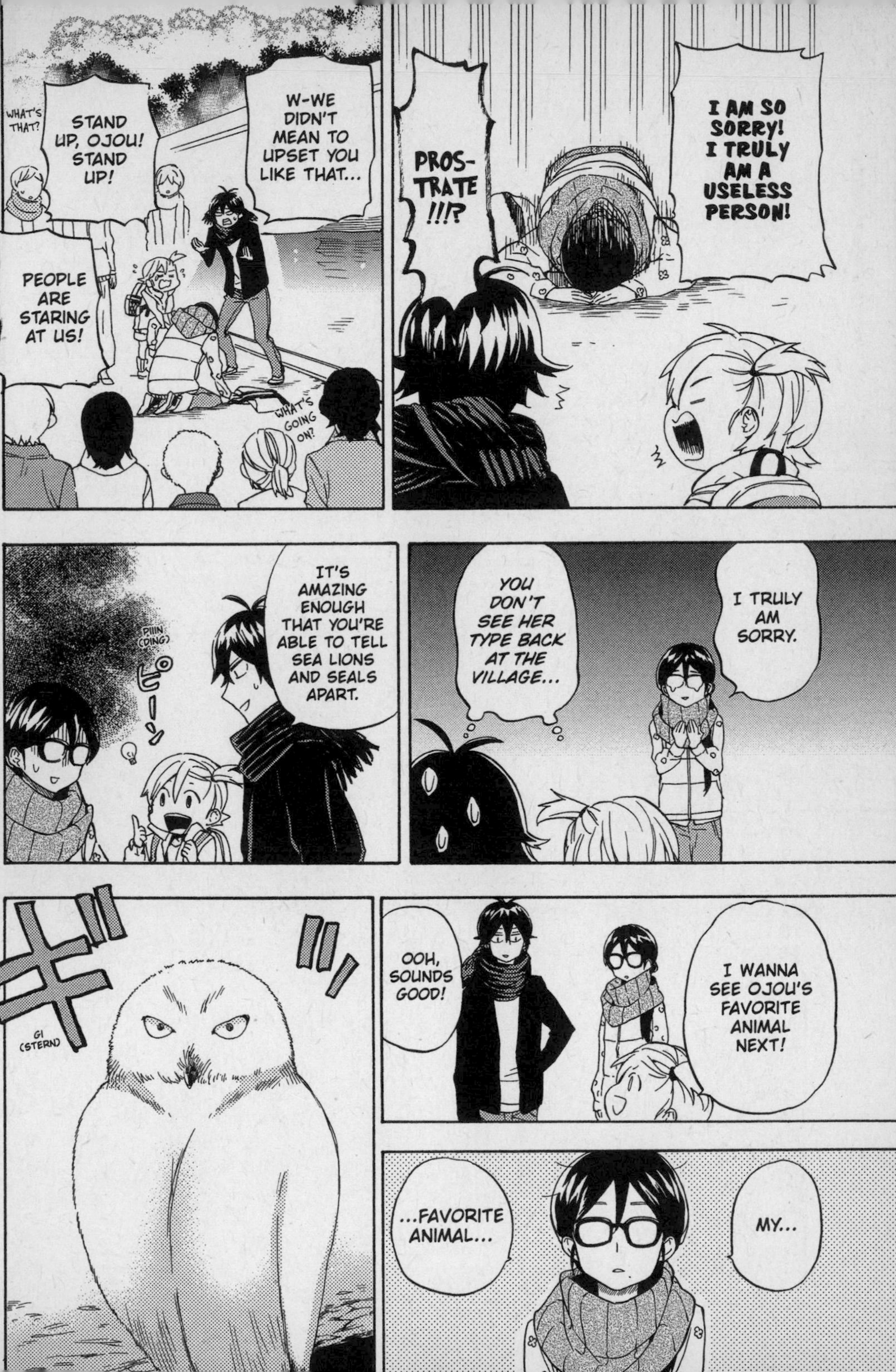
I AM SO SORRY! I TRULY AM A USELESS PERSON!
PROS-TRATE!!!?
W-WE DIDN'T MEAN TO UPSET YOU LIKE THAT...
STAND UP, OJOU! STAND UP!
WHAT'S THAT?
PEOPLE ARE STARING AT US!
WHAT'S GOING ON?
I TRULY AM SORRY.
YOU DON'T SEE HER TYPE BACK AT THE VILLAGE...
IT'S AMAZING ENOUGH THAT YOU'RE ABLE TO TELL SEA LIONS AND SEALS APART.
PIIN (DING)
I WANNA SEE OJOU'S FAVORITE ANIMAL NEXT!
OOH, SOUNDS GOOD!
MY...
...FAVORITE ANIMAL...
GI (STERN)

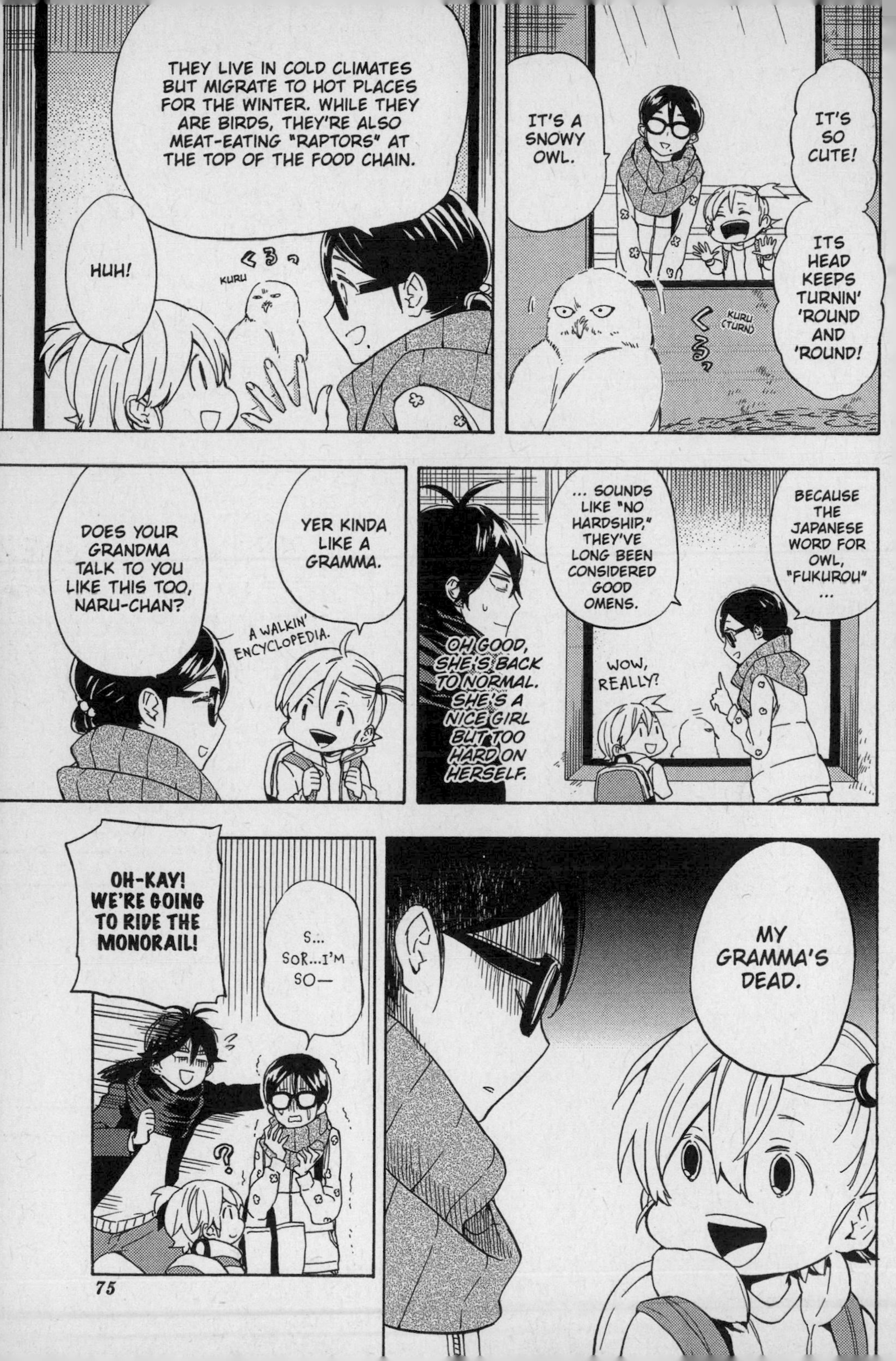
IT'S SO CUTE!
IT'S A SNOWY OWL.
ITS HEAD KEEPS TURNIN' 'ROUND AND 'ROUND!
KURU (TURN)
THEY LIVE IN COLD CLIMATES BUT MIGRATE TO HOT PLACES FOR THE WINTER. WHILE THEY ARE BIRDS, THEY'RE ALSO MEAT-EATING "RAPTORS" AT THE TOP OF THE FOOD CHAIN.
HUH!
KURU
BECAUSE THE JAPANESE WORD FOR OWL, "FUKUROU"...
... SOUNDS LIKE "NO HARDSHIP," THEY'VE LONG BEEN CONSIDERED GOOD OMENS.
WOW, REALLY?
OH GOOD, SHE'S BACK TO NORMAL. SHE'S A NICE GIRL BUT TOO HARD ON HERSELF.
YER KINDA LIKE A GRAMMA.
DOES YOUR GRANDMA TALK TO YOU LIKE THIS TOO, NARU-CHAN?
A WALKIN' ENCYCLOPEDIA.
MY GRAMMA'S DEAD.
S... SOR...I'M SO—
OH-KAY! WE'RE GOING TO RIDE THE MONORAIL!

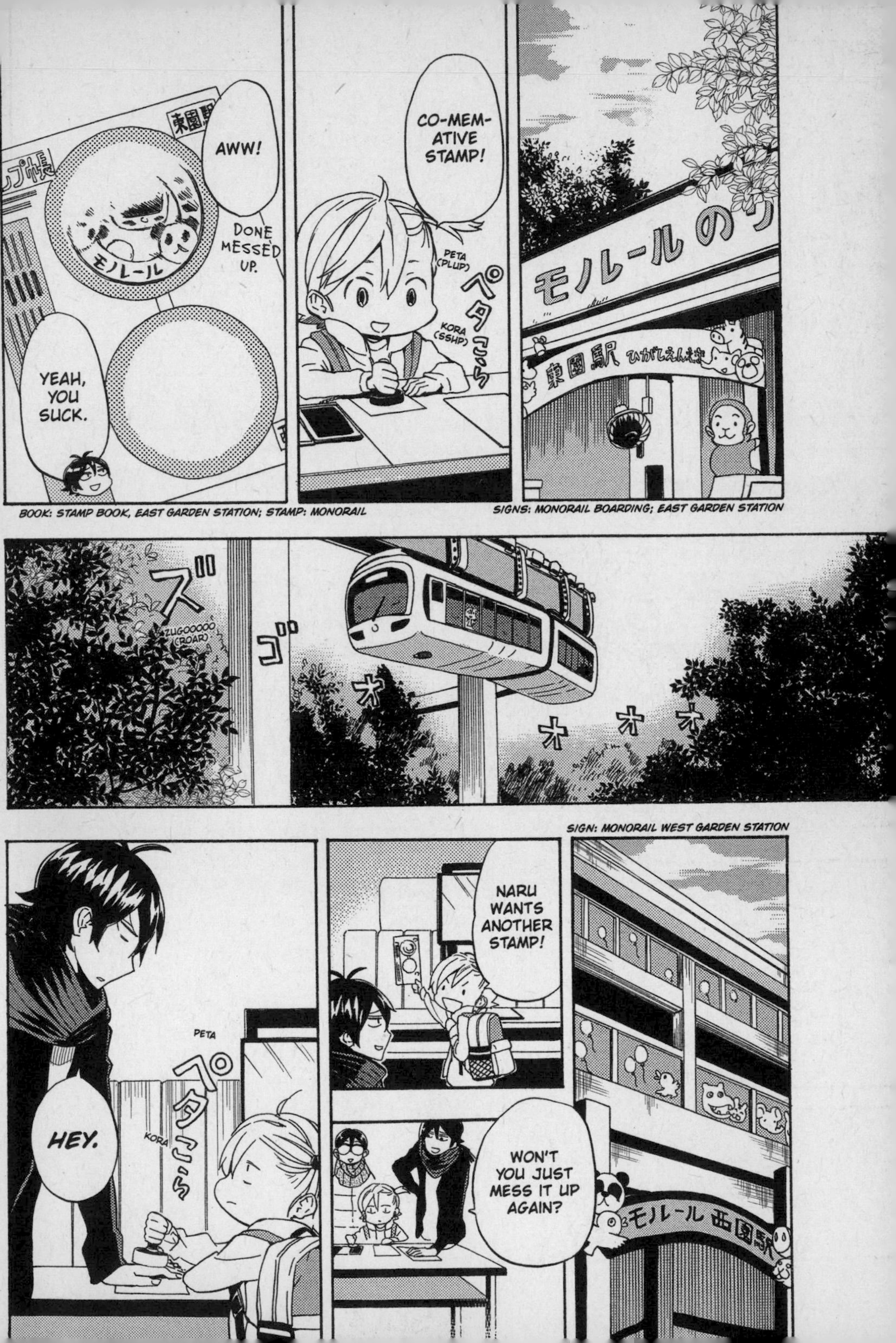
SIGNS: MONORAIL BOARDING; EAST GARDEN STATION
CO-MEM-ATIVE STAMP!
PETA (PLUP)
KORA (SSHP)
AWW!
DONE MESSED UP.
YEAH, YOU SUCK.
BOOK: STAMP BOOK, EAST GARDEN STATION; STAMP: MONORAIL
ZUGOOOOO (ROAR)
SIGN: MONORAIL WEST GARDEN STATION
NARU WANTS ANOTHER STAMP!
WON'T YOU JUST MESS IT UP AGAIN?
PETA
KORA
HEY.

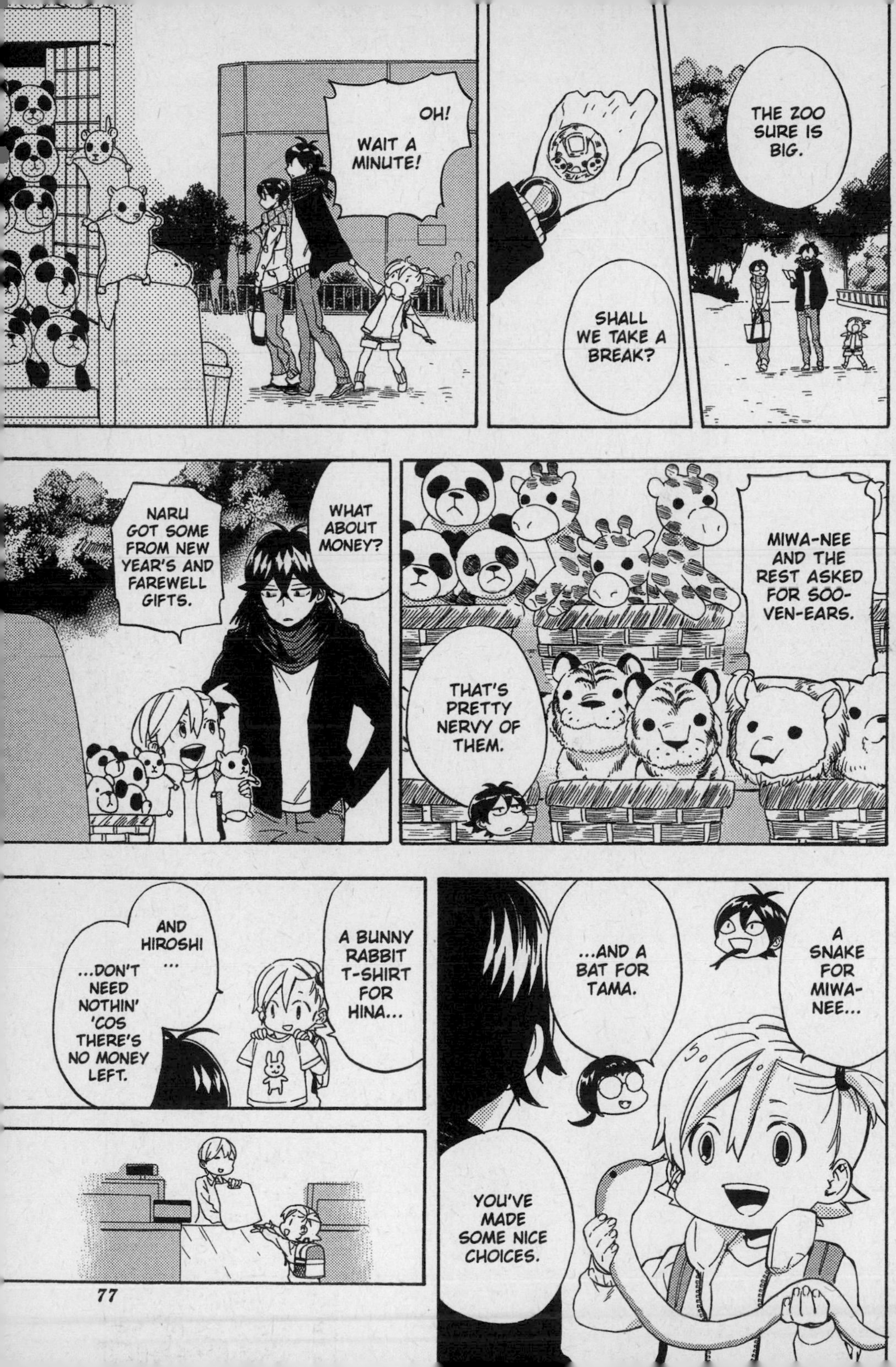
THE ZOO SURE IS BIG.
SHALL WE TAKE A BREAK?
OH!
WAIT A MINUTE!
MIWA-NEE AND THE REST ASKED FOR SOO-VEN-EARS.
THAT'S PRETTY NERVY OF THEM.
WHAT ABOUT MONEY?
NARU GOT SOME FROM NEW YEAR'S AND FAREWELL GIFTS.
A SNAKE FOR MIWA-NEE...
...AND A BAT FOR TAMA.
YOU'VE MADE SOME NICE CHOICES.
A BUNNY RABBIT T-SHIRT FOR HINA...
AND HIROSHI ...
...DON'T NEED NOTHIN' 'COS THERE'S NO MONEY LEFT.

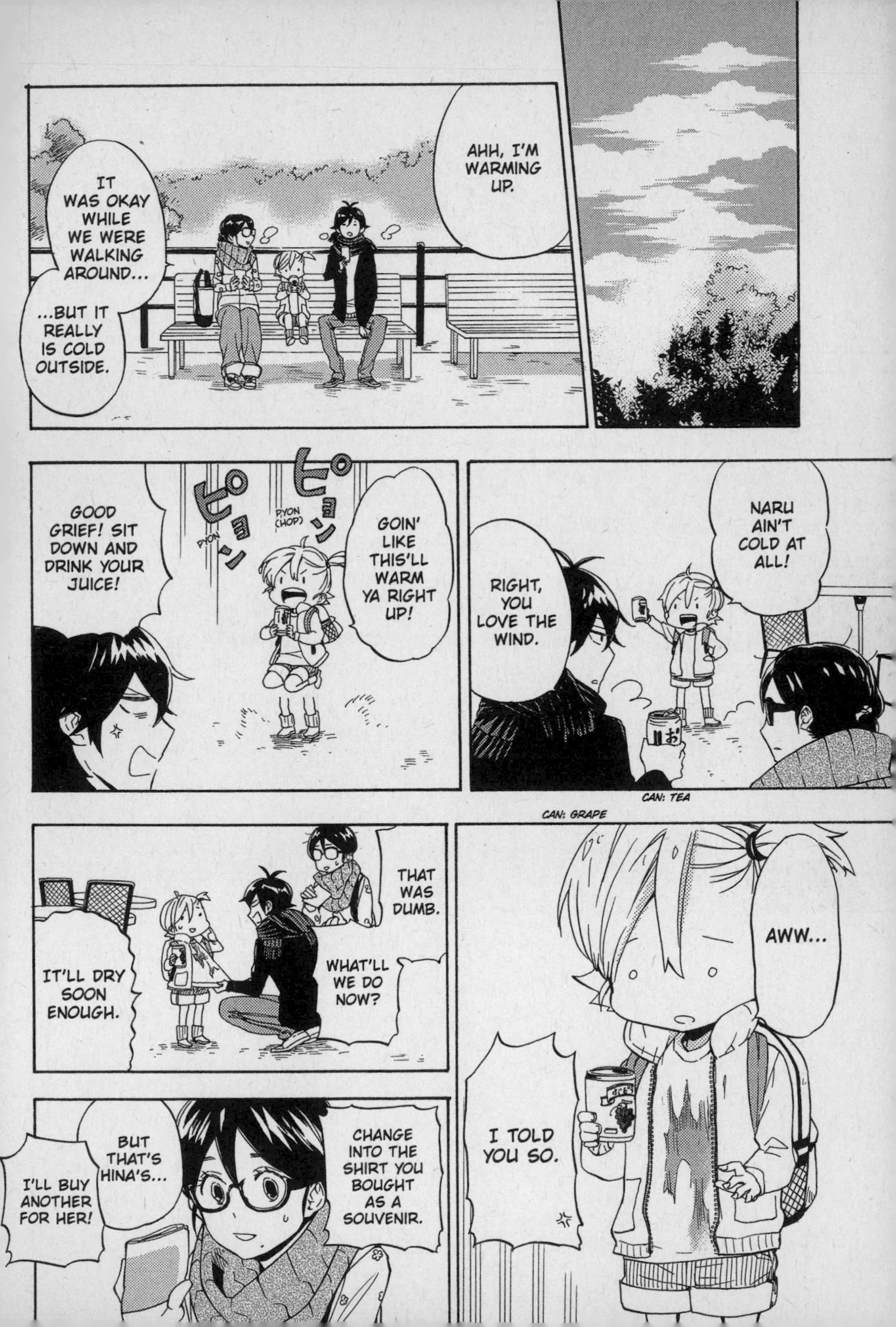
AHH, I'M WARMING UP.
IT WAS OKAY WHILE WE WERE WALKING AROUND...
...BUT IT REALLY IS COLD OUTSIDE.
NARU AIN'T COLD AT ALL!
RIGHT, YOU LOVE THE WIND.
CAN: TEA
ピョン
PYON (HOP)
ピョン
PYON
GOIN' LIKE THIS'LL WARM YA RIGHT UP!
GOOD GRIEF! SIT DOWN AND DRINK YOUR JUICE!
CAN: GRAPE
AWW...
I TOLD YOU SO.
THAT WAS DUMB.
WHAT'LL WE DO NOW?
IT'LL DRY SOON ENOUGH.
CHANGE INTO THE SHIRT YOU BOUGHT AS A SOUVENIR.
BUT THAT'S HINA'S...
I'LL BUY ANOTHER FOR HER!

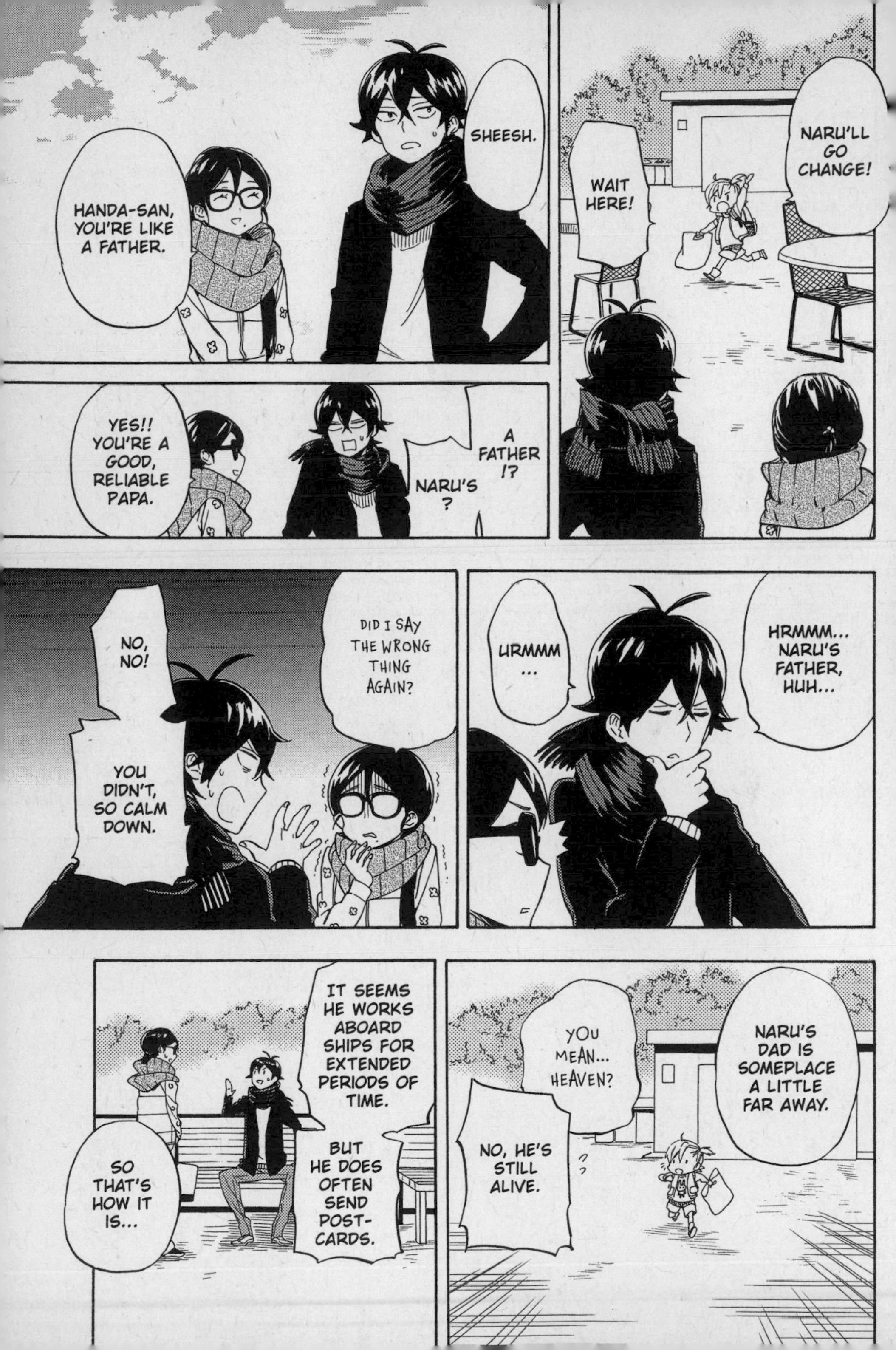
NARU'LL GO CHANGE!
WAIT HERE!
SHEESH.
HANDA-SAN, YOU'RE LIKE A FATHER.
A FATHER !?
NARU'S ?
YES!! YOU'RE A GOOD, RELIABLE PAPA.
HRMMM... NARU'S FATHER, HUH...
URMMM ...
DID I SAY THE WRONG THING AGAIN?
NO, NO!
YOU DIDN'T, SO CALM DOWN.
NARU'S DAD IS SOMEPLACE A LITTLE FAR AWAY.
YOU MEAN... HEAVEN?
NO, HE'S STILL ALIVE.
IT SEEMS HE WORKS ABOARD SHIPS FOR EXTENDED PERIODS OF TIME.
BUT HE DOES OFTEN SEND POST-CARDS.
SO THAT'S HOW IT IS...

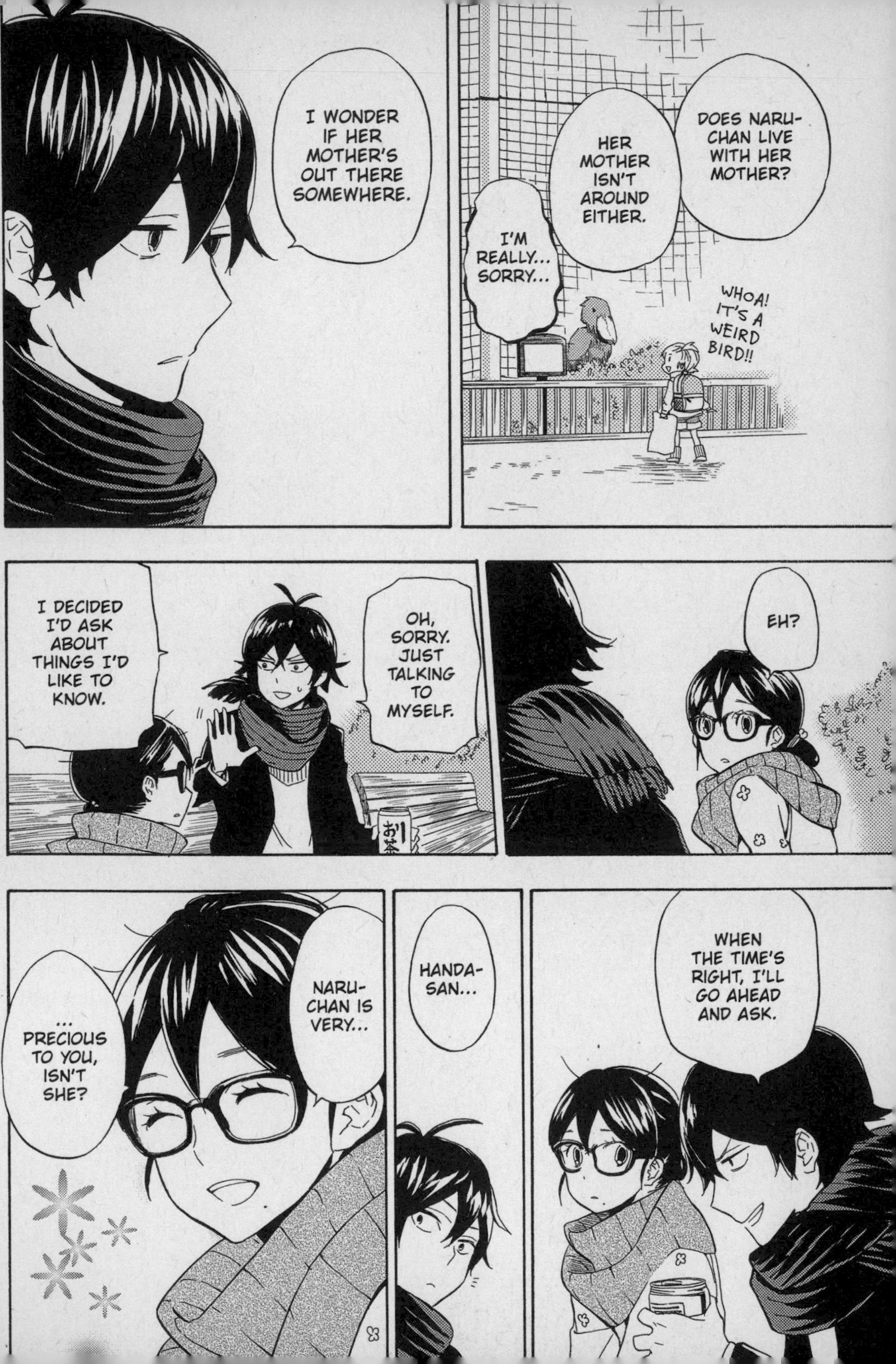
DOES NARU-CHAN LIVE WITH HER MOTHER?
HER MOTHER ISN'T AROUND EITHER.
I'M REALLY... SORRY...
WHOA! IT'S A WEIRD BIRD!!
I WONDER IF HER MOTHER'S OUT THERE SOMEWHERE.
EH?
OH, SORRY. JUST TALKING TO MYSELF.
I DECIDED I'D ASK ABOUT THINGS I'D LIKE TO KNOW.
WHEN THE TIME'S RIGHT, I'LL GO AHEAD AND ASK.
HANDA-SAN...
NARU-CHAN IS VERY...
...PRECIOUS TO YOU, ISN'T SHE?

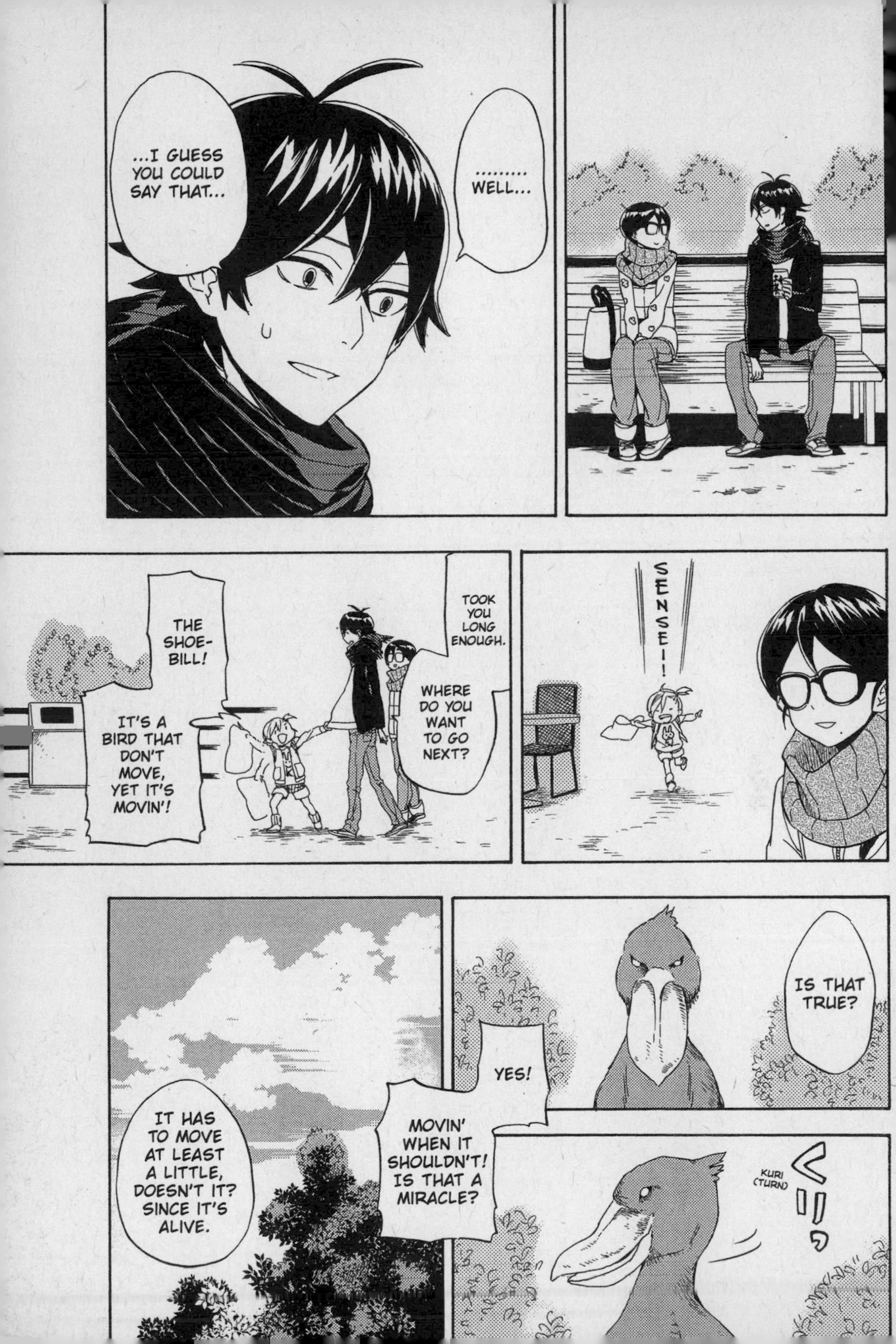
....
WELL...
...I GUESS YOU COULD SAY THAT...
SENSEI!!
TOOK YOU LONG ENOUGH.
WHERE DO YOU WANT TO GO NEXT?
THE SHOE-BILL!
IT'S A BIRD THAT DON'T MOVE, YET IT'S MOVIN'!
IS THAT TRUE?
YES!
KURI (TURN)
MOVIN' WHEN IT SHOULDN'T! IS THAT A MIRACLE?
IT HAS TO MOVE AT LEAST A LITTLE, DOESN'T IT? SINCE IT'S ALIVE.

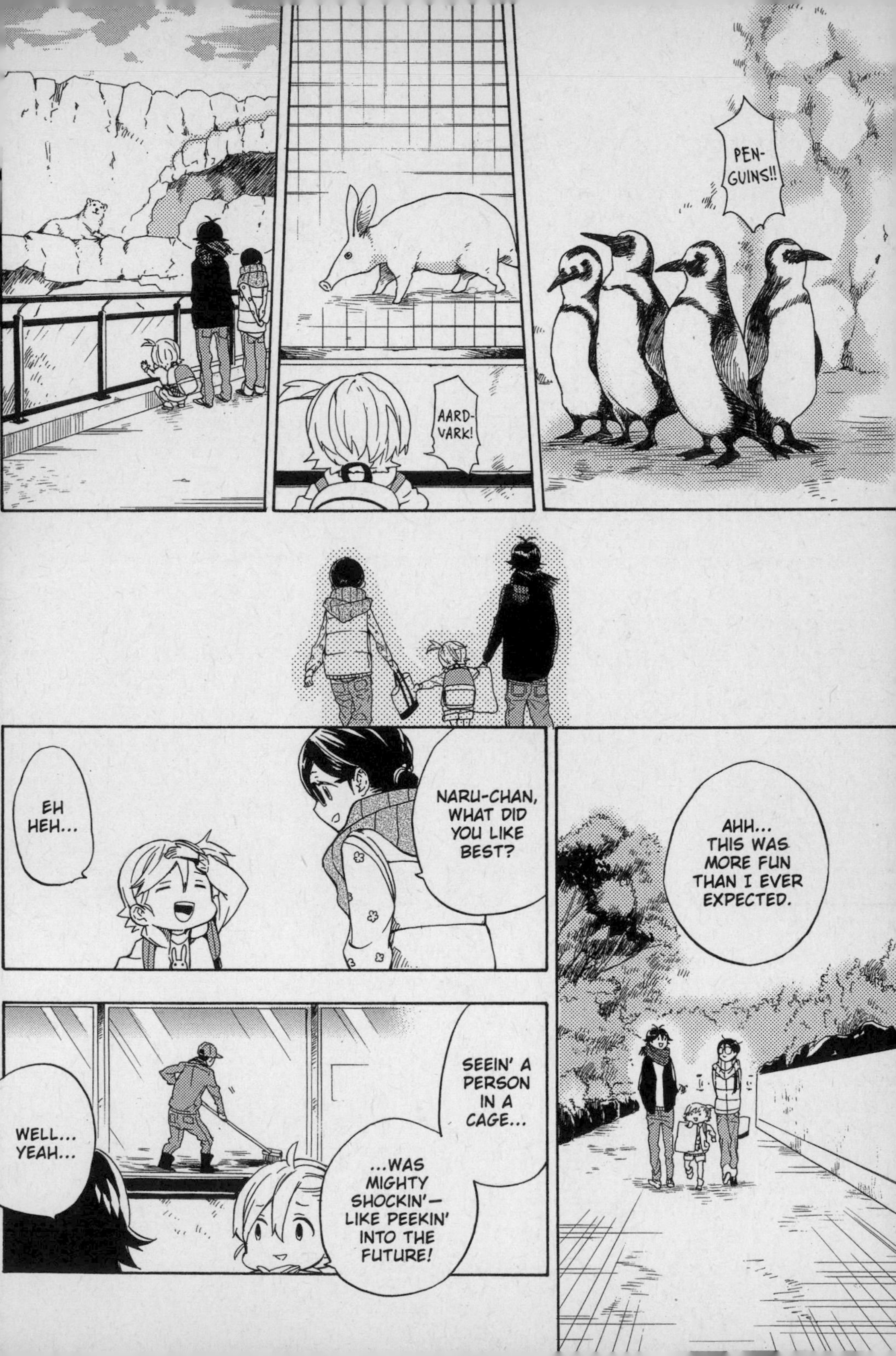
PEN-GUINS!!
AARD-VARK!
AHH... THIS WAS MORE FUN THAN I EVER EXPECTED.
NARU-CHAN, WHAT DID YOU LIKE BEST?
EH HEH...
SEEIN' A PERSON IN A CAGE...
...WAS MIGHTY SHOCKIN'—LIKE PEEKIN' INTO THE FUTURE!
WELL... YEAH...

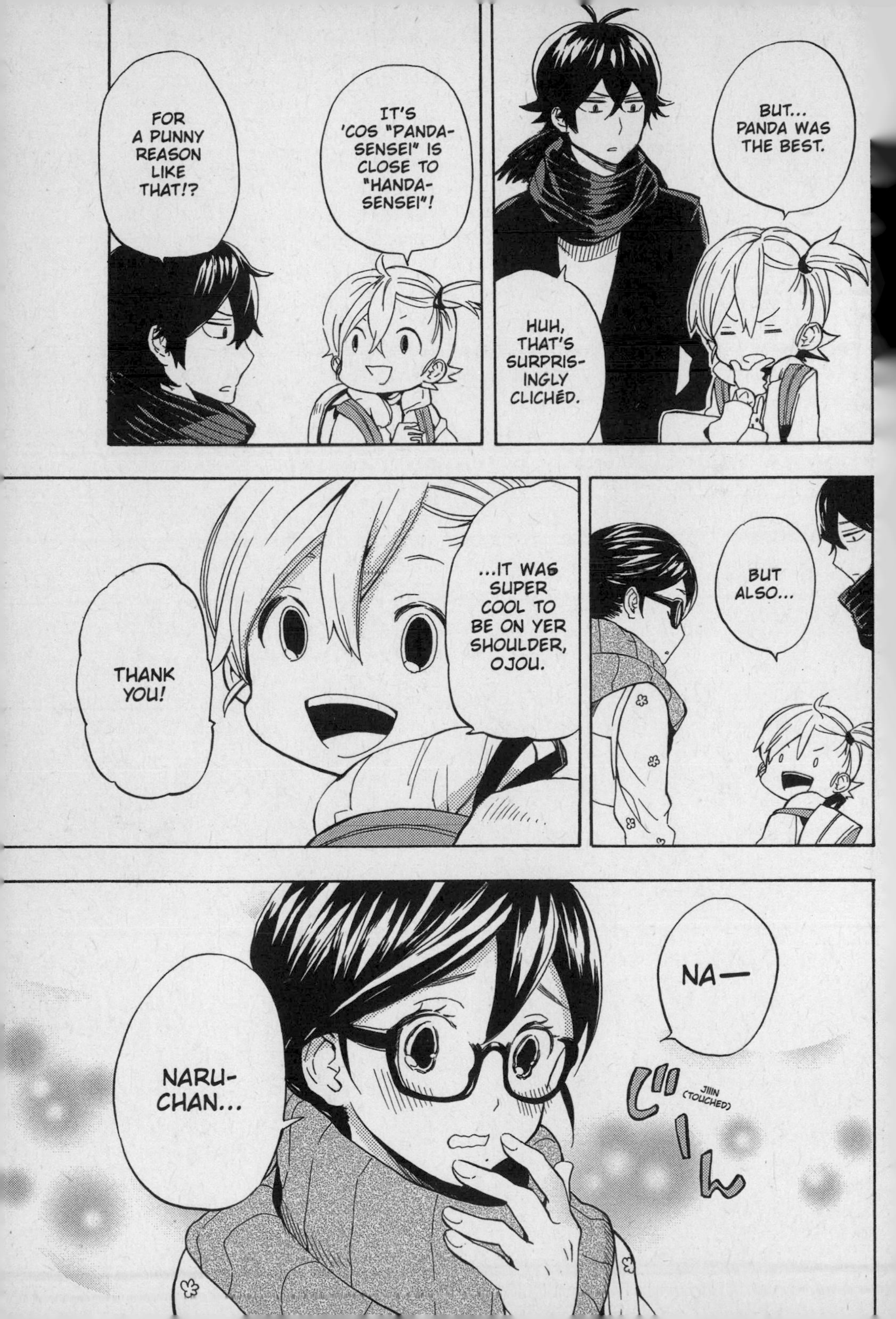
BUT... PANDA WAS THE BEST.
HUH, THAT'S SURPRISINGLY CLICHÉD.
IT'S 'COS "PANDA-SENSEI" IS CLOSE TO "HANDA-SENSEI"!
FOR A PUNNY REASON LIKE THAT!?
BUT ALSO...
...IT WAS SUPER COOL TO BE ON YER SHOULDER, OJOU.
THANK YOU!
NA—
NARU-CHAN...
じーん
JIIIN (TOUCHED)

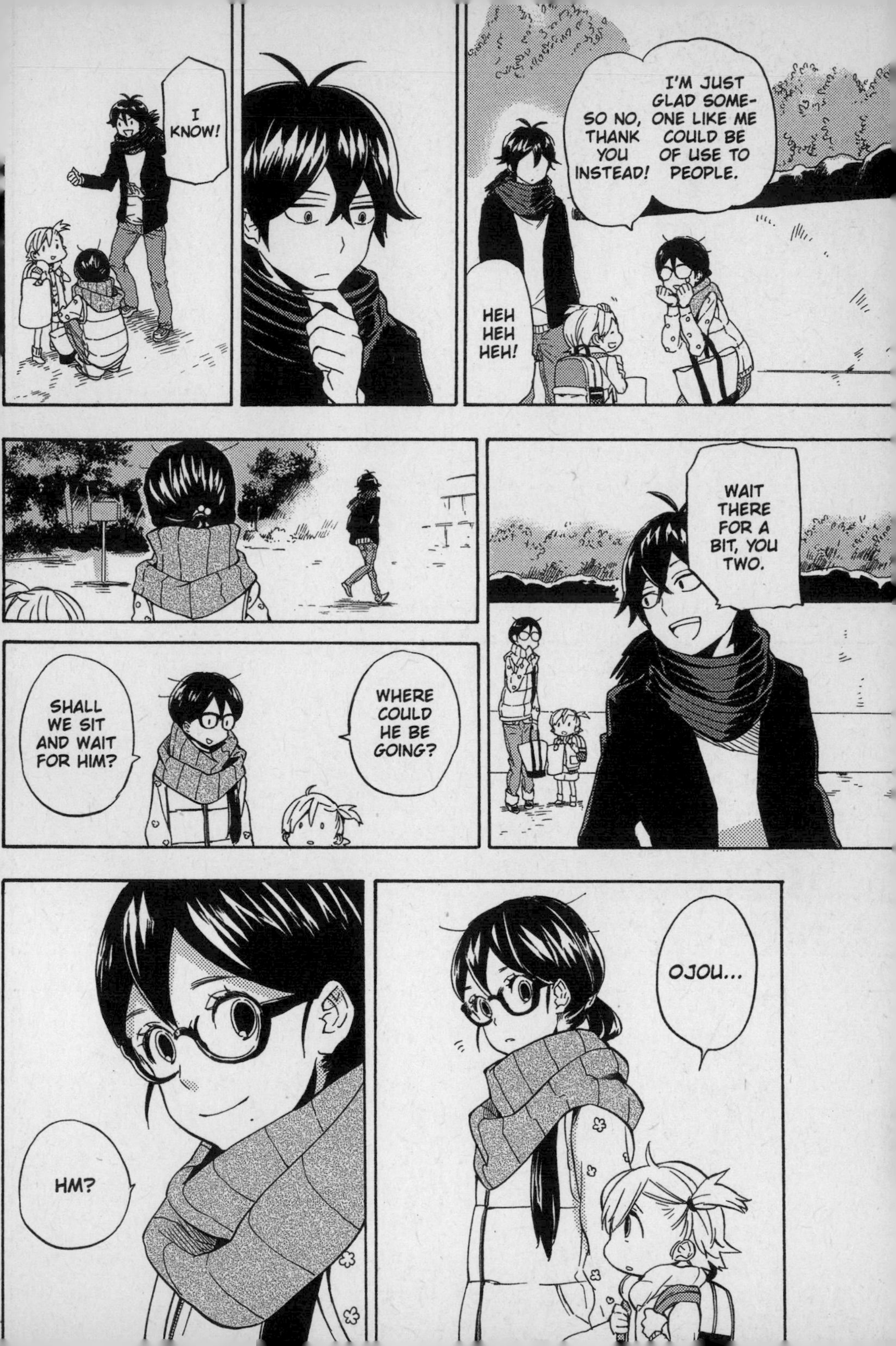
I'M JUST GLAD SOME-ONE LIKE ME COULD BE OF USE TO PEOPLE.
SO NO, THANK YOU INSTEAD!
HEH HEH HEH!
I KNOW!
WAIT THERE FOR A BIT, YOU TWO.
WHERE COULD HE BE GOING?
SHALL WE SIT AND WAIT FOR HIM?
OJOU...
HM?

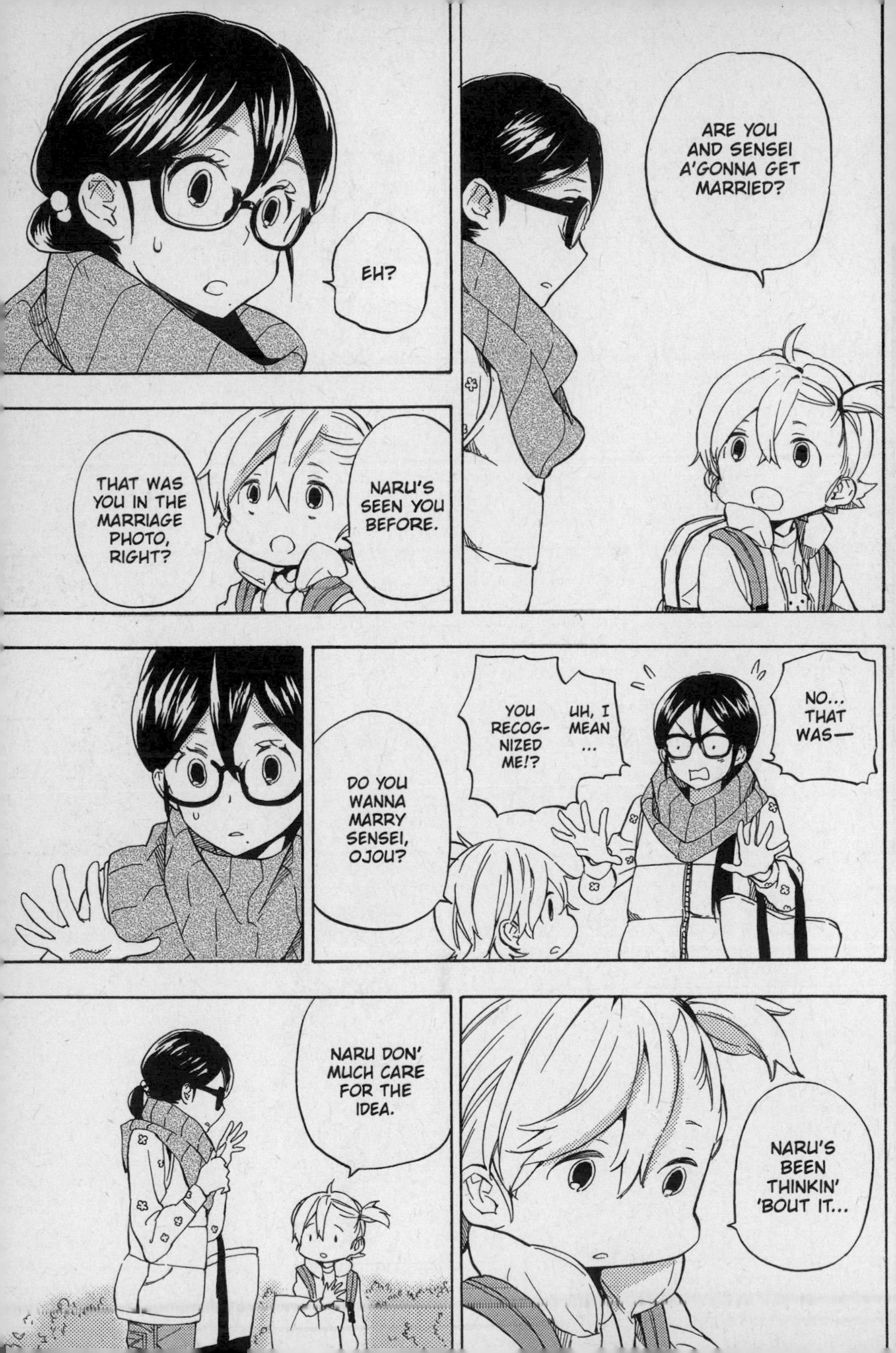
ARE YOU AND SENSEI A'GONNA GET MARRIED?
EH?
NARU'S SEEN YOU BEFORE.
THAT WAS YOU IN THE MARRIAGE PHOTO, RIGHT?
NO... THAT WAS—
UH, I MEAN ...
YOU RECOG-NIZED ME!?
DO YOU WANNA MARRY SENSEI, OJOU?
NARU'S BEEN THINKIN' 'BOUT IT...
NARU DON' MUCH CARE FOR THE IDEA.

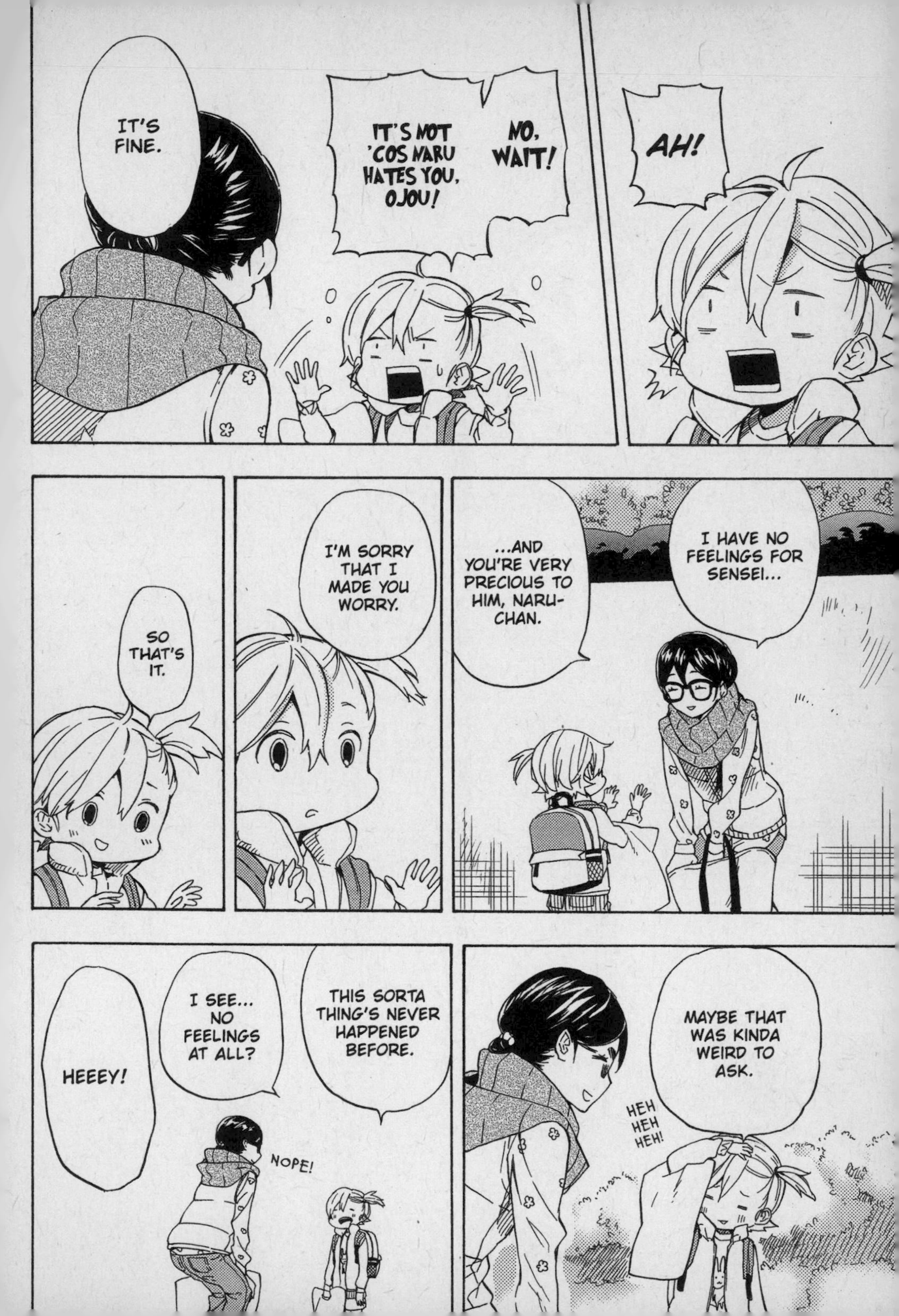
AH!
NO, WAIT!
IT'S NOT 'COS NARU HATES YOU, OJOU!
IT'S FINE.
I HAVE NO FEELINGS FOR SENSEI...
...AND YOU'RE VERY PRECIOUS TO HIM, NARU-CHAN.
I'M SORRY THAT I MADE YOU WORRY.
SO THAT'S IT.
MAYBE THAT WAS KINDA WEIRD TO ASK.
HEH HEH HEH!
THIS SORTA THING'S NEVER HAPPENED BEFORE.
I SEE... NO FEELINGS AT ALL?
NOPE!
HEEEY!

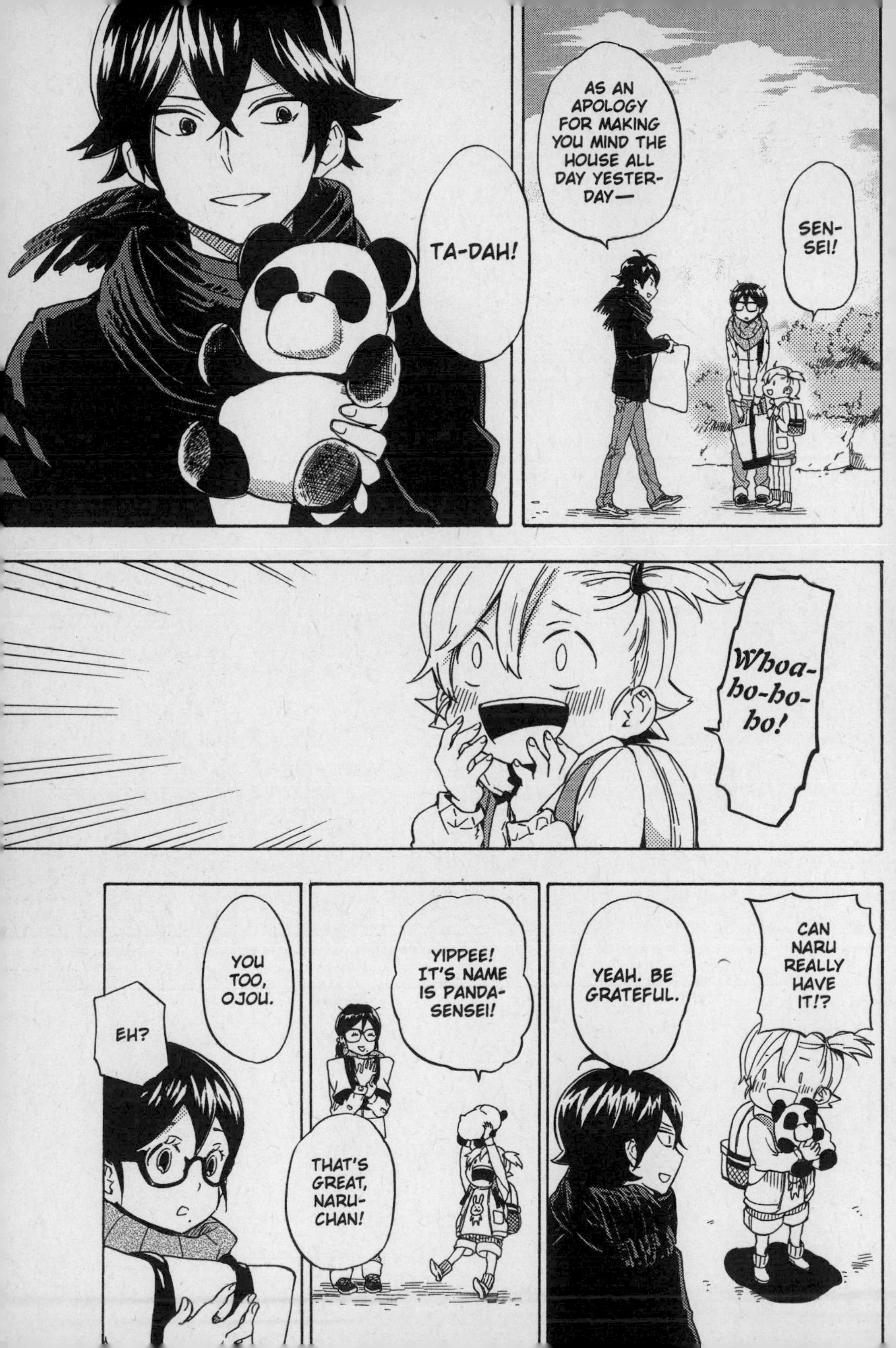
SEN-SEI!
AS AN APOLOGY FOR MAKING YOU MIND THE HOUSE ALL DAY YESTER-DAY—
TA-DAH!
Whoa-ho-ho-ho!
CAN NARU REALLY HAVE IT!?
YEAH. BE GRATEFUL.
YIPPEE! IT'S NAME IS PANDA-SENSEI!
THAT'S GREAT, NARU-CHAN!
YOU TOO, OJOU.
EH?

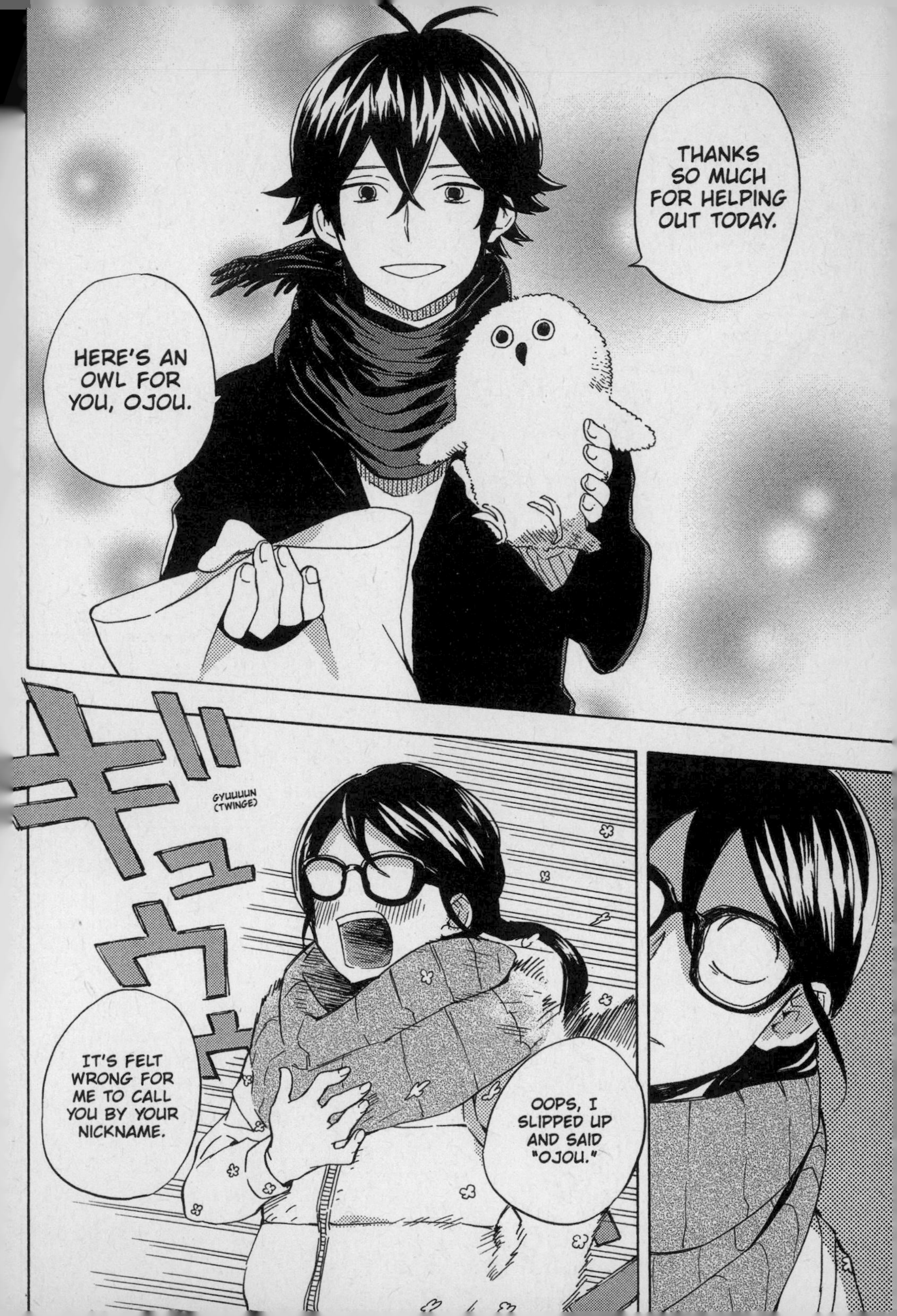
THANKS SO MUCH FOR HELPING OUT TODAY.
HERE'S AN OWL FOR YOU, OJOU.
OOPS, I SLIPPED UP AND SAID "OJOU."
IT'S FELT WRONG FOR ME TO CALL YOU BY YOUR NICKNAME.
GYUUUUN (TWINGE)

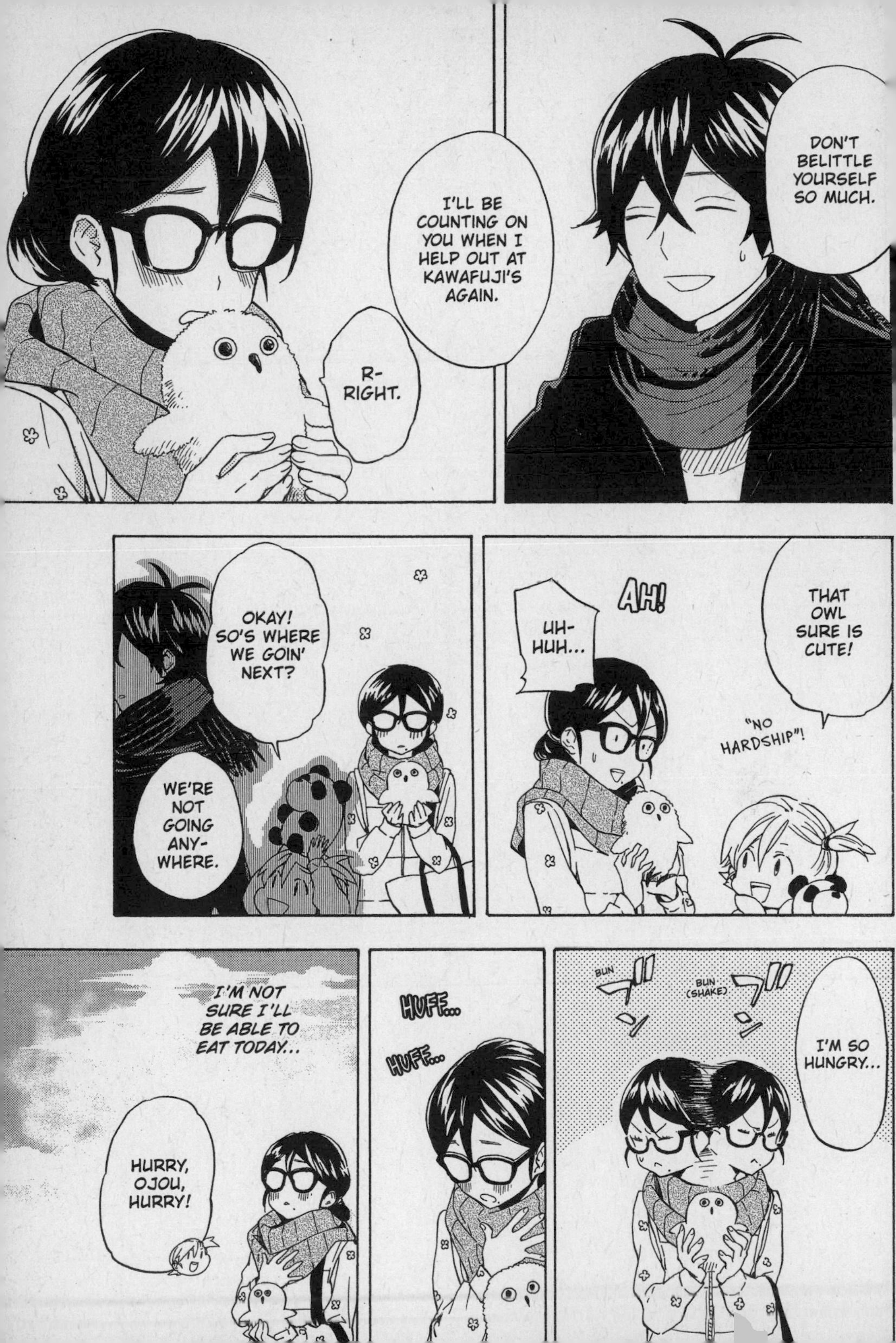
DON'T BELITTLE YOURSELF SO MUCH.
I'LL BE COUNTING ON YOU WHEN I HELP OUT AT KAWAFUJI'S AGAIN.
R-RIGHT.
THAT OWL SURE IS CUTE!
AH!
UH-HUH...
"NO HARDSHIP"!
OKAY! SO'S WHERE WE GOIN' NEXT?
WE'RE NOT GOING ANY-WHERE.
BUN
BUN (SHAKE)
I'M SO HUNGRY...
HUFF...
HUFF...
I'M NOT SURE I'LL BE ABLE TO EAT TODAY...
HURRY, OJOU, HURRY!

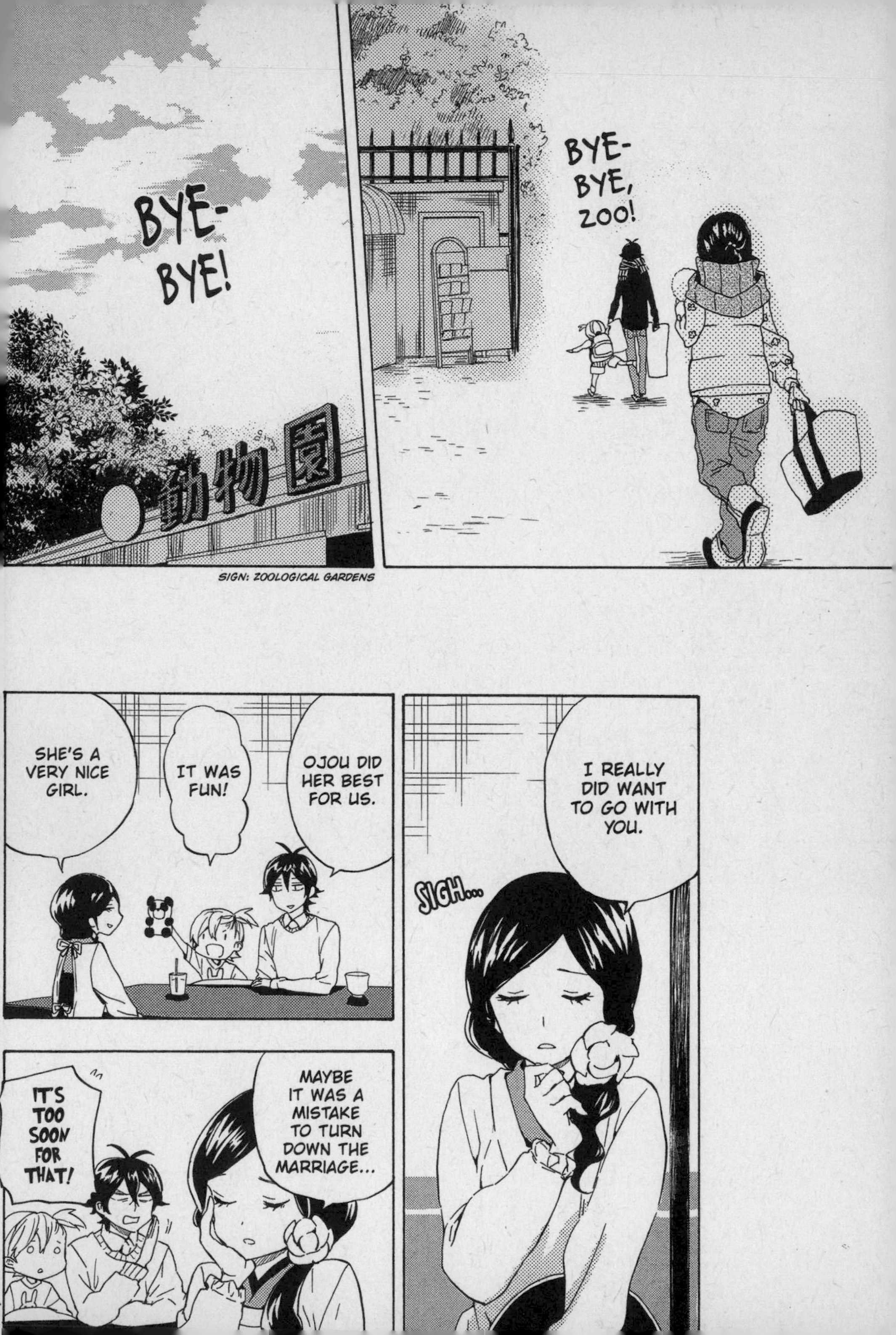
BYE-BYE, ZOO!
BYE-BYE!
SIGN: ZOOLOGICAL GARDENS
I REALLY DID WANT TO GO WITH YOU.
SIGH...
OJOU DID HER BEST FOR US.
IT WAS FUN!
SHE'S A VERY NICE GIRL.
MAYBE IT WAS A MISTAKE TO TURN DOWN THE MARRIAGE...
IT'S TOO SOON FOR THAT!

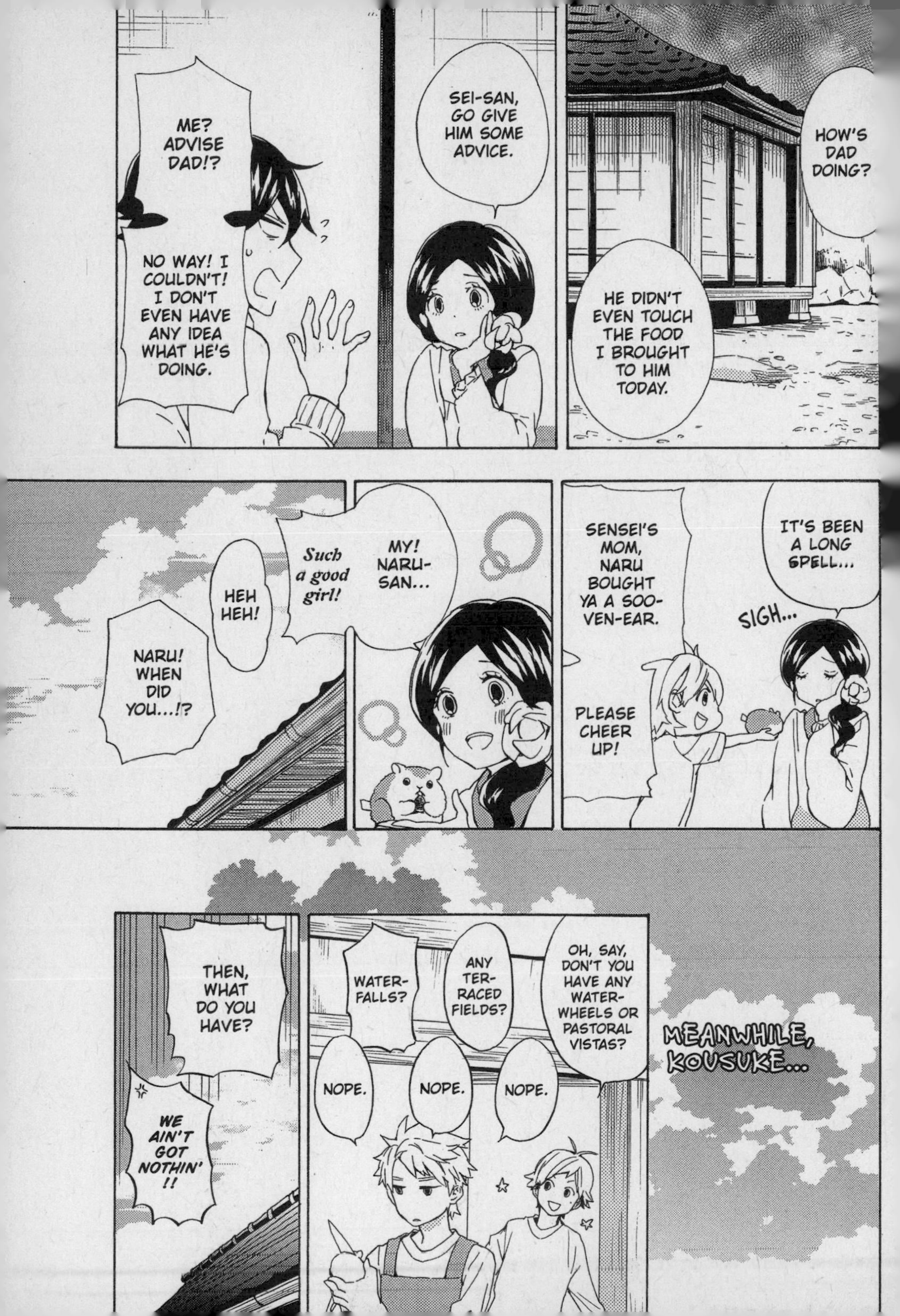
HOW'S DAD DOING?
HE DIDN'T EVEN TOUCH THE FOOD I BROUGHT TO HIM TODAY.
SEI-SAN, GO GIVE HIM SOME ADVICE.
ME? ADVISE DAD!?
NO WAY! I COULDN'T! I DON'T EVEN HAVE ANY IDEA WHAT HE'S DOING.
IT'S BEEN A LONG SPELL...
SIGH...
SENSEI'S MOM, NARU BOUGHT YA A SOO-VEN-EAR.
PLEASE CHEER UP!
MY! NARU-SAN...
Such a good girl!
HEH HEH!
NARU! WHEN DID YOU...!?
MEANWHILE, KOUSUKE...
OH, SAY, DON'T YOU HAVE ANY WATER-WHEELS OR PASTORAL VISTAS?
NOPE.
ANY TER-RACED FIELDS?
NOPE.
WATER-FALLS?
NOPE.
THEN, WHAT DO YOU HAVE?
WE AIN'T GOT NOTHIN' !!

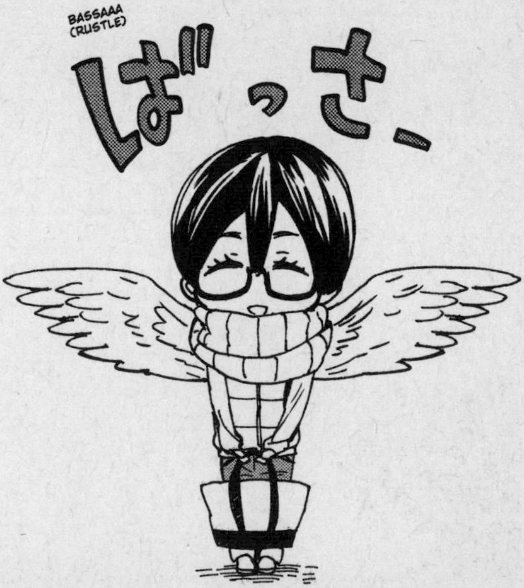
BASSAAA (RUSTLE)
ばっさー

ZOO BONUS

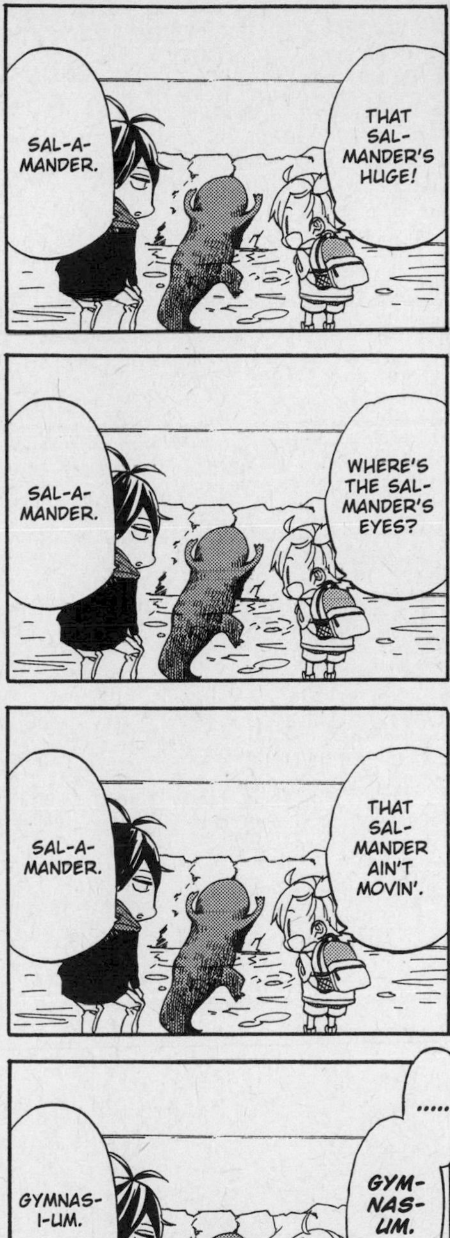
THAT SAL-MANDER'S HUGE!
SAL-A-MANDER.
WHERE'S THE SAL-MANDER'S EYES?
SAL-A-MANDER.
THAT SAL-MANDER AIN'T MOVIN'.
SAL-A-MANDER.
......
GYM-NAS-UM.
GYMNAS-I-UM.

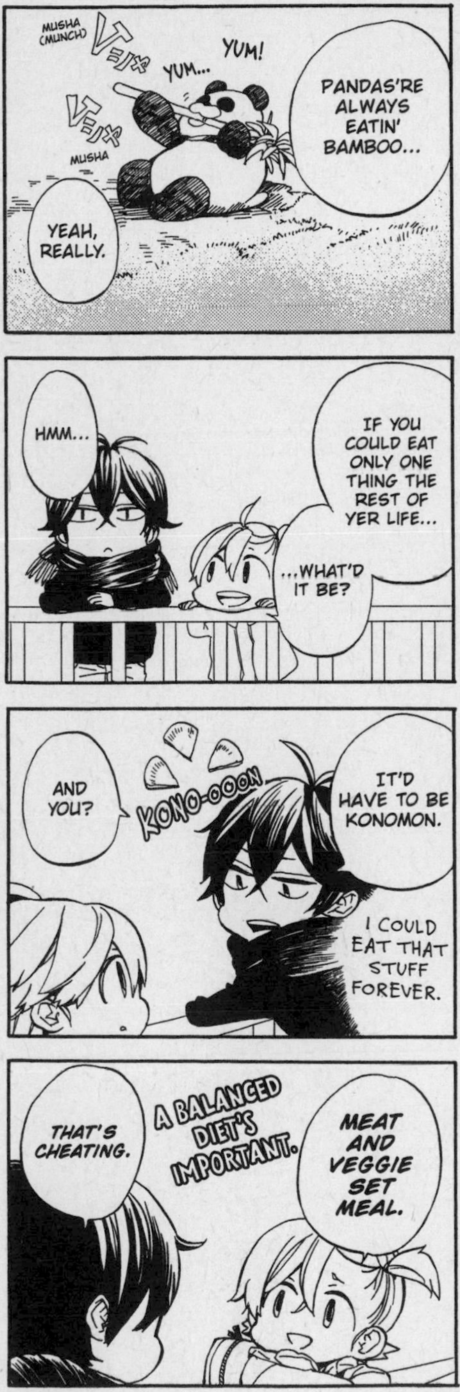
PANDAS'RE ALWAYS EATIN' BAMBOO...
YUM!
YUM...
MUSHA (MUNCH)
MUSHA
YEAH, REALLY.
IF YOU COULD EAT ONLY ONE THING THE REST OF YER LIFE...
...WHAT'D IT BE?
HMM...
IT'D HAVE TO BE KONOMON.
I COULD EAT THAT STUFF FOREVER.
KONO-OOON
AND YOU?
MEAT AND VEGGIE SET MEAL.
A BALANCED DIET'S IMPORTANT.
THAT'S CHEATING.

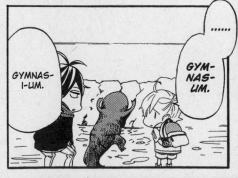

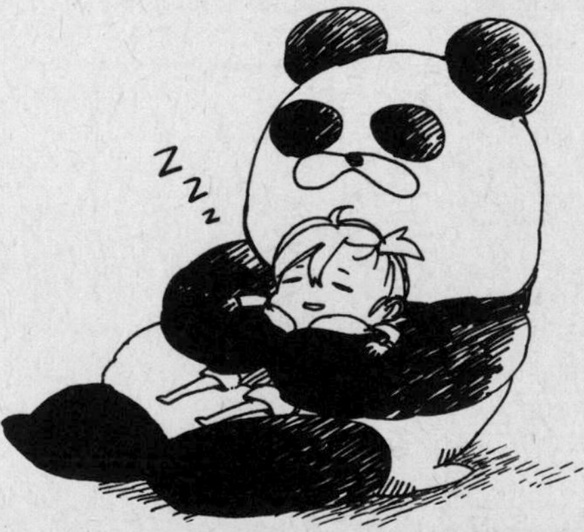
Zzz

Act.97
KOUSUKE WA HIMASON SHICHO
(Translation: Kousuke Is Acting Unemployed)

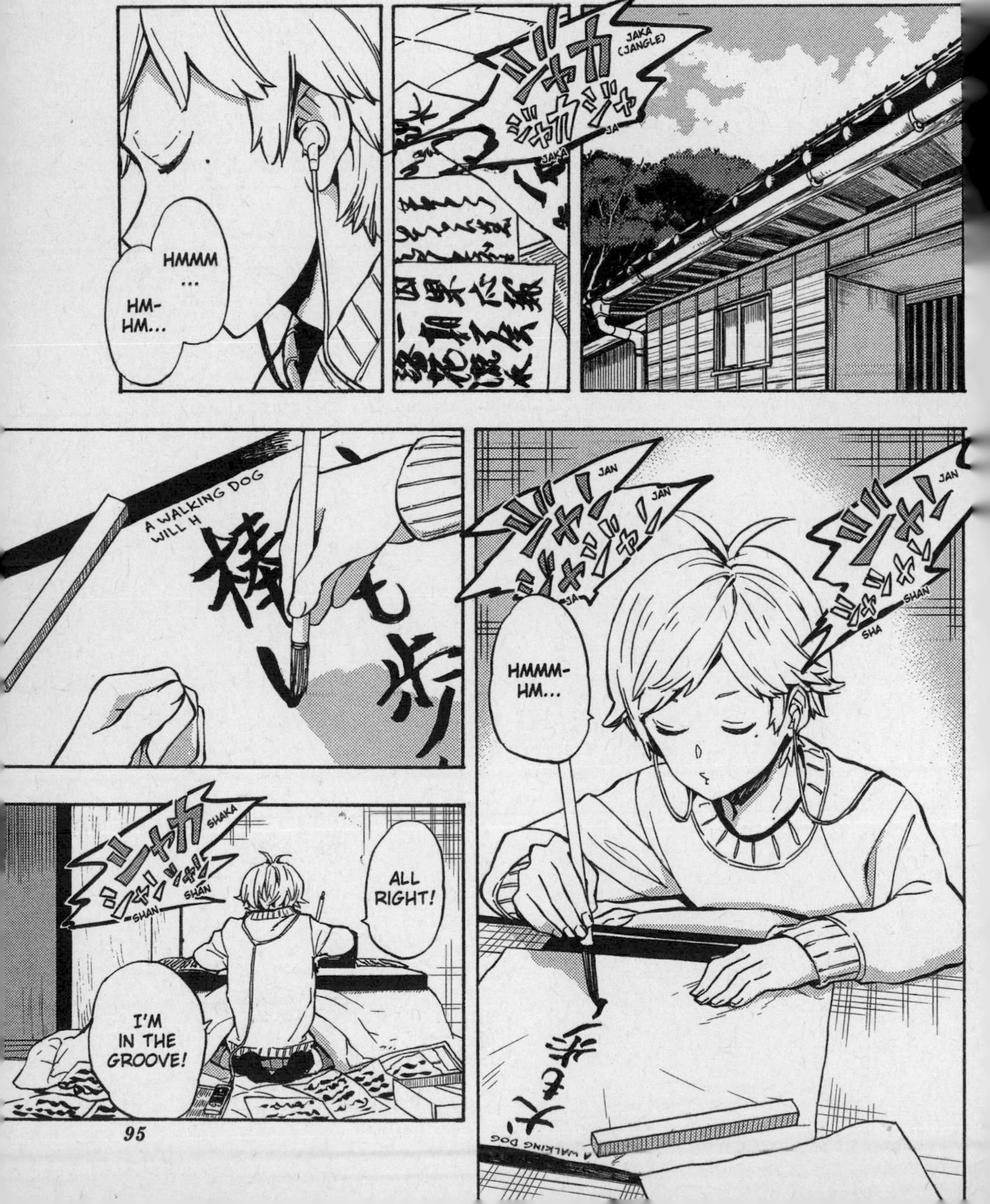

JAKA (JANGLE)
JA
JAKA
HMMM ...
HM-HM...
JAN
JAN
JA
JAN
SHAN
SHA
HMMM-HM...
A WALKING DOG
A WALKING DOG WILL H
SHAKA
SHAN
SHAN
ALL RIGHT!
I'M IN THE GROOVE!

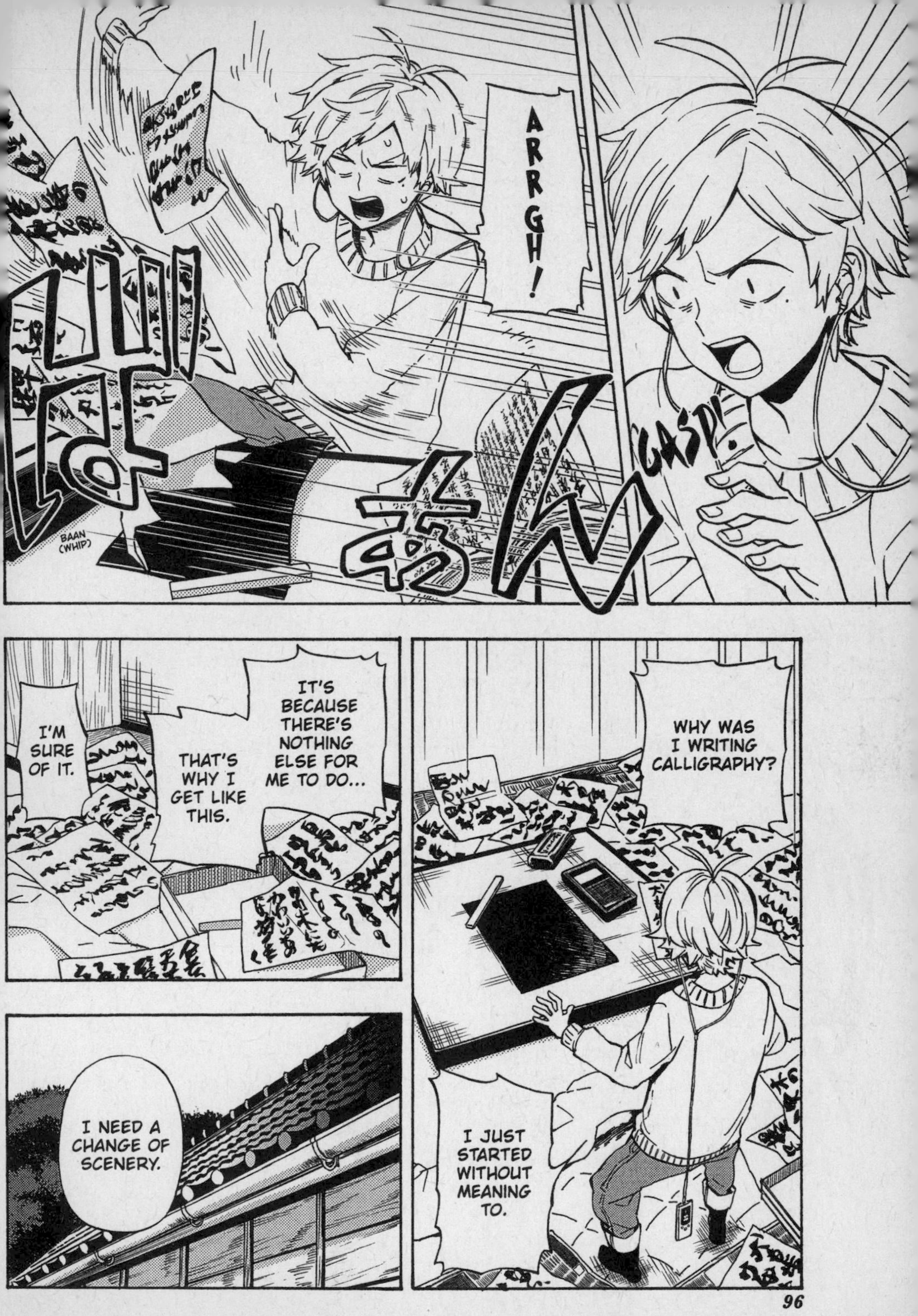
GASP!
ARRGH!
BAAN (WHIP)
WHY WAS I WRITING CALLIGRAPHY?
I JUST STARTED WITHOUT MEANING TO.
IT'S BECAUSE THERE'S NOTHING ELSE FOR ME TO DO...
THAT'S WHY I GET LIKE THIS.
I'M SURE OF IT.
I NEED A CHANGE OF SCENERY.

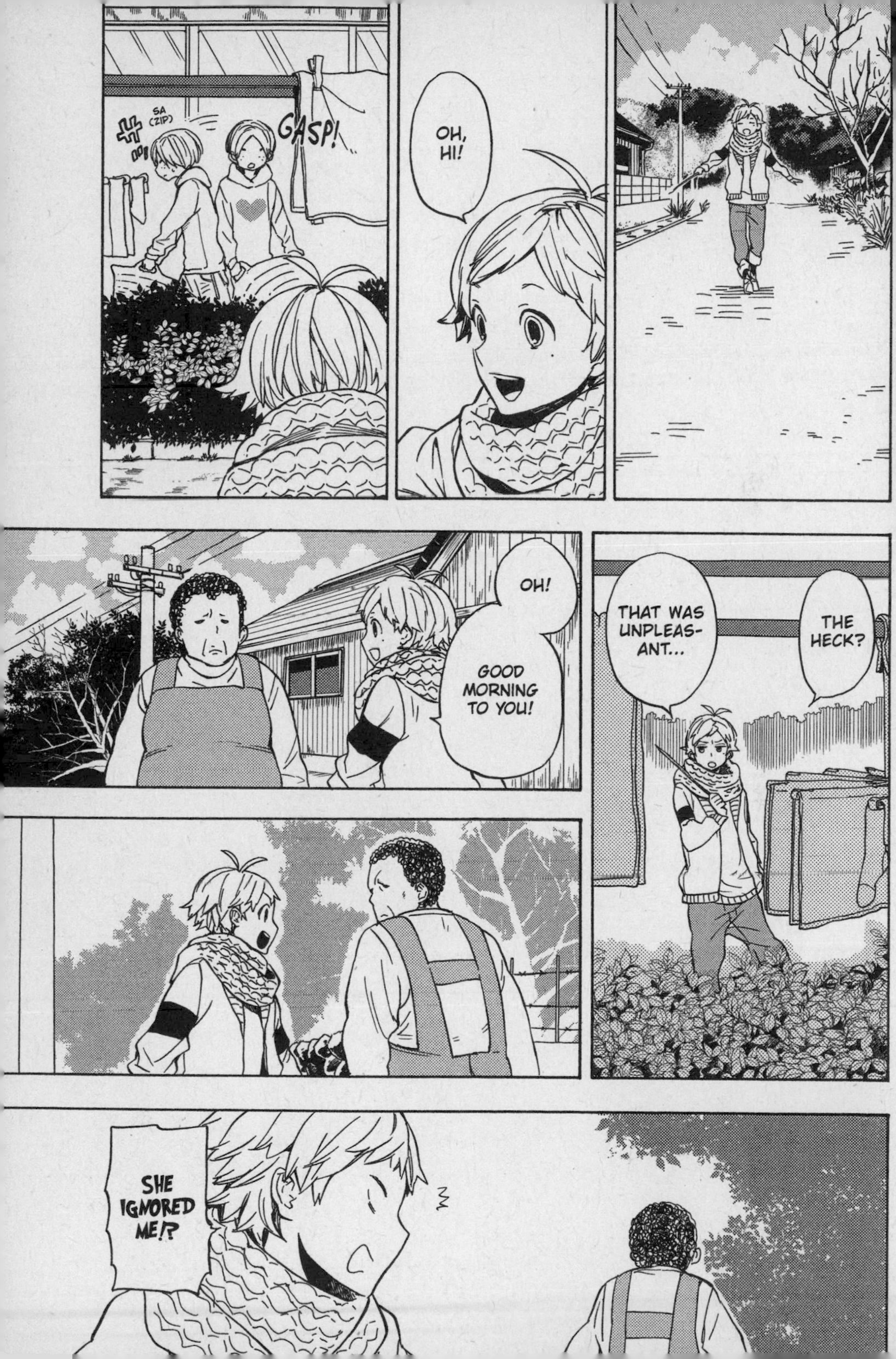
OH, HI!
SA (ZIP)
GASP!
THE HECK?
THAT WAS UNPLEAS-ANT...
OH!
GOOD MORNING TO YOU!
SHE IGNORED ME!?

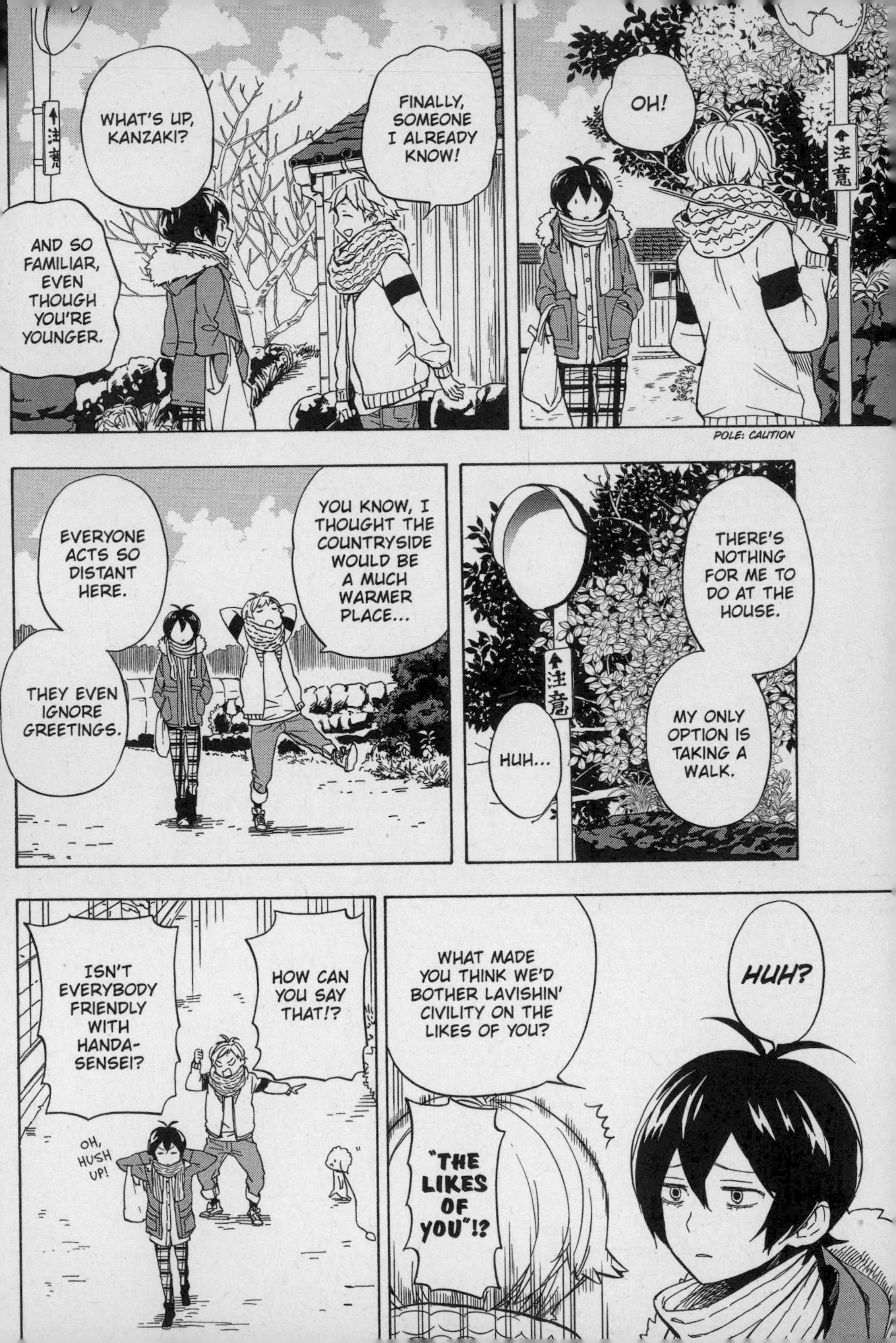
注意
OH!
FINALLY, SOMEONE I ALREADY KNOW!
WHAT'S UP, KANZAKI?
AND SO FAMILIAR, EVEN THOUGH YOU'RE YOUNGER.
注意
POLE: CAUTION
THERE'S NOTHING FOR ME TO DO AT THE HOUSE.
MY ONLY OPTION IS TAKING A WALK.
注意
HUH...
YOU KNOW, I THOUGHT THE COUNTRYSIDE WOULD BE A MUCH WARMER PLACE...
EVERYONE ACTS SO DISTANT HERE.
THEY EVEN IGNORE GREETINGS.
HUH?
WHAT MADE YOU THINK WE'D BOTHER LAVISHIN' CIVILITY ON THE LIKES OF YOU?
"THE LIKES OF YOU"!?
HOW CAN YOU SAY THAT!?
ISN'T EVERYBODY FRIENDLY WITH HANDA-SENSEI?
OH, HUSH UP!

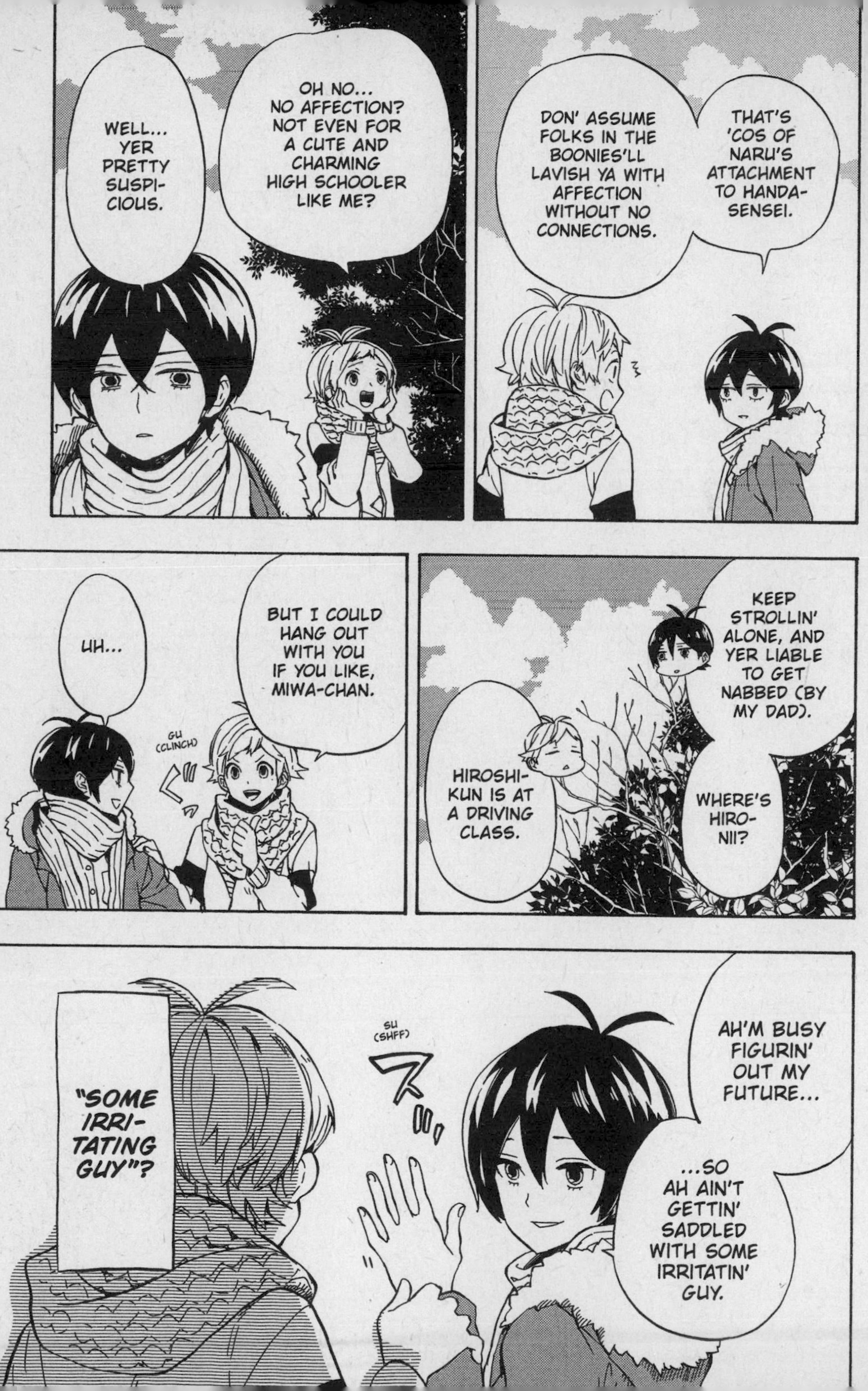
THAT'S 'COS OF NARU'S ATTACHMENT TO HANDA-SENSEI.
DON' ASSUME FOLKS IN THE BOONIES'LL LAVISH YA WITH AFFECTION WITHOUT NO CONNECTIONS.
OH NO... NO AFFECTION? NOT EVEN FOR A CUTE AND CHARMING HIGH SCHOOLER LIKE ME?
WELL... YER PRETTY SUSPI-CIOUS.
KEEP STROLLIN' ALONE, AND YER LIABLE TO GET NABBED (BY MY DAD).
WHERE'S HIRO-NII?
HIROSHI-KUN IS AT A DRIVING CLASS.
BUT I COULD HANG OUT WITH YOU IF YOU LIKE, MIWA-CHAN.
GU (CLINCH)
UH...
AH'M BUSY FIGURIN' OUT MY FUTURE...
...SO AH AIN'T GETTIN' SADDLED WITH SOME IRRITATIN' GUY.
SU (SHFF)
"SOME IRRI-TATING GUY"?

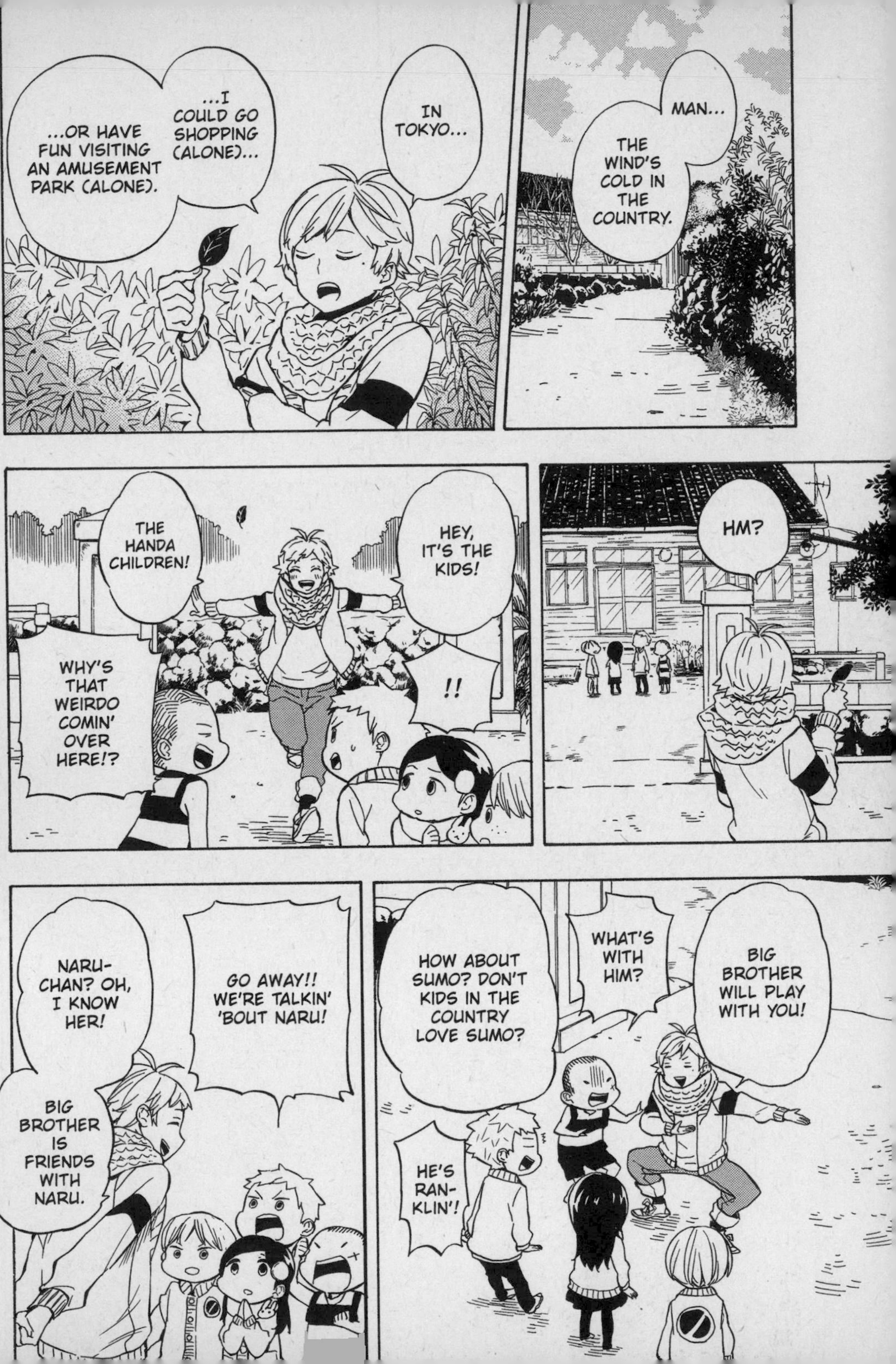
MAN...
THE WIND'S COLD IN THE COUNTRY.
IN TOKYO...
...I COULD GO SHOPPING (ALONE)...
...OR HAVE FUN VISITING AN AMUSEMENT PARK (ALONE).
HM?
HEY, IT'S THE KIDS!
THE HANDA CHILDREN!
!!
WHY'S THAT WEIRDO COMIN' OVER HERE!?
BIG BROTHER WILL PLAY WITH YOU!
WHAT'S WITH HIM?
HOW ABOUT SUMO? DON'T KIDS IN THE COUNTRY LOVE SUMO?
HE'S RAN-KLIN'!
GO AWAY!! WE'RE TALKIN' 'BOUT NARU!
NARU-CHAN? OH, I KNOW HER!
BIG BROTHER IS FRIENDS WITH NARU.

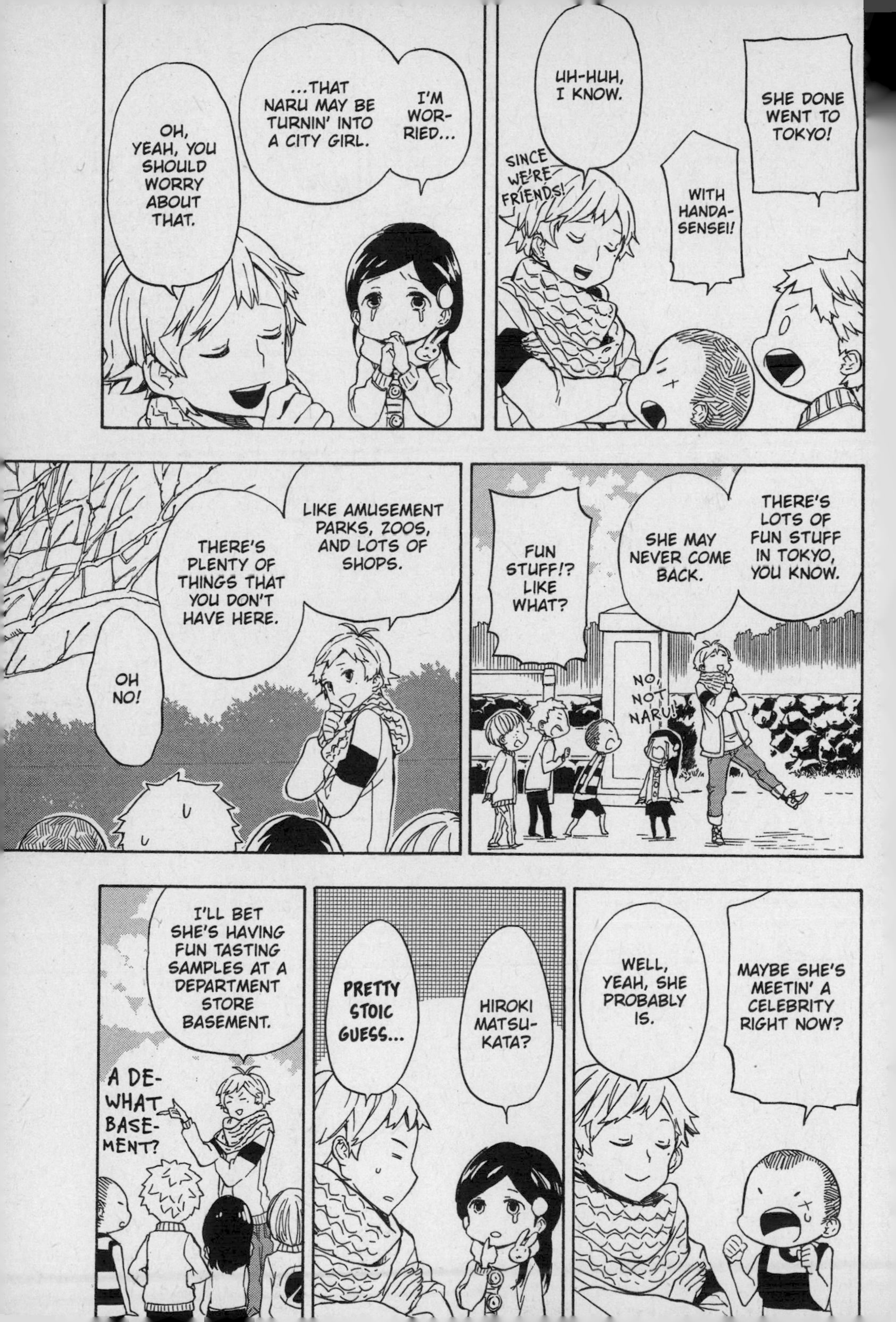
SHE DONE WENT TO TOKYO!
WITH HANDA-SENSEI!
UH-HUH, I KNOW.
SINCE WE'RE FRIENDS!
I'M WORRIED...
...THAT NARU MAY BE TURNIN' INTO A CITY GIRL.
OH, YEAH, YOU SHOULD WORRY ABOUT THAT.
THERE'S LOTS OF FUN STUFF IN TOKYO, YOU KNOW.
SHE MAY NEVER COME BACK.
FUN STUFF!? LIKE WHAT?
NO, NOT NARU!
LIKE AMUSEMENT PARKS, ZOOS, AND LOTS OF SHOPS.
THERE'S PLENTY OF THINGS THAT YOU DON'T HAVE HERE.
OH NO!
MAYBE SHE'S MEETIN' A CELEBRITY RIGHT NOW?
WELL, YEAH, SHE PROBABLY IS.
HIROKI MATSUKATA?
PRETTY STOIC GUESS...
I'LL BET SHE'S HAVING FUN TASTING SAMPLES AT A DEPARTMENT STORE BASEMENT.
A DE-WHAT BASEMENT?

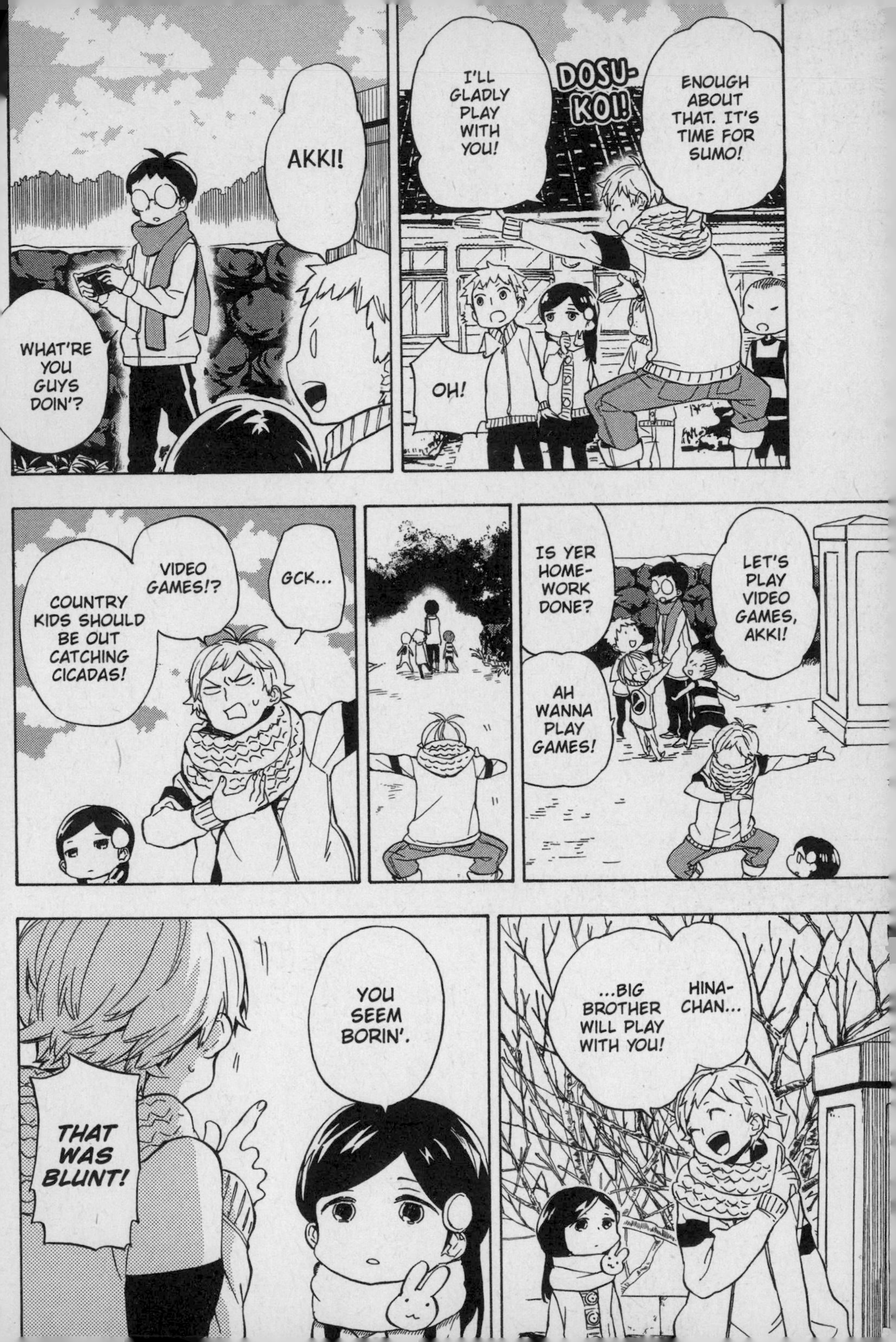
ENOUGH ABOUT THAT. IT'S TIME FOR SUMO!
DOSU-KOI!
I'LL GLADLY PLAY WITH YOU!
OH!
AKKI!
WHAT'RE YOU GUYS DOIN'?
LET'S PLAY VIDEO GAMES, AKKI!
IS YER HOME-WORK DONE?
AH WANNA PLAY GAMES!
GCK...
VIDEO GAMES!?
COUNTRY KIDS SHOULD BE OUT CATCHING CICADAS!
HINA-CHAN...
...BIG BROTHER WILL PLAY WITH YOU!
YOU SEEM BORIN'.
THAT WAS BLUNT!

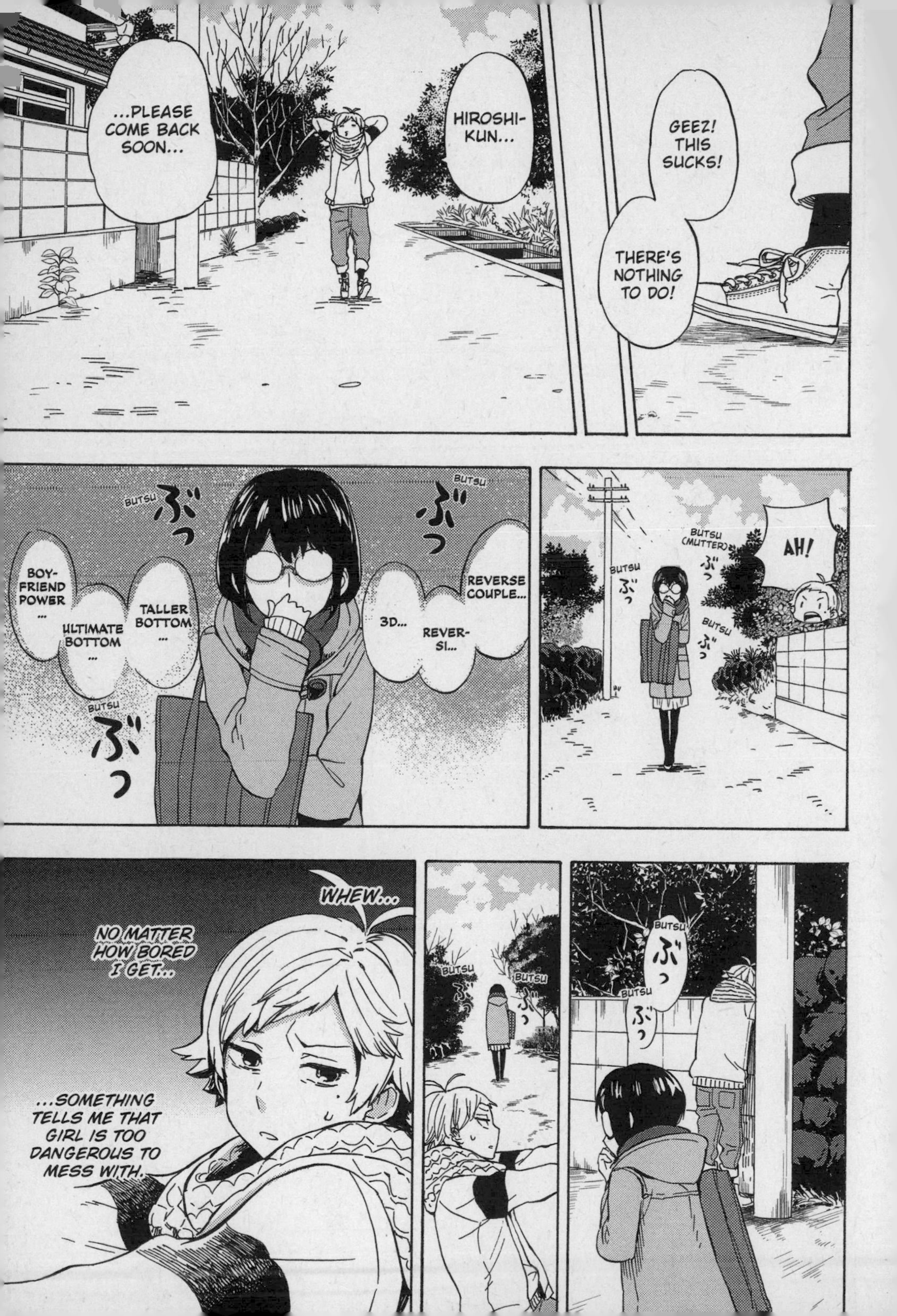
GEEZ! THIS SUCKS!
THERE'S NOTHING TO DO!
HIROSHI-KUN...
...PLEASE COME BACK SOON...
AH!
BUTSU (MUTTER)
ぶっ
BUTSU
ぶっ
BUTSU
ぶっ
BUTSU
ぶっ
REVERSE COUPLE...
REVERSI...
3D...
BUTSU
ぶっ
TALLER BOTTOM...
BOY-FRIEND POWER...
ULTIMATE BOTTOM...
BUTSU
ぶっ
BUTSU
ぶっ
BUTSU
ぶっ
BUTSU
ぶっ
BUTSU
ぶっ
WHEW...
NO MATTER HOW BORED I GET...
...SOMETHING TELLS ME THAT GIRL IS TOO DANGEROUS TO MESS WITH.

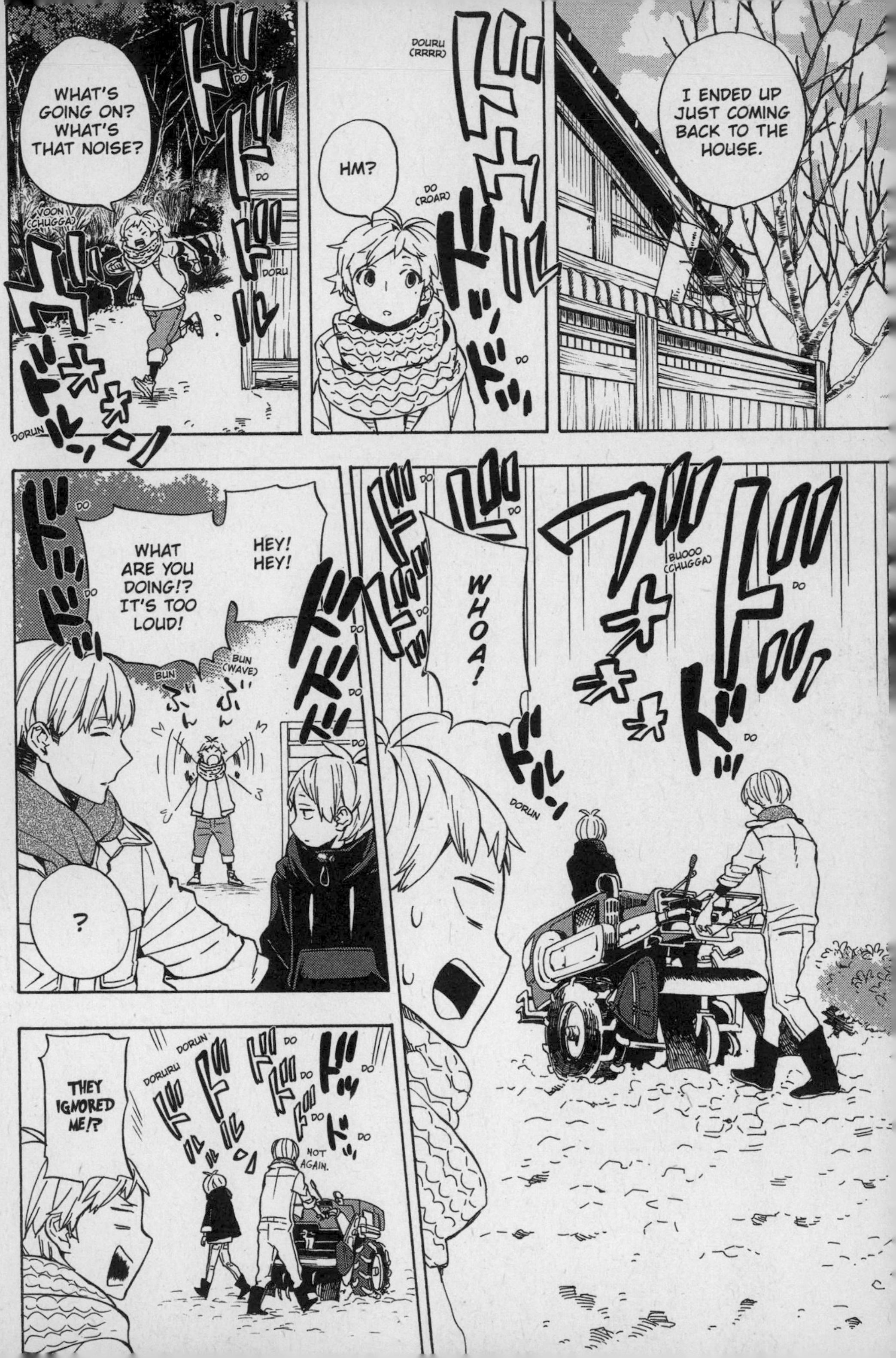
I ENDED UP JUST COMING BACK TO THE HOUSE.
DOURU (RRRR)
HM?
DO (ROAR)
DO
WHAT'S GOING ON? WHAT'S THAT NOISE?
DO
DO
VOON (CHUGGA)
DORU
DORUN
DO
DO
BUOOO (CHUGGA)
DO
DO
DO
WHOA!
DO
DORUN
DO
HEY! HEY!
WHAT ARE YOU DOING!? IT'S TOO LOUD!
BUN (WAVE)
BUN
DO
DO
?
THEY IGNORED ME!?
DORURU
DORUN
DO
DO
DO
DO
DO
NOT AGAIN.

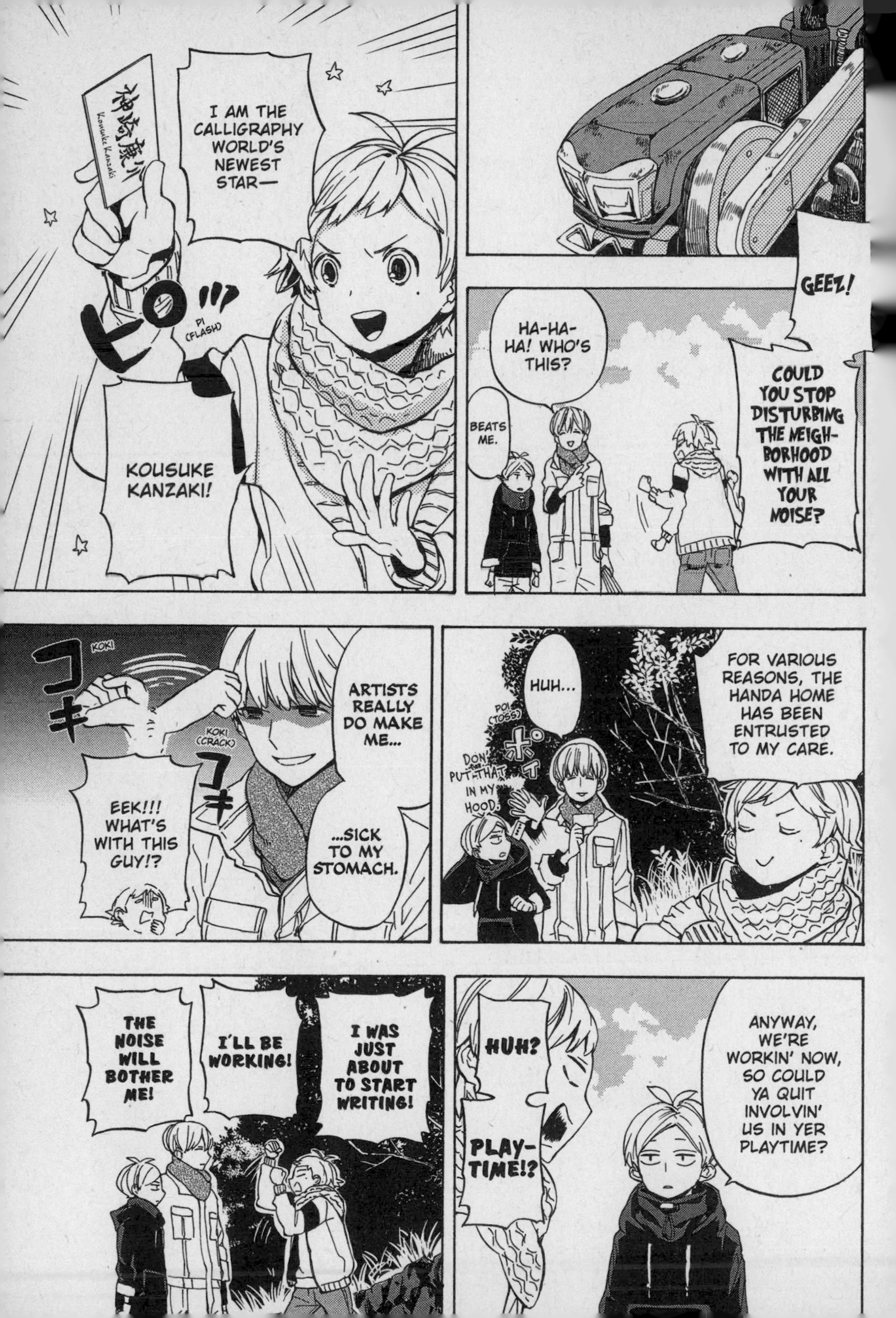

GEEZ!
HA-HA-HA! WHO'S THIS?
BEATS ME.
COULD YOU STOP DISTURBING THE NEIGHBORHOOD WITH ALL YOUR NOISE?
神崎康介
Kousuke Kanzaki
I AM THE CALLIGRAPHY WORLD'S NEWEST STAR—
ピロッ
PI (FLASH)
KOUSUKE KANZAKI!
FOR VARIOUS REASONS, THE HANDA HOME HAS BEEN ENTRUSTED TO MY CARE.
HUH...
ポイ
POI (TOSS)
DON'T PUT THAT IN MY HOOD.
ARTISTS REALLY DO MAKE ME...
コキ
KOKI
コキ
KOKI (CRACK)
EEK!!! WHAT'S WITH THIS GUY!?
...SICK TO MY STOMACH.
ANYWAY, WE'RE WORKIN' NOW, SO COULD YA QUIT INVOLVIN' US IN YER PLAYTIME?
HUH?
PLAY-TIME!?
I WAS JUST ABOUT TO START WRITING!
I'LL BE WORKING!
THE NOISE WILL BOTHER ME!

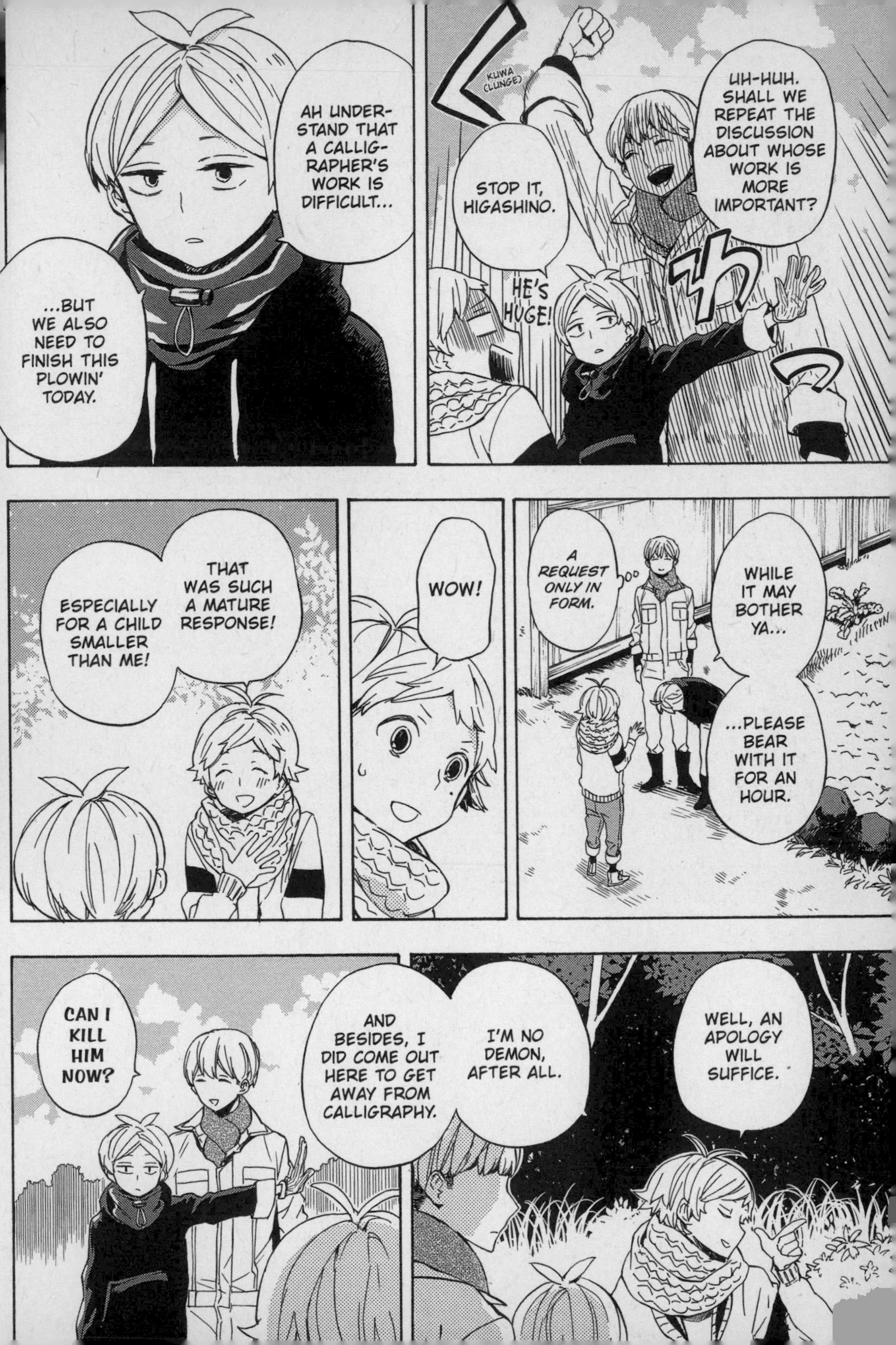
KUWA (LUNGE)
UH-HUH. SHALL WE REPEAT THE DISCUSSION ABOUT WHOSE WORK IS MORE IMPORTANT?
STOP IT, HIGASHINO.
HE'S HUGE!
AH UNDERSTAND THAT A CALLIGRAPHER'S WORK IS DIFFICULT...
...BUT WE ALSO NEED TO FINISH THIS PLOWIN' TODAY.
WHILE IT MAY BOTHER YA...
...PLEASE BEAR WITH IT FOR AN HOUR.
A REQUEST ONLY IN FORM.
WOW!
THAT WAS SUCH A MATURE RESPONSE!
ESPECIALLY FOR A CHILD SMALLER THAN ME!
WELL, AN APOLOGY WILL SUFFICE.
I'M NO DEMON, AFTER ALL.
AND BESIDES, I DID COME OUT HERE TO GET AWAY FROM CALLIGRAPHY.
CAN I KILL HIM NOW?

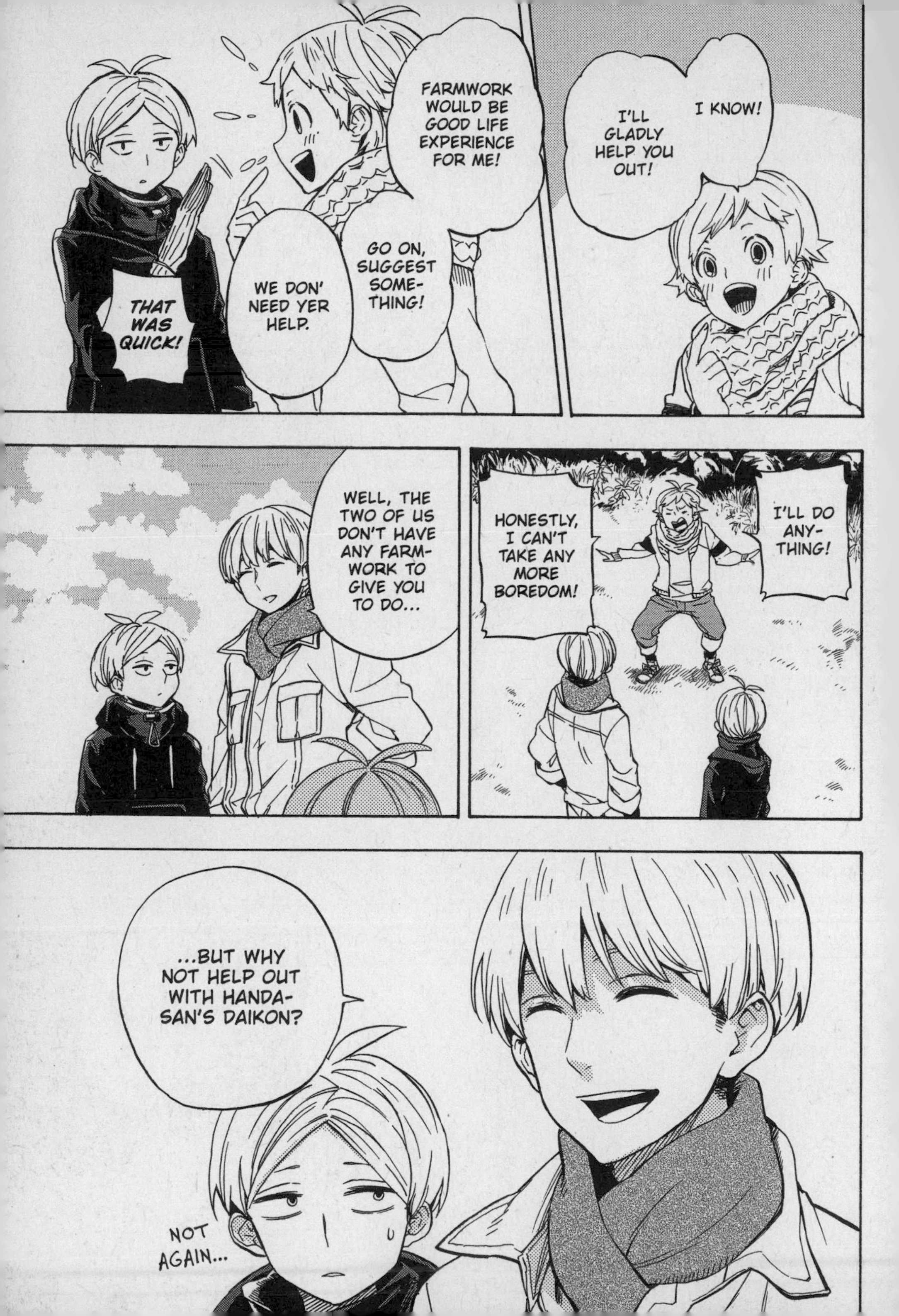
I KNOW!
I'LL GLADLY HELP YOU OUT!
FARMWORK WOULD BE GOOD LIFE EXPERIENCE FOR ME!
GO ON, SUGGEST SOME-THING!
WE DON' NEED YER HELP.
THAT WAS QUICK!
I'LL DO ANY-THING!
HONESTLY, I CAN'T TAKE ANY MORE BOREDOM!
WELL, THE TWO OF US DON'T HAVE ANY FARM-WORK TO GIVE YOU TO DO...
...BUT WHY NOT HELP OUT WITH HANDA-SAN'S DAIKON?
NOT AGAIN...

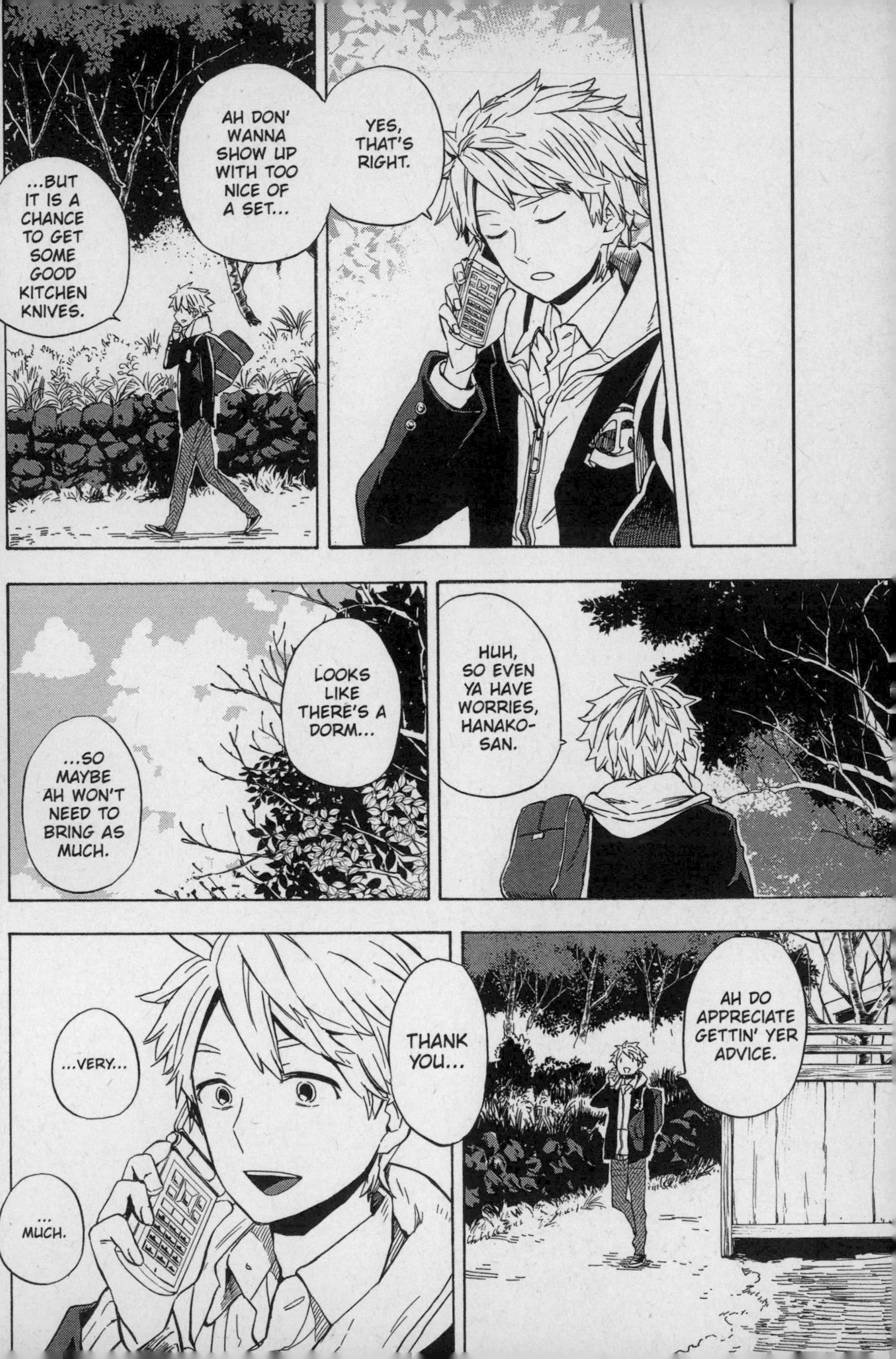
YES, THAT'S RIGHT.
AH DON' WANNA SHOW UP WITH TOO NICE OF A SET...
...BUT IT IS A CHANCE TO GET SOME GOOD KITCHEN KNIVES.
HUH, SO EVEN YA HAVE WORRIES, HANAKO-SAN.
LOOKS LIKE THERE'S A DORM...
...SO MAYBE AH WON'T NEED TO BRING AS MUCH.
AH DO APPRECIATE GETTIN' YER ADVICE.
THANK YOU...
...VERY...
... MUCH.

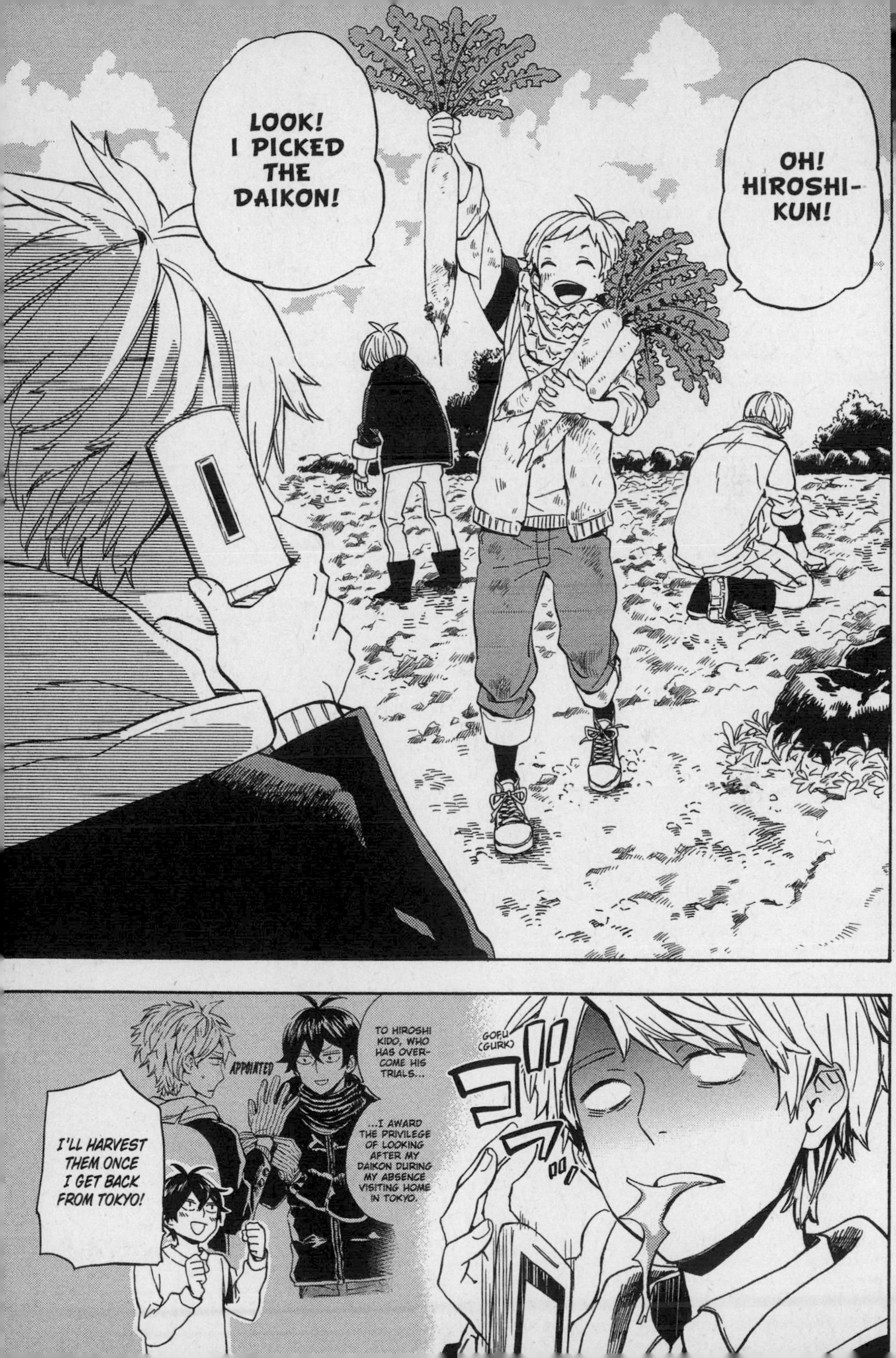
OH! HIROSHI-KUN!
LOOK! I PICKED THE DAIKON!
GOFU (GURK)
TO HIROSHI KIDO, WHO HAS OVERCOME HIS TRIALS...
...I AWARD THE PRIVILEGE OF LOOKING AFTER MY DAIKON DURING MY ABSENCE VISITING HOME IN TOKYO.
APPOINTED
I'LL HARVEST THEM ONCE I GET BACK FROM TOKYO!

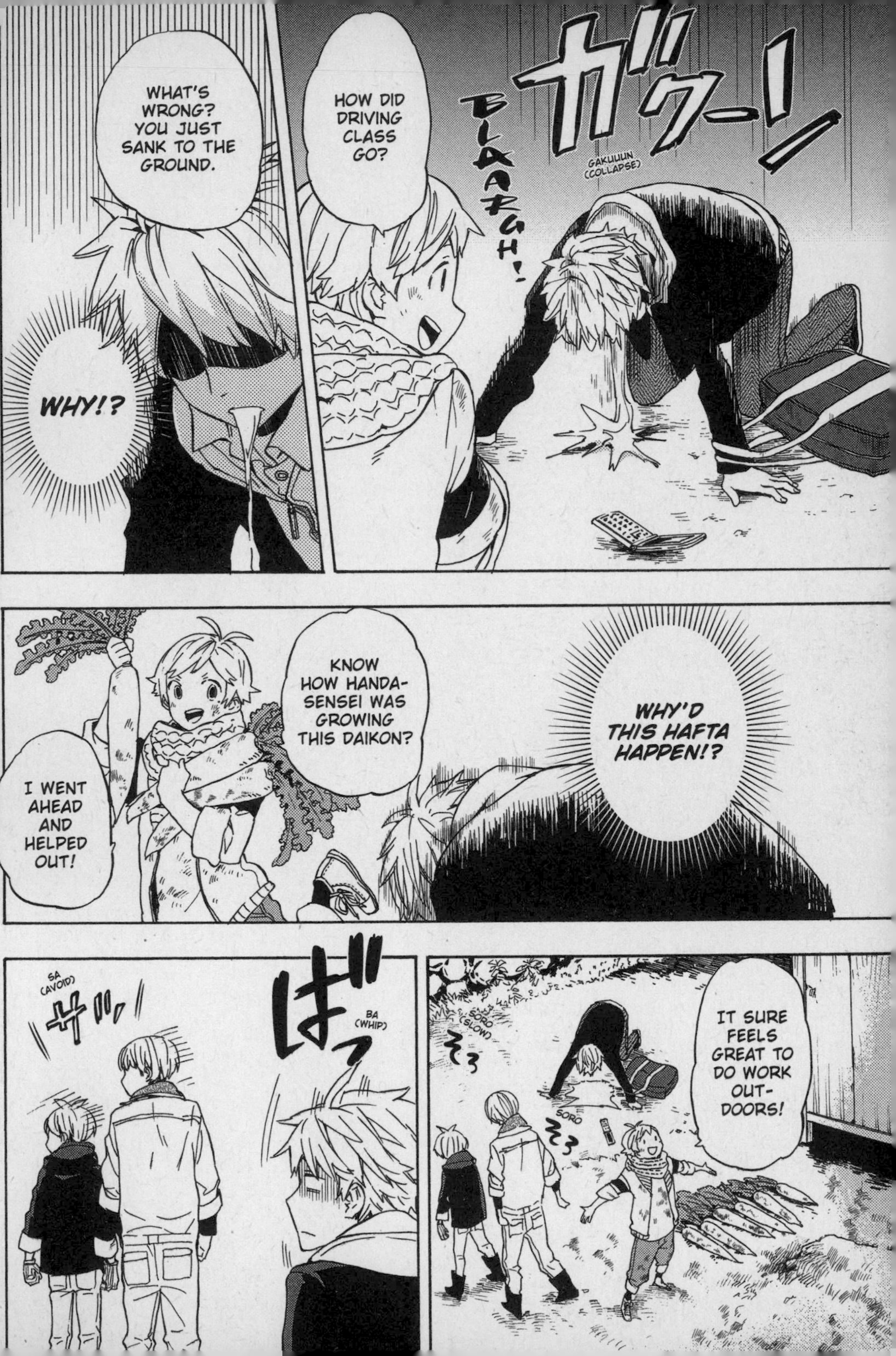
ガクーン
GAKUUUN (COLLAPSE)
BLAAARGH!
HOW DID DRIVING CLASS GO?
WHAT'S WRONG? YOU JUST SANK TO THE GROUND.
WHY!?
WHY'D THIS HAFTA HAPPEN!?
KNOW HOW HANDA-SENSEI WAS GROWING THIS DAIKON?
I WENT AHEAD AND HELPED OUT!
IT SURE FEELS GREAT TO DO WORK OUT-DOORS!
そろ
SORO (SLOW)
そろ
SORO
ばっ
BA (WHIP)
サッ
SA (AVOID)

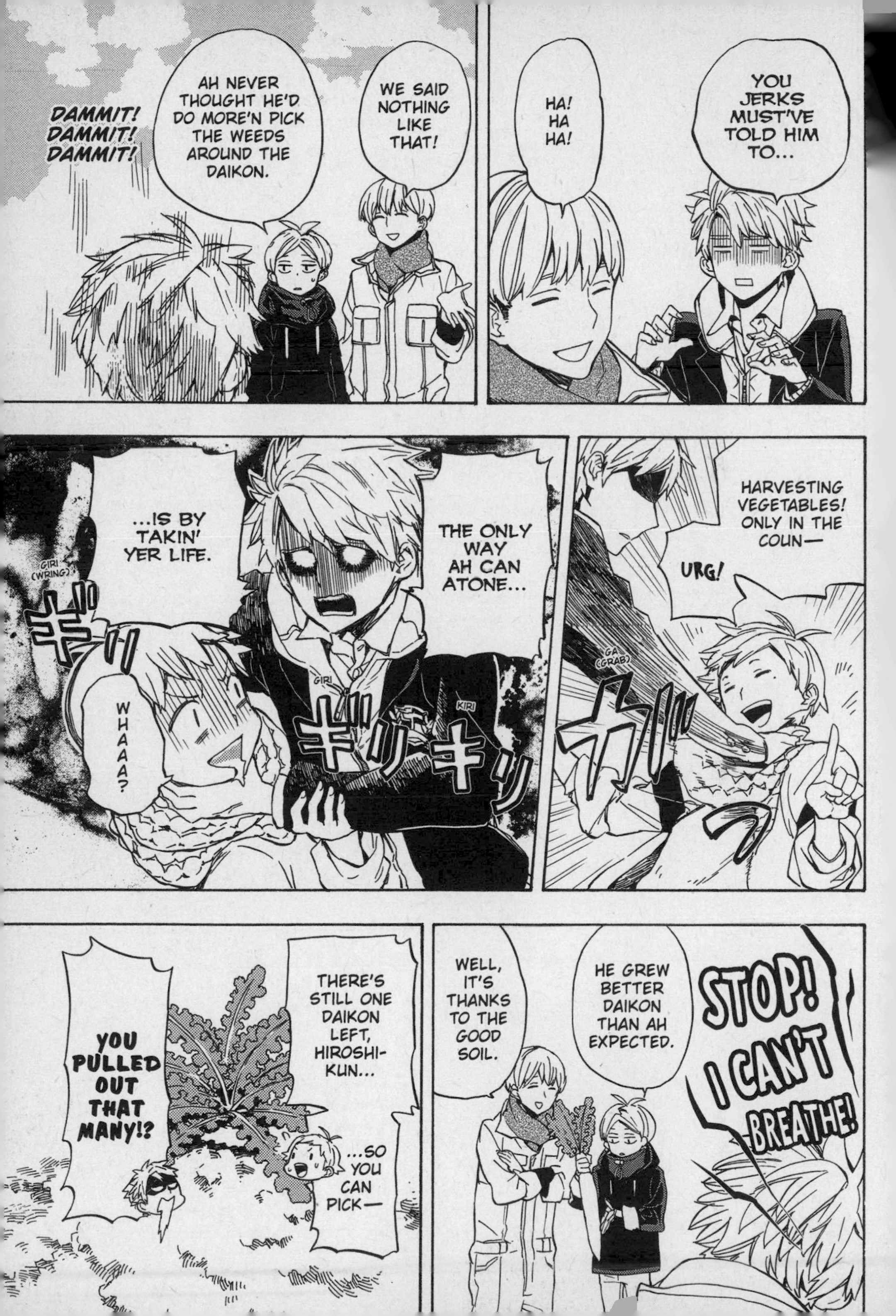
YOU JERKS MUST'VE TOLD HIM TO...
HA! HA HA!
WE SAID NOTHING LIKE THAT!
AH NEVER THOUGHT HE'D DO MORE'N PICK THE WEEDS AROUND THE DAIKON.
DAMMIT! DAMMIT! DAMMIT!
HARVESTING VEGETABLES! ONLY IN THE COUN—
URG!
GA (GRAB)
THE ONLY WAY AH CAN ATONE...
...IS BY TAKIN' YER LIFE.
GIRI
KIRI
GIRI (WRING)
WHAAAA?
STOP! I CAN'T BREATHE!
HE GREW BETTER DAIKON THAN AH EXPECTED.
WELL, IT'S THANKS TO THE GOOD SOIL.
THERE'S STILL ONE DAIKON LEFT, HIROSHI-KUN...
...SO YOU CAN PICK—
YOU PULLED OUT THAT MANY!?

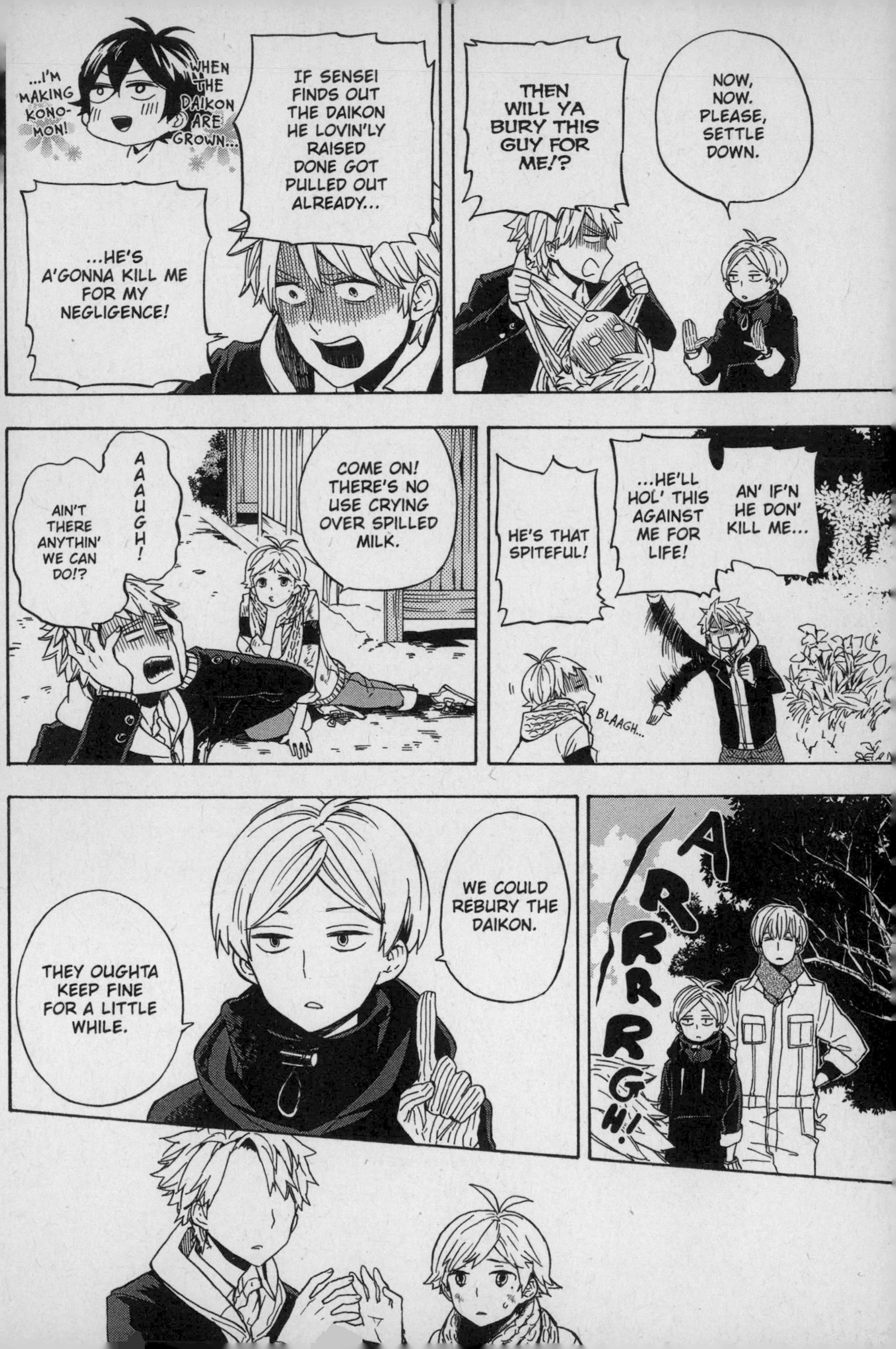
NOW, NOW. PLEASE, SETTLE DOWN.
THEN WILL YA BURY THIS GUY FOR ME!?
IF SENSEI FINDS OUT THE DAIKON HE LOVIN'LY RAISED DONE GOT PULLED OUT ALREADY...
WHEN THE DAIKON ARE GROWN...
...I'M MAKING KONO-MON!
...HE'S A'GONNA KILL ME FOR MY NEGLIGENCE!
AN' IF'N HE DON' KILL ME...
...HE'LL HOL' THIS AGAINST ME FOR LIFE!
HE'S THAT SPITEFUL!
BLAAGH...
COME ON! THERE'S NO USE CRYING OVER SPILLED MILK.
AAAAUGH!
AIN'T THERE ANYTHIN' WE CAN DO!?
ARRRRGH!
WE COULD REBURY THE DAIKON.
THEY OUGHTA KEEP FINE FOR A LITTLE WHILE.

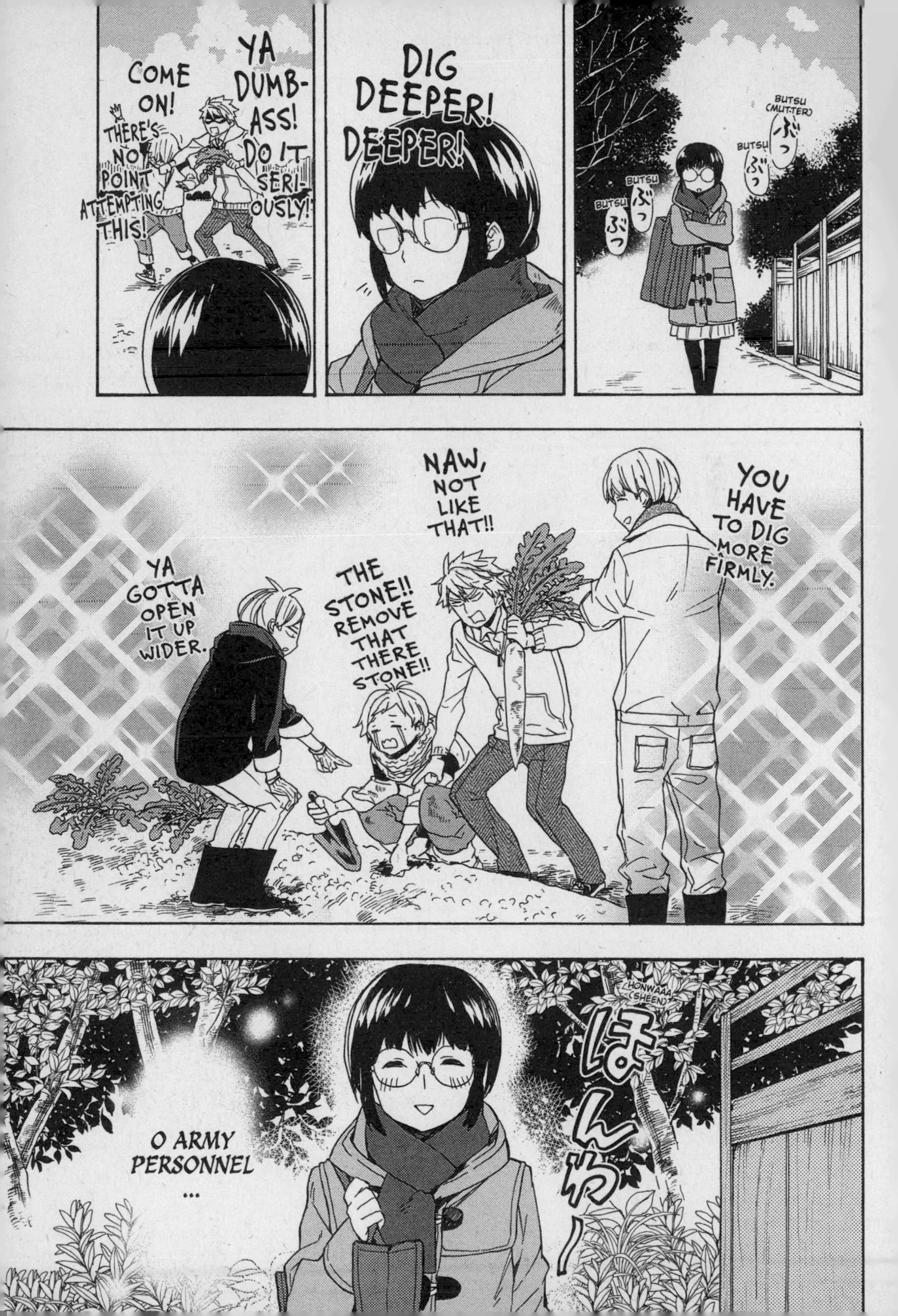
BUTSU (MUTTER) ぶっ
BUTSU ぶっ
BUTSU ぶっ
BUTSU ぶっ
DIG DEEPER! DEEPER!
YA DUMB-ASS! DO IT SERI-OUSLY!
COME ON! THERE'S NO POINT ATTEMPTING THIS!
YOU HAVE TO DIG MORE FIRMLY.
NAW, NOT LIKE THAT!!
THE STONE!! REMOVE THAT THERE STONE!!
YA GOTTA OPEN IT UP WIDER.
HONWAAA (SHEEN)
ほんわ～
O ARMY PERSONNEL ...

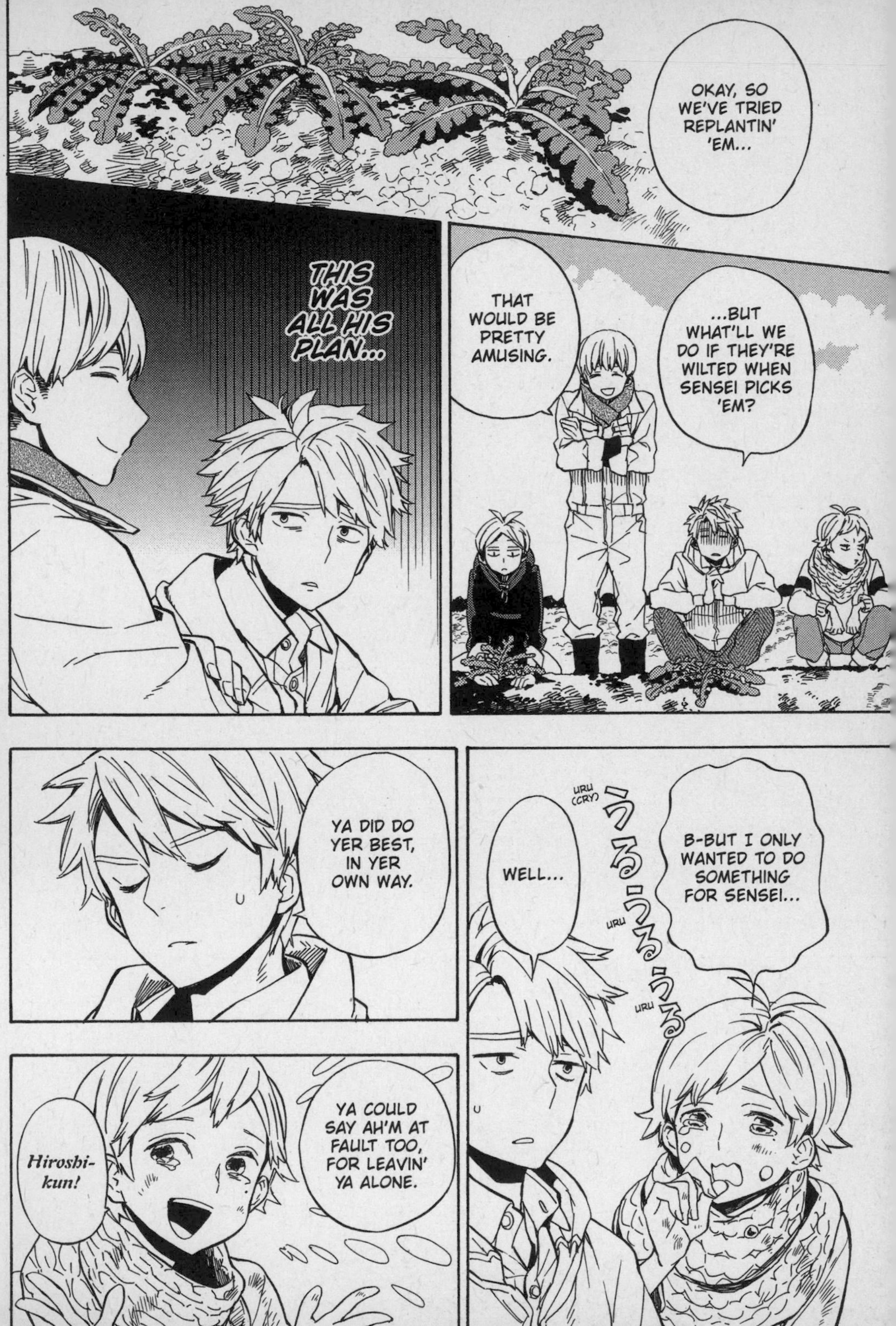
OKAY, SO WE'VE TRIED REPLANTIN' 'EM...
...BUT WHAT'LL WE DO IF THEY'RE WILTED WHEN SENSEI PICKS 'EM?
THAT WOULD BE PRETTY AMUSING.
THIS WAS ALL HIS PLAN...
B-BUT I ONLY WANTED TO DO SOMETHING FOR SENSEI...
うる URU (CRY)
うる URU
うる URU
WELL...
YA DID DO YER BEST, IN YER OWN WAY.
YA COULD SAY AH'M AT FAULT TOO, FOR LEAVIN' YA ALONE.
Hiroshi-kun!

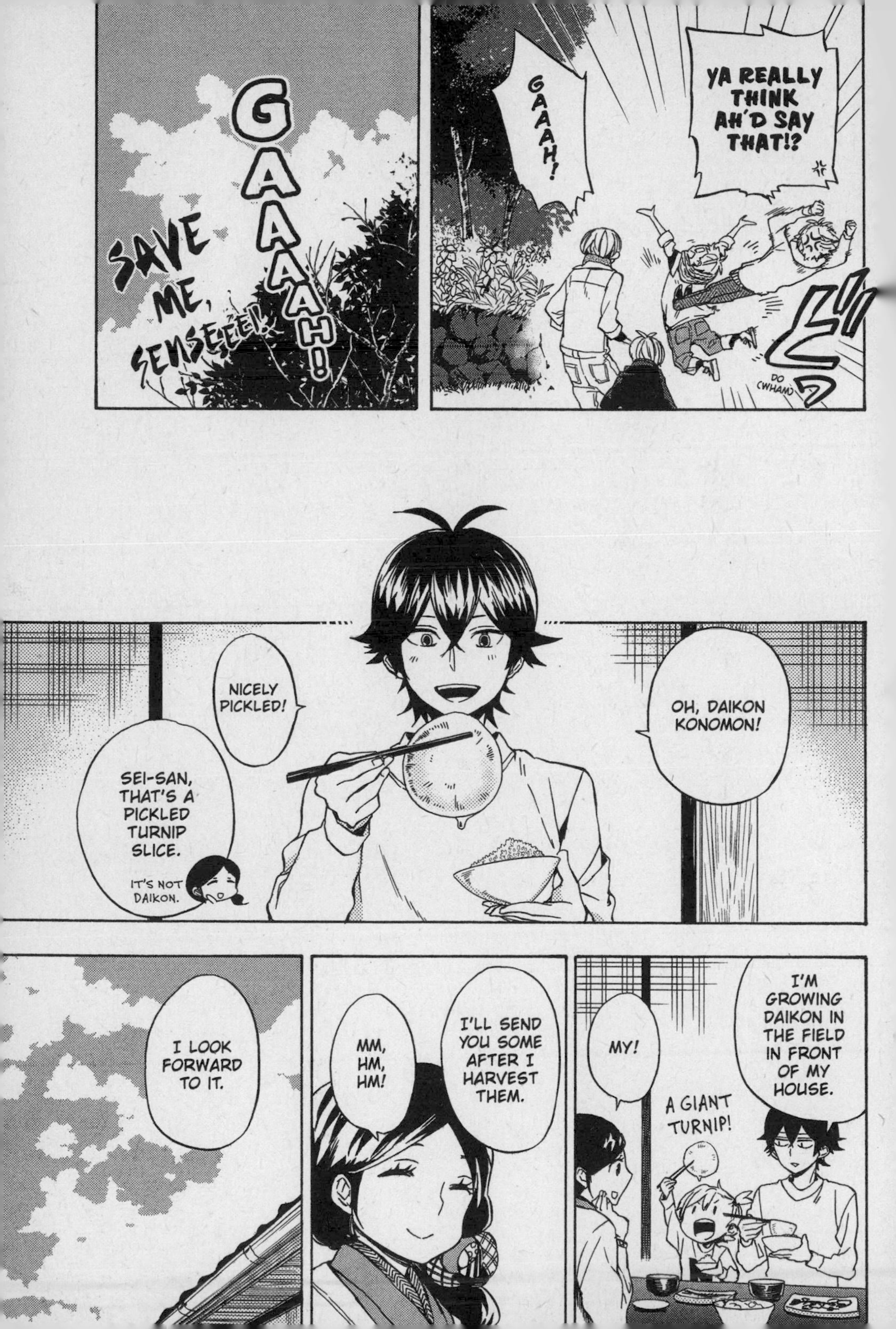
YA REALLY THINK AH'D SAY THAT!?
GAAAH!
DO (WHAM)
GAAAAAH!
SAVE ME, SENSEEE!
OH, DAIKON KONOMON!
NICELY PICKLED!
SEI-SAN, THAT'S A PICKLED TURNIP SLICE.
IT'S NOT DAIKON.
I'M GROWING DAIKON IN THE FIELD IN FRONT OF MY HOUSE.
MY!
A GIANT TURNIP!
I'LL SEND YOU SOME AFTER I HARVEST THEM.
MM, HM, HM!
I LOOK FORWARD TO IT.

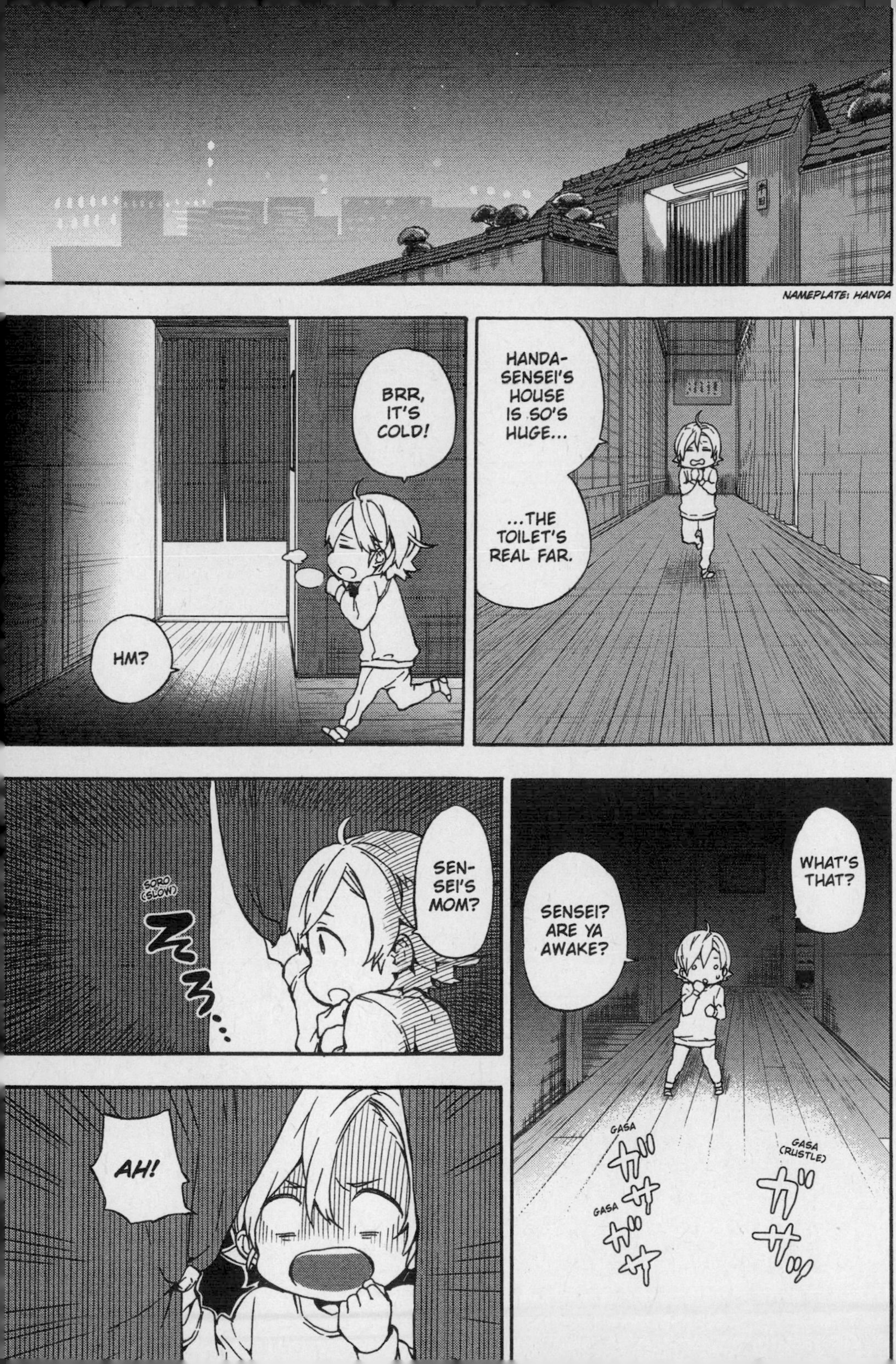
NAMEPLATE: HANDA
HANDA-SENSEI'S HOUSE IS SO'S HUGE...
...THE TOILET'S REAL FAR.
BRR, IT'S COLD!
HM?
WHAT'S THAT?
SENSEI? ARE YA AWAKE?
GASA (RUSTLE)
GASA
GASA
SEN-SEI'S MOM?
SORO (SLOW)
AH!

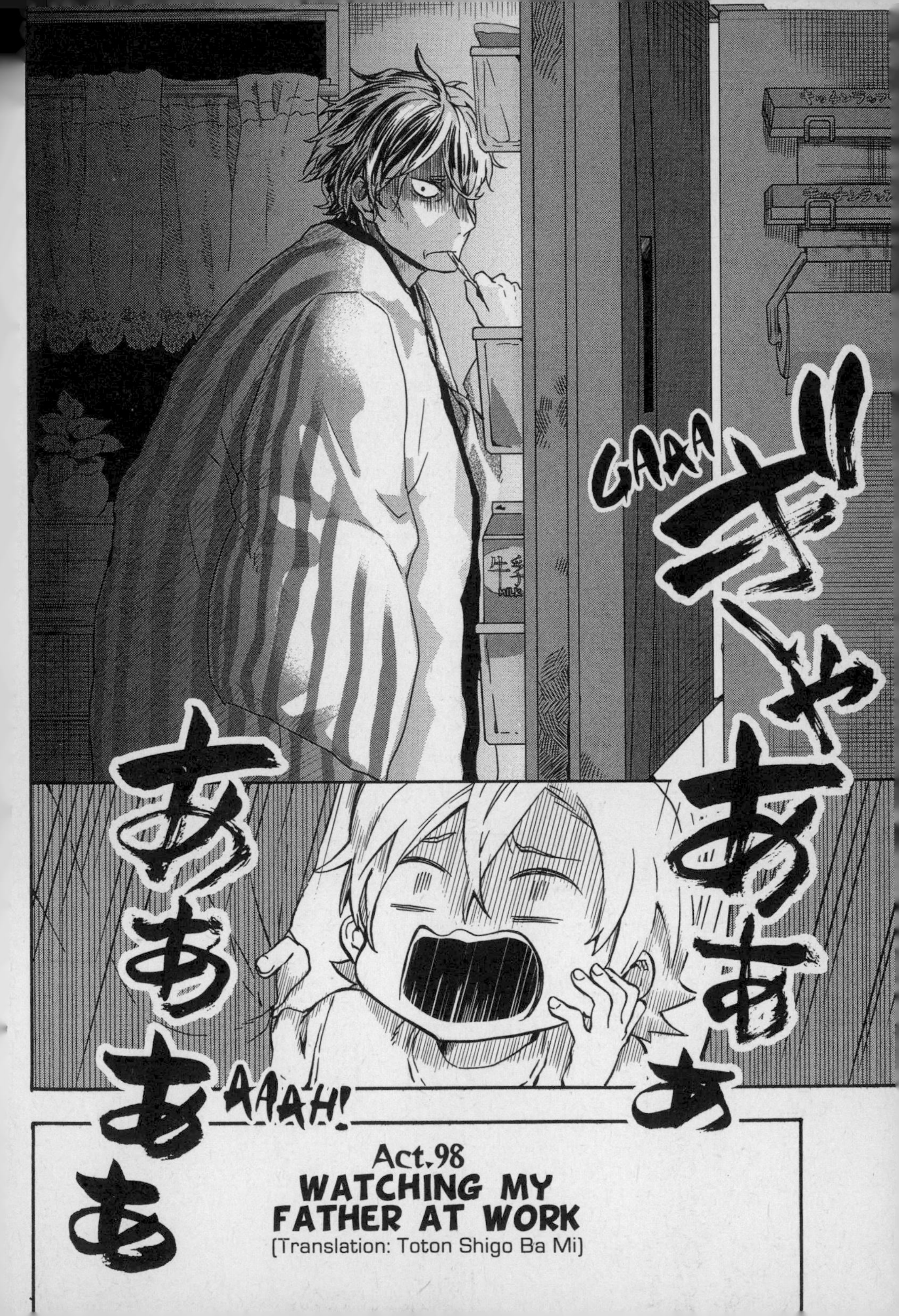
GAAA
AAAH!

Act.98
WATCHING MY FATHER AT WORK
(Translation: Toton Shigo Ba Mi)

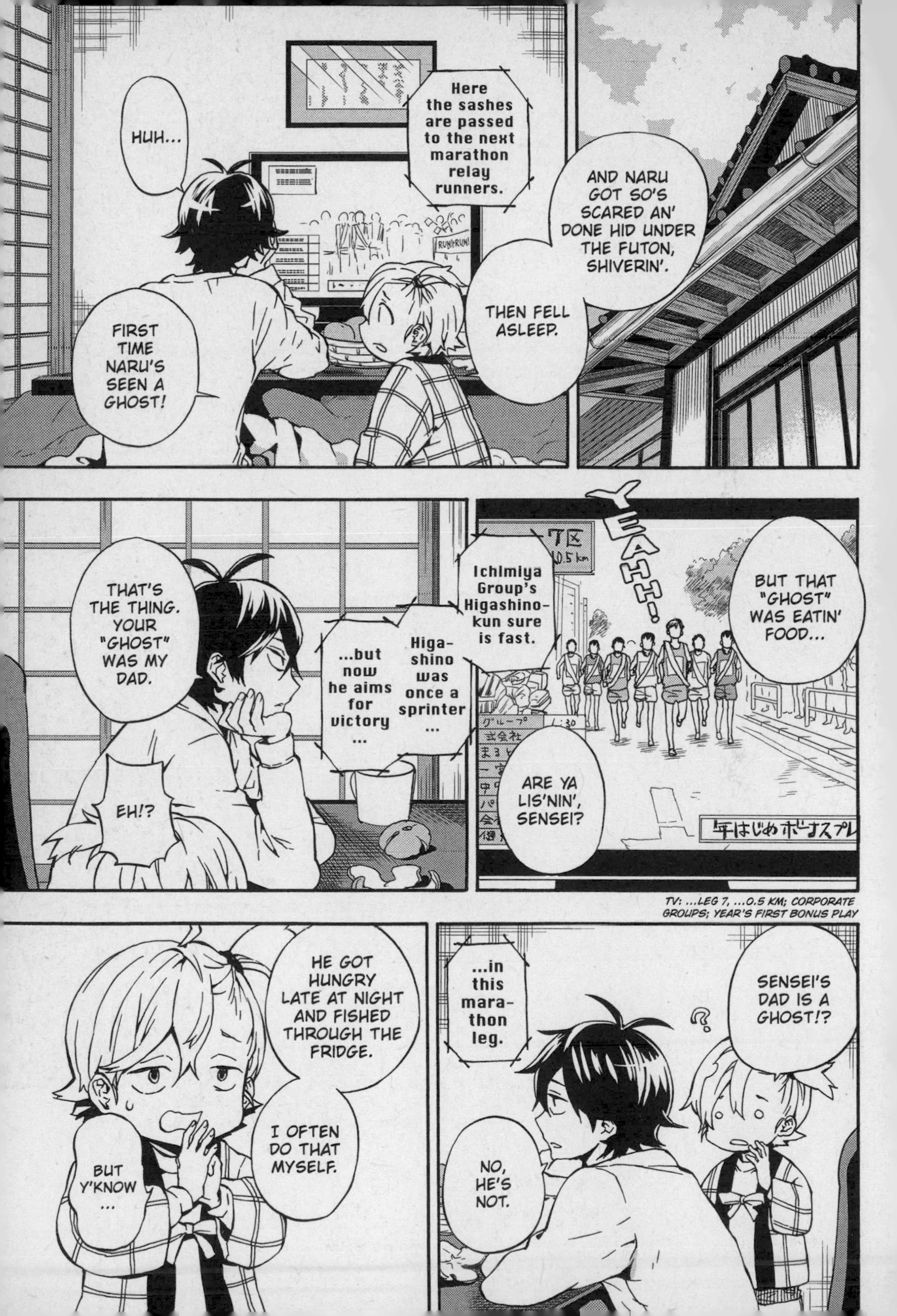
AND NARU GOT SO'S SCARED AN' DONE HID UNDER THE FUTON, SHIVERIN'.
THEN FELL ASLEEP.
Here the sashes are passed to the next marathon relay runners.
HUH...
RUN! RUN!
FIRST TIME NARU'S SEEN A GHOST!
YEAHH!
BUT THAT "GHOST" WAS EATIN' FOOD...
Ichimiya Group's Higashino-kun sure is fast.
ARE YA LIS'NIN', SENSEI?
TV: ...LEG 7, ...0.5 KM; CORPORATE GROUPS; YEAR'S FIRST BONUS PLAY
Higa-shino was once a sprinter...
...but now he aims for victory...
THAT'S THE THING. YOUR "GHOST" WAS MY DAD.
EH!?
SENSEI'S DAD IS A GHOST!?
?
...in this mara-thon leg.
NO, HE'S NOT.
HE GOT HUNGRY LATE AT NIGHT AND FISHED THROUGH THE FRIDGE.
I OFTEN DO THAT MYSELF.
BUT Y'KNOW...

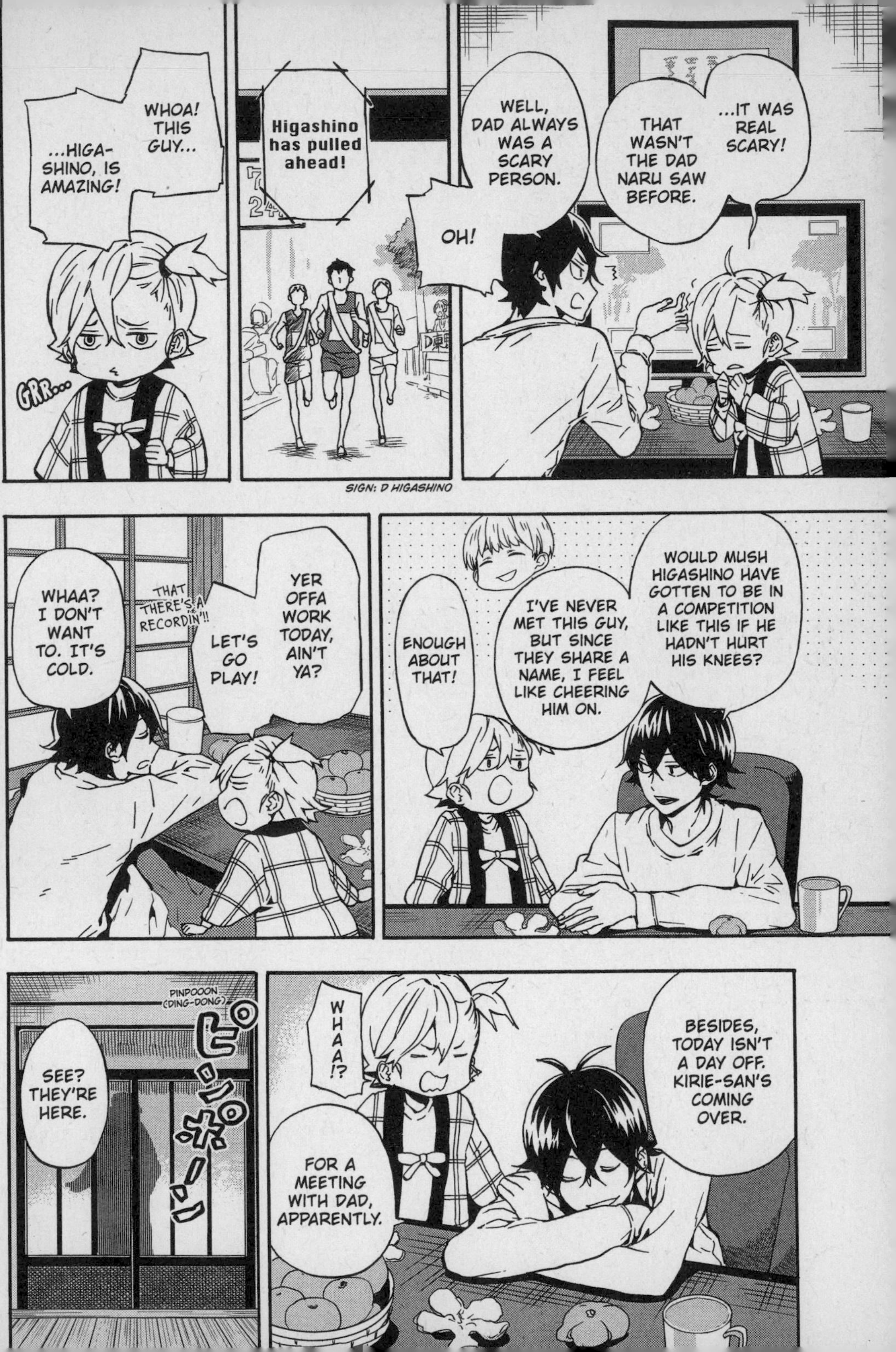
...IT WAS REAL SCARY!
THAT WASN'T THE DAD NARU SAW BEFORE.
WELL, DAD ALWAYS WAS A SCARY PERSON.
OH!
Higashino has pulled ahead!
WHOA! THIS GUY...
...HIGA-SHINO, IS AMAZING!
GRR...
SIGN: D HIGASHINO
WOULD MUSH HIGASHINO HAVE GOTTEN TO BE IN A COMPETITION LIKE THIS IF HE HADN'T HURT HIS KNEES?
I'VE NEVER MET THIS GUY, BUT SINCE THEY SHARE A NAME, I FEEL LIKE CHEERING HIM ON.
ENOUGH ABOUT THAT!
YER OFFA WORK TODAY, AIN'T YA?
LET'S GO PLAY!
THAT THERE'S A RECORDIN'!!
WHAA? I DON'T WANT TO. IT'S COLD.
BESIDES, TODAY ISN'T A DAY OFF. KIRIE-SAN'S COMING OVER.
WHAAA!?
FOR A MEETING WITH DAD, APPARENTLY.
PINPOOON (DING-DONG)
SEE? THEY'RE HERE.

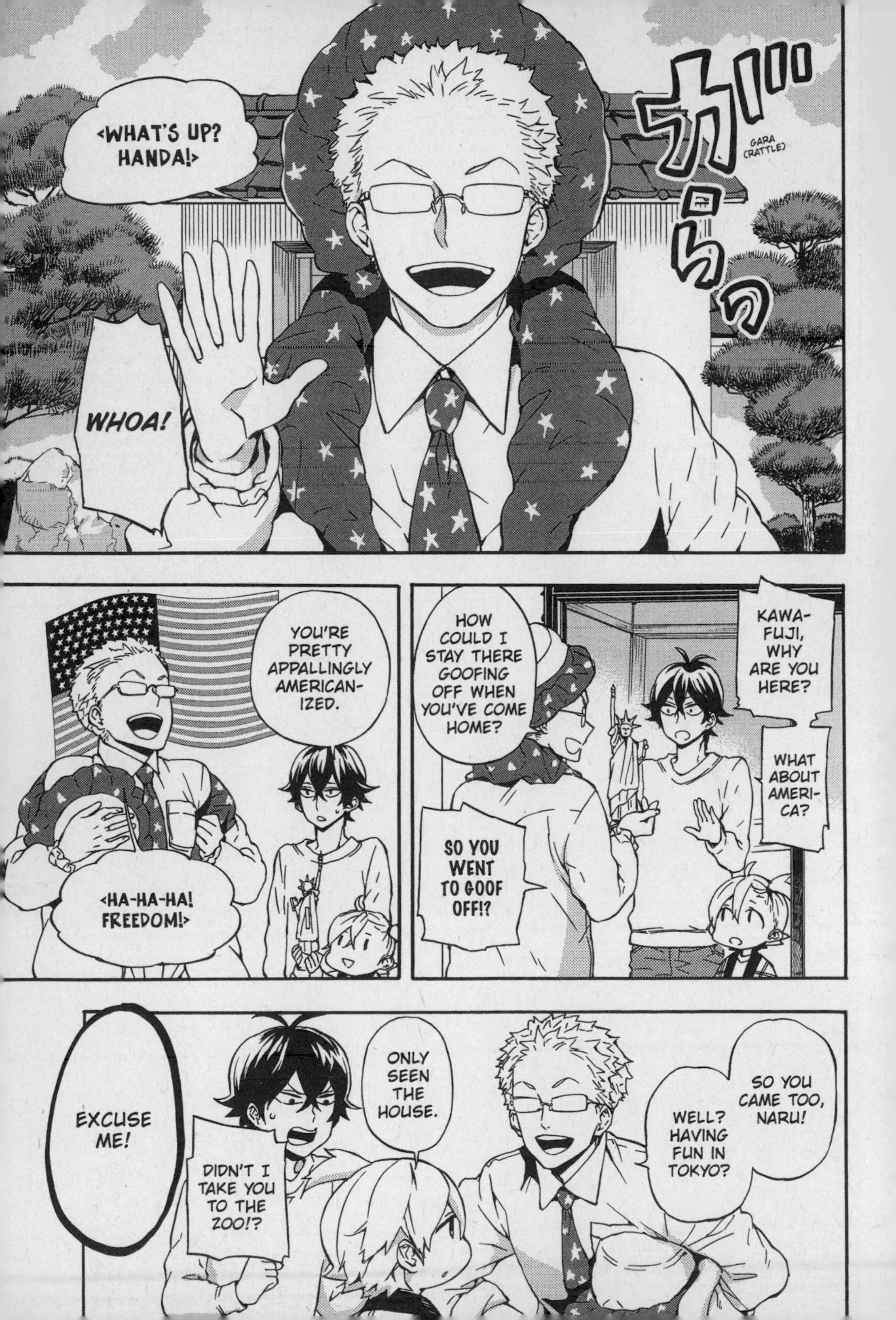
GARA (RATTLE)
<WHAT'S UP? HANDA!>
WHOA!
KAWA-FUJI, WHY ARE YOU HERE?
WHAT ABOUT AMERICA?
HOW COULD I STAY THERE GOOFING OFF WHEN YOU'VE COME HOME?
SO YOU WENT TO GOOF OFF!?
YOU'RE PRETTY APPALLINGLY AMERICAN-IZED.
<HA-HA-HA! FREEDOM!>
SO YOU CAME TOO, NARU!
WELL? HAVING FUN IN TOKYO?
ONLY SEEN THE HOUSE.
EXCUSE ME!
DIDN'T I TAKE YOU TO THE ZOO!?

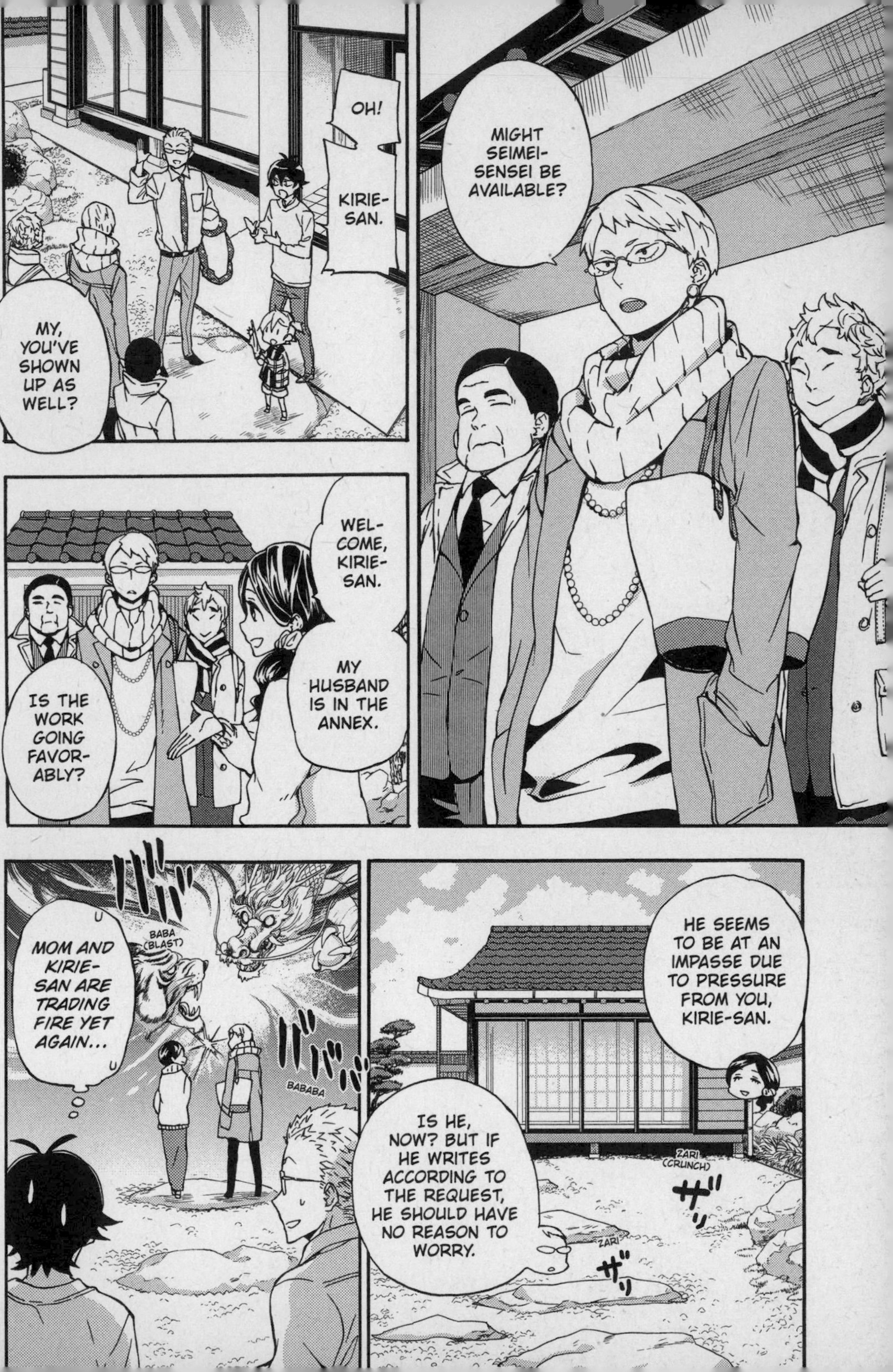
MIGHT SEIMEI-SENSEI BE AVAILABLE?
OH!
KIRIE-SAN.
MY, YOU'VE SHOWN UP AS WELL?
WEL-COME, KIRIE-SAN.
MY HUSBAND IS IN THE ANNEX.
IS THE WORK GOING FAVOR-ABLY?
HE SEEMS TO BE AT AN IMPASSE DUE TO PRESSURE FROM YOU, KIRIE-SAN.
IS HE, NOW? BUT IF HE WRITES ACCORDING TO THE REQUEST, HE SHOULD HAVE NO REASON TO WORRY.
ZARI (CRUNCH)
ZARI
BABA (BLAST)
MOM AND KIRIE-SAN ARE TRADING FIRE YET AGAIN...
BABABA

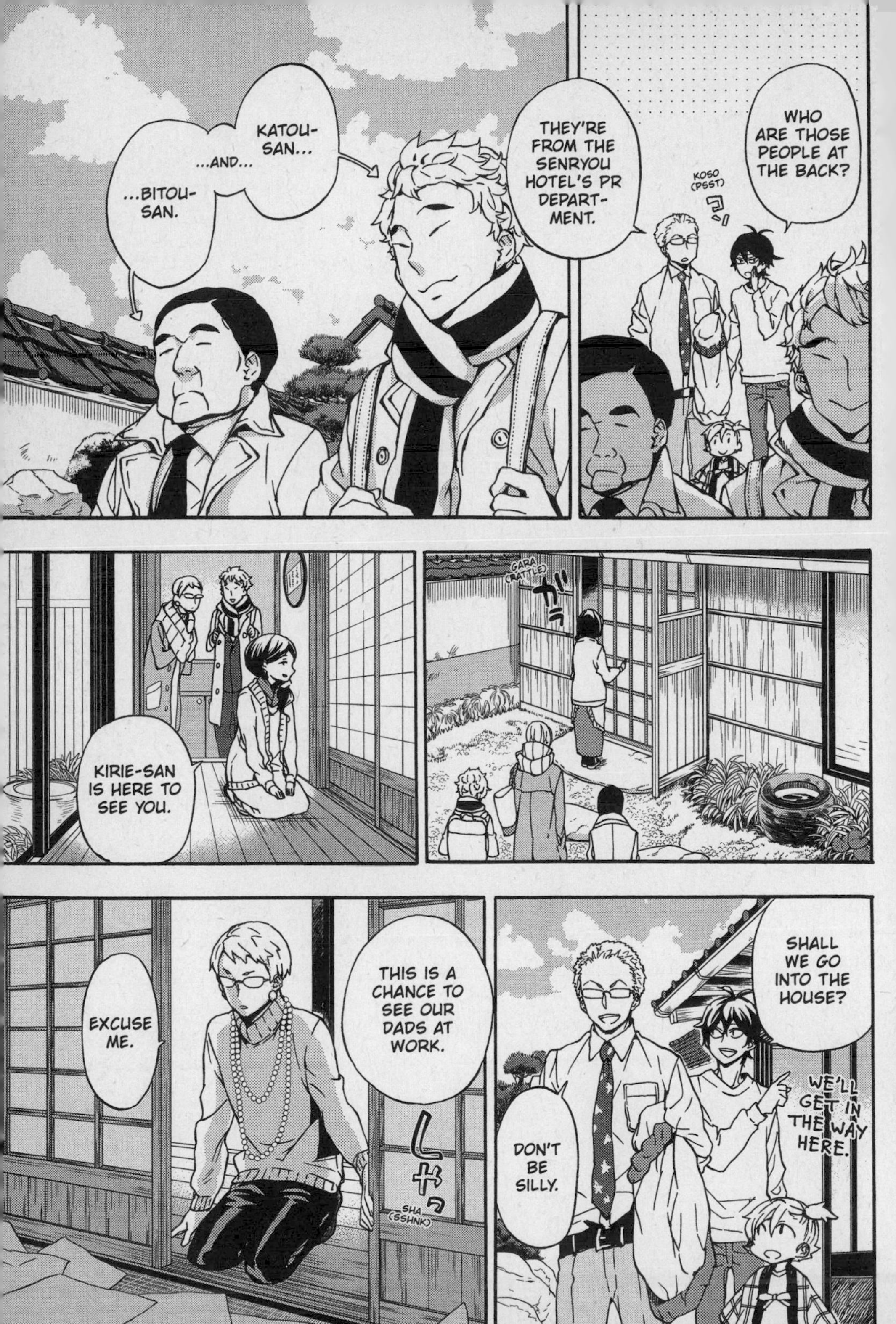
KOSO (PSST)
WHO ARE THOSE PEOPLE AT THE BACK?
THEY'RE FROM THE SENRYOU HOTEL'S PR DEPARTMENT.
KATOU-SAN...
...AND...
...BITOU-SAN.
GARA (RATTLE)
KIRIE-SAN IS HERE TO SEE YOU.
SHALL WE GO INTO THE HOUSE?
WE'LL GET IN THE WAY HERE.
DON'T BE SILLY.
THIS IS A CHANCE TO SEE OUR DADS AT WORK.
EXCUSE ME.
SHA (SSHNK)

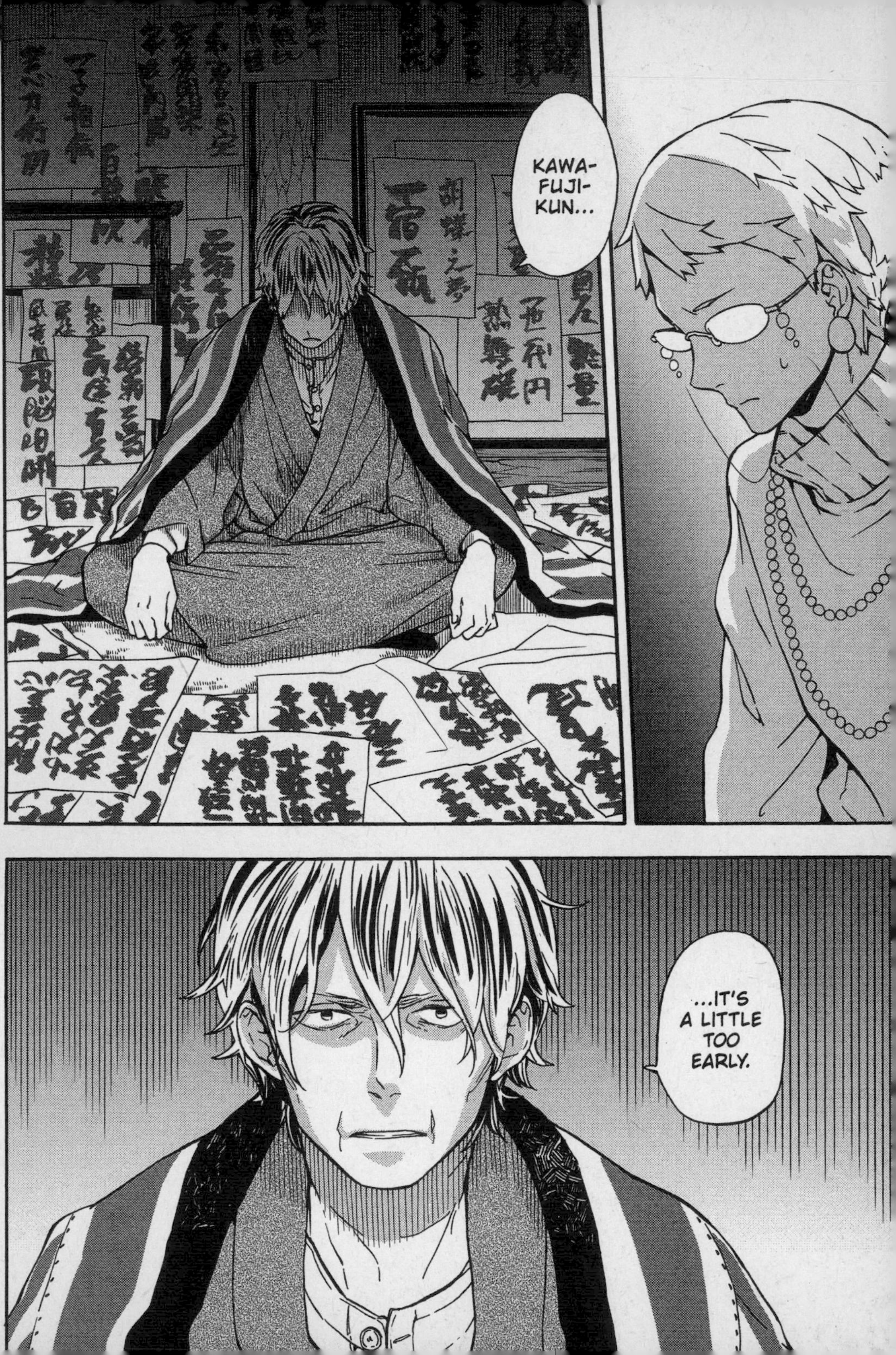
KAWA-FUJI-KUN...
...IT'S A LITTLE TOO EARLY.

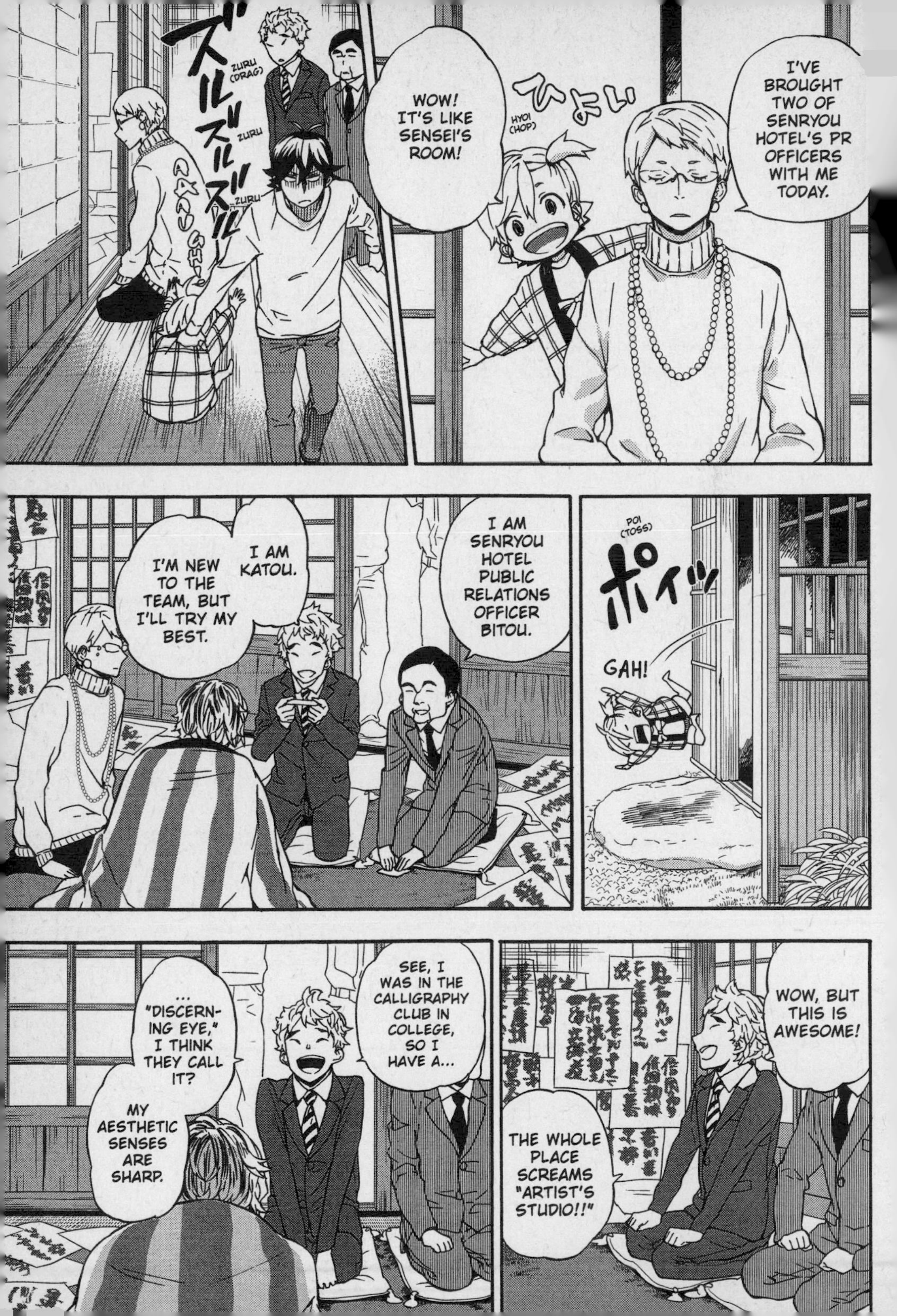
I'VE BROUGHT TWO OF SENRYOU HOTEL'S PR OFFICERS WITH ME TODAY.
ひょい
HYOI (HOP)
WOW! IT'S LIKE SENSEI'S ROOM!
ズルズルズル
ZURU (DRAG)
ZURU
ZURU
POI (TOSS)
ポイッ
GAH!
I AM SENRYOU HOTEL PUBLIC RELATIONS OFFICER BITOU.
I AM KATOU.
I'M NEW TO THE TEAM, BUT I'LL TRY MY BEST.
WOW, BUT THIS IS AWESOME!
THE WHOLE PLACE SCREAMS "ARTIST'S STUDIO!!"
SEE, I WAS IN THE CALLIGRAPHY CLUB IN COLLEGE, SO I HAVE A...
... "DISCERNING-EYE," I THINK THEY CALL IT?
MY AESTHETIC SENSES ARE SHARP.

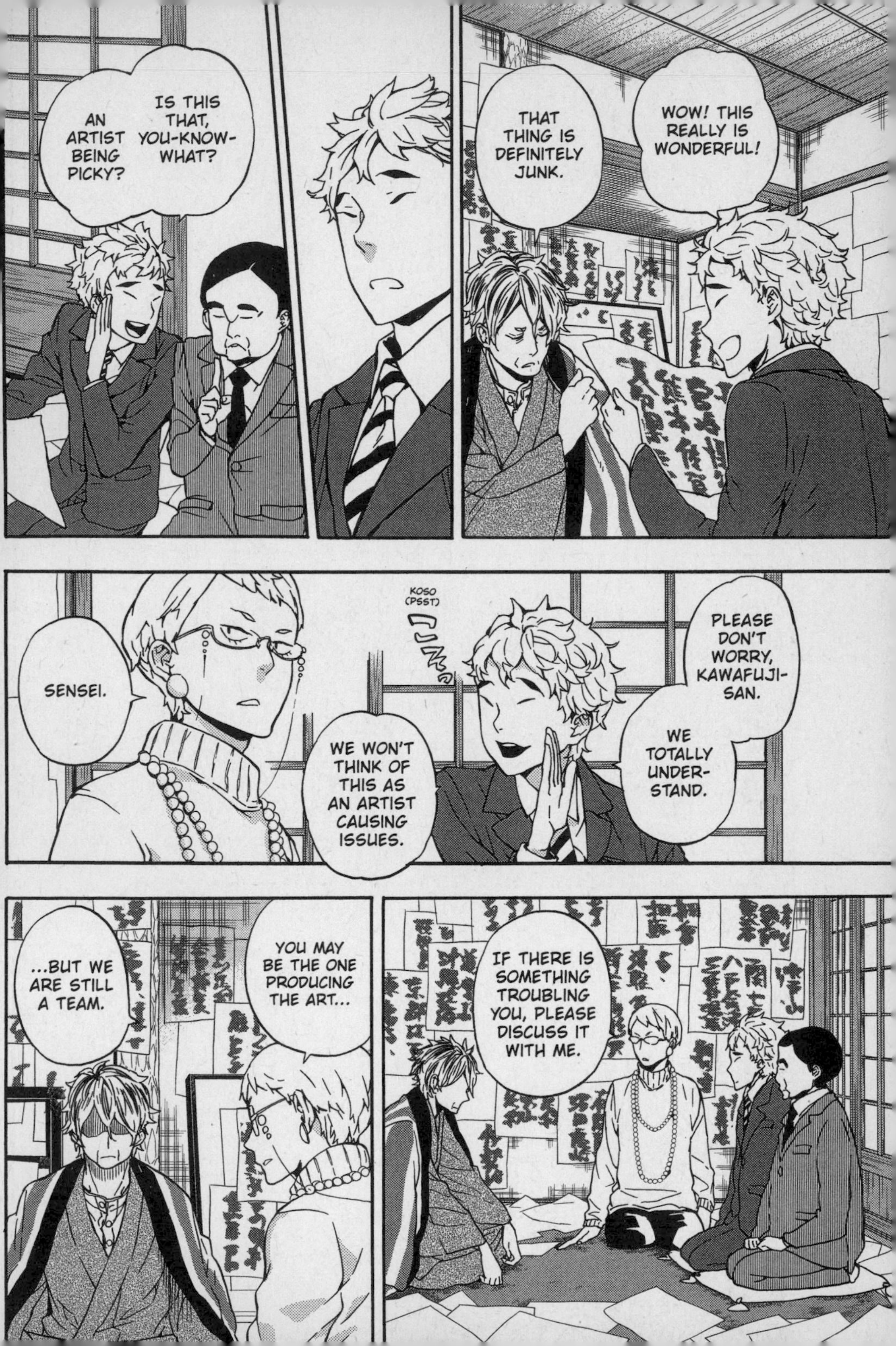
WOW! THIS REALLY IS WONDERFUL!
THAT THING IS DEFINITELY JUNK.
IS THIS THAT, YOU-KNOW-WHAT?
AN ARTIST BEING PICKY?
PLEASE DON'T WORRY, KAWAFUJI-SAN.
WE TOTALLY UNDER-STAND.
KOSO (PSST)
WE WON'T THINK OF THIS AS AN ARTIST CAUSING ISSUES.
SENSEI.
IF THERE IS SOMETHING TROUBLING YOU, PLEASE DISCUSS IT WITH ME.
YOU MAY BE THE ONE PRODUCING THE ART...
...BUT WE ARE STILL A TEAM.

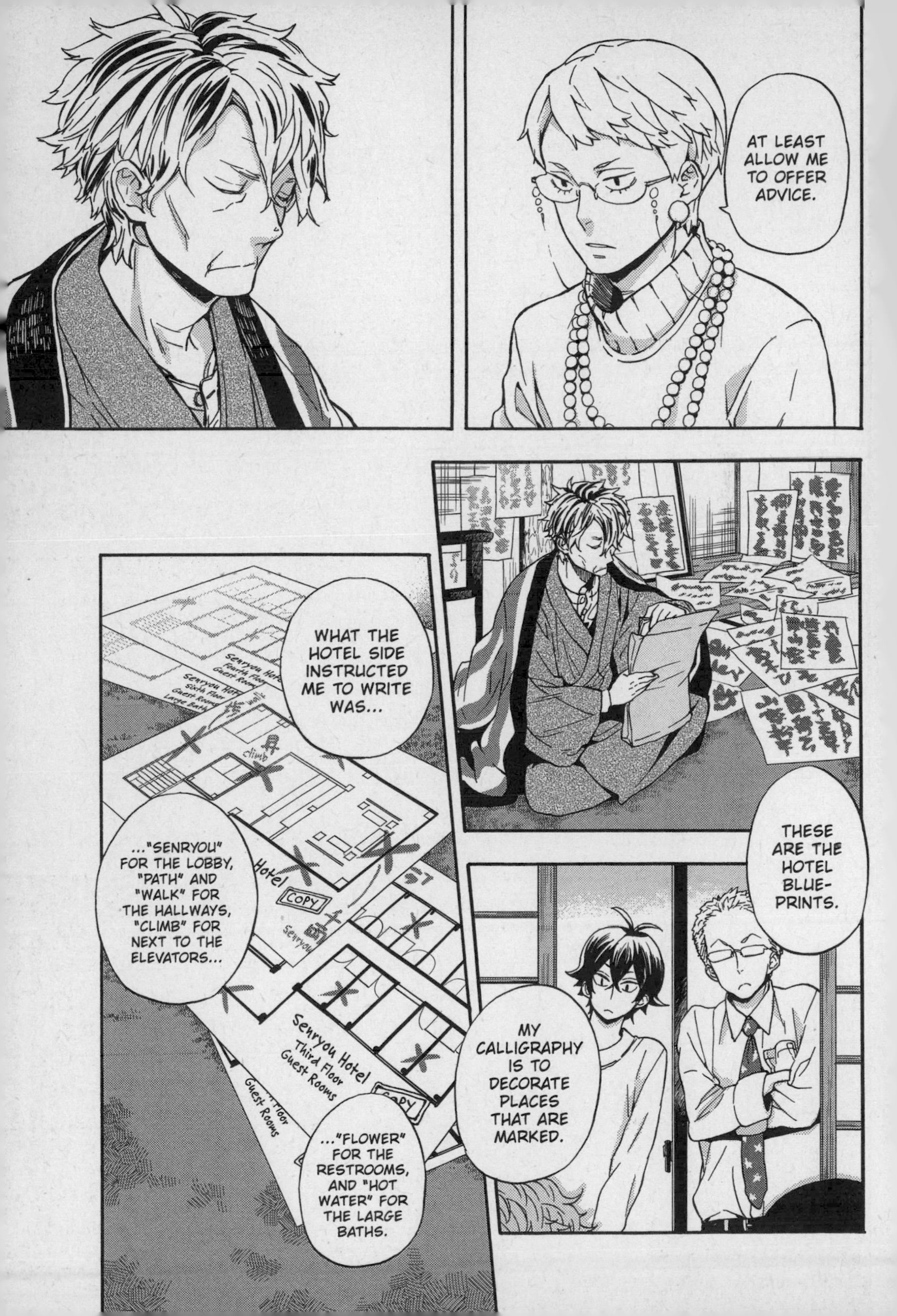
AT LEAST ALLOW ME TO OFFER ADVICE.
THESE ARE THE HOTEL BLUE-PRINTS.
MY CALLIGRAPHY IS TO DECORATE PLACES THAT ARE MARKED.
WHAT THE HOTEL SIDE INSTRUCTED ME TO WRITE WAS...
..."SENRYOU" FOR THE LOBBY, "PATH" AND "WALK" FOR THE HALLWAYS, "CLIMB" FOR NEXT TO THE ELEVATORS...
..."FLOWER" FOR THE RESTROOMS, AND "HOT WATER" FOR THE LARGE BATHS.
Senryou Hotel Fourth Floor Guest Rooms
Senryou Hotel Sixth Floor Guest Rooms Large Baths
climb
Hotel
COPY
Senryou
Senryou Hotel Third Floor Guest Rooms
COPY
Floor Guest Rooms

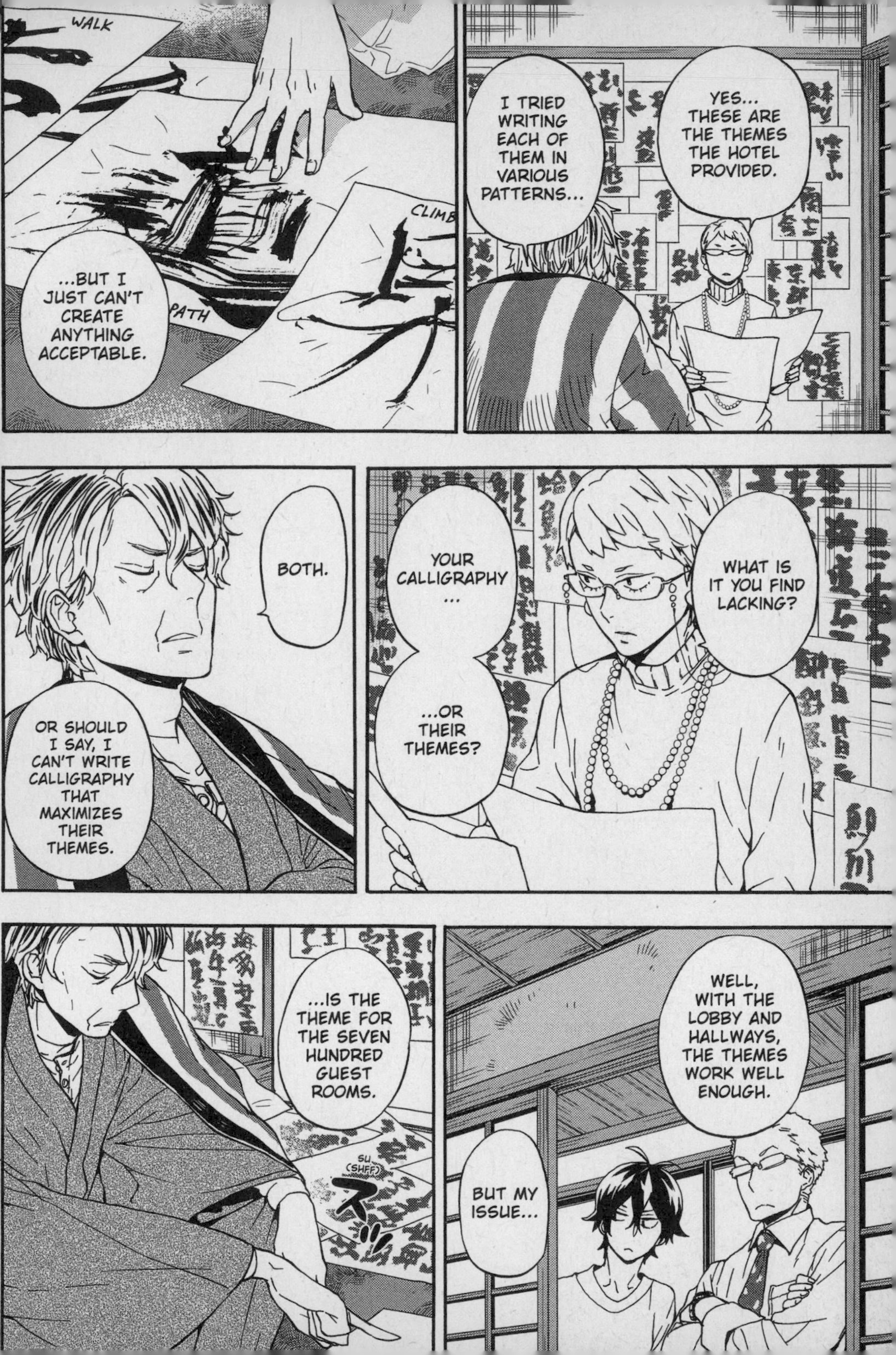
YES... THESE ARE THE THEMES THE HOTEL PROVIDED.
I TRIED WRITING EACH OF THEM IN VARIOUS PATTERNS...
WALK
CLIMB
PATH
...BUT I JUST CAN'T CREATE ANYTHING ACCEPTABLE.
WHAT IS IT YOU FIND LACKING?
YOUR CALLIGRAPHY ...
...OR THEIR THEMES?
BOTH.
OR SHOULD I SAY, I CAN'T WRITE CALLIGRAPHY THAT MAXIMIZES THEIR THEMES.
WELL, WITH THE LOBBY AND HALLWAYS, THE THEMES WORK WELL ENOUGH.
BUT MY ISSUE...
...IS THE THEME FOR THE SEVEN HUNDRED GUEST ROOMS.
SU (SHFF)

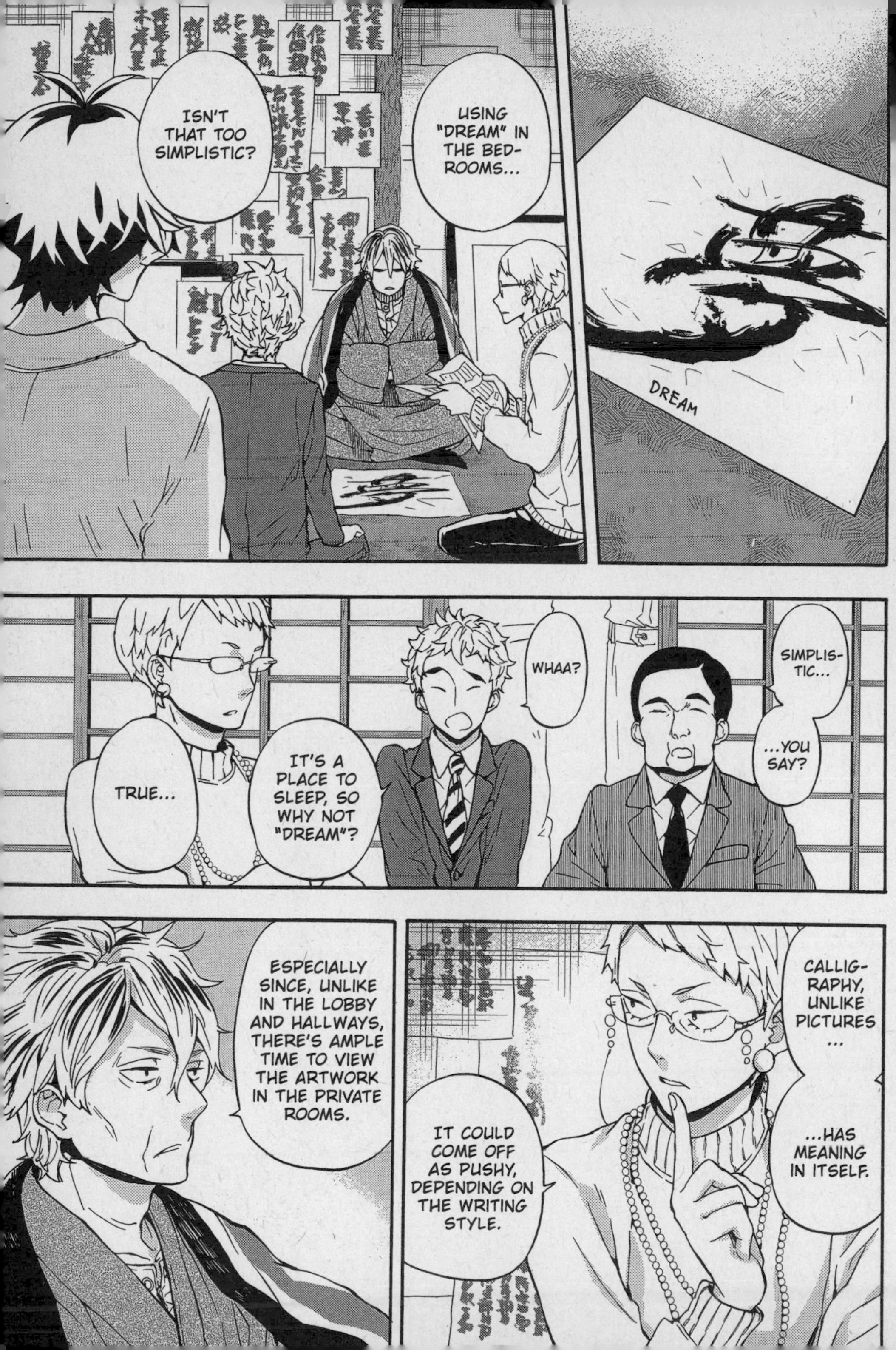
DREAM
USING "DREAM" IN THE BED-ROOMS...
ISN'T THAT TOO SIMPLISTIC?
SIMPLIS-TIC...
...YOU SAY?
WHAA?
IT'S A PLACE TO SLEEP, SO WHY NOT "DREAM"?
TRUE...
CALLIG-RAPHY, UNLIKE PICTURES...
...HAS MEANING IN ITSELF.
IT COULD COME OFF AS PUSHY, DEPENDING ON THE WRITING STYLE.
ESPECIALLY SINCE, UNLIKE IN THE LOBBY AND HALLWAYS, THERE'S AMPLE TIME TO VIEW THE ARTWORK IN THE PRIVATE ROOMS.

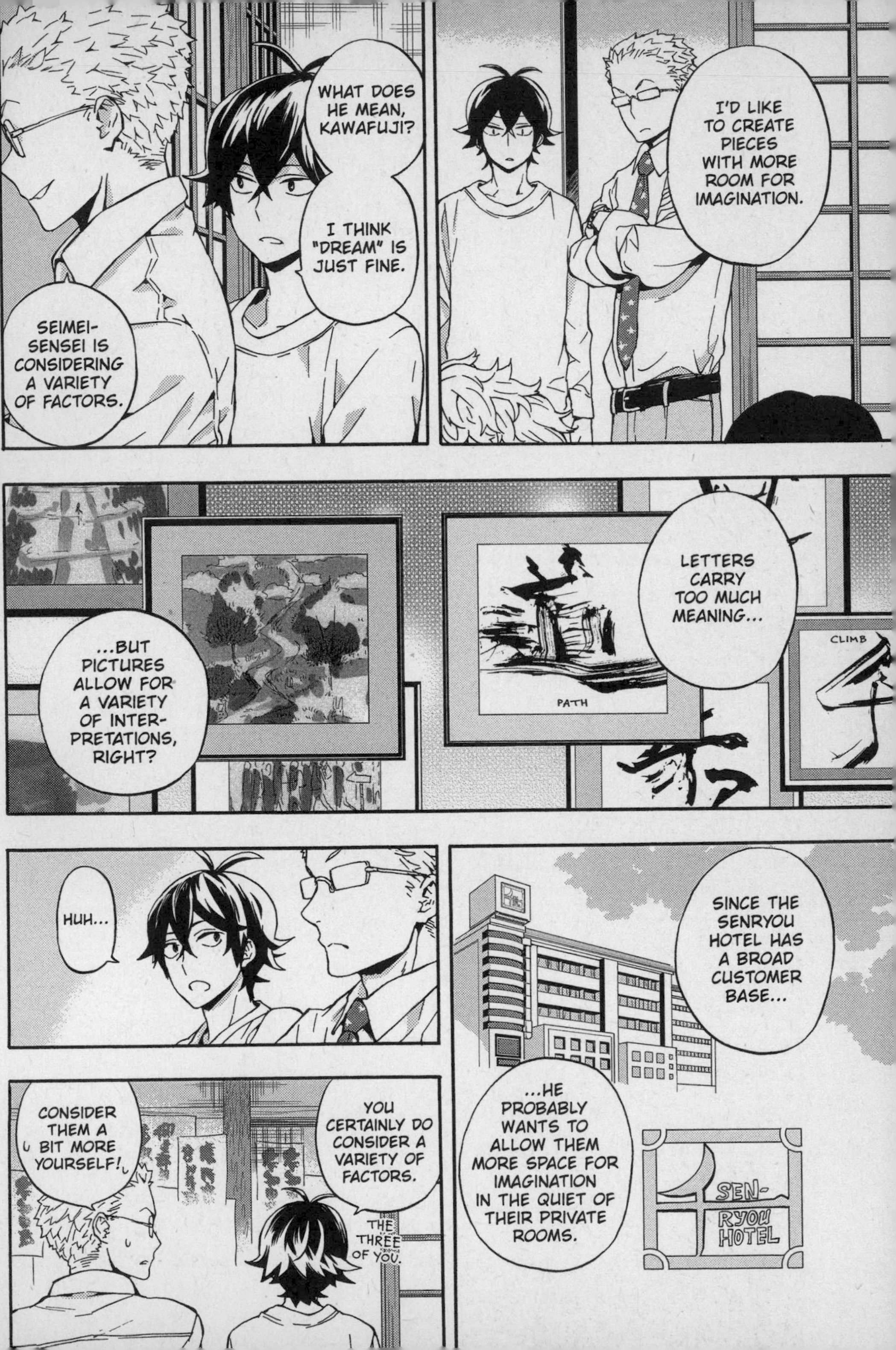
I'D LIKE TO CREATE PIECES WITH MORE ROOM FOR IMAGINATION.
WHAT DOES HE MEAN, KAWAFUJI?
I THINK "DREAM" IS JUST FINE.
SEIMEI-SENSEI IS CONSIDERING A VARIETY OF FACTORS.
LETTERS CARRY TOO MUCH MEANING...
CLIMB
PATH
...BUT PICTURES ALLOW FOR A VARIETY OF INTER-PRETATIONS, RIGHT?
SINCE THE SENRYOU HOTEL HAS A BROAD CUSTOMER BASE...
SEN-RYOU HOTEL
...HE PROBABLY WANTS TO ALLOW THEM MORE SPACE FOR IMAGINATION IN THE QUIET OF THEIR PRIVATE ROOMS.
HUH...
YOU CERTAINLY DO CONSIDER A VARIETY OF FACTORS.
THE THREE OF YOU.
CONSIDER THEM A BIT MORE YOURSELF!

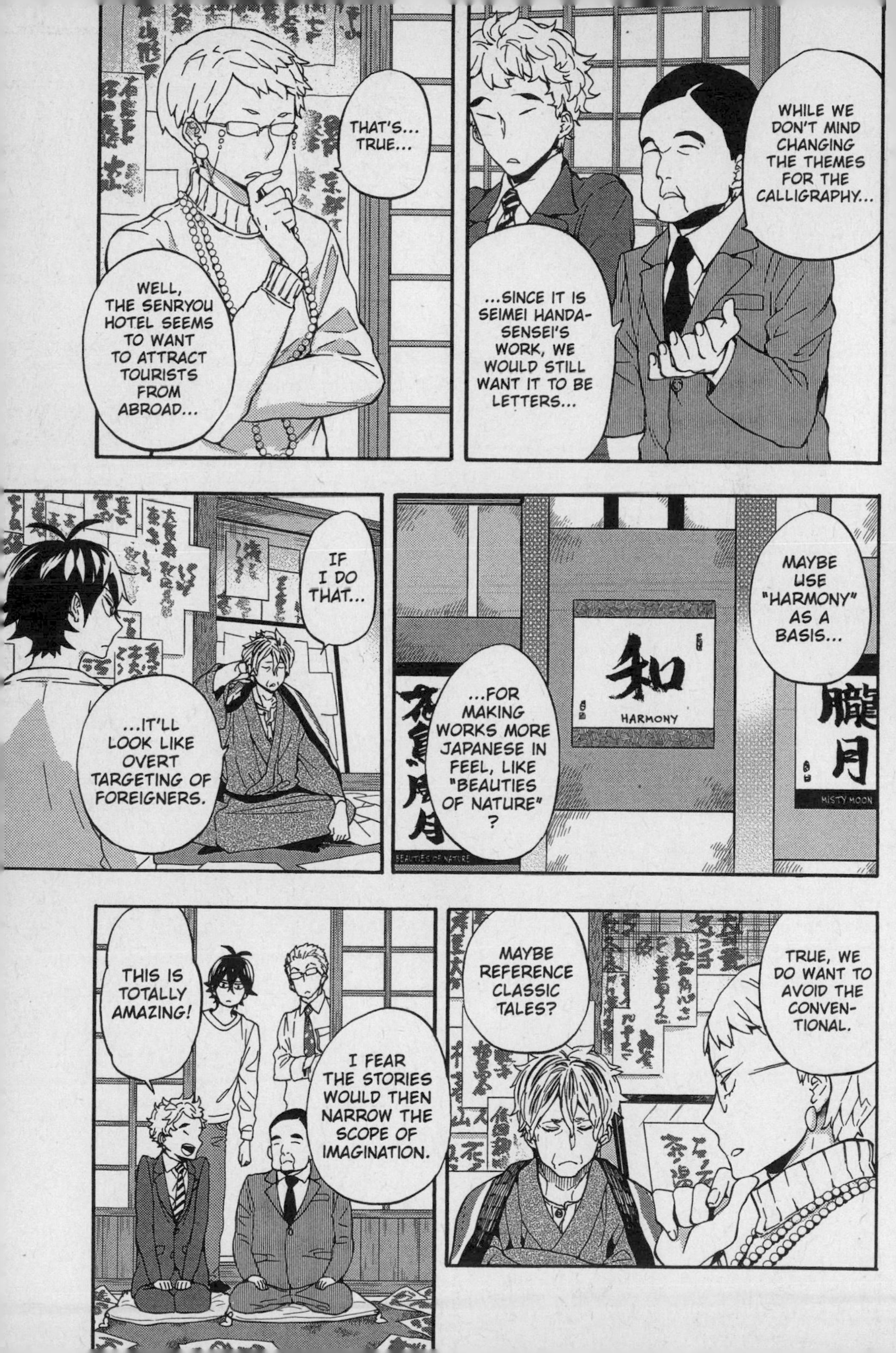
WHILE WE DON'T MIND CHANGING THE THEMES FOR THE CALLIGRAPHY...
...SINCE IT IS SEIMEI HANDA-SENSEI'S WORK, WE WOULD STILL WANT IT TO BE LETTERS...
THAT'S... TRUE...
WELL, THE SENRYOU HOTEL SEEMS TO WANT TO ATTRACT TOURISTS FROM ABROAD...
MAYBE USE "HARMONY" AS A BASIS...
MISTY MOON
HARMONY
...FOR MAKING WORKS MORE JAPANESE IN FEEL, LIKE "BEAUTIES OF NATURE"?
BEAUTIES OF NATURE
IF I DO THAT...
...IT'LL LOOK LIKE OVERT TARGETING OF FOREIGNERS.
TRUE, WE DO WANT TO AVOID THE CONVENTIONAL.
MAYBE REFERENCE CLASSIC TALES?
I FEAR THE STORIES WOULD THEN NARROW THE SCOPE OF IMAGINATION.
THIS IS TOTALLY AMAZING!

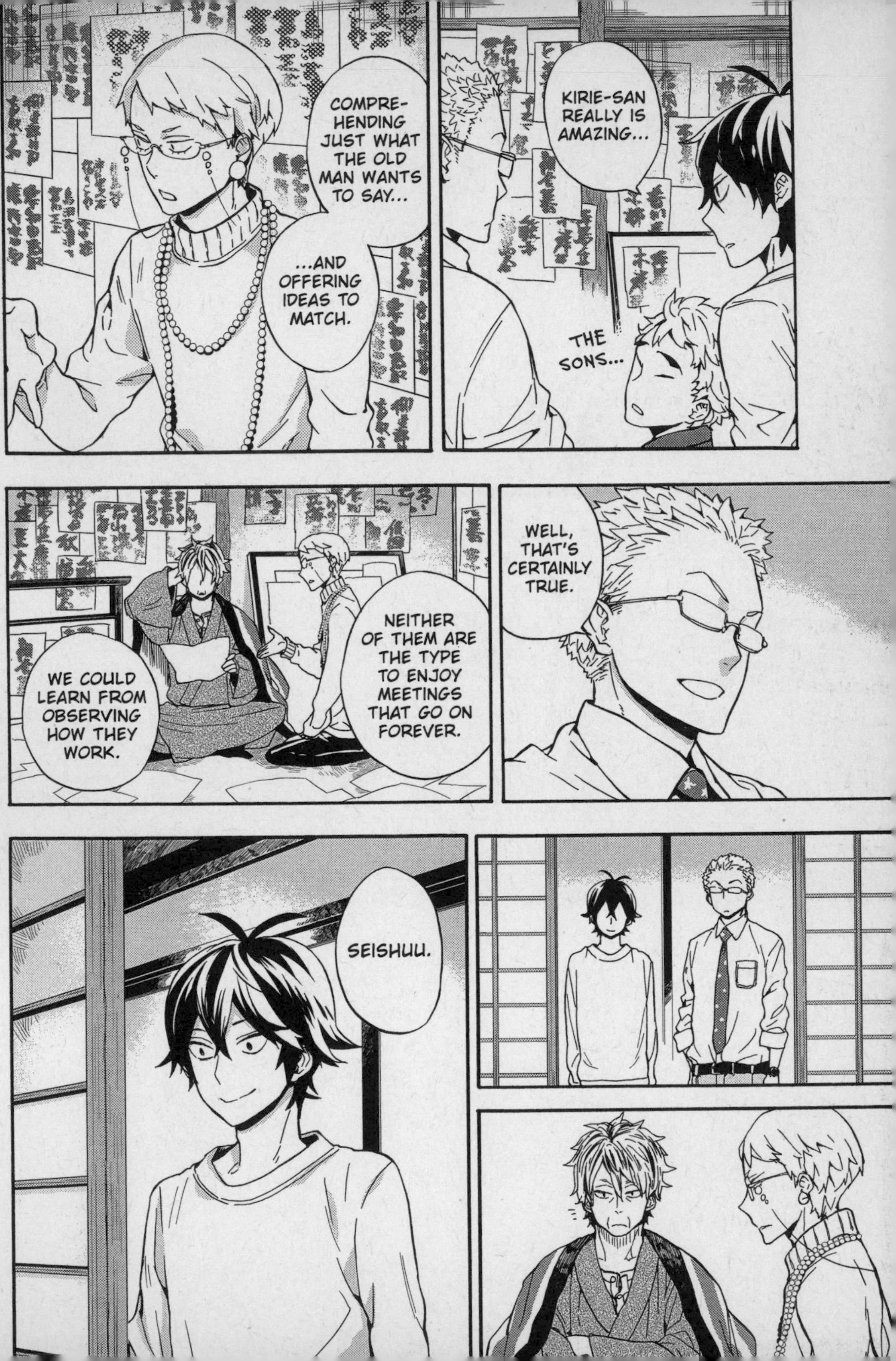
KIRIE-SAN REALLY IS AMAZING...
THE SONS...
COMPRE-HENDING JUST WHAT THE OLD MAN WANTS TO SAY...
...AND OFFERING IDEAS TO MATCH.
WELL, THAT'S CERTAINLY TRUE.
NEITHER OF THEM ARE THE TYPE TO ENJOY MEETINGS THAT GO ON FOREVER.
WE COULD LEARN FROM OBSERVING HOW THEY WORK.
SEISHUU.

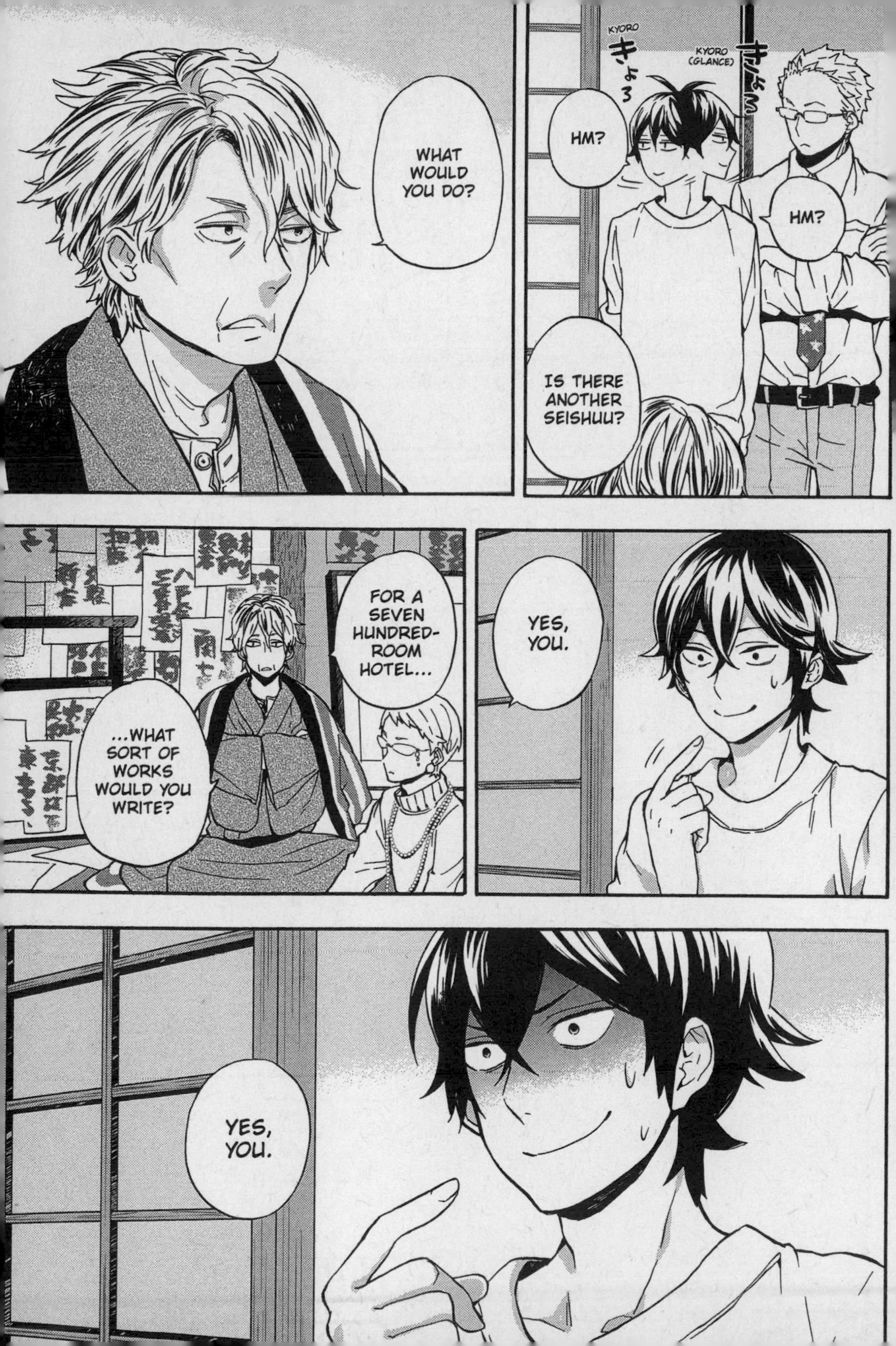
KYORO (GLANCE)
HM?
KYORO
HM?
IS THERE ANOTHER SEISHUU?
WHAT WOULD YOU DO?
YES, YOU.
FOR A SEVEN HUNDRED-ROOM HOTEL...
...WHAT SORT OF WORKS WOULD YOU WRITE?
YES, YOU.

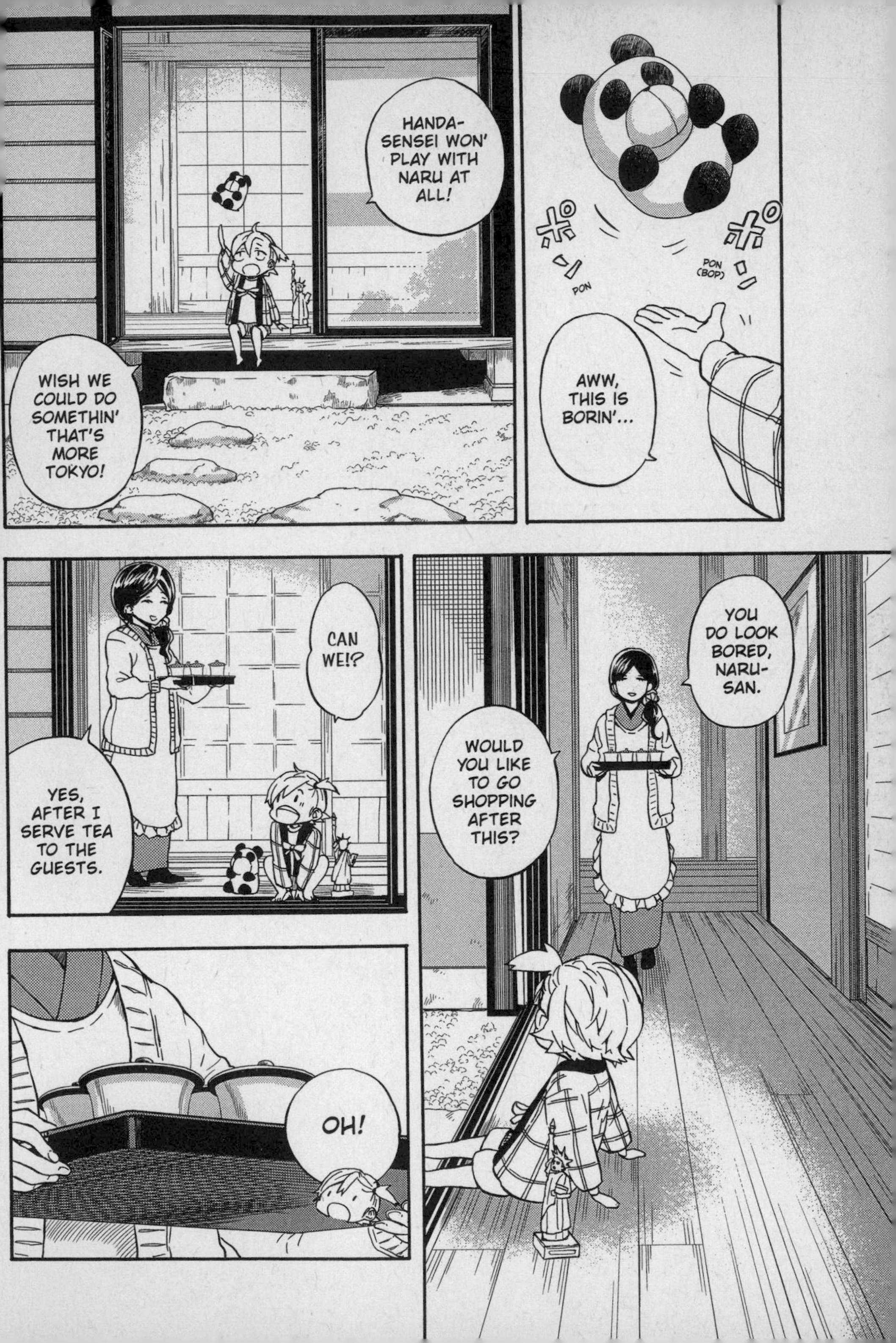
ポン
PON (BOP)
ポン
PON
AWW, THIS IS BORIN'...
HANDA-SENSEI WON' PLAY WITH NARU AT ALL!
WISH WE COULD DO SOMETHIN' THAT'S MORE TOKYO!
YOU DO LOOK BORED, NARU-SAN.
WOULD YOU LIKE TO GO SHOPPING AFTER THIS?
CAN WE!?
YES, AFTER I SERVE TEA TO THE GUESTS.
OH!

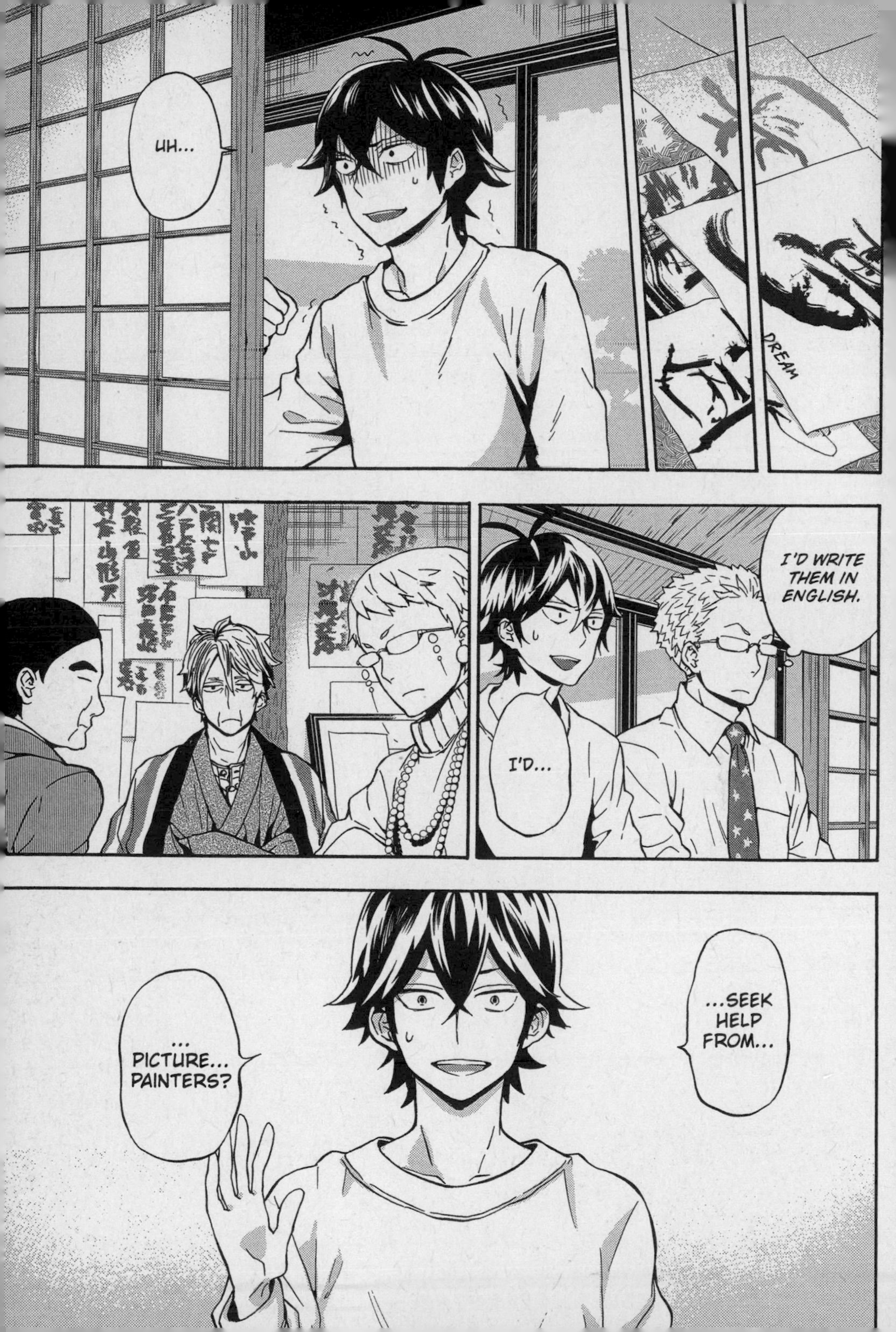
UH...
DREAM
I'D WRITE THEM IN ENGLISH.
I'D...
...SEEK HELP FROM...
... PICTURE... PAINTERS?

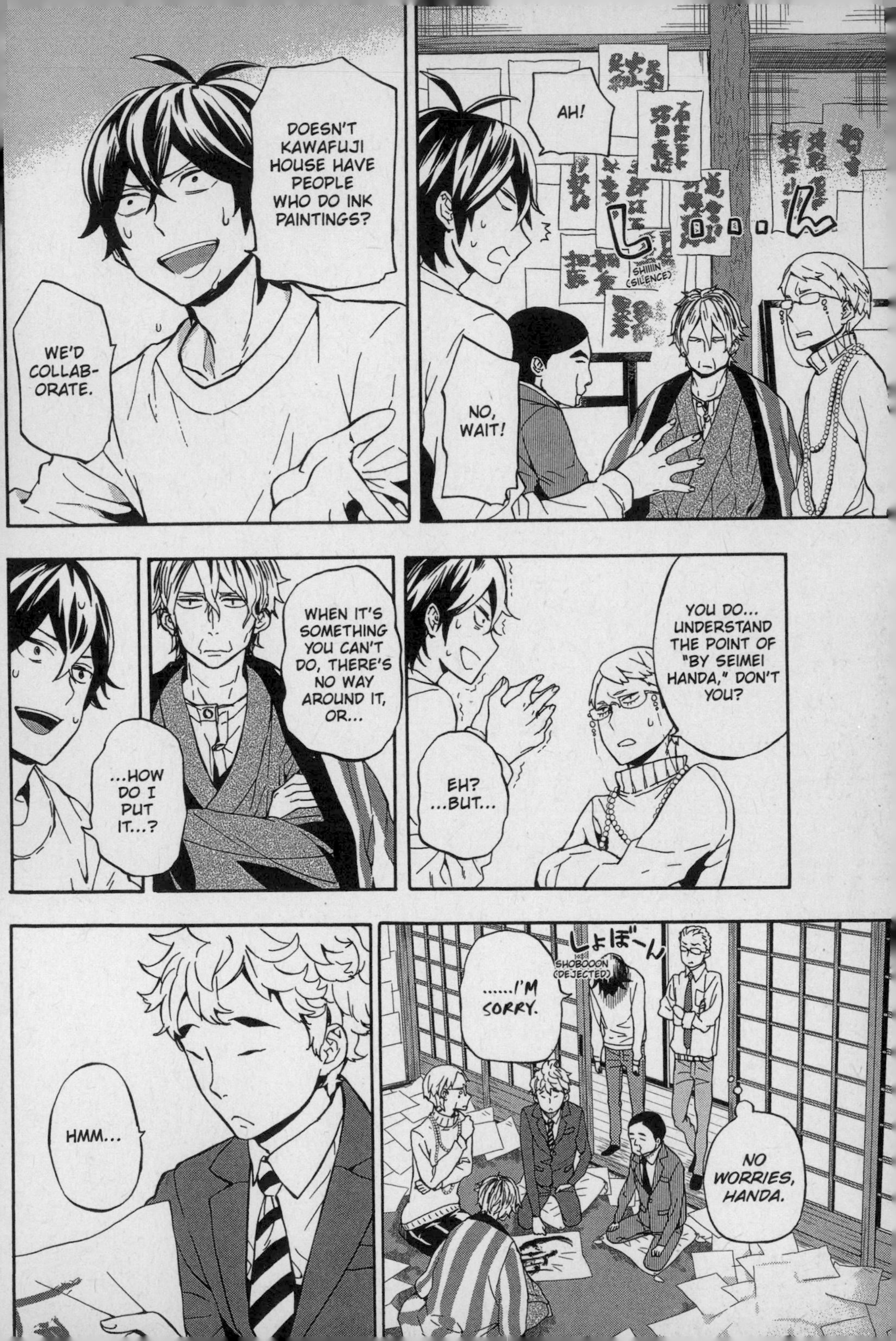
DOESN'T KAWAFUJI HOUSE HAVE PEOPLE WHO DO INK PAINTINGS?
WE'D COLLAB-ORATE.
AH!
しーん
SHIIIN (SILENCE)
NO, WAIT!
WHEN IT'S SOMETHING YOU CAN'T DO, THERE'S NO WAY AROUND IT, OR...
...HOW DO I PUT IT...?
YOU DO... UNDERSTAND THE POINT OF "BY SEIMEI HANDA," DON'T YOU?
EH? ...BUT...
HMM...
しょぼ~ん
SHOBOOON (DEJECTED)
......I'M SORRY.
NO WORRIES, HANDA.

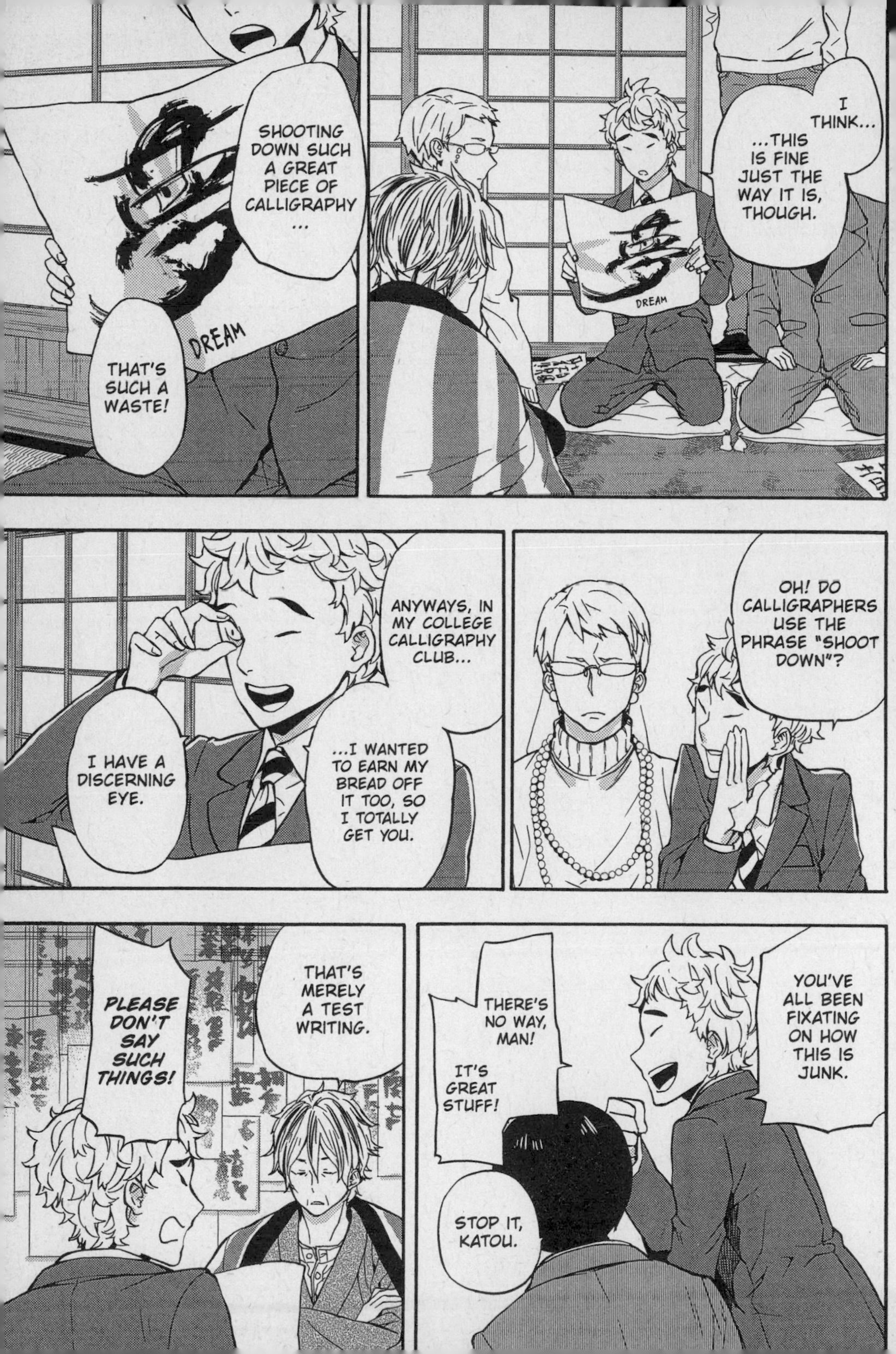
I THINK...
...THIS IS FINE JUST THE WAY IT IS, THOUGH.
DREAM
SHOOTING DOWN SUCH A GREAT PIECE OF CALLIGRAPHY ...
DREAM
THAT'S SUCH A WASTE!
OH! DO CALLIGRAPHERS USE THE PHRASE "SHOOT DOWN"?
ANYWAYS, IN MY COLLEGE CALLIGRAPHY CLUB...
...I WANTED TO EARN MY BREAD OFF IT TOO, SO I TOTALLY GET YOU.
I HAVE A DISCERNING EYE.
YOU'VE ALL BEEN FIXATING ON HOW THIS IS JUNK.
THERE'S NO WAY, MAN!
IT'S GREAT STUFF!
STOP IT, KATOU.
THAT'S MERELY A TEST WRITING.
PLEASE DON'T SAY SUCH THINGS!

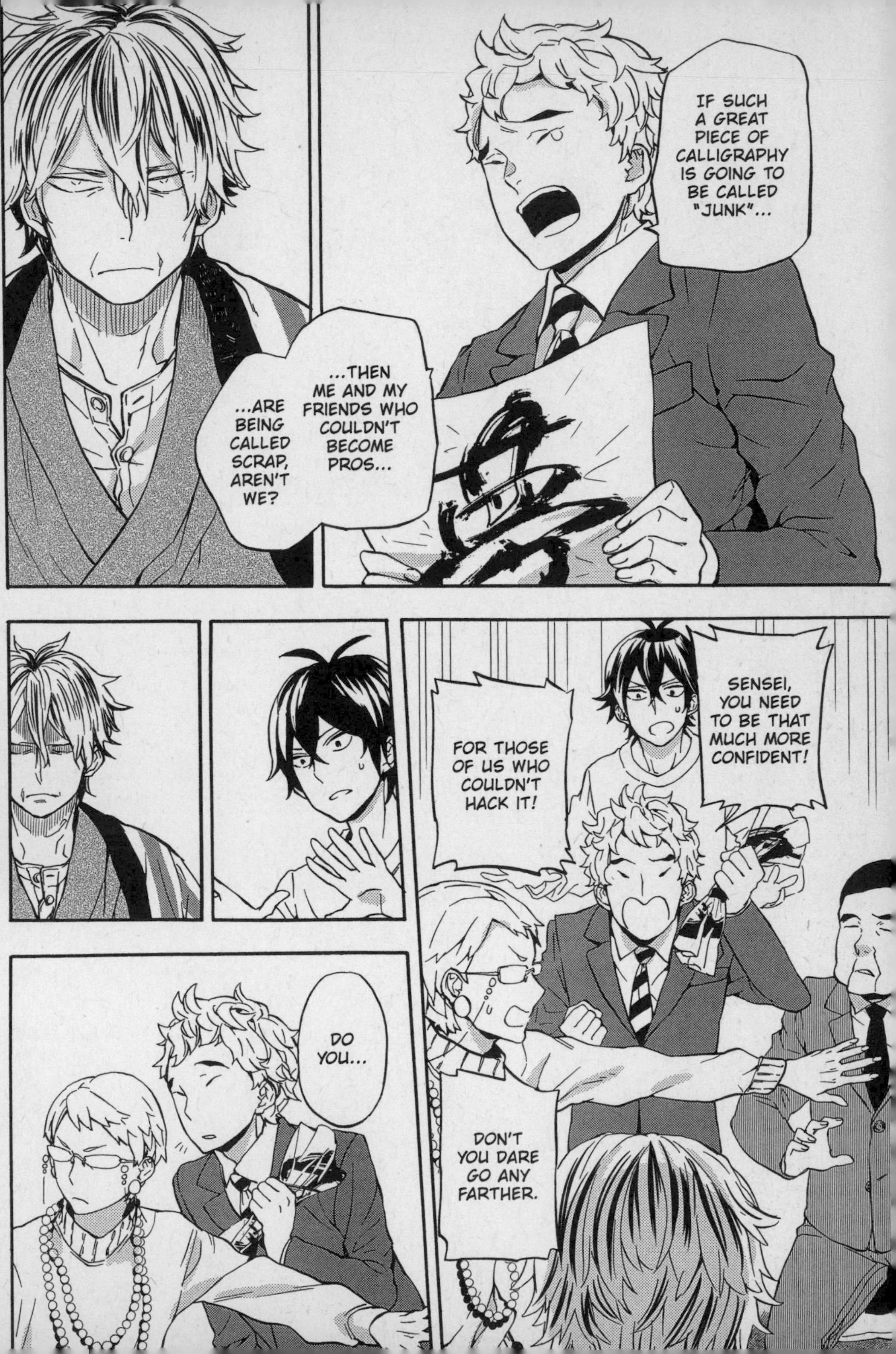
IF SUCH A GREAT PIECE OF CALLIGRAPHY IS GOING TO BE CALLED "JUNK"...
...THEN ME AND MY FRIENDS WHO COULDN'T BECOME PROS...
...ARE BEING CALLED SCRAP, AREN'T WE?
SENSEI, YOU NEED TO BE THAT MUCH MORE CONFIDENT!
FOR THOSE OF US WHO COULDN'T HACK IT!
DON'T YOU DARE GO ANY FARTHER.
DO YOU...

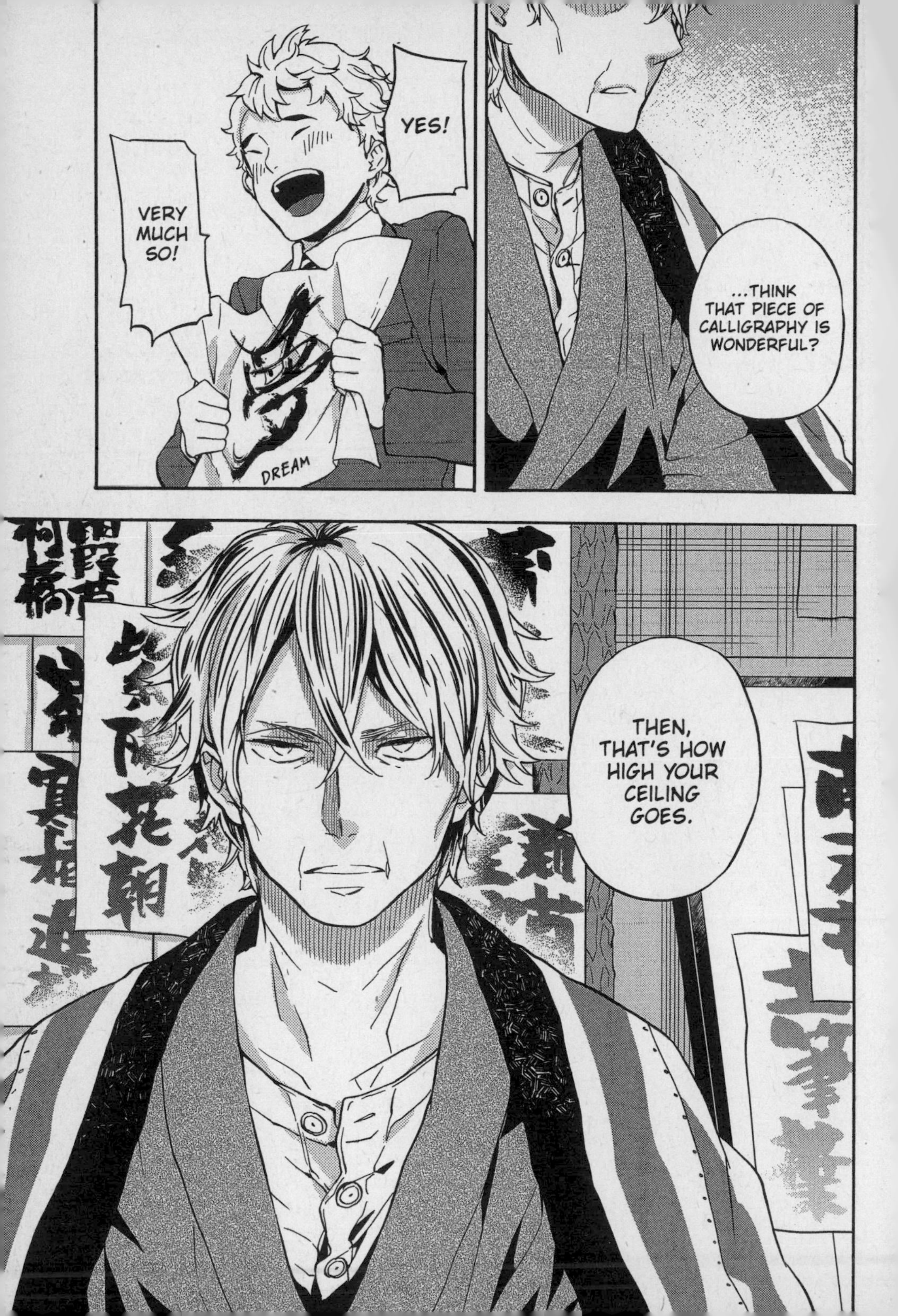
...THINK THAT PIECE OF CALLIGRAPHY IS WONDERFUL?
YES!
VERY MUCH SO!
DREAM
THEN, THAT'S HOW HIGH YOUR CEILING GOES.

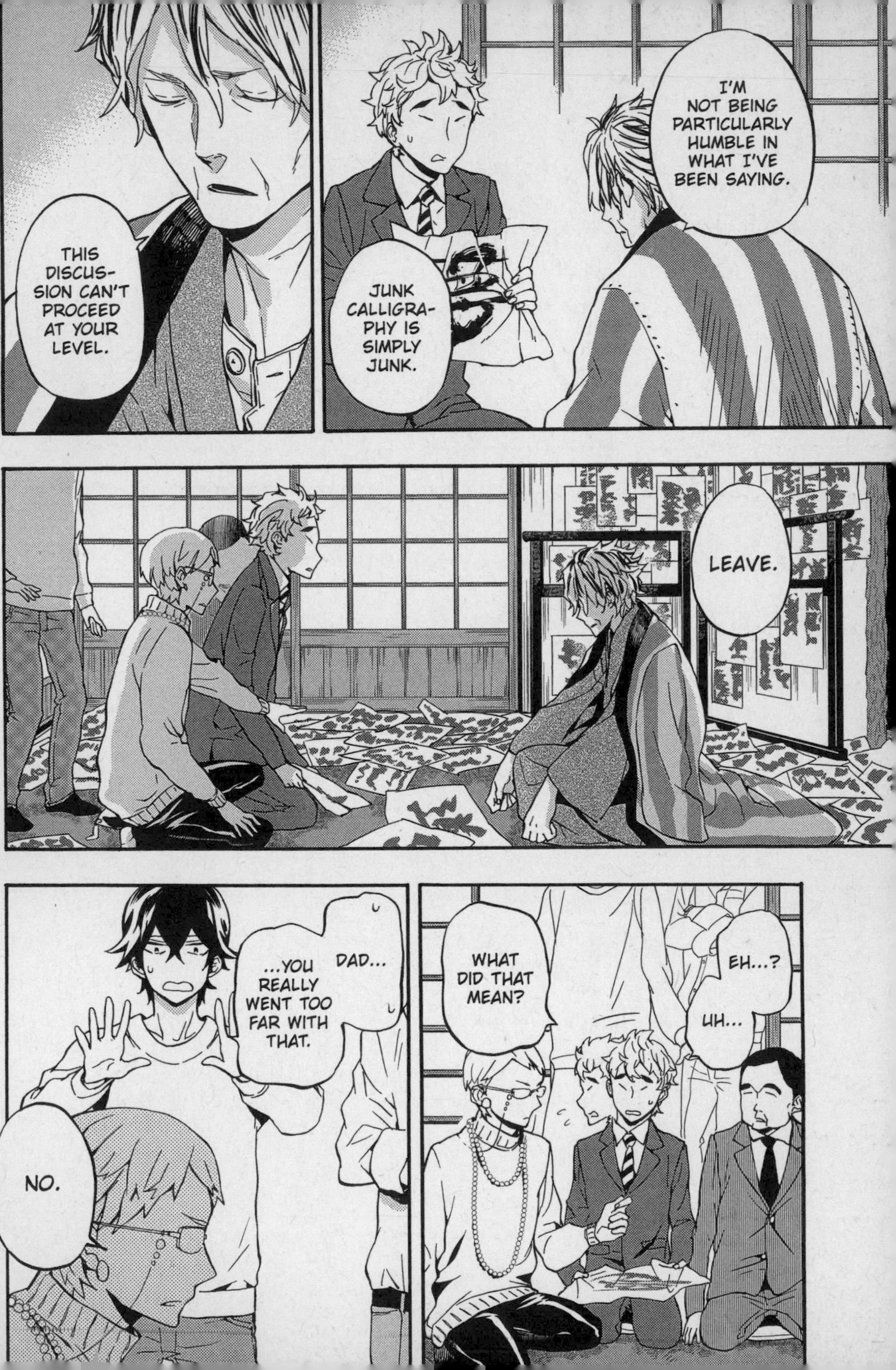
I'M NOT BEING PARTICULARLY HUMBLE IN WHAT I'VE BEEN SAYING.
JUNK CALLIGRAPHY IS SIMPLY JUNK.
THIS DISCUSSION CAN'T PROCEED AT YOUR LEVEL.
LEAVE.
EH...?
UH...
WHAT DID THAT MEAN?
DAD...
...YOU REALLY WENT TOO FAR WITH THAT.
NO.

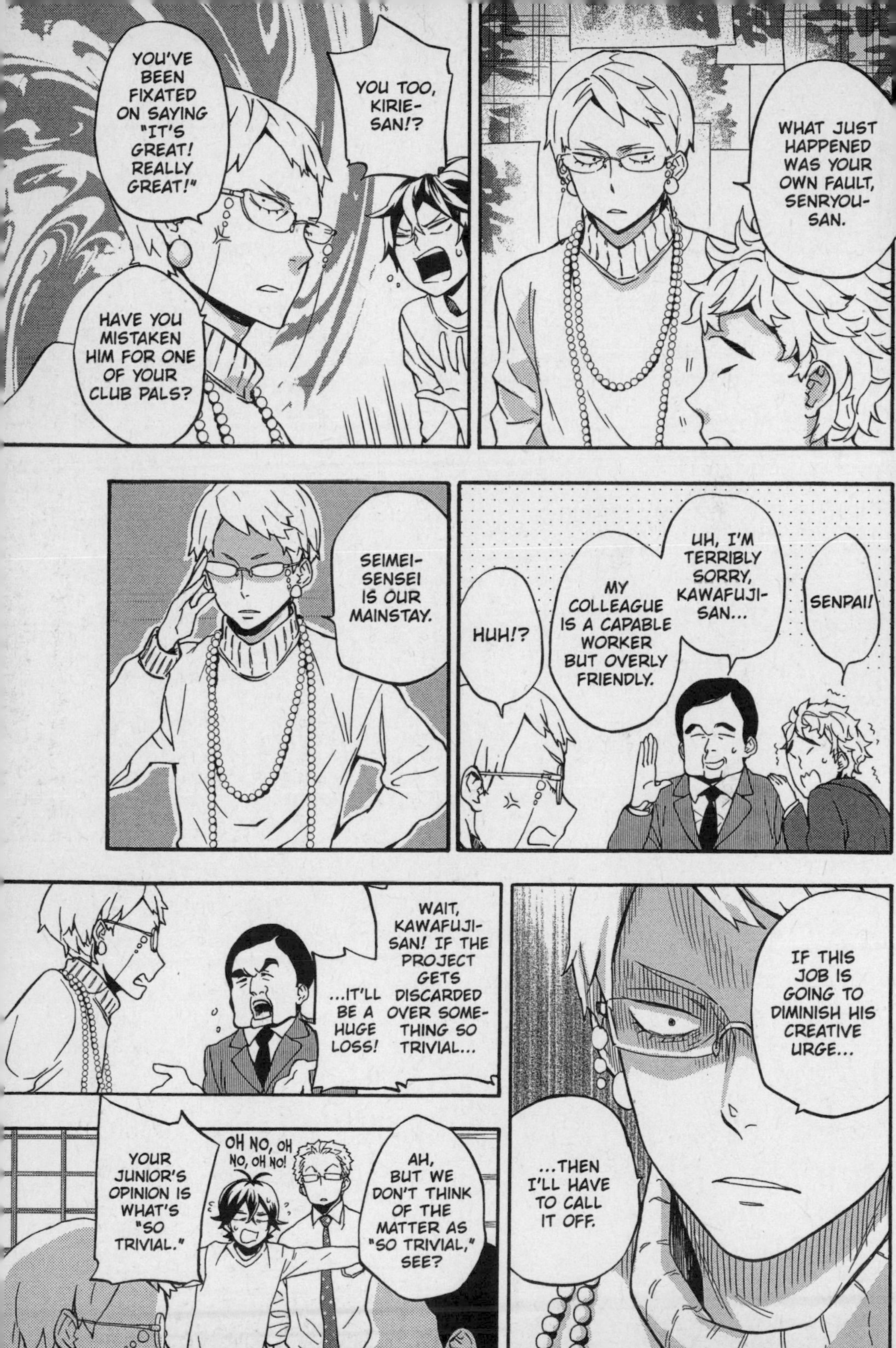
WHAT JUST HAPPENED WAS YOUR OWN FAULT, SENRYOU-SAN.
YOU TOO, KIRIE-SAN!?
YOU'VE BEEN FIXATED ON SAYING "IT'S GREAT! REALLY GREAT!"
HAVE YOU MISTAKEN HIM FOR ONE OF YOUR CLUB PALS?
SENPAI!
UH, I'M TERRIBLY SORRY, KAWAFUJI-SAN...
MY COLLEAGUE IS A CAPABLE WORKER BUT OVERLY FRIENDLY.
HUH!?
SEIMEI-SENSEI IS OUR MAINSTAY.
IF THIS JOB IS GOING TO DIMINISH HIS CREATIVE URGE...
...THEN I'LL HAVE TO CALL IT OFF.
WAIT, KAWAFUJI-SAN! IF THE PROJECT GETS DISCARDED OVER SOMETHING SO TRIVIAL...
...IT'LL BE A HUGE LOSS!
AH, BUT WE DON'T THINK OF THE MATTER AS "SO TRIVIAL," SEE?
OH NO, OH NO, OH NO!
YOUR JUNIOR'S OPINION IS WHAT'S "SO TRIVIAL."

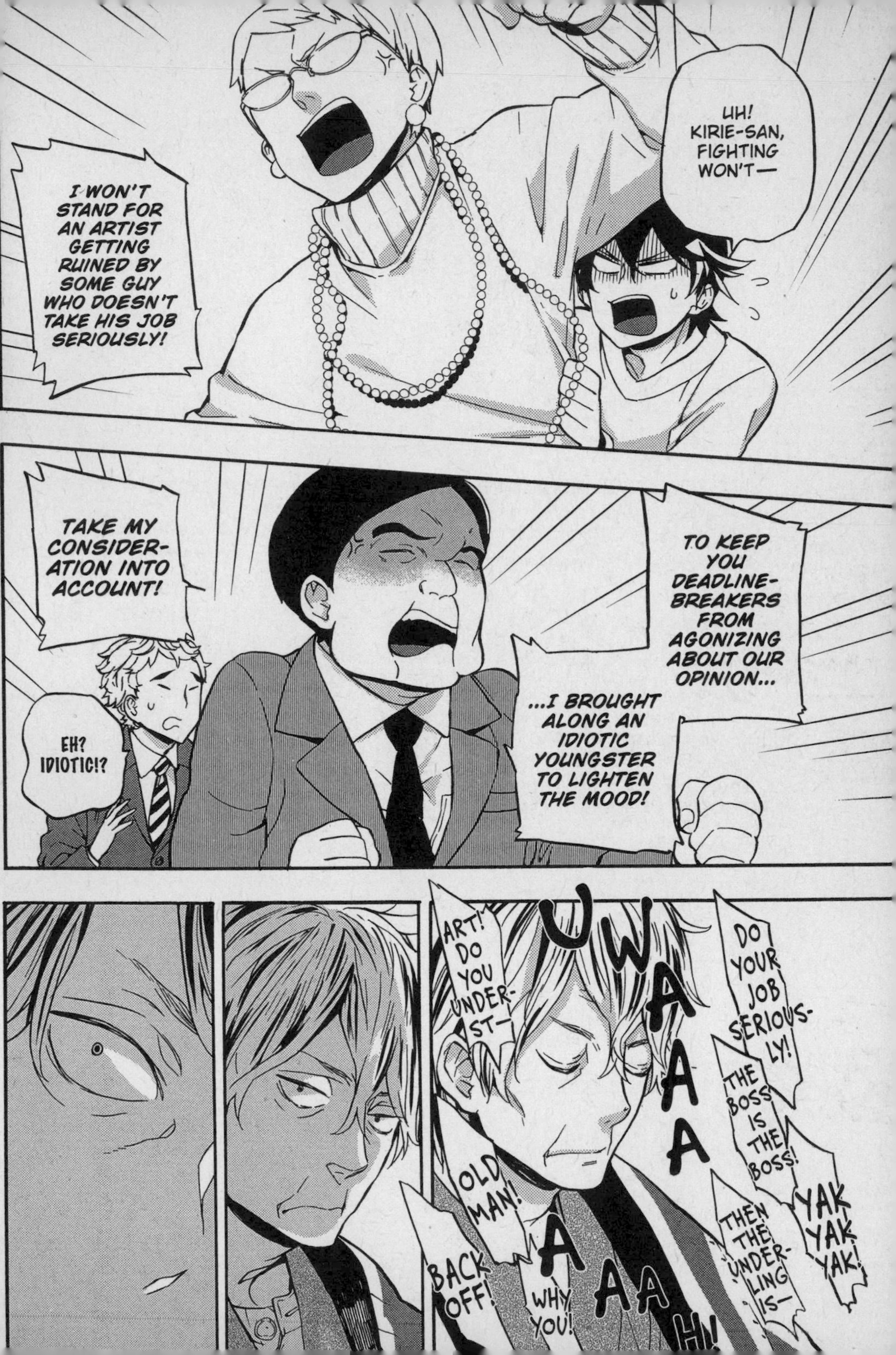
UH! KIRIE-SAN, FIGHTING WON'T—
I WON'T STAND FOR AN ARTIST GETTING RUINED BY SOME GUY WHO DOESN'T TAKE HIS JOB SERIOUSLY!
TO KEEP YOU DEADLINE-BREAKERS FROM AGONIZING ABOUT OUR OPINION...
...I BROUGHT ALONG AN IDIOTIC YOUNGSTER TO LIGHTEN THE MOOD!
TAKE MY CONSIDER-ATION INTO ACCOUNT!
EH? IDIOTIC!?
DO YOUR JOB SERIOUS-LY!
YAK YAK YAK!
THE BOSS IS THE BOSS!
THEN THE UNDER-LING IS—
UWAAAAAAAH!
ART! DO YOU UNDER-ST—
OLD MAN!
WHY YOU!
BACK OFF!

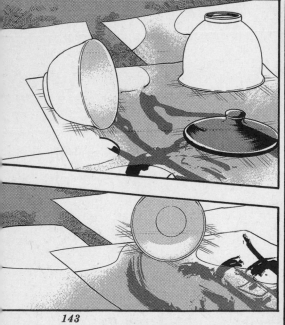

DOSAA
(WHUMP)

GASHAN
(SPLASH)

GASHA

GASHAN

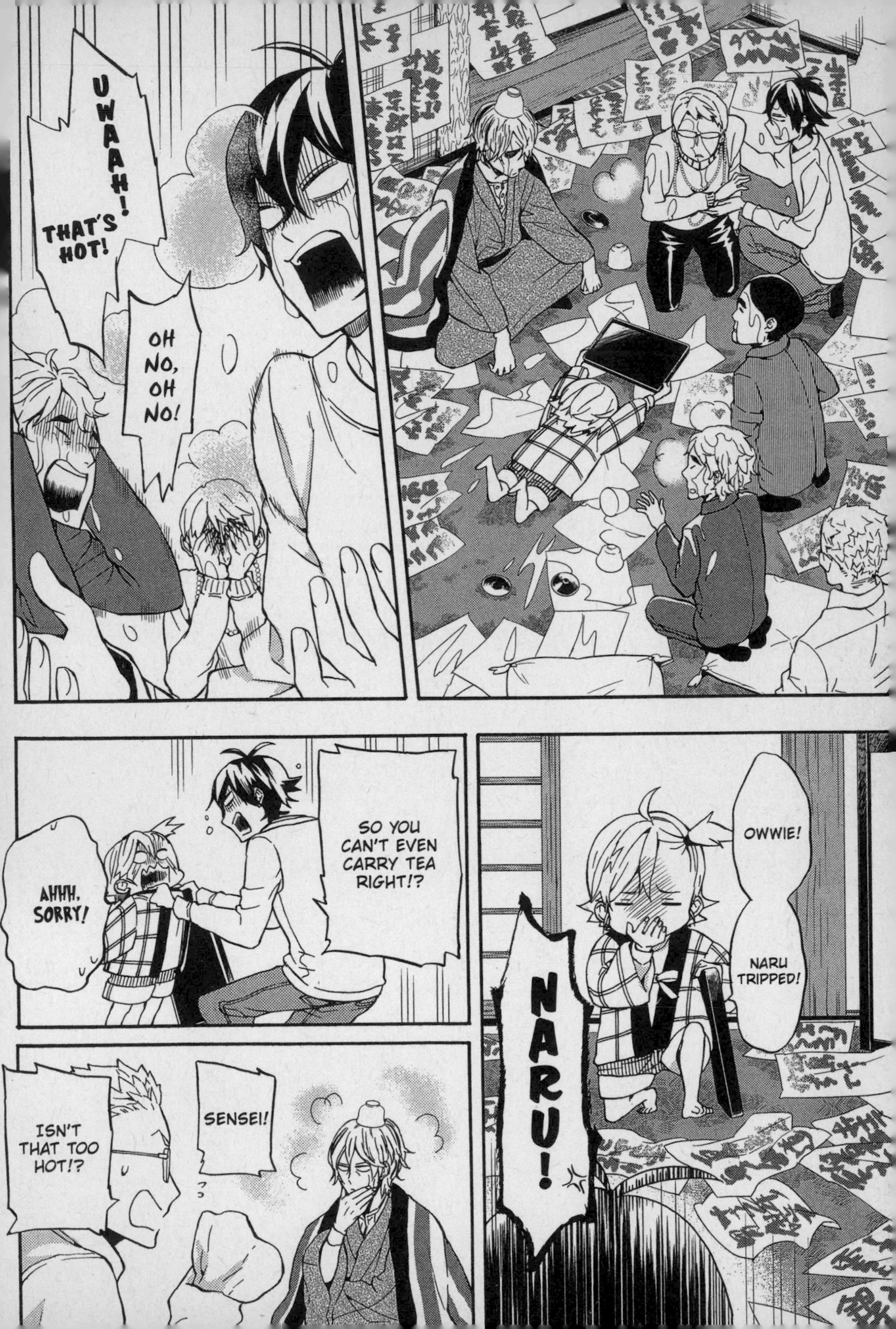
UWAAH! THAT'S HOT!
OH NO, OH NO!
OWWIE!
NARU TRIPPED!
NARU!
SO YOU CAN'T EVEN CARRY TEA RIGHT!?
AHHH, SORRY!
SENSEI!
ISN'T THAT TOO HOT!?

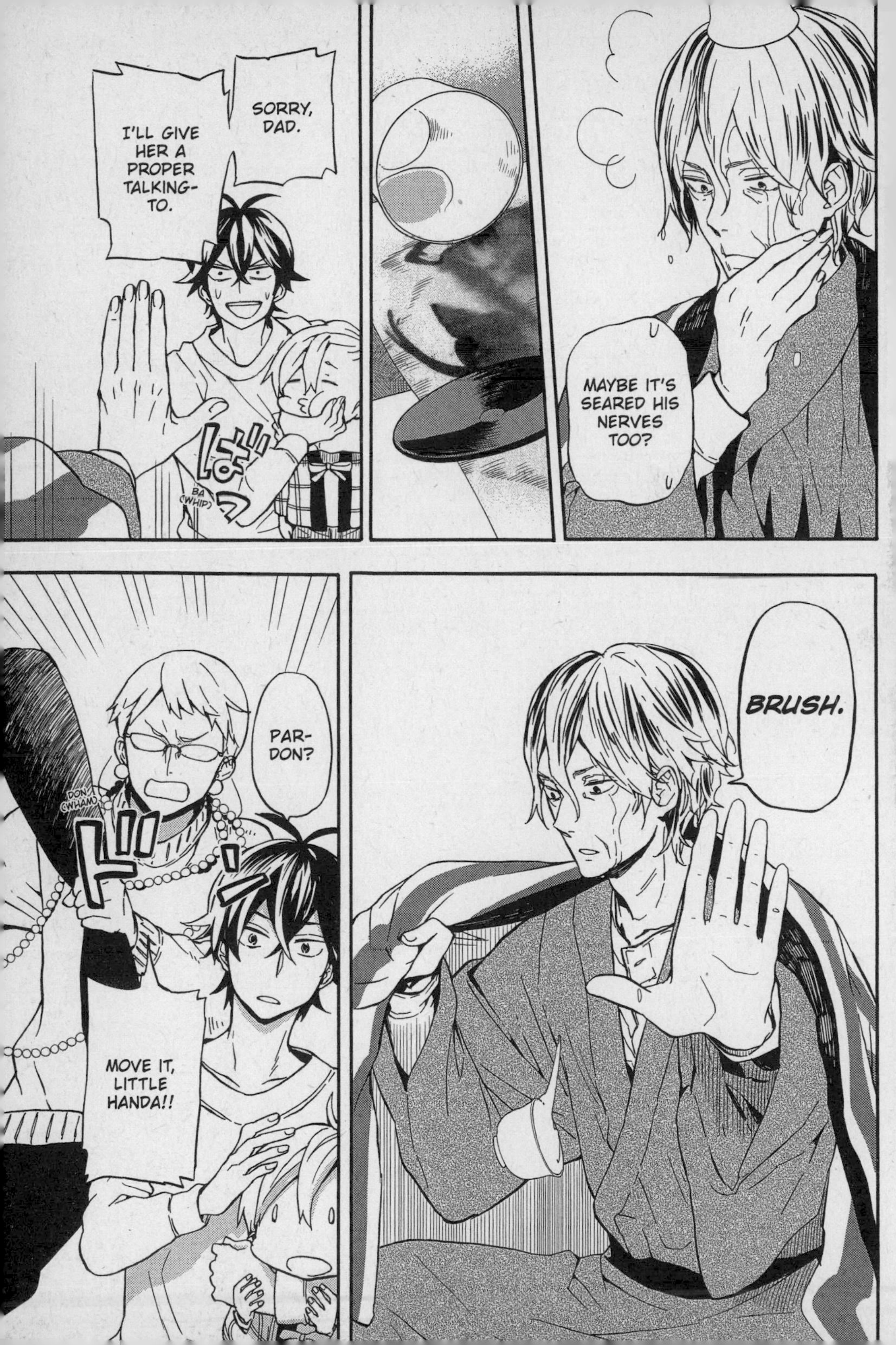
MAYBE IT'S SEARED HIS NERVES TOO?
SORRY, DAD.
I'LL GIVE HER A PROPER TALKING-TO.
BA (WHIP)
BRUSH.
PAR-DON?
DON (WHAM)
MOVE IT, LITTLE HANDA!!

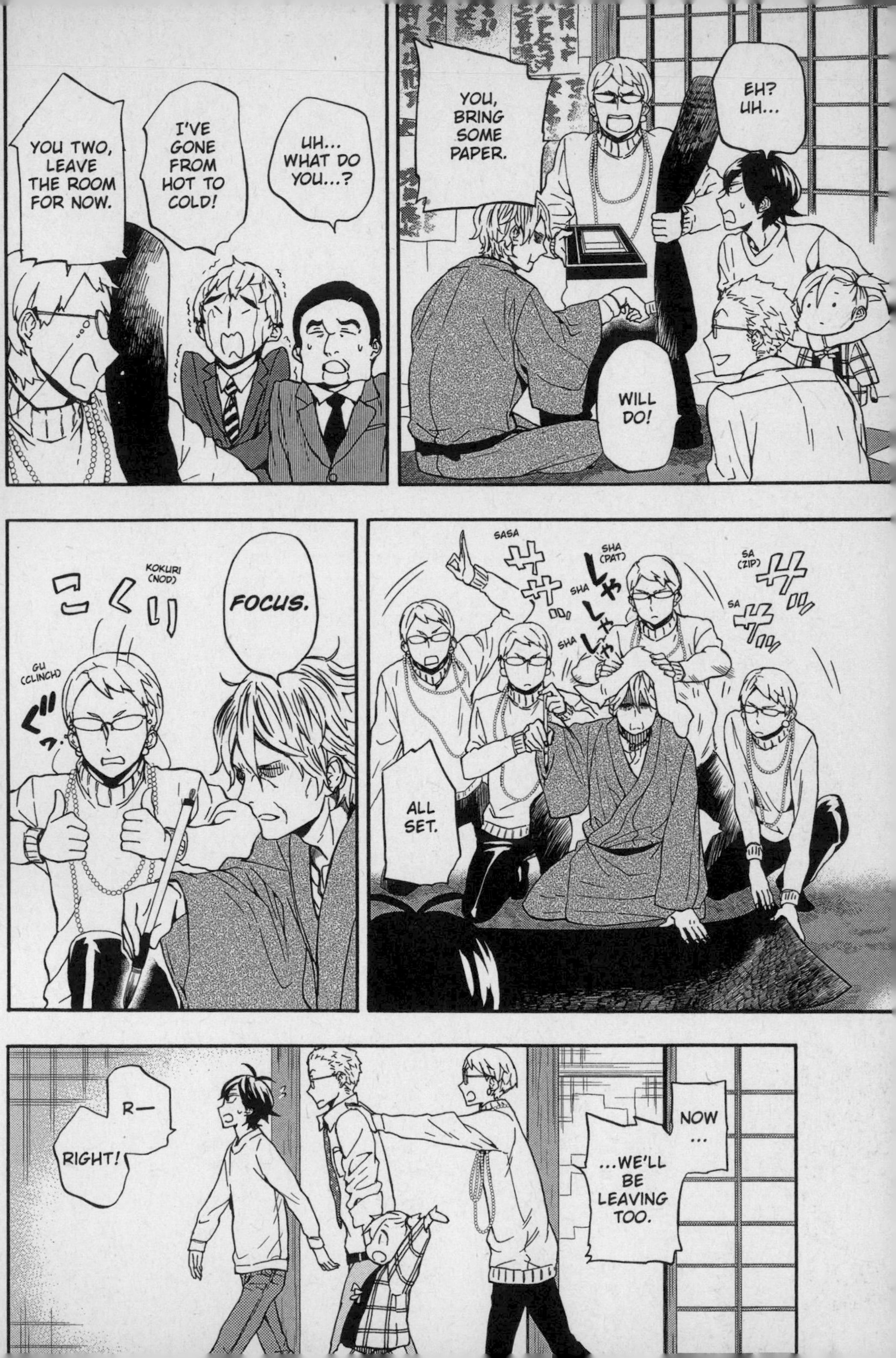
EH? UH...
YOU, BRING SOME PAPER.
WILL DO!
UH... WHAT DO YOU...?
I'VE GONE FROM HOT TO COLD!
YOU TWO, LEAVE THE ROOM FOR NOW.
SA (ZIP)
SA
SHA (PAT)
SHA
SHA
SASA
ALL SET.
FOCUS.
KOKURI (NOD)
GU (CLINCH)
NOW...
...WE'LL BE LEAVING TOO.
R—
RIGHT!

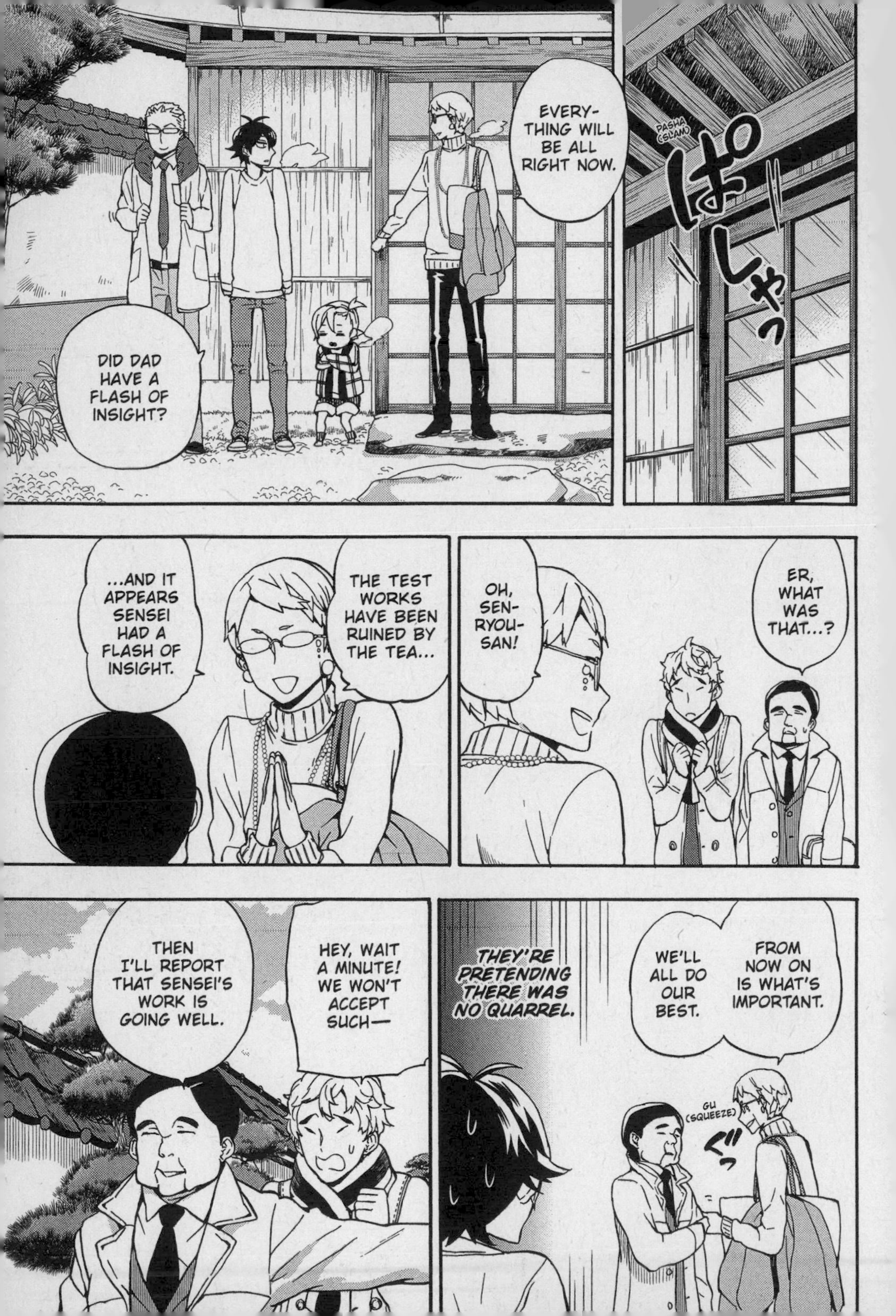
PASHA (SLAM)
ぱしゃっ
EVERY-THING WILL BE ALL RIGHT NOW.
DID DAD HAVE A FLASH OF INSIGHT?
ER, WHAT WAS THAT...?
OH, SEN-RYOU-SAN!
THE TEST WORKS HAVE BEEN RUINED BY THE TEA...
...AND IT APPEARS SENSEI HAD A FLASH OF INSIGHT.
FROM NOW ON IS WHAT'S IMPORTANT.
WE'LL ALL DO OUR BEST.
GU (SQUEEZE)
ぐっ
THEY'RE PRETENDING THERE WAS NO QUARREL.
HEY, WAIT A MINUTE! WE WON'T ACCEPT SUCH—
THEN I'LL REPORT THAT SENSEI'S WORK IS GOING WELL.

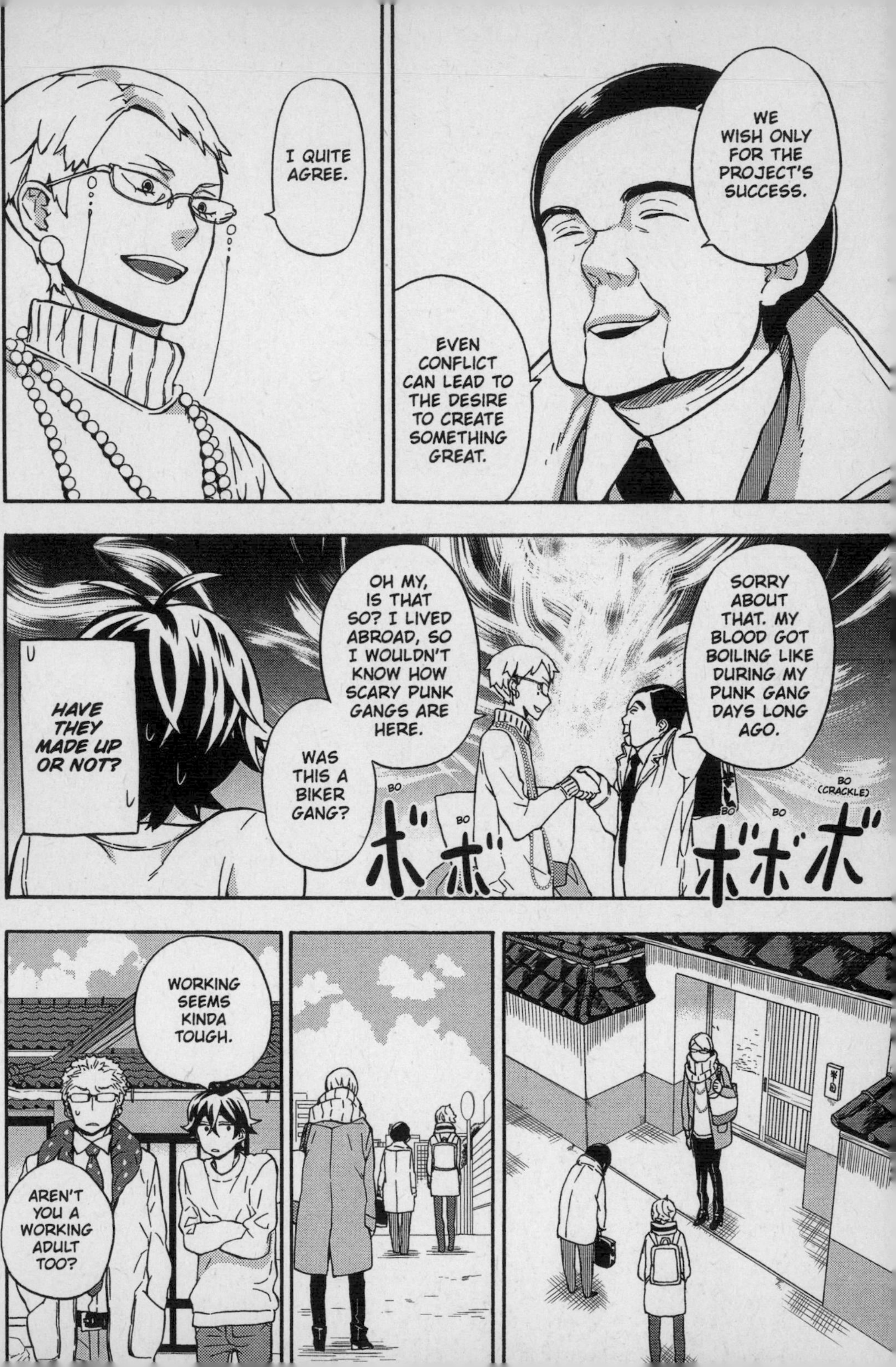
WE WISH ONLY FOR THE PROJECT'S SUCCESS.
EVEN CONFLICT CAN LEAD TO THE DESIRE TO CREATE SOMETHING GREAT.
I QUITE AGREE.
SORRY ABOUT THAT. MY BLOOD GOT BOILING LIKE DURING MY PUNK GANG DAYS LONG AGO.
BO (CRACKLE)
BO BO
ボボボ
OH MY, IS THAT SO? I LIVED ABROAD, SO I WOULDN'T KNOW HOW SCARY PUNK GANGS ARE HERE.
WAS THIS A BIKER GANG?
BO BO
ボボ
HAVE THEY MADE UP OR NOT?
WORKING SEEMS KINDA TOUGH.
AREN'T YOU A WORKING ADULT TOO?

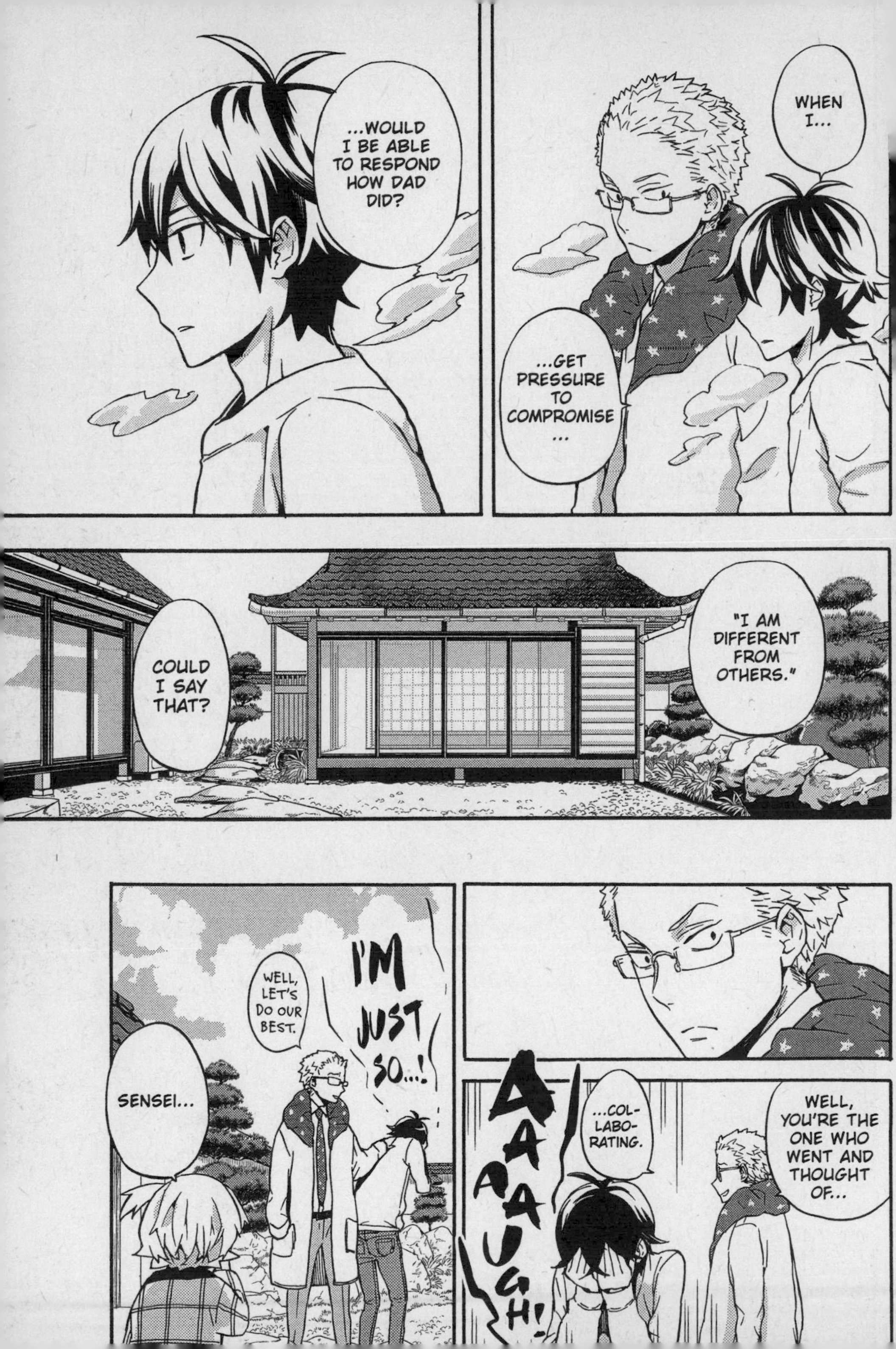
WHEN I...
...GET PRESSURE TO COMPROMISE ...
...WOULD I BE ABLE TO RESPOND HOW DAD DID?
"I AM DIFFERENT FROM OTHERS."
COULD I SAY THAT?
WELL, YOU'RE THE ONE WHO WENT AND THOUGHT OF...
...COL-LABO-RATING.
AAAAAUGH!
I'M JUST SO...!
WELL, LET'S DO OUR BEST.
SENSEI...

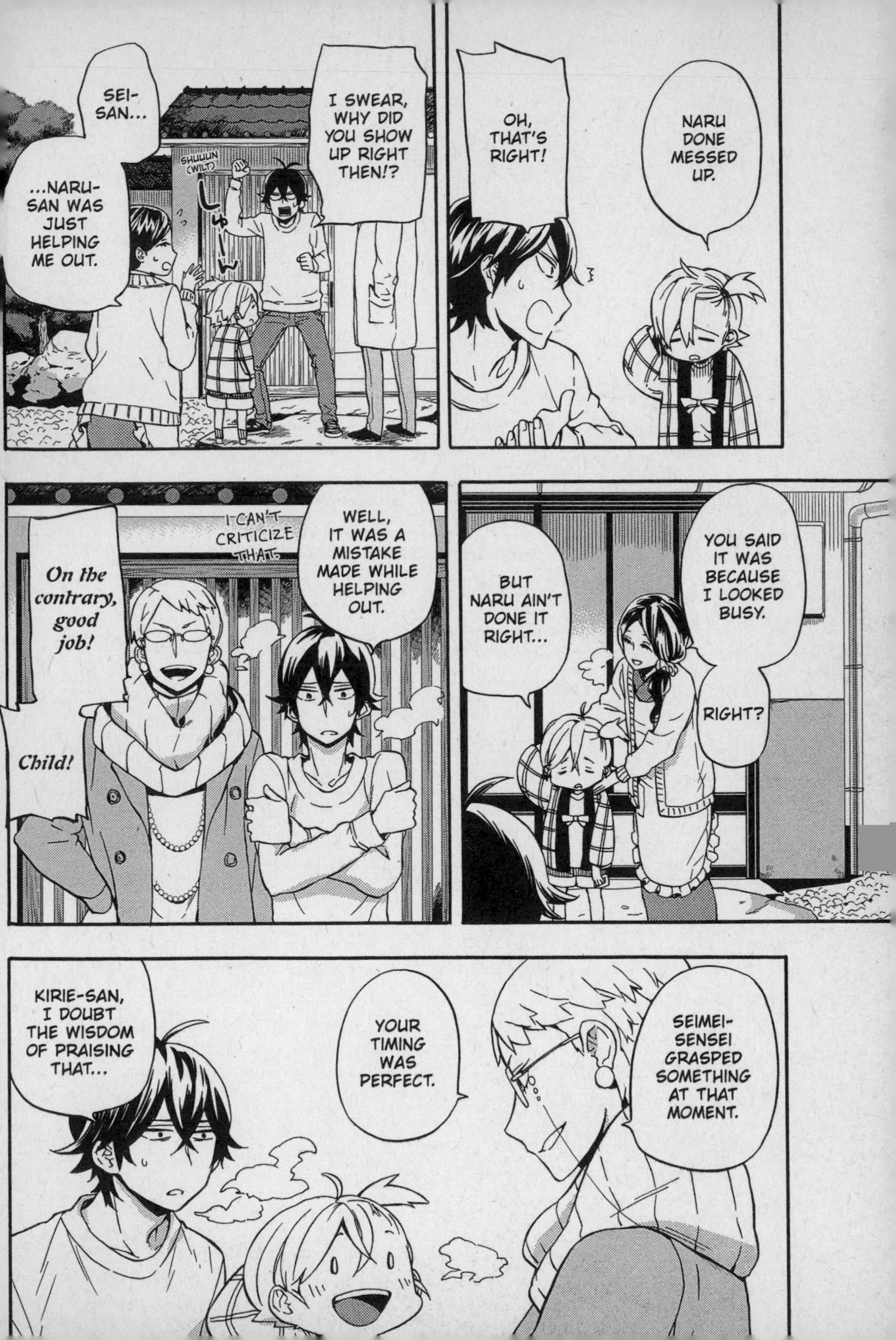
NARU DONE MESSED UP.
OH, THAT'S RIGHT!
I SWEAR, WHY DID YOU SHOW UP RIGHT THEN!?
SHUUUN (WILT)
SEI-SAN...
...NARU-SAN WAS JUST HELPING ME OUT.
YOU SAID IT WAS BECAUSE I LOOKED BUSY.
RIGHT?
BUT NARU AIN'T DONE IT RIGHT...
WELL, IT WAS A MISTAKE MADE WHILE HELPING OUT.
I CAN'T CRITICIZE THAT.
On the contrary, good job!
Child!
SEIMEI-SENSEI GRASPED SOMETHING AT THAT MOMENT.
YOUR TIMING WAS PERFECT.
KIRIE-SAN, I DOUBT THE WISDOM OF PRAISING THAT...

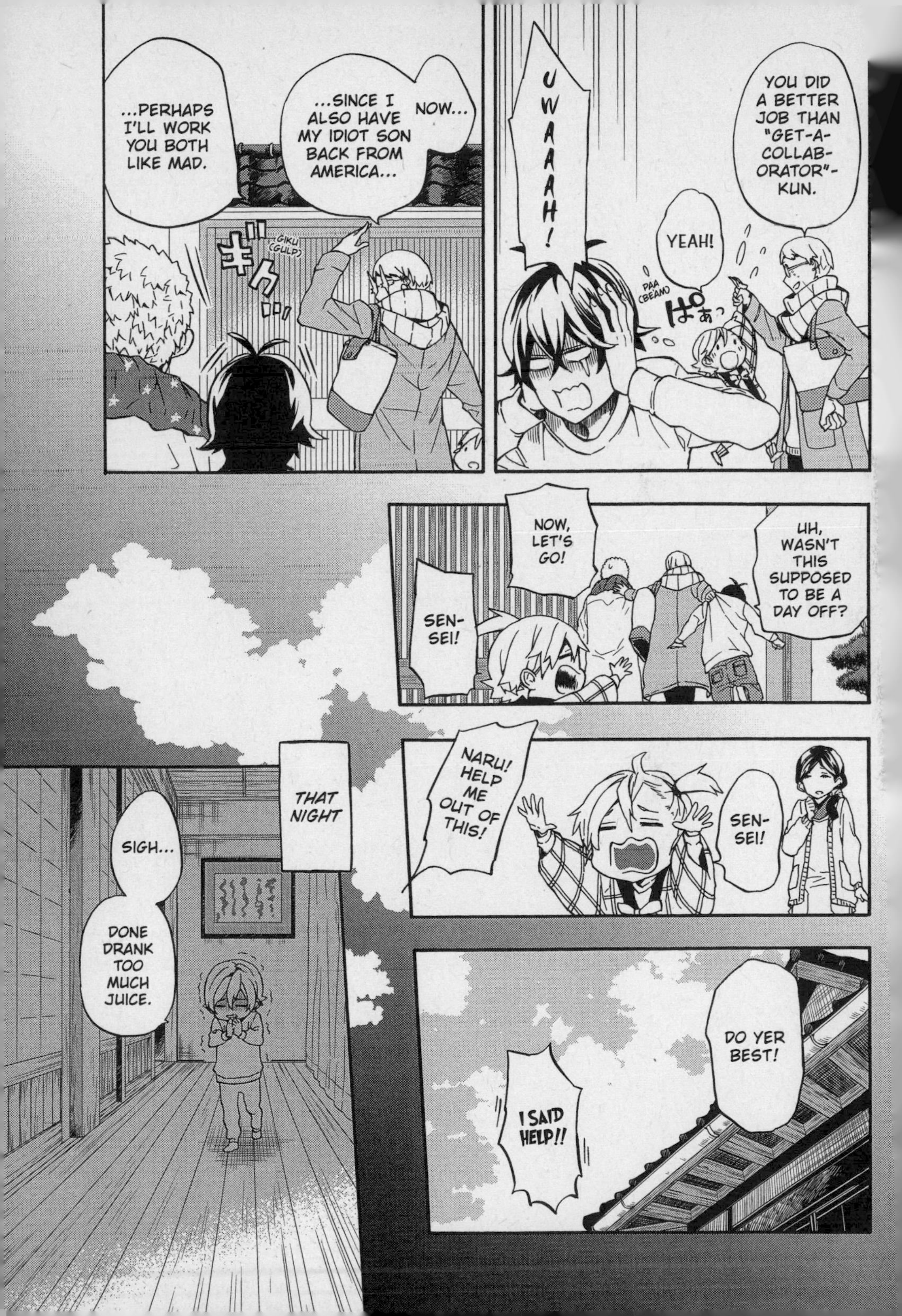
YOU DID A BETTER JOB THAN "GET-A-COLLABORATOR"-KUN.
YEAH!
PAA (BEAM)
ぱあっ
UWAAAAH!
NOW...
...SINCE I ALSO HAVE MY IDIOT SON BACK FROM AMERICA...
...PERHAPS I'LL WORK YOU BOTH LIKE MAD.
GIKU (GULP)
ギクッ
UH, WASN'T THIS SUPPOSED TO BE A DAY OFF?
NOW, LET'S GO!
SEN-SEI!
SEN-SEI!
NARU! HELP ME OUT OF THIS!
DO YER BEST!
I SAID HELP!!
THAT NIGHT
SIGH...
DONE DRANK TOO MUCH JUICE.

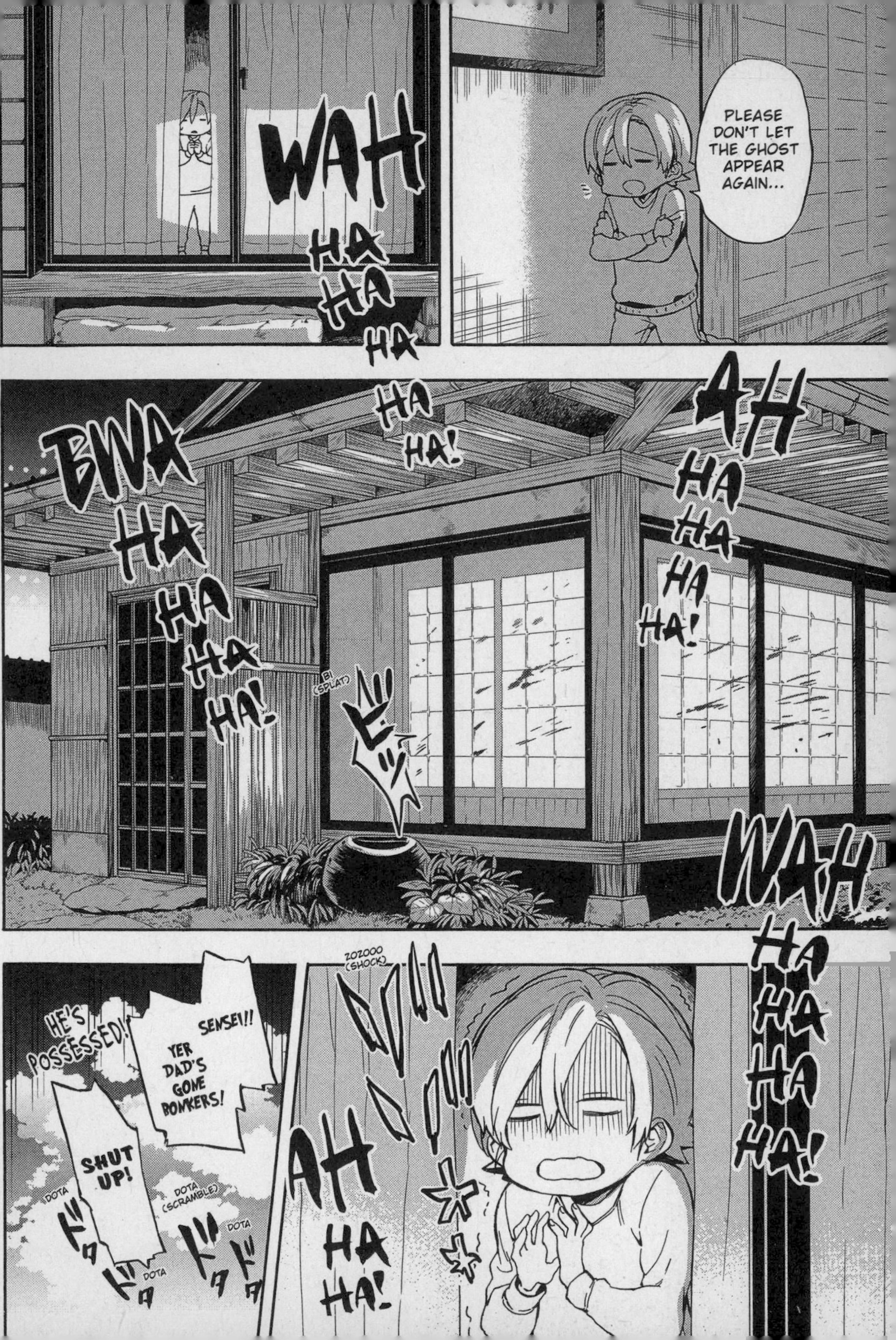
PLEASE DON'T LET THE GHOST APPEAR AGAIN...
WAH HA HA HA
AH HA HA HA HA HA!
HA HA!
BWA HA HA HA HA!
BI (SPLAT)
WAH HA HA HA HA HA!
ZOZOOO (SHOCK)
AH HA HA!
SENSEI!!
YER DAD'S GONE BONKERS!
HE'S POSSESSED!
SHUT UP!
DOTA (SCRAMBLE)
DOTA
DOTA
DOTA

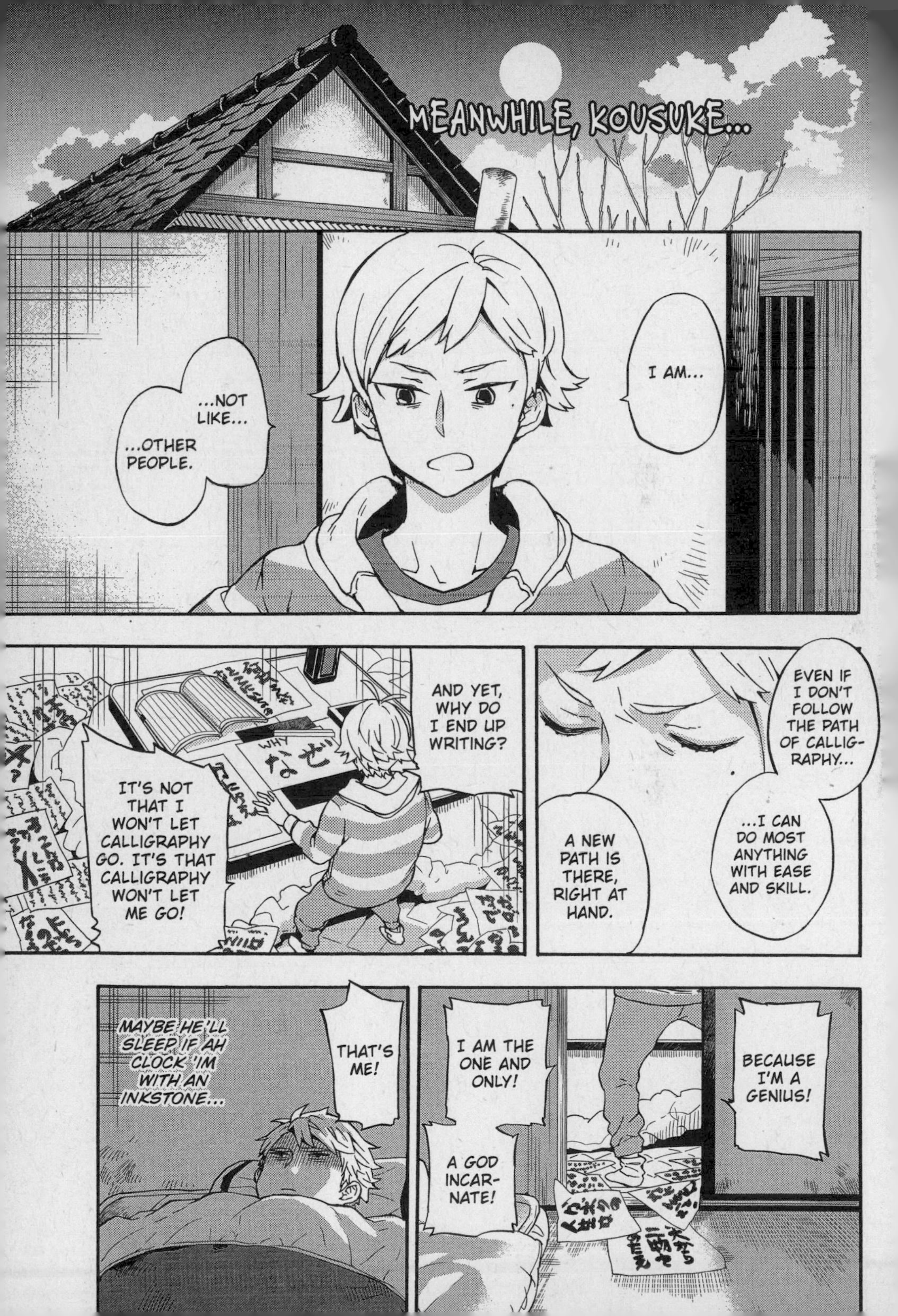
MEANWHILE, KOUSUKE...
I AM...
...NOT LIKE...
...OTHER PEOPLE.
EVEN IF I DON'T FOLLOW THE PATH OF CALLIG-RAPHY...
...I CAN DO MOST ANYTHING WITH EASE AND SKILL.
A NEW PATH IS THERE, RIGHT AT HAND.
AND YET, WHY DO I END UP WRITING?
WHY
なぜ
IT'S NOT THAT I WON'T LET CALLIGRAPHY GO. IT'S THAT CALLIGRAPHY WON'T LET ME GO!
BECAUSE I'M A GENIUS!
I AM THE ONE AND ONLY!
A GOD INCAR-NATE!
THAT'S ME!
MAYBE HE'LL SLEEP IF AH CLOCK 'IM WITH AN INKSTONE...

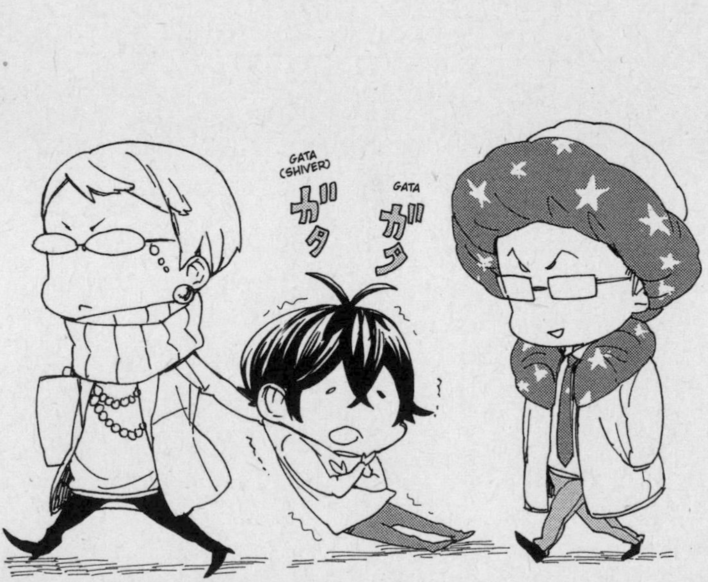
GATA
(SHIVER)
ガタ
GATA
ガタ

Act.99
GOING HOME?
[Translation: Modo?]

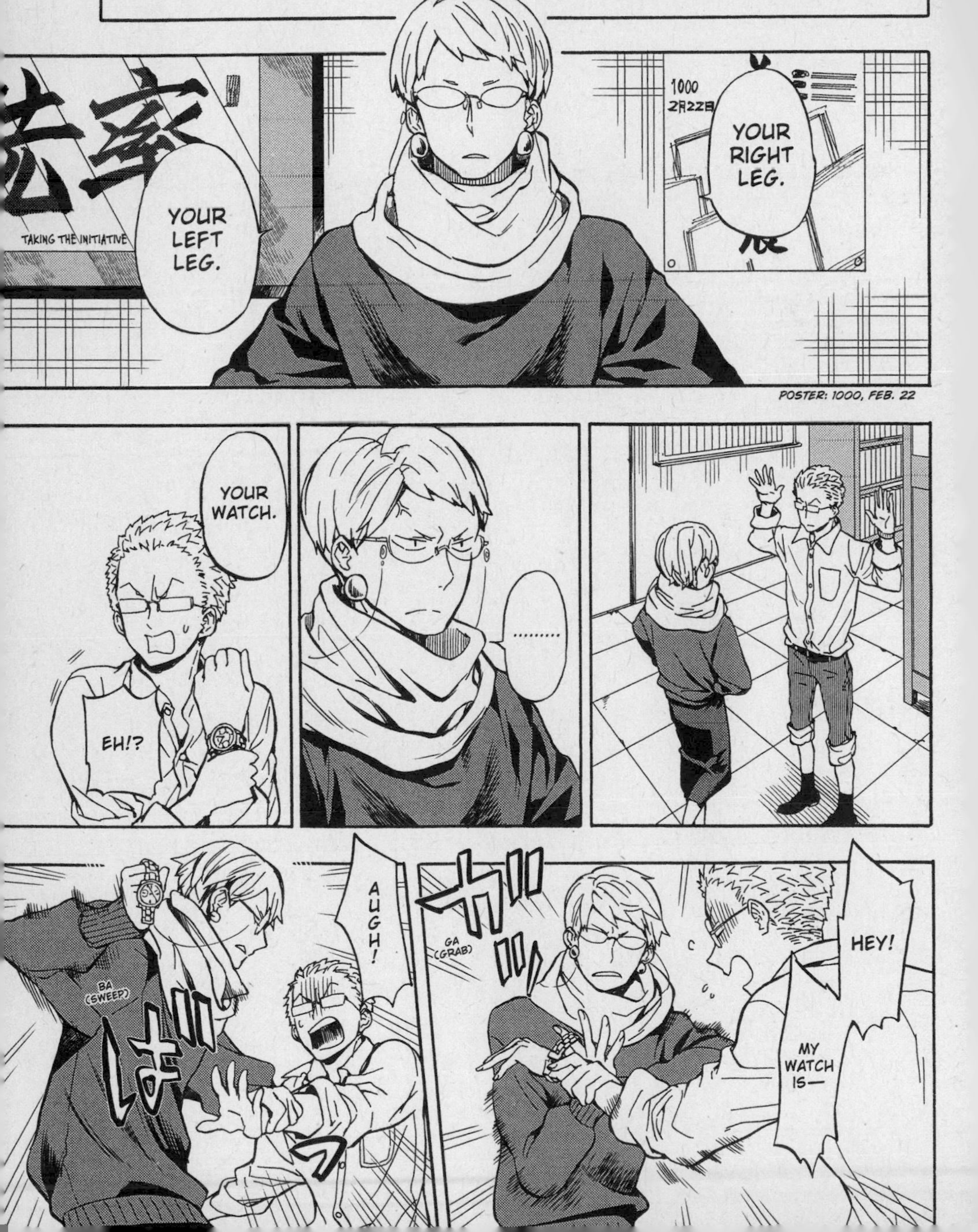
YOUR RIGHT LEG.
1000
2月22日
YOUR LEFT LEG.
TAKING THE INITIATIVE
POSTER: 1000, FEB. 22
....
YOUR WATCH.
EH!?
HEY!
MY WATCH IS—
GA (GRAB)
AUGH!
BA (SWEEP)

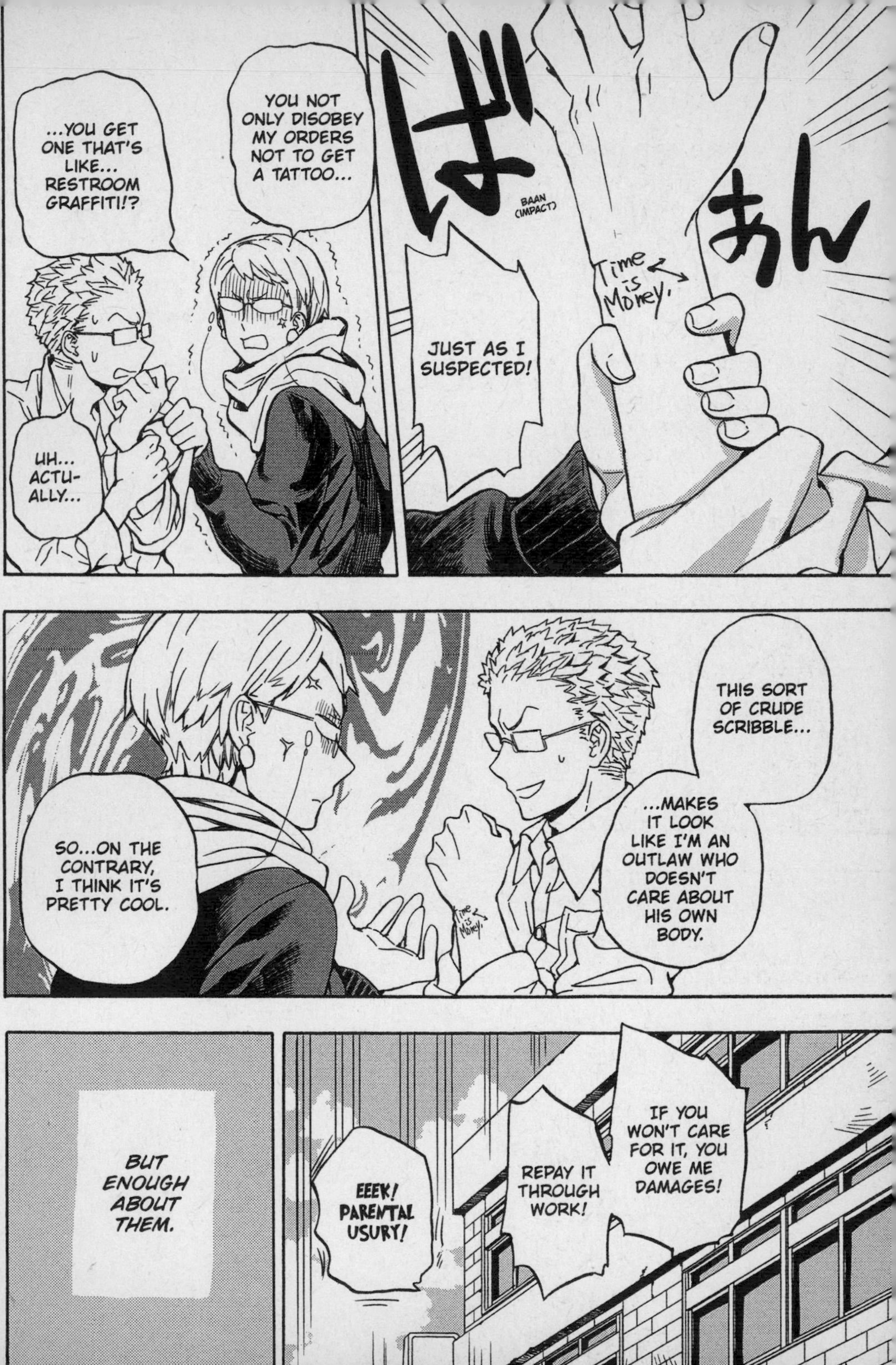
ばあん
BAAN (IMPACT)
Time is Money.
JUST AS I SUSPECTED!
YOU NOT ONLY DISOBEY MY ORDERS NOT TO GET A TATTOO...
...YOU GET ONE THAT'S LIKE... RESTROOM GRAFFITI!?
UH... ACTU-ALLY...
THIS SORT OF CRUDE SCRIBBLE...
...MAKES IT LOOK LIKE I'M AN OUTLAW WHO DOESN'T CARE ABOUT HIS OWN BODY.
Time is Money.
SO...ON THE CONTRARY, I THINK IT'S PRETTY COOL.
IF YOU WON'T CARE FOR IT, YOU OWE ME DAMAGES!
REPAY IT THROUGH WORK!
EEEK! PARENTAL USURY!
BUT ENOUGH ABOUT THEM.

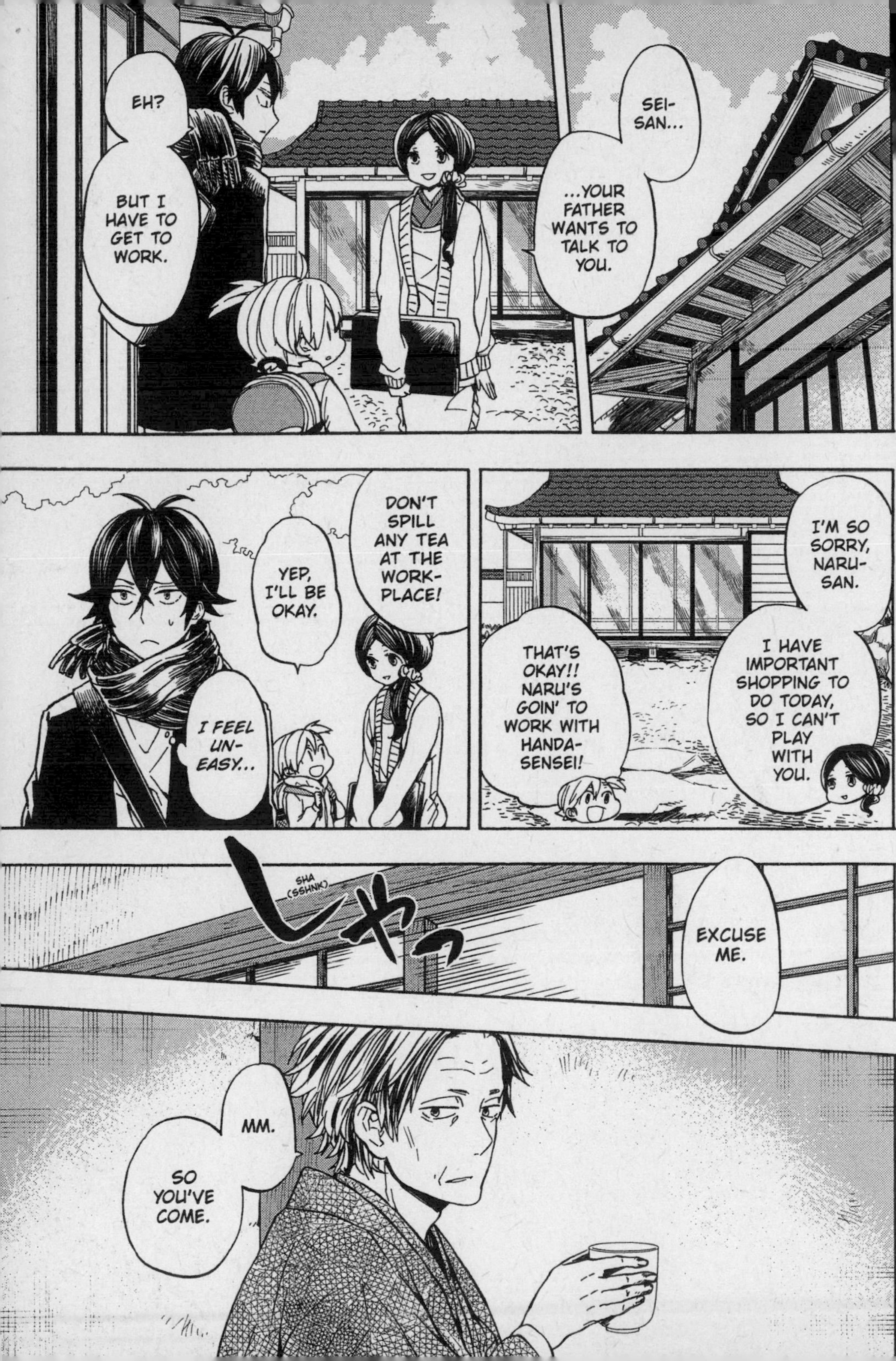
SEI-SAN...
...YOUR FATHER WANTS TO TALK TO YOU.
EH?
BUT I HAVE TO GET TO WORK.
I'M SO SORRY, NARU-SAN.
I HAVE IMPORTANT SHOPPING TO DO TODAY, SO I CAN'T PLAY WITH YOU.
THAT'S OKAY!! NARU'S GOIN' TO WORK WITH HANDA-SENSEI!
DON'T SPILL ANY TEA AT THE WORK-PLACE!
YEP, I'LL BE OKAY.
I FEEL UN-EASY...
しゃっ
SHA (SSHNK)
EXCUSE ME.
MM.
SO YOU'VE COME.

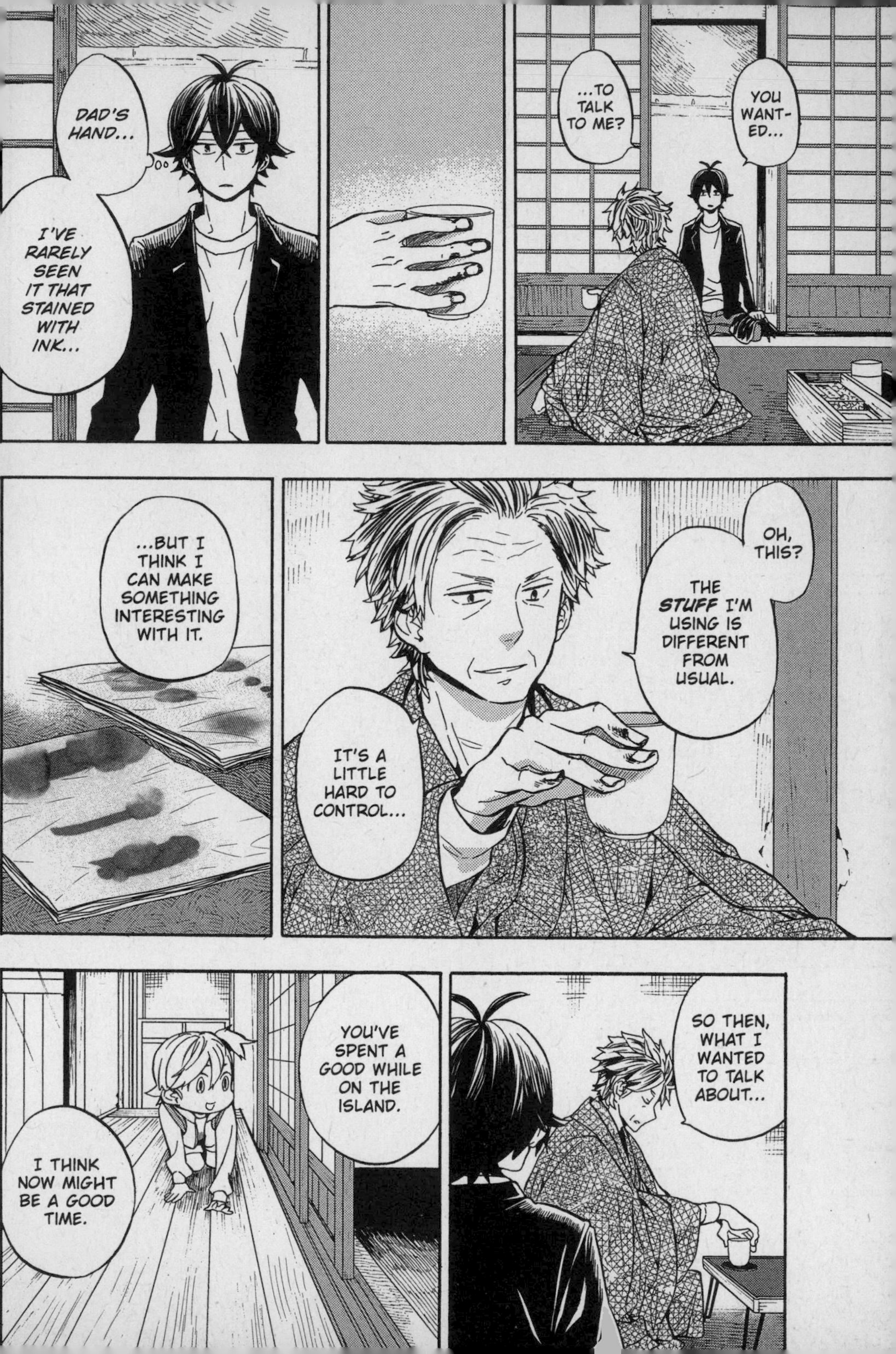
YOU WANT-ED...
...TO TALK TO ME?
DAD'S HAND...
I'VE RARELY SEEN IT THAT STAINED WITH INK...
OH, THIS?
THE STUFF I'M USING IS DIFFERENT FROM USUAL.
IT'S A LITTLE HARD TO CONTROL...
...BUT I THINK I CAN MAKE SOMETHING INTERESTING WITH IT.
SO THEN, WHAT I WANTED TO TALK ABOUT...
YOU'VE SPENT A GOOD WHILE ON THE ISLAND.
I THINK NOW MIGHT BE A GOOD TIME.

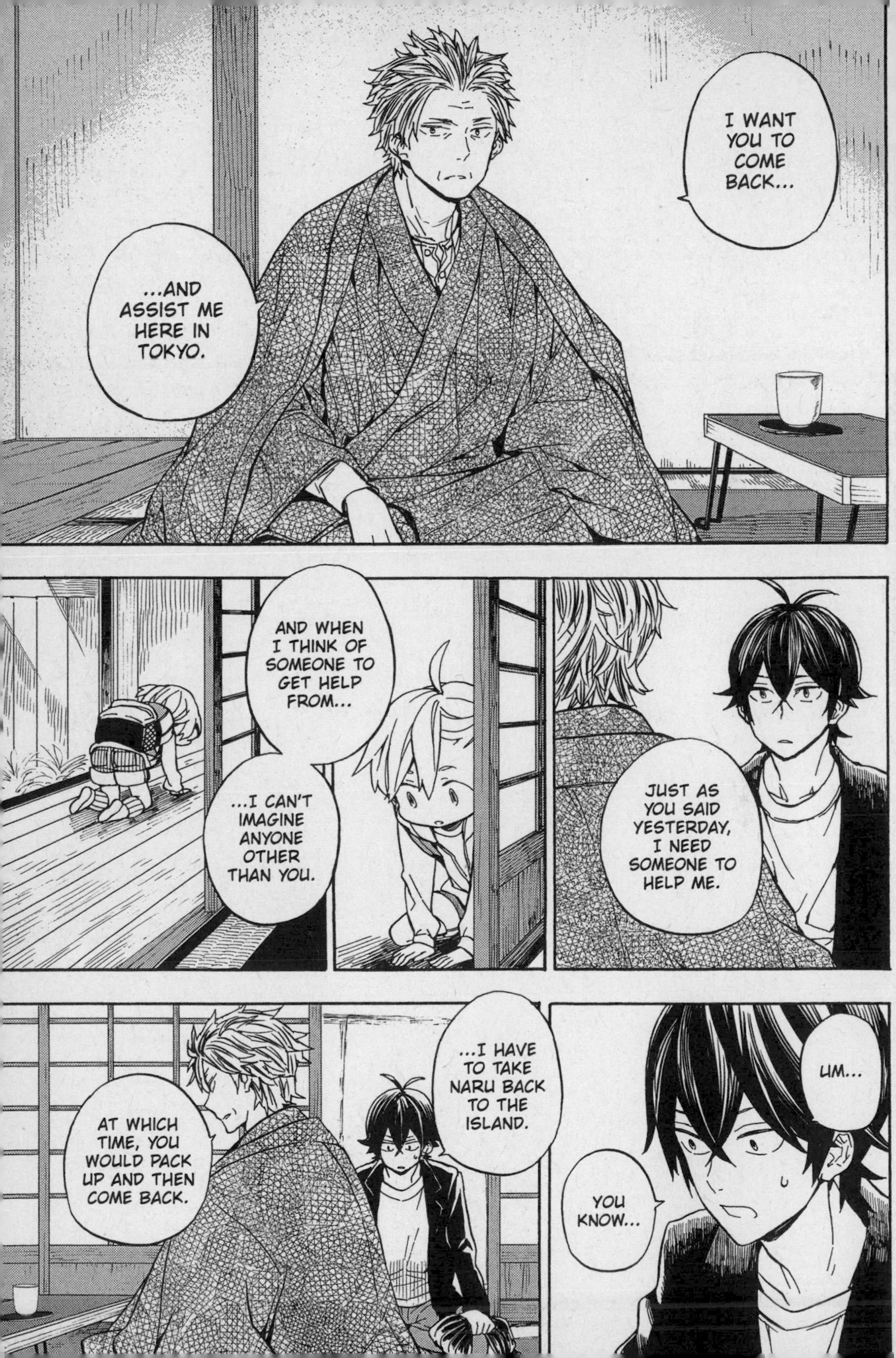
I WANT YOU TO COME BACK...
...AND ASSIST ME HERE IN TOKYO.
JUST AS YOU SAID YESTERDAY, I NEED SOMEONE TO HELP ME.
AND WHEN I THINK OF SOMEONE TO GET HELP FROM...
...I CAN'T IMAGINE ANYONE OTHER THAN YOU.
UM...
YOU KNOW...
...I HAVE TO TAKE NARU BACK TO THE ISLAND.
AT WHICH TIME, YOU WOULD PACK UP AND THEN COME BACK.

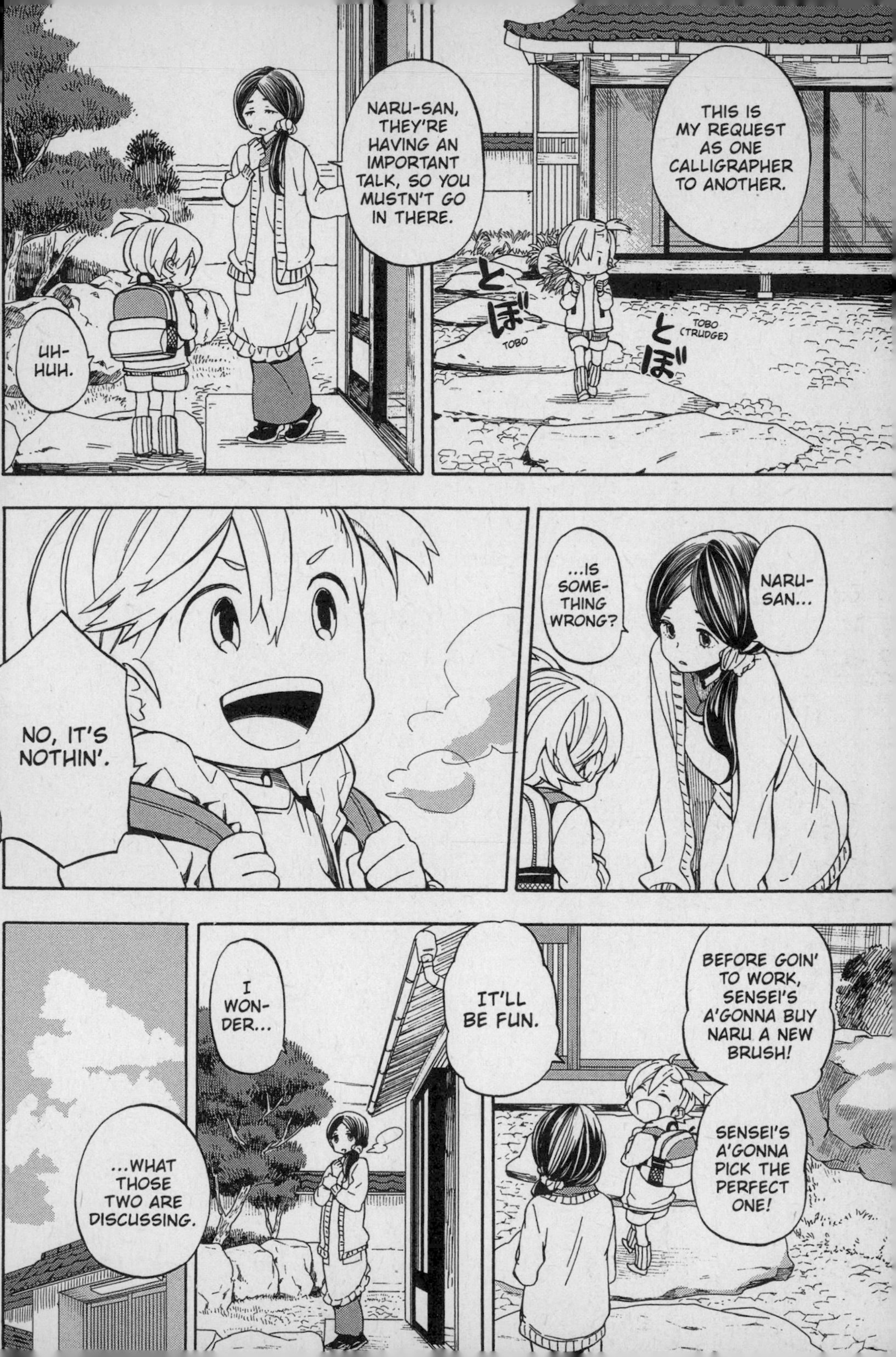
THIS IS MY REQUEST AS ONE CALLIGRAPHER TO ANOTHER.
とぼ
TOBO
とぼ
TOBO (TRUDGE)
NARU-SAN, THEY'RE HAVING AN IMPORTANT TALK, SO YOU MUSTN'T GO IN THERE.
UH-HUH.
NARU-SAN...
...IS SOMETHING WRONG?
NO, IT'S NOTHIN'.
BEFORE GOIN' TO WORK, SENSEI'S A'GONNA BUY NARU A NEW BRUSH!
SENSEI'S A'GONNA PICK THE PERFECT ONE!
IT'LL BE FUN.
I WONDER...
...WHAT THOSE TWO ARE DISCUSSING.

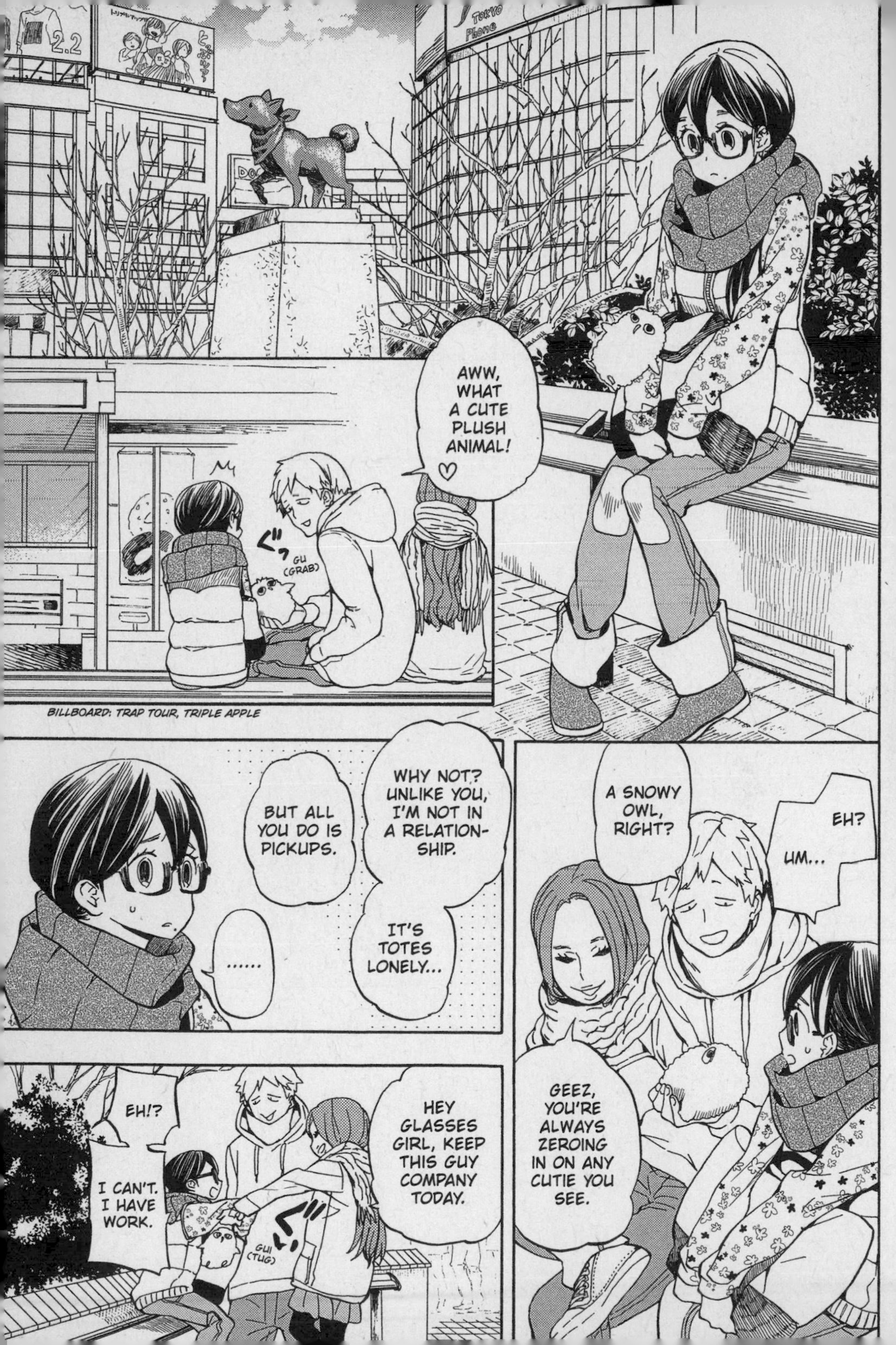
AWW, WHAT A CUTE PLUSH ANIMAL! ♡
GU (GRAB)
BILLBOARD: TRAP TOUR, TRIPLE APPLE
EH?
UM...
A SNOWY OWL, RIGHT?
GEEZ, YOU'RE ALWAYS ZEROING IN ON ANY CUTIE YOU SEE.
WHY NOT? UNLIKE YOU, I'M NOT IN A RELATION-SHIP.
IT'S TOTES LONELY...
BUT ALL YOU DO IS PICKUPS.
......
HEY GLASSES GIRL, KEEP THIS GUY COMPANY TODAY.
GUI (TUG)
EH!?
I CAN'T. I HAVE WORK.

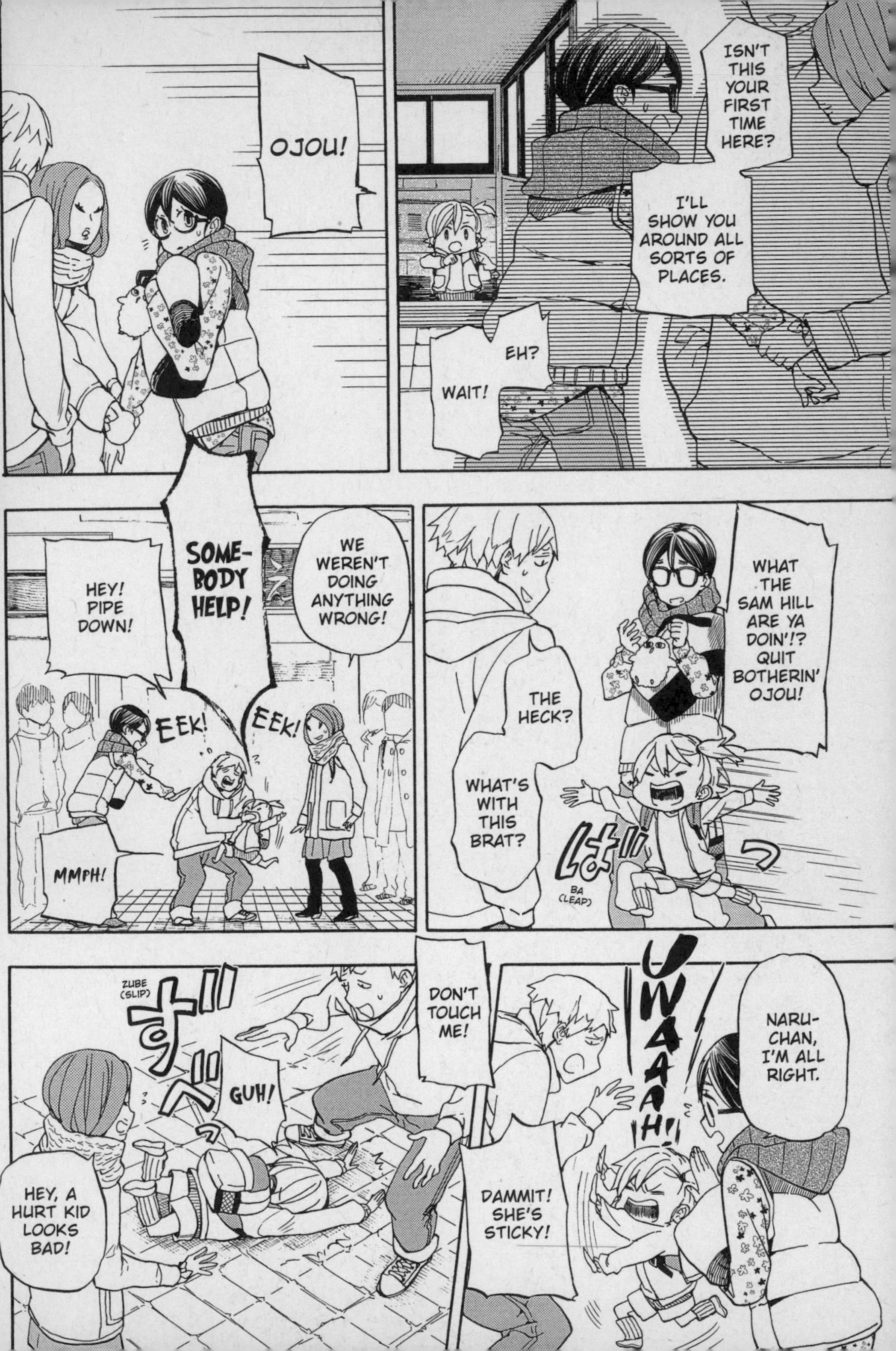

ISN'T THIS YOUR FIRST TIME HERE?
I'LL SHOW YOU AROUND ALL SORTS OF PLACES.
EH?
WAIT!
OJOU!
WHAT THE SAM HILL ARE YA DOIN'!? QUIT BOTHERIN' OJOU!
THE HECK?
WHAT'S WITH THIS BRAT?
BA (LEAP)
WE WEREN'T DOING ANYTHING WRONG!
SOME-BODY HELP!
HEY! PIPE DOWN!
EEK!
EEK!
MMPH!
NARU-CHAN, I'M ALL RIGHT.
UWAAAH!!
DAMMIT! SHE'S STICKY!
DON'T TOUCH ME!
GUH!
ZUBE (SLIP)
HEY, A HURT KID LOOKS BAD!

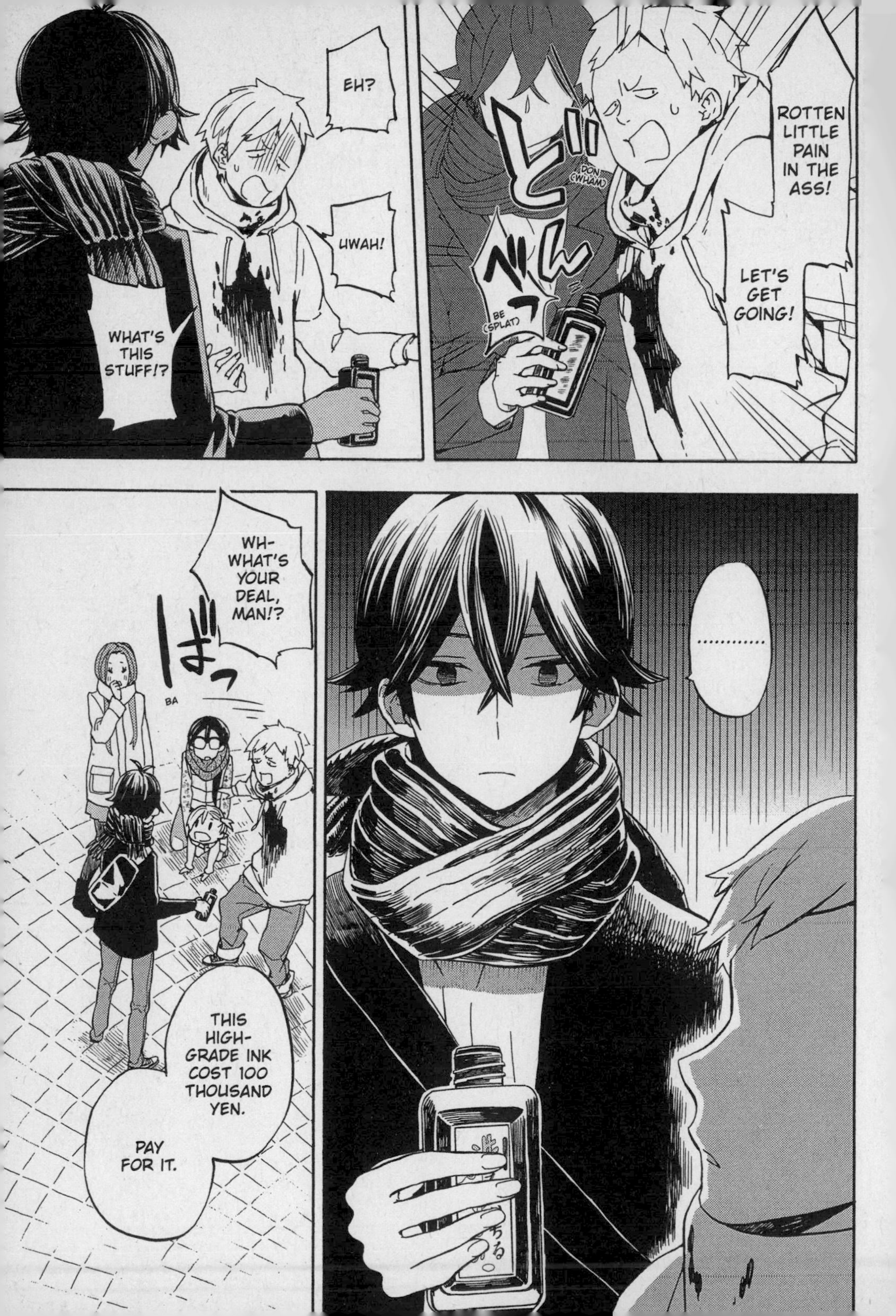
ROTTEN LITTLE PAIN IN THE ASS!
DON (WHAM)
BE (SPLAT)
LET'S GET GOING!
EH?
UWAH!
WHAT'S THIS STUFF!?
......
WH-WHAT'S YOUR DEAL, MAN!?
BA
THIS HIGH-GRADE INK COST 100 THOUSAND YEN.
PAY FOR IT.

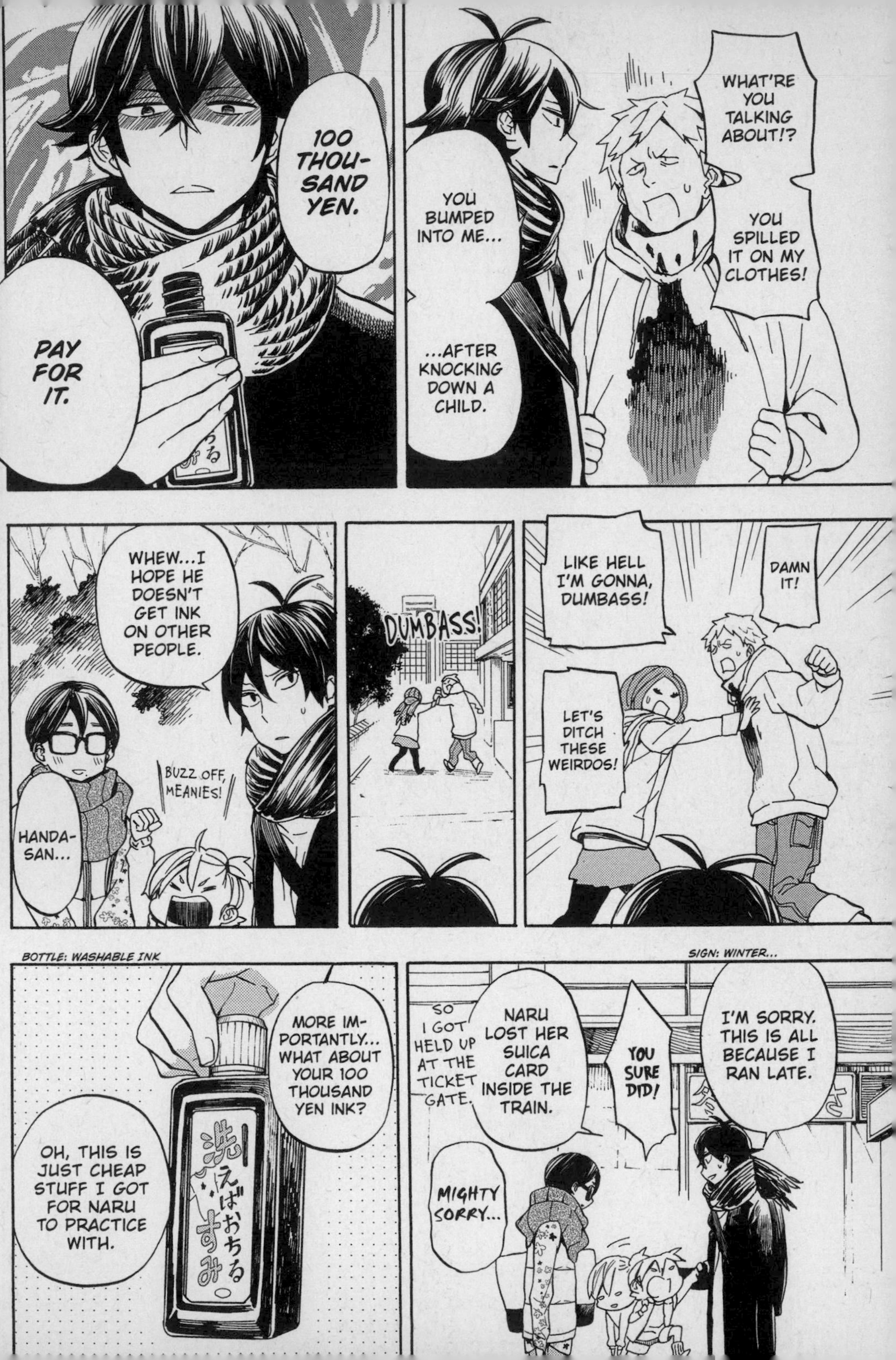
WHAT'RE YOU TALKING ABOUT!?
YOU SPILLED IT ON MY CLOTHES!
YOU BUMPED INTO ME...
...AFTER KNOCKING DOWN A CHILD.
100 THOUSAND YEN.
PAY FOR IT.
DAMN IT!
LIKE HELL I'M GONNA, DUMBASS!
LET'S DITCH THESE WEIRDOS!
DUMBASS!
WHEW...I HOPE HE DOESN'T GET INK ON OTHER PEOPLE.
BUZZ OFF, MEANIES!
HANDA-SAN...
SIGN: WINTER...
BOTTLE: WASHABLE INK
I'M SORRY. THIS IS ALL BECAUSE I RAN LATE.
YOU SURE DID!
NARU LOST HER SUICA CARD INSIDE THE TRAIN.
SO I GOT HELD UP AT THE TICKET GATE.
MIGHTY SORRY...
MORE IMPORTANTLY... WHAT ABOUT YOUR 100 THOUSAND YEN INK?
OH, THIS IS JUST CHEAP STUFF I GOT FOR NARU TO PRACTICE WITH.
洗えばおちるすみ

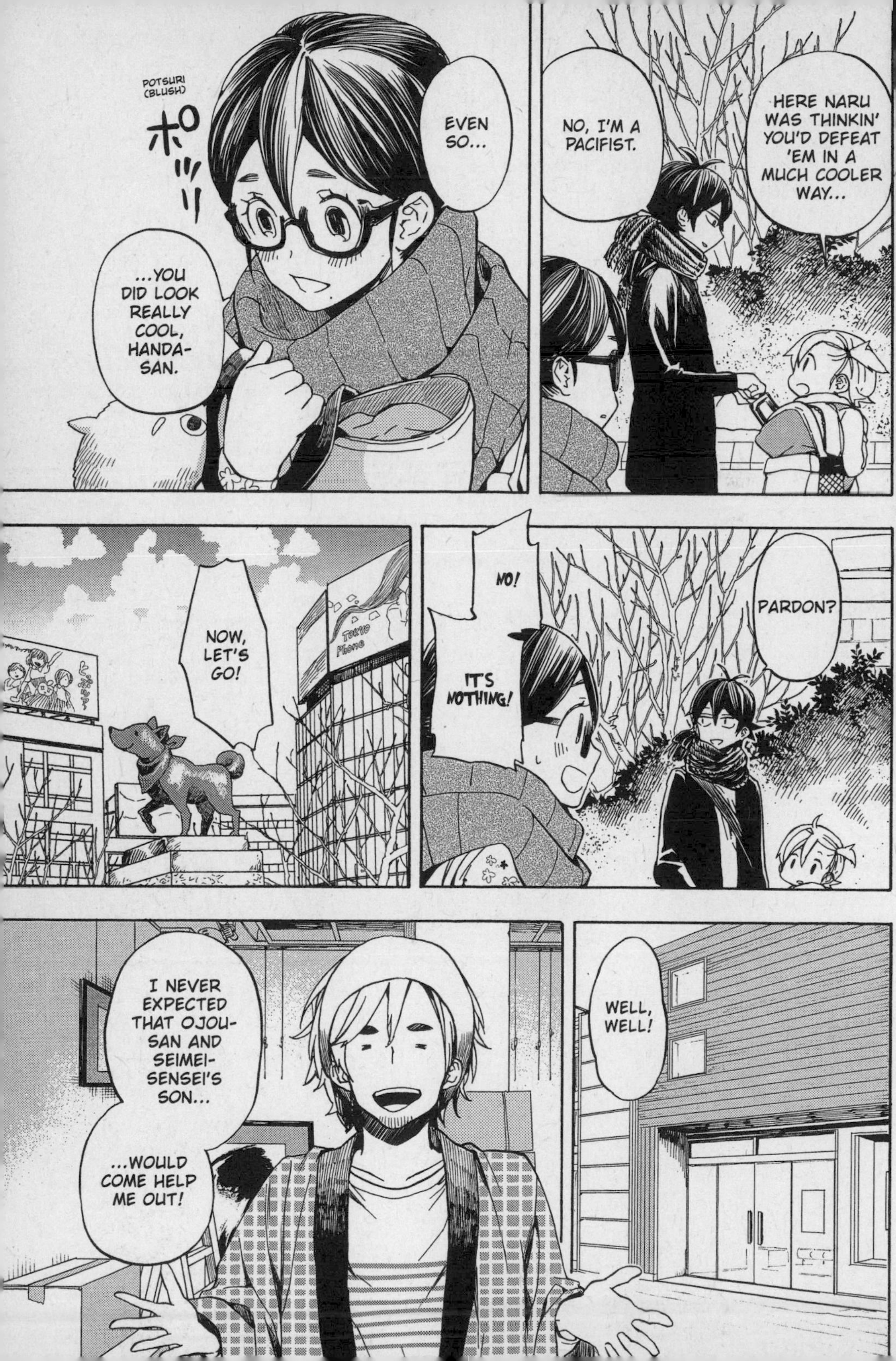
HERE NARU WAS THINKIN' YOU'D DEFEAT 'EM IN A MUCH COOLER WAY...
NO, I'M A PACIFIST.
EVEN SO...
POTSURI (BLUSH)
ポッ
...YOU DID LOOK REALLY COOL, HANDA-SAN.
PARDON?
NO!
IT'S NOTHING!
NOW, LET'S GO!
WELL, WELL!
I NEVER EXPECTED THAT OJOU-SAN AND SEIMEI-SENSEI'S SON...
...WOULD COME HELP ME OUT!

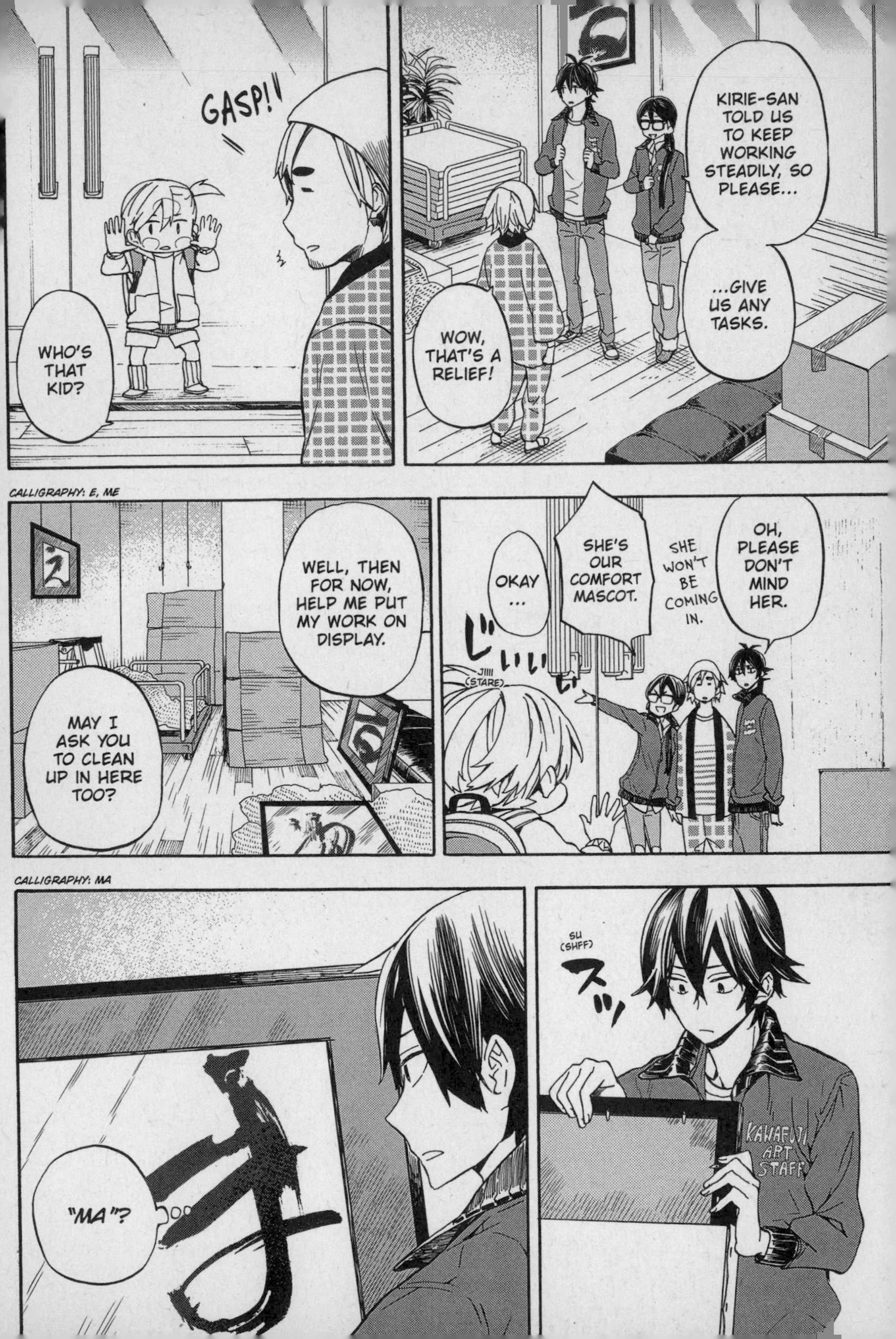
KIRIE-SAN TOLD US TO KEEP WORKING STEADILY, SO PLEASE...
...GIVE US ANY TASKS.
WOW, THAT'S A RELIEF!
GASP!!
WHO'S THAT KID?
CALLIGRAPHY: E, ME
OH, PLEASE DON'T MIND HER.
SHE WON'T BE COMING IN.
SHE'S OUR COMFORT MASCOT.
OKAY...
JIIII (STARE)
WELL, THEN FOR NOW, HELP ME PUT MY WORK ON DISPLAY.
MAY I ASK YOU TO CLEAN UP IN HERE TOO?
CALLIGRAPHY: MA
SU (SHFF)
KAWAFUJI ART STAFF
"MA"?

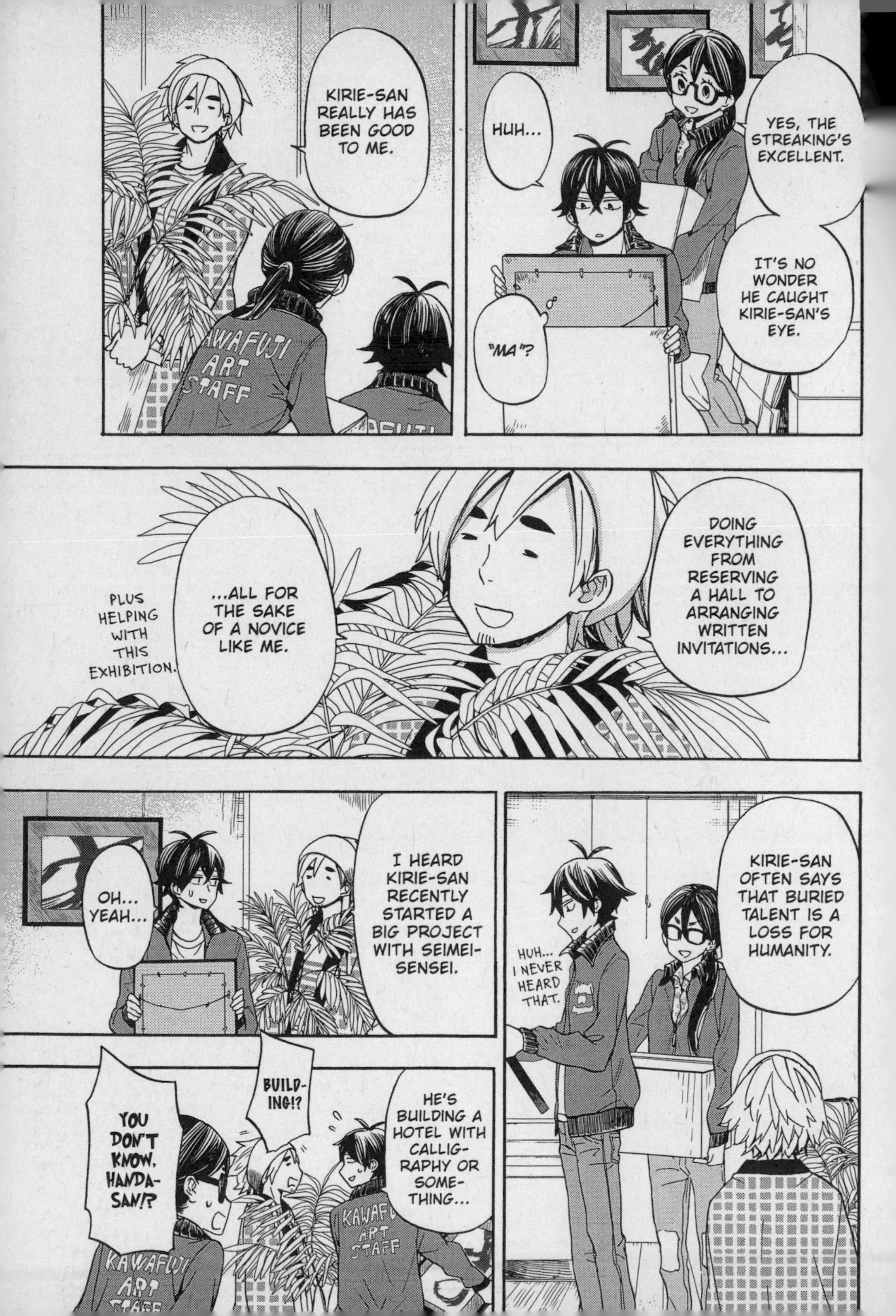
YES, THE STREAKING'S EXCELLENT.
IT'S NO WONDER HE CAUGHT KIRIE-SAN'S EYE.
HUH...
"MA"?
KIRIE-SAN REALLY HAS BEEN GOOD TO ME.
KAWAFUJI ART STAFF
DOING EVERYTHING FROM RESERVING A HALL TO ARRANGING WRITTEN INVITATIONS...
...ALL FOR THE SAKE OF A NOVICE LIKE ME.
PLUS HELPING WITH THIS EXHIBITION.
KIRIE-SAN OFTEN SAYS THAT BURIED TALENT IS A LOSS FOR HUMANITY.
HUH... I NEVER HEARD THAT.
I HEARD KIRIE-SAN RECENTLY STARTED A BIG PROJECT WITH SEIMEI-SENSEI.
OH... YEAH...
HE'S BUILDING A HOTEL WITH CALLIG-RAPHY OR SOME-THING...
BUILD-ING!?
YOU DON'T KNOW, HANDA-SAN!?
KAWAFU ART STAFF
KAWAFUJI ART STAFF

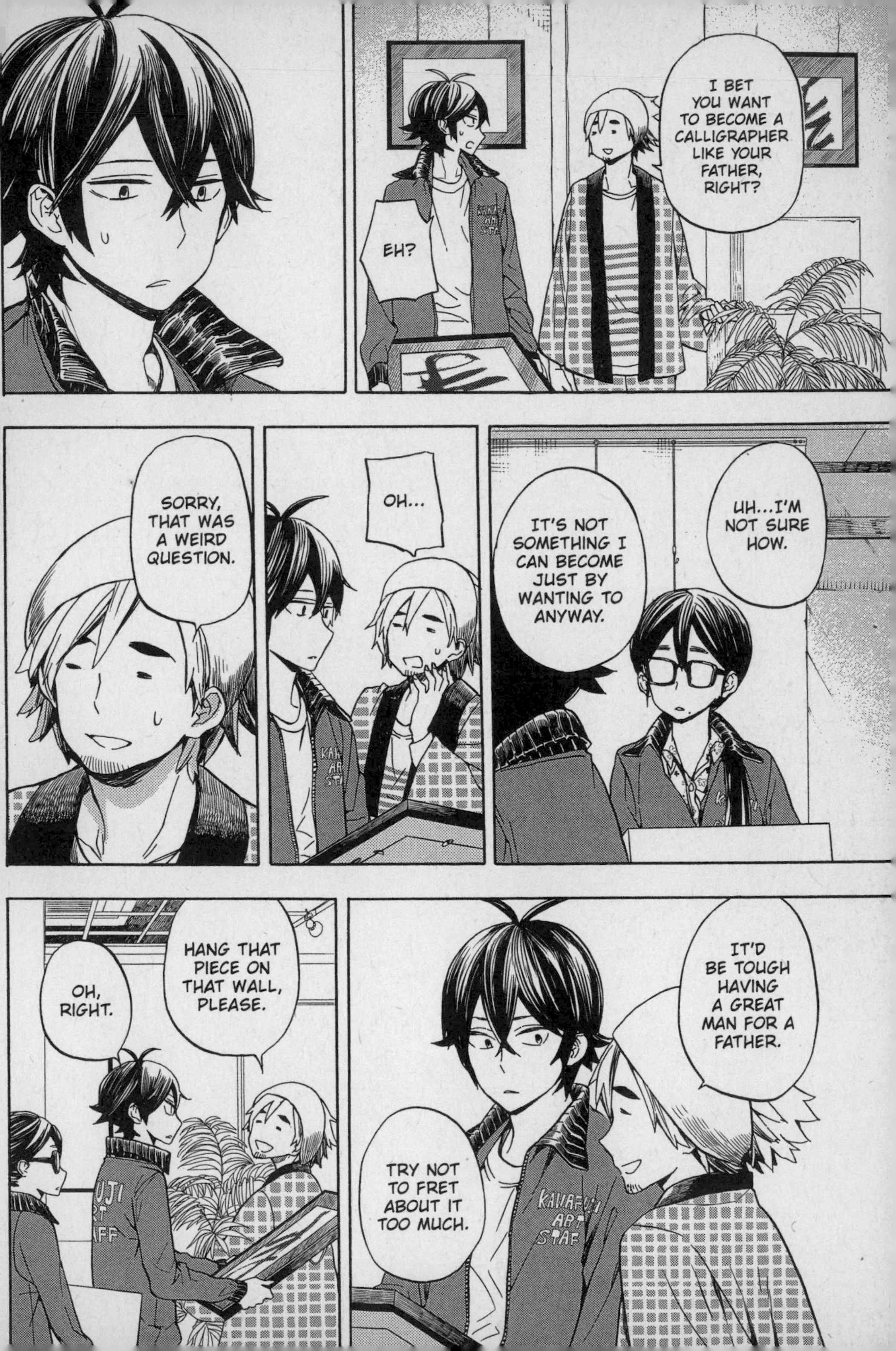
I BET YOU WANT TO BECOME A CALLIGRAPHER LIKE YOUR FATHER, RIGHT?
EH?
UH...I'M NOT SURE HOW.
IT'S NOT SOMETHING I CAN BECOME JUST BY WANTING TO ANYWAY.
OH...
SORRY, THAT WAS A WEIRD QUESTION.
IT'D BE TOUGH HAVING A GREAT MAN FOR A FATHER.
TRY NOT TO FRET ABOUT IT TOO MUCH.
HANG THAT PIECE ON THAT WALL, PLEASE.
OH, RIGHT.

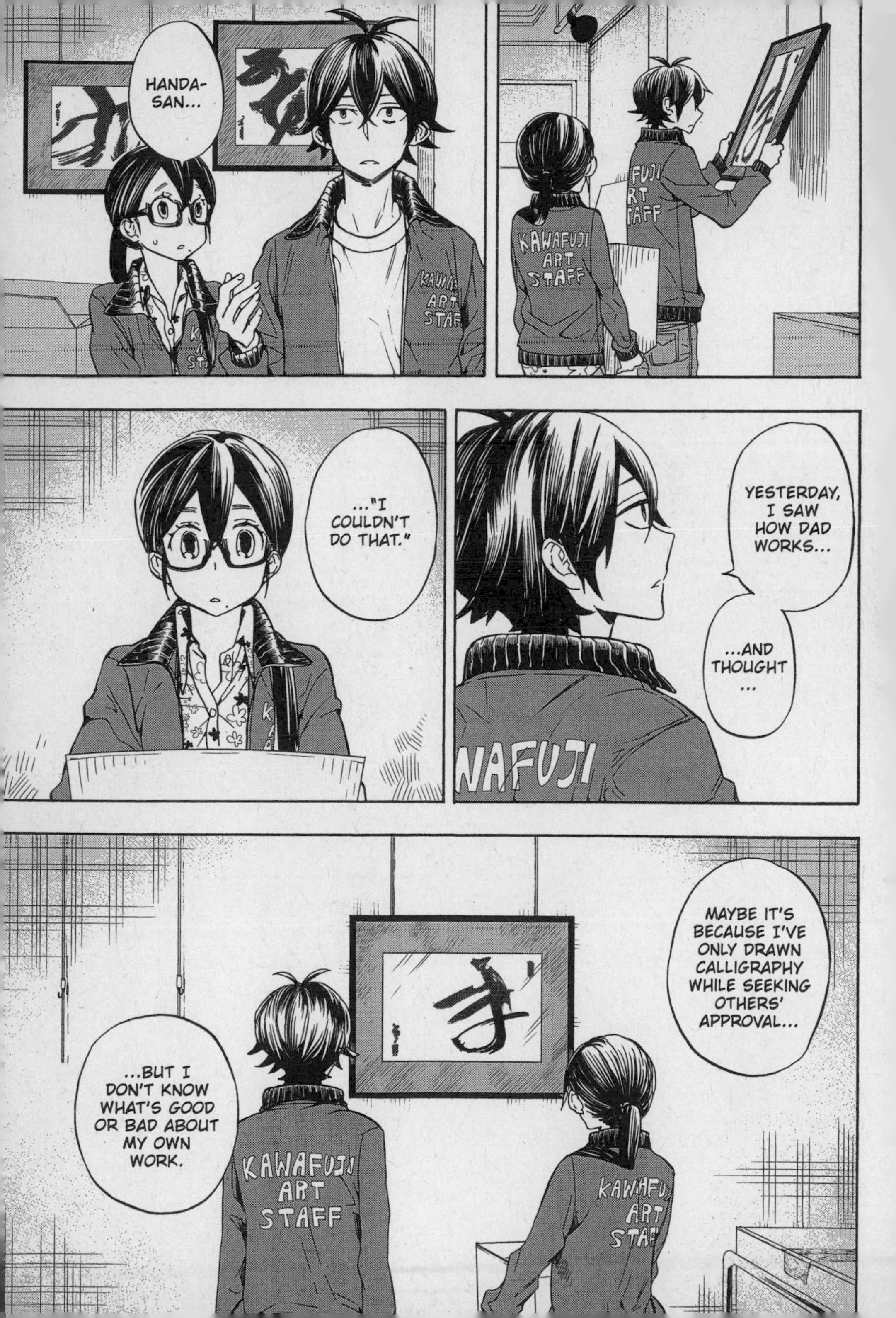
HANDA-SAN...
YESTERDAY, I SAW HOW DAD WORKS...
...AND THOUGHT...
..."I COULDN'T DO THAT."
MAYBE IT'S BECAUSE I'VE ONLY DRAWN CALLIGRAPHY WHILE SEEKING OTHERS' APPROVAL...
...BUT I DON'T KNOW WHAT'S GOOD OR BAD ABOUT MY OWN WORK.

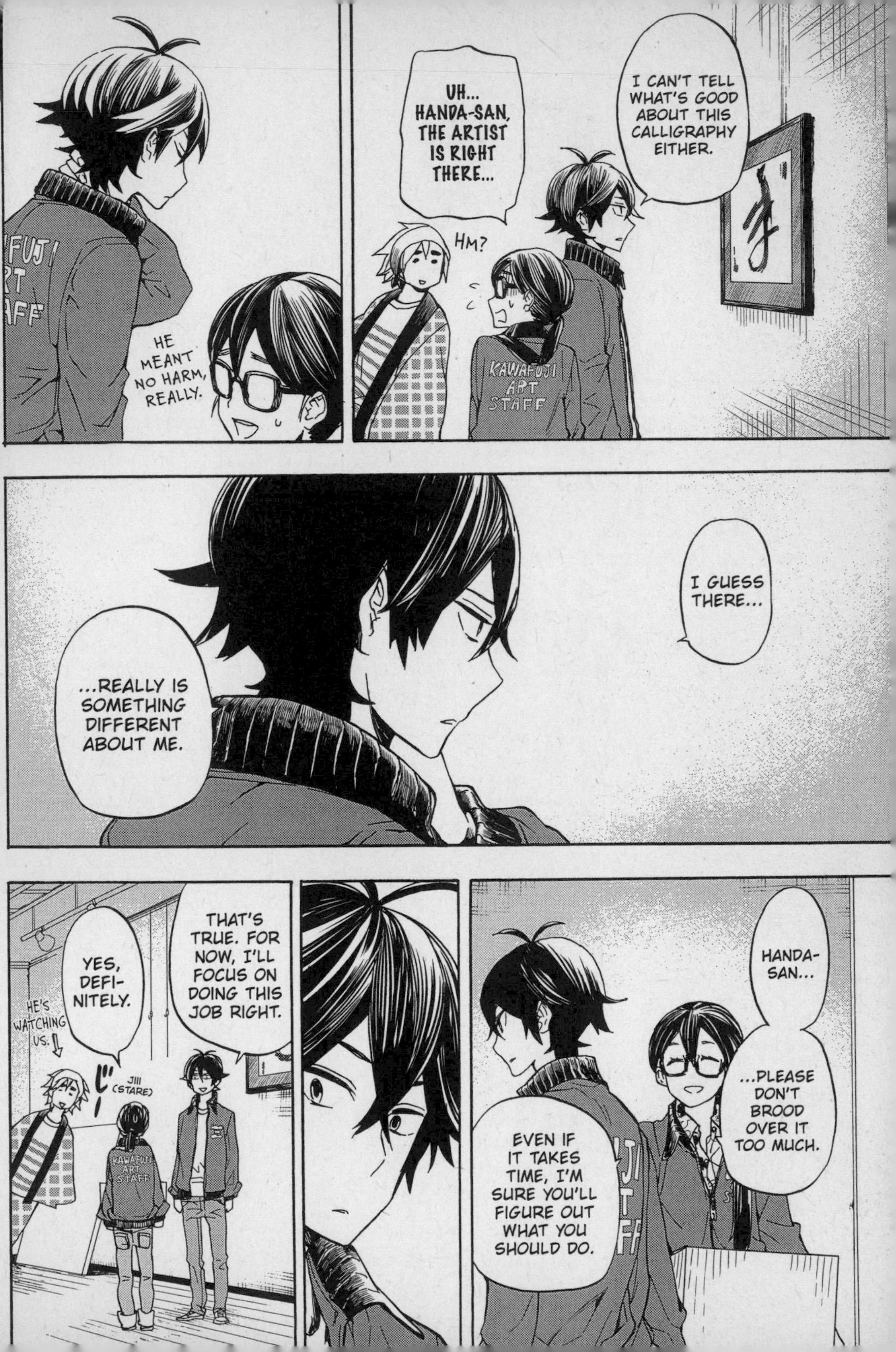

I CAN'T TELL WHAT'S GOOD ABOUT THIS CALLIGRAPHY EITHER.
UH... HANDA-SAN, THE ARTIST IS RIGHT THERE...
HM?
KAWAFUJI ART STAFF
HE MEANT NO HARM, REALLY.
I GUESS THERE...
...REALLY IS SOMETHING DIFFERENT ABOUT ME.
HANDA-SAN...
...PLEASE DON'T BROOD OVER IT TOO MUCH.
EVEN IF IT TAKES TIME, I'M SURE YOU'LL FIGURE OUT WHAT YOU SHOULD DO.
THAT'S TRUE. FOR NOW, I'LL FOCUS ON DOING THIS JOB RIGHT.
YES, DEFI-NITELY.
HE'S WATCHING US.
JIII (STARE)
KAWAFUJI ART STAFF

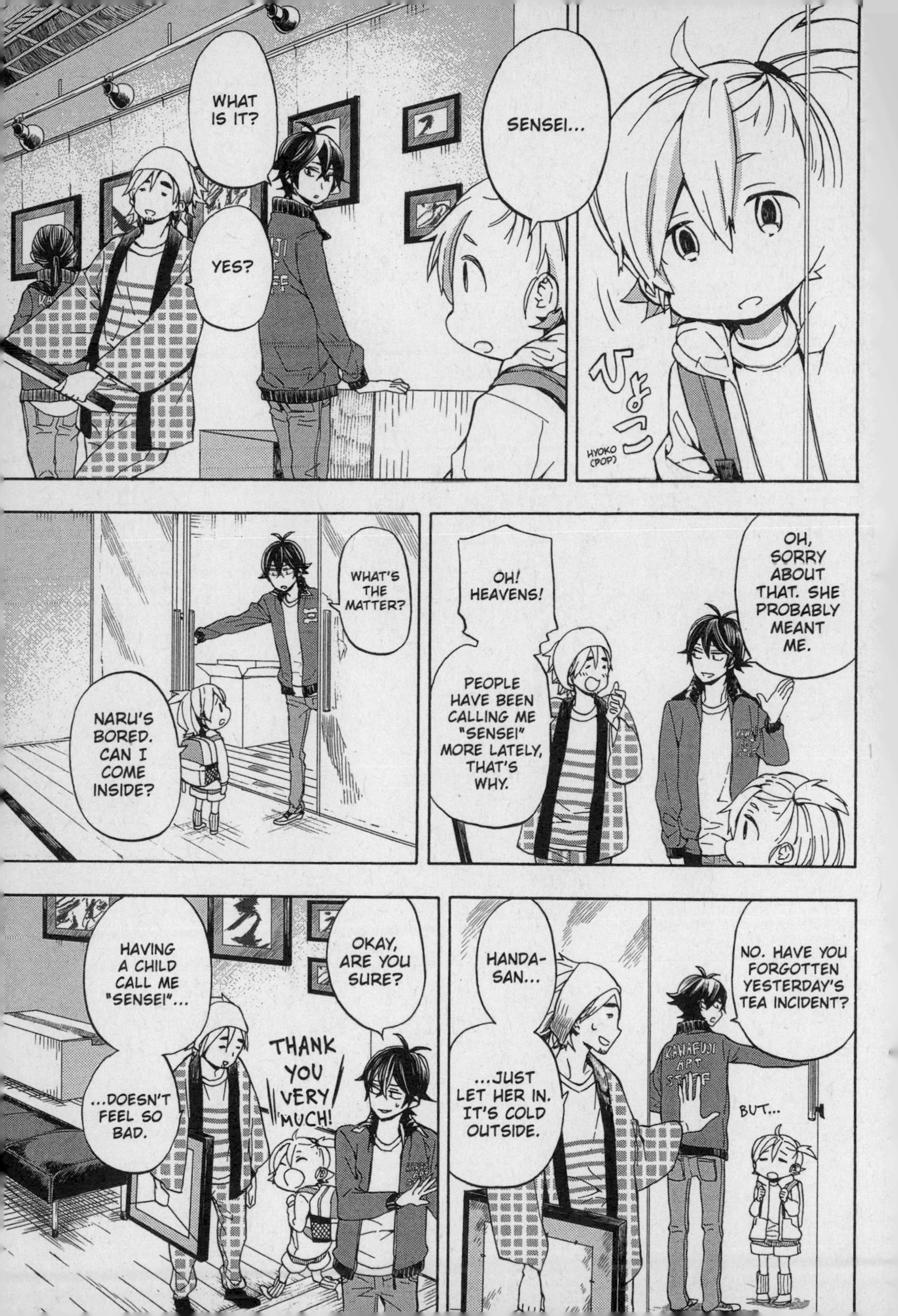
ひょこ
HYOKO (POP)
SENSEI...
WHAT IS IT?
YES?
OH, SORRY ABOUT THAT. SHE PROBABLY MEANT ME.
OH! HEAVENS!
PEOPLE HAVE BEEN CALLING ME "SENSEI" MORE LATELY, THAT'S WHY.
WHAT'S THE MATTER?
NARU'S BORED. CAN I COME INSIDE?
NO. HAVE YOU FORGOTTEN YESTERDAY'S TEA INCIDENT?
HANDA-SAN...
...JUST LET HER IN. IT'S COLD OUTSIDE.
BUT...
OKAY, ARE YOU SURE?
HAVING A CHILD CALL ME "SENSEI"...
THANK YOU VERY MUCH!
...DOESN'T FEEL SO BAD.

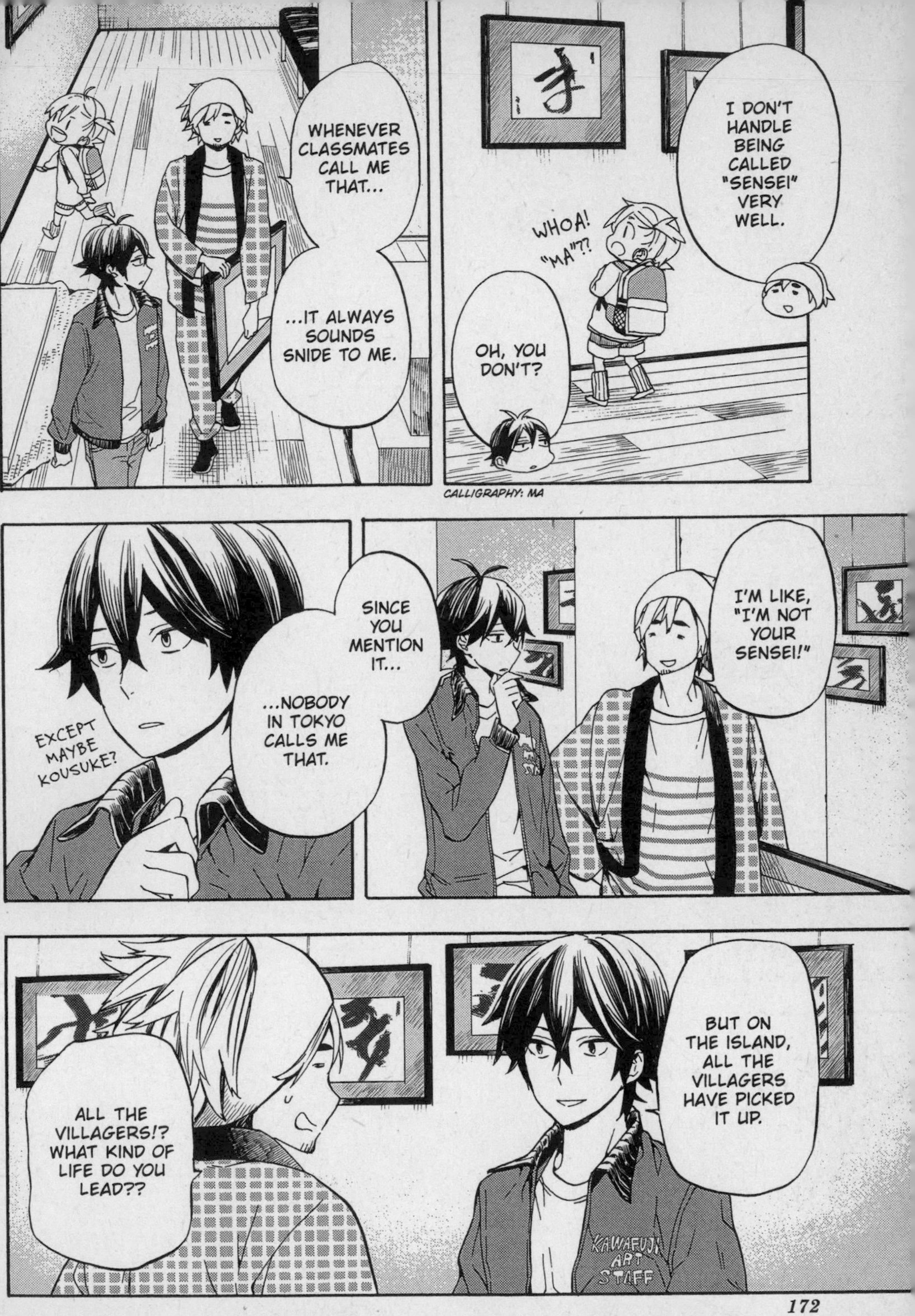
I DON'T HANDLE BEING CALLED "SENSEI" VERY WELL.
WHOA! "MA"??
OH, YOU DON'T?
CALLIGRAPHY: MA
WHENEVER CLASSMATES CALL ME THAT...
...IT ALWAYS SOUNDS SNIDE TO ME.
I'M LIKE, "I'M NOT YOUR SENSEI!"
SINCE YOU MENTION IT...
...NOBODY IN TOKYO CALLS ME THAT.
EXCEPT MAYBE KOUSUKE?
BUT ON THE ISLAND, ALL THE VILLAGERS HAVE PICKED IT UP.
KAWAFUJI ART STAFF
ALL THE VILLAGERS!? WHAT KIND OF LIFE DO YOU LEAD??

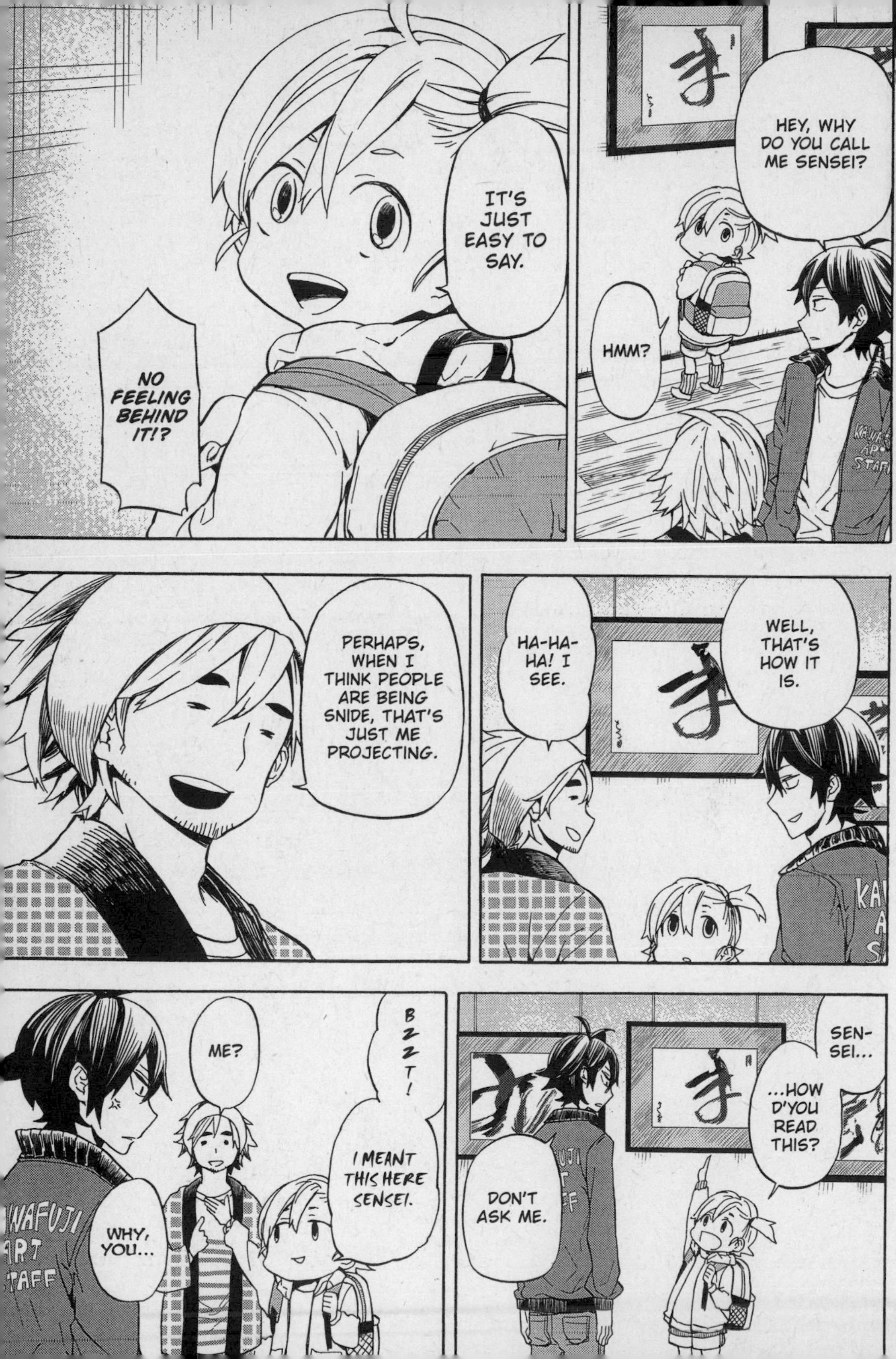
HEY, WHY DO YOU CALL ME SENSEI?
HMM?
IT'S JUST EASY TO SAY.
NO FEELING BEHIND IT!?
WELL, THAT'S HOW IT IS.
HA-HA-HA! I SEE.
PERHAPS, WHEN I THINK PEOPLE ARE BEING SNIDE, THAT'S JUST ME PROJECTING.
SENSEI...
...HOW D'YOU READ THIS?
DON'T ASK ME.
ME?
BZZT!
I MEANT THIS HERE SENSEI.
WHY, YOU...

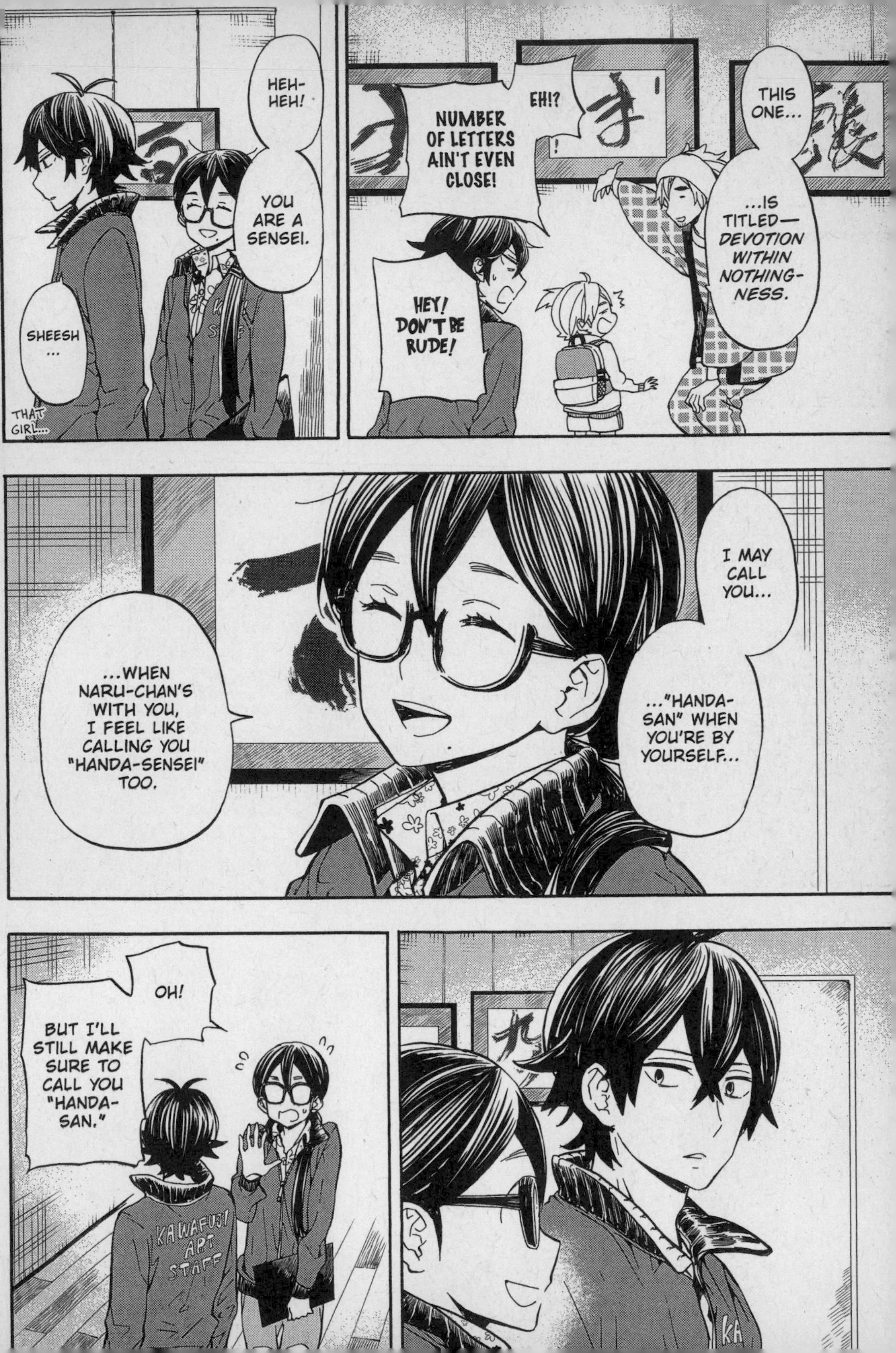
THIS ONE...
...IS TITLED—DEVOTION WITHIN NOTHINGNESS.
EH!?
NUMBER OF LETTERS AIN'T EVEN CLOSE!
HEY! DON'T BE RUDE!
HEH-HEH!
YOU ARE A SENSEI.
SHEESH...
THAT GIRL...
I MAY CALL YOU...
..."HANDA-SAN" WHEN YOU'RE BY YOURSELF...
...WHEN NARU-CHAN'S WITH YOU, I FEEL LIKE CALLING YOU "HANDA-SENSEI" TOO.
OH!
BUT I'LL STILL MAKE SURE TO CALL YOU "HANDA-SAN."
KAWAFUJI APT STAFF

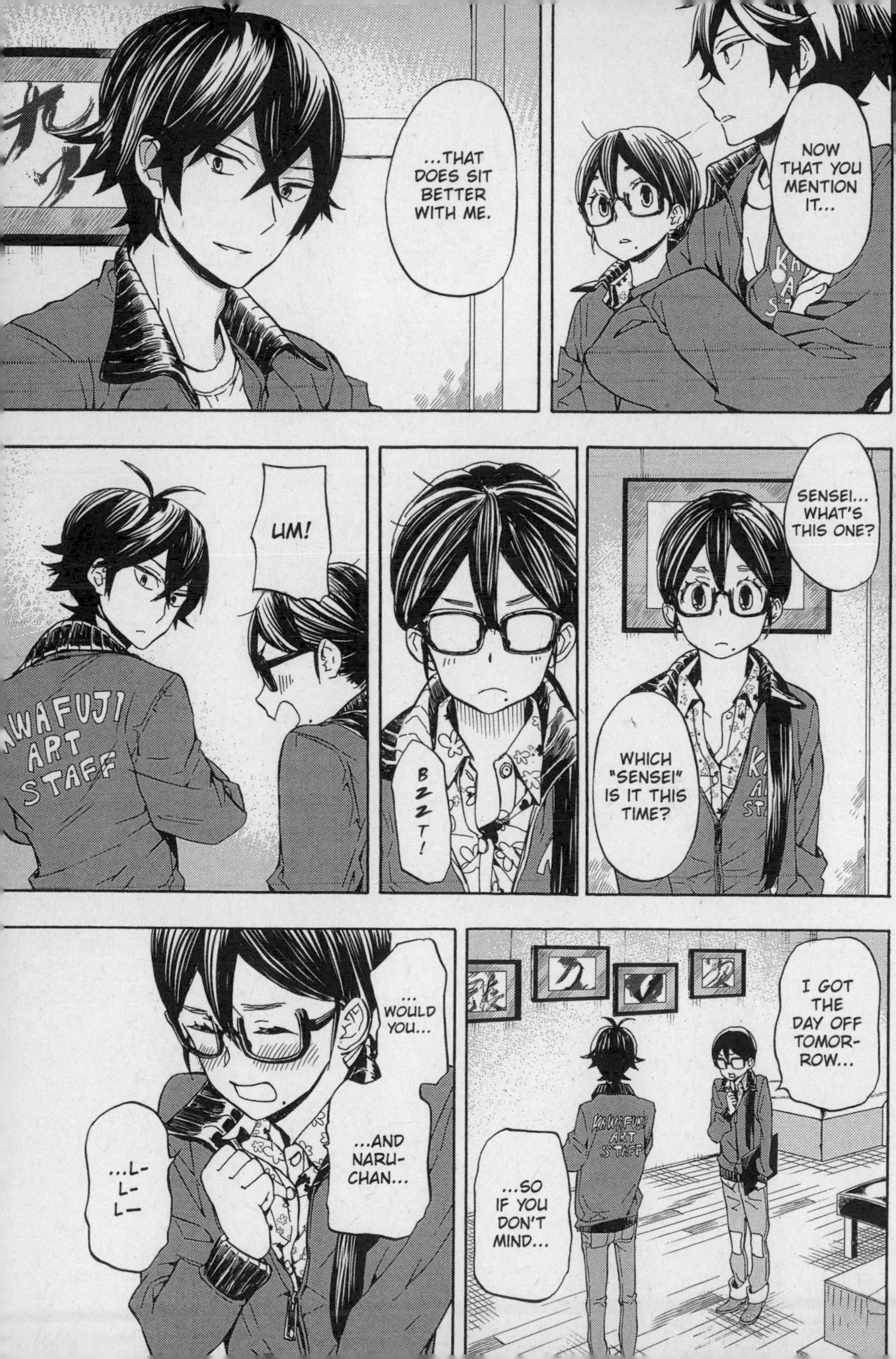
NOW THAT YOU MENTION IT...
...THAT DOES SIT BETTER WITH ME.
SENSEI... WHAT'S THIS ONE?
WHICH "SENSEI" IS IT THIS TIME?
BZZT!
UM!
KAWAFUJI ART STAFF
I GOT THE DAY OFF TOMOR-ROW...
...SO IF YOU DON'T MIND...
...WOULD YOU...
...AND NARU-CHAN...
...L- L- L—

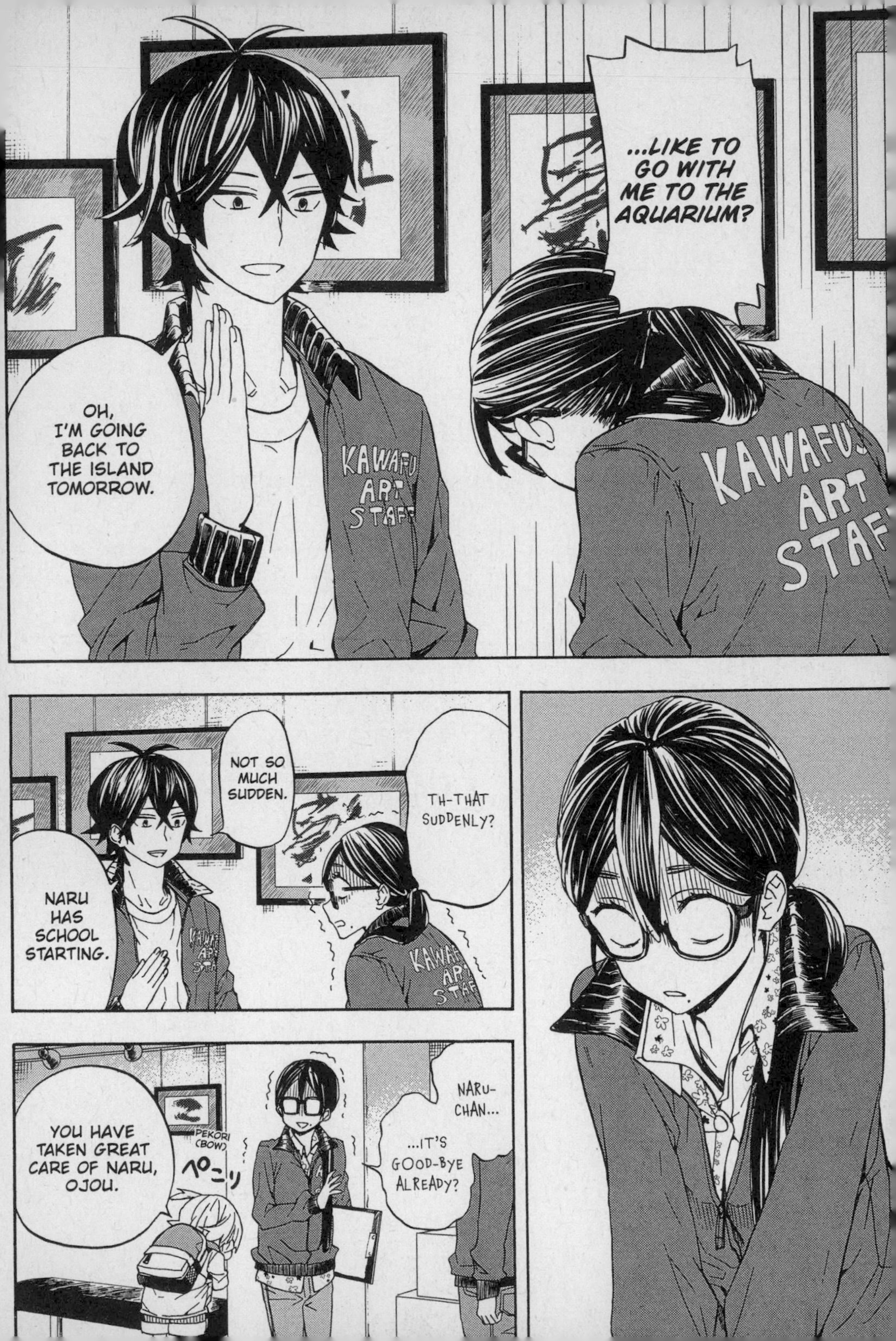
...LIKE TO GO WITH ME TO THE AQUARIUM?
OH, I'M GOING BACK TO THE ISLAND TOMORROW.
TH-THAT SUDDENLY?
NOT SO MUCH SUDDEN.
NARU HAS SCHOOL STARTING.
NARU-CHAN...
...IT'S GOOD-BYE ALREADY?
PEKORI (BOW)
ぺこり
YOU HAVE TAKEN GREAT CARE OF NARU, OJOU.

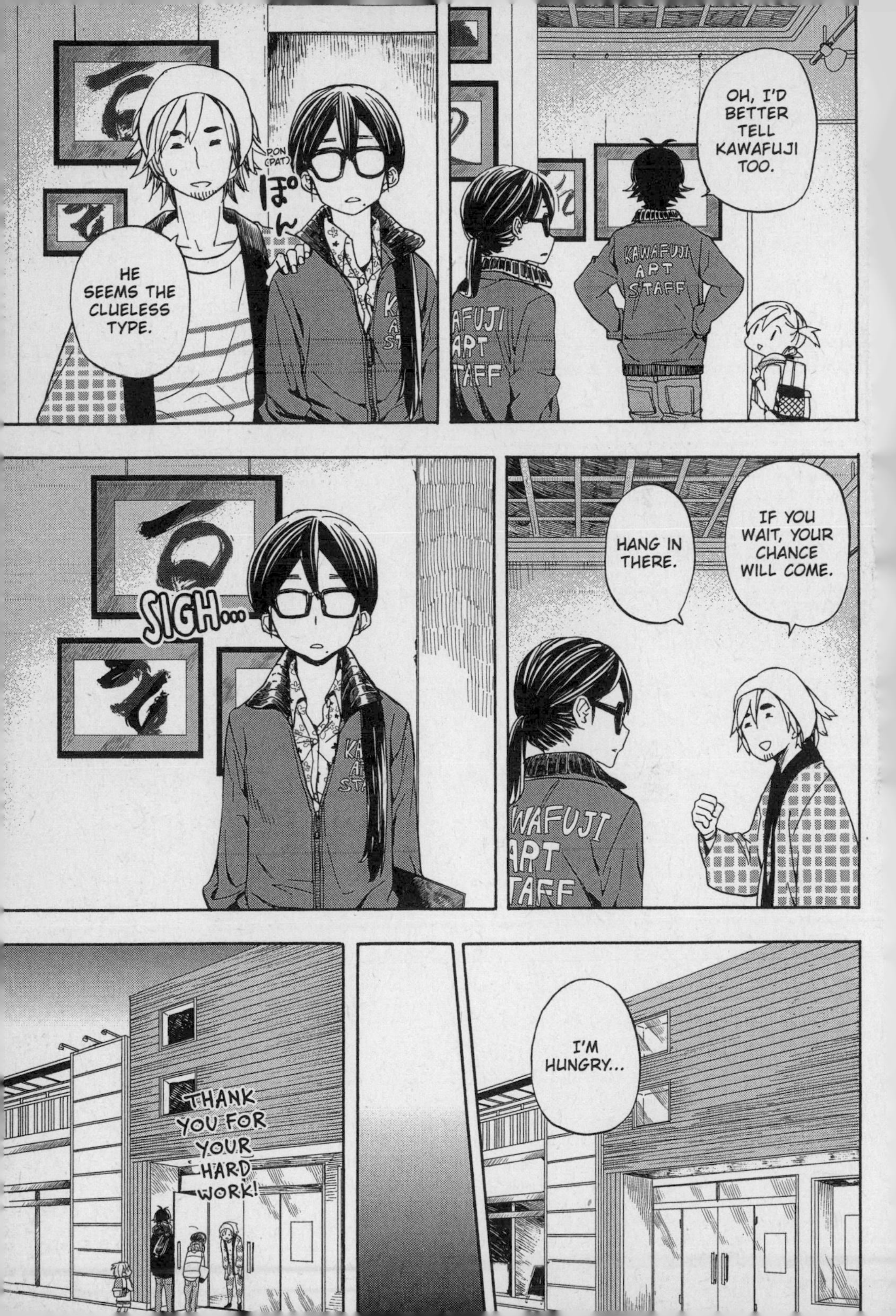
OH, I'D BETTER TELL KAWAFUJI TOO.
KAWAFUJI ART STAFF
PON (PAT)
ぽん
HE SEEMS THE CLUELESS TYPE.
IF YOU WAIT, YOUR CHANCE WILL COME.
HANG IN THERE.
SIGH...
I'M HUNGRY...
THANK YOU FOR YOUR HARD WORK!

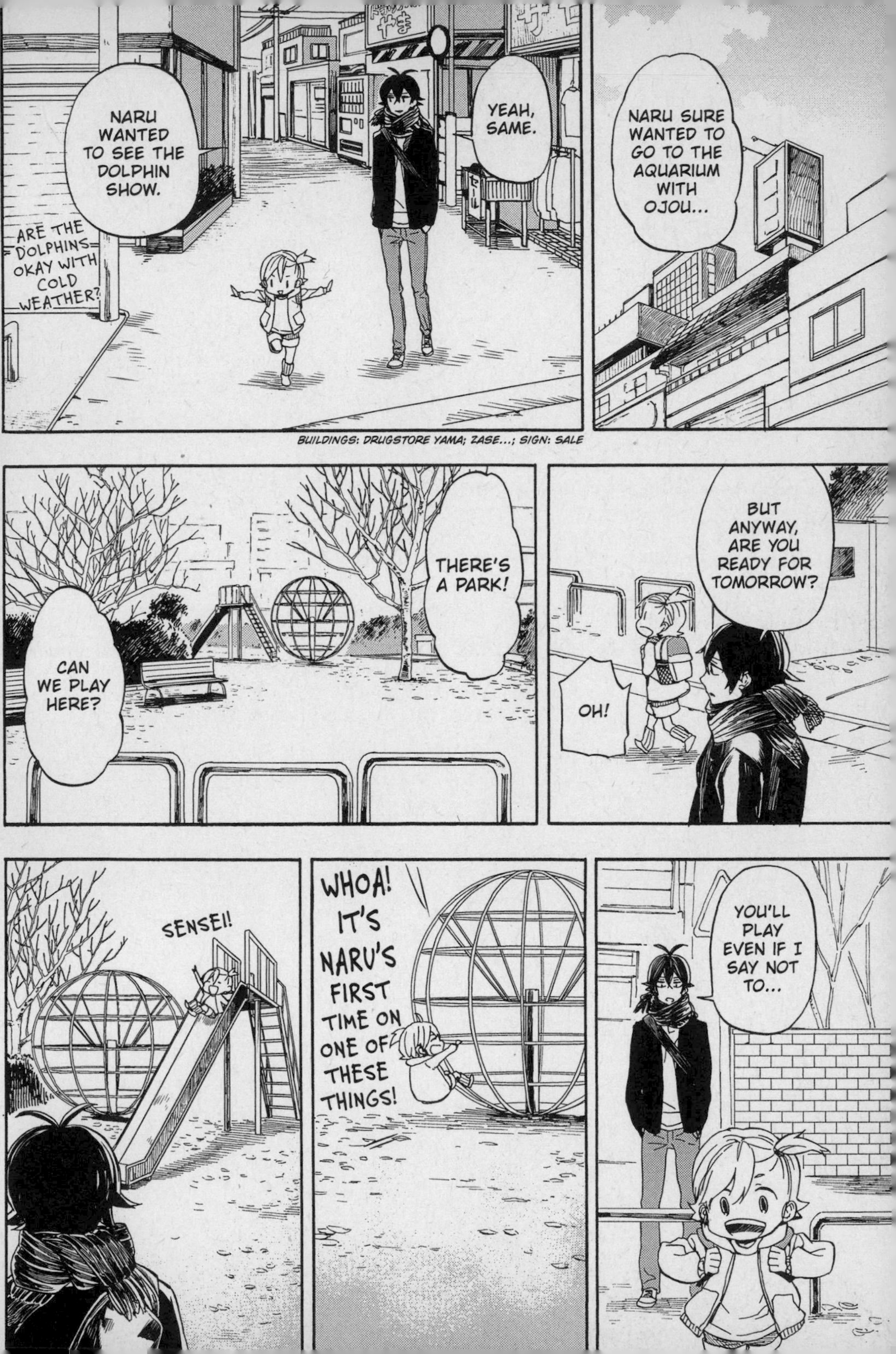
NARU SURE WANTED TO GO TO THE AQUARIUM WITH OJOU...
YEAH, SAME.
NARU WANTED TO SEE THE DOLPHIN SHOW.
ARE THE DOLPHINS OKAY WITH COLD WEATHER?
BUILDINGS: DRUGSTORE YAMA; ZASE...; SIGN: SALE
BUT ANYWAY, ARE YOU READY FOR TOMORROW?
OH!
THERE'S A PARK!
CAN WE PLAY HERE?
YOU'LL PLAY EVEN IF I SAY NOT TO...
WHOA! IT'S NARU'S FIRST TIME ON ONE OF THESE THINGS!
SENSEI!

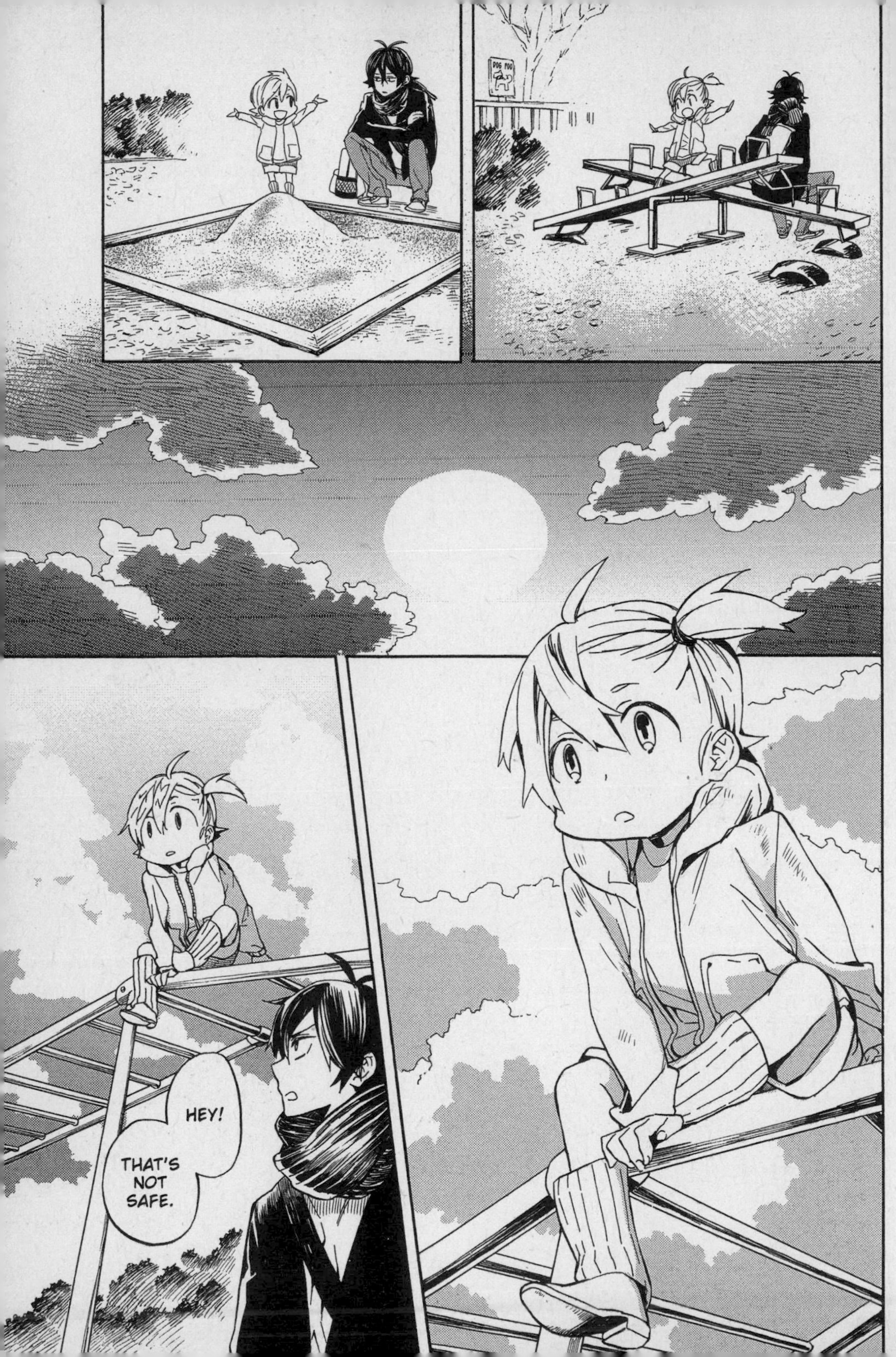
HEY!
THAT'S NOT SAFE.

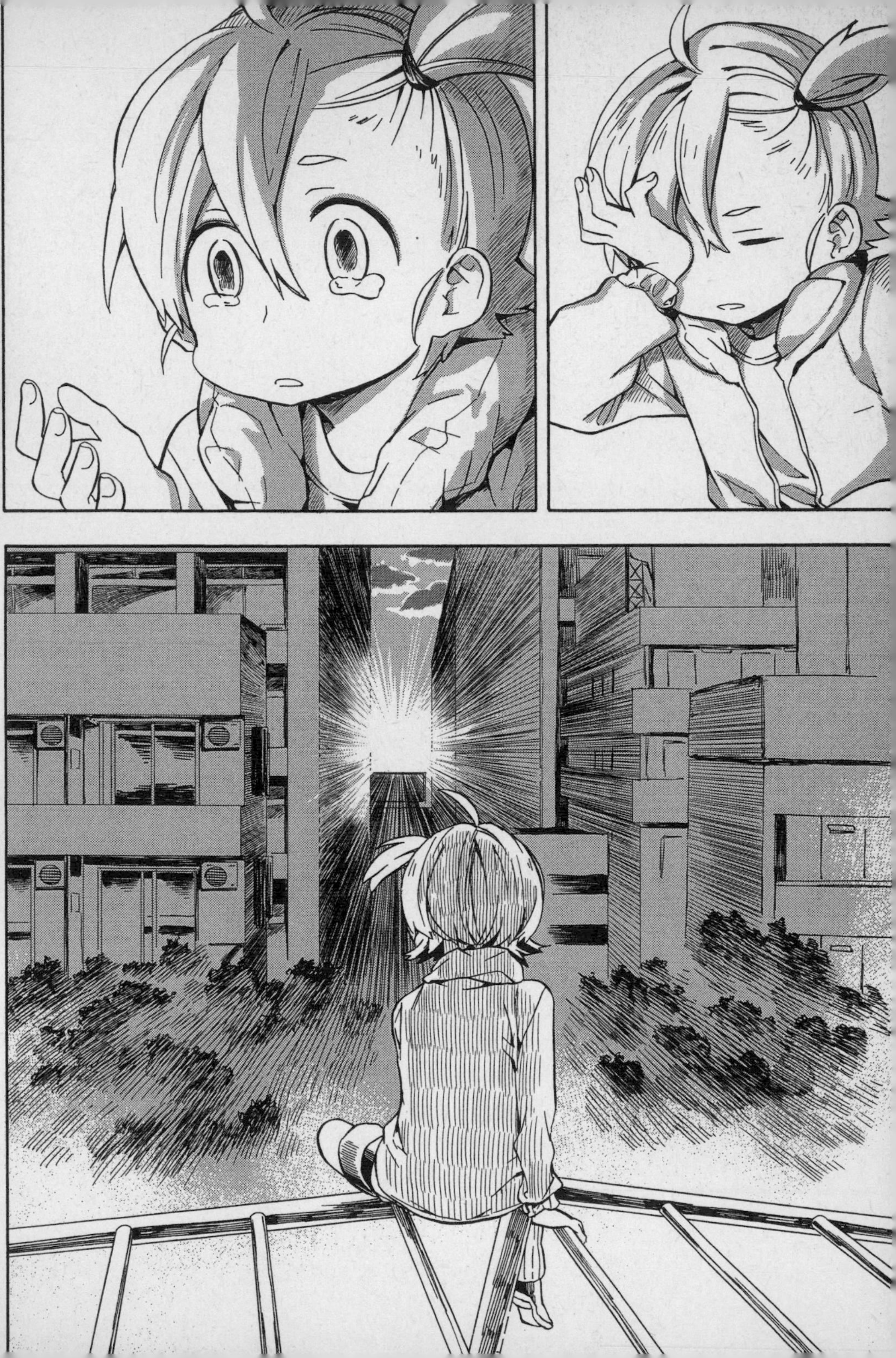

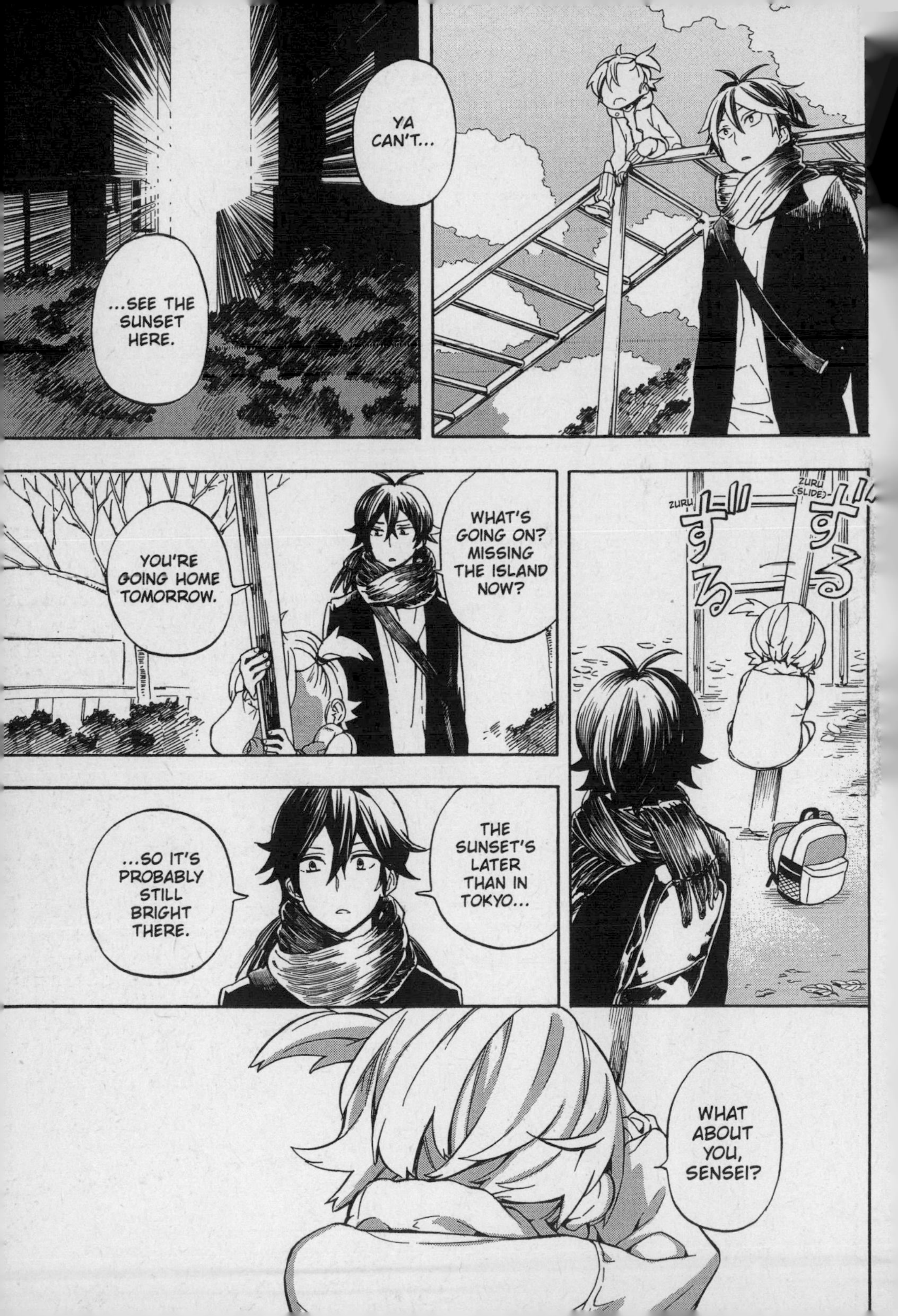
YA CAN'T...
...SEE THE SUNSET HERE.
ずる ZURU (SLIDE)
ずる ZURU
WHAT'S GOING ON? MISSING THE ISLAND NOW?
YOU'RE GOING HOME TOMORROW.
THE SUNSET'S LATER THAN IN TOKYO...
...SO IT'S PROBABLY STILL BRIGHT THERE.
WHAT ABOUT YOU, SENSEI?

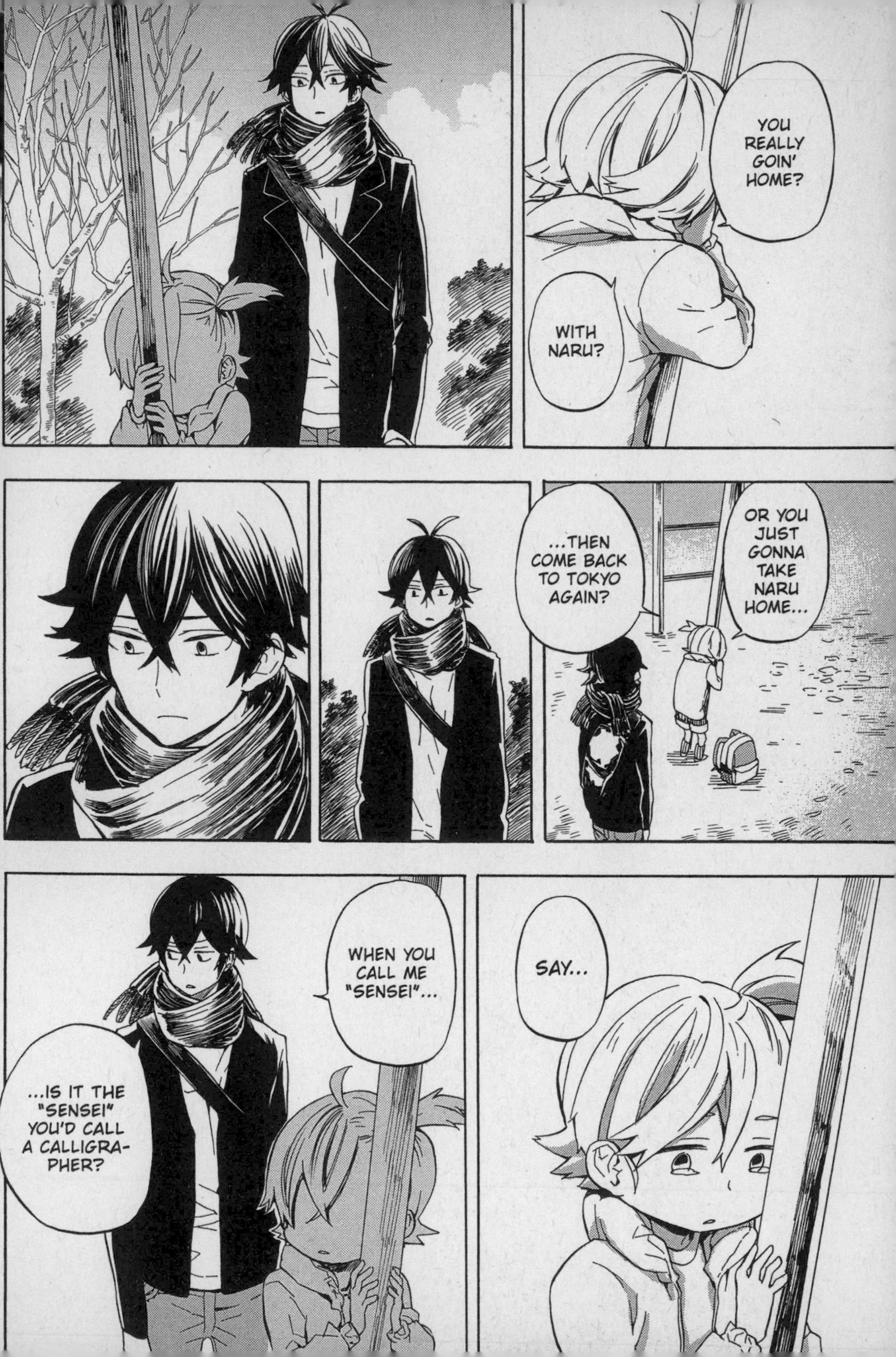
YOU REALLY GOIN' HOME?
WITH NARU?
OR YOU JUST GONNA TAKE NARU HOME...
...THEN COME BACK TO TOKYO AGAIN?
SAY...
WHEN YOU CALL ME "SENSEI"...
...IS IT THE "SENSEI" YOU'D CALL A CALLIGRA-PHER?

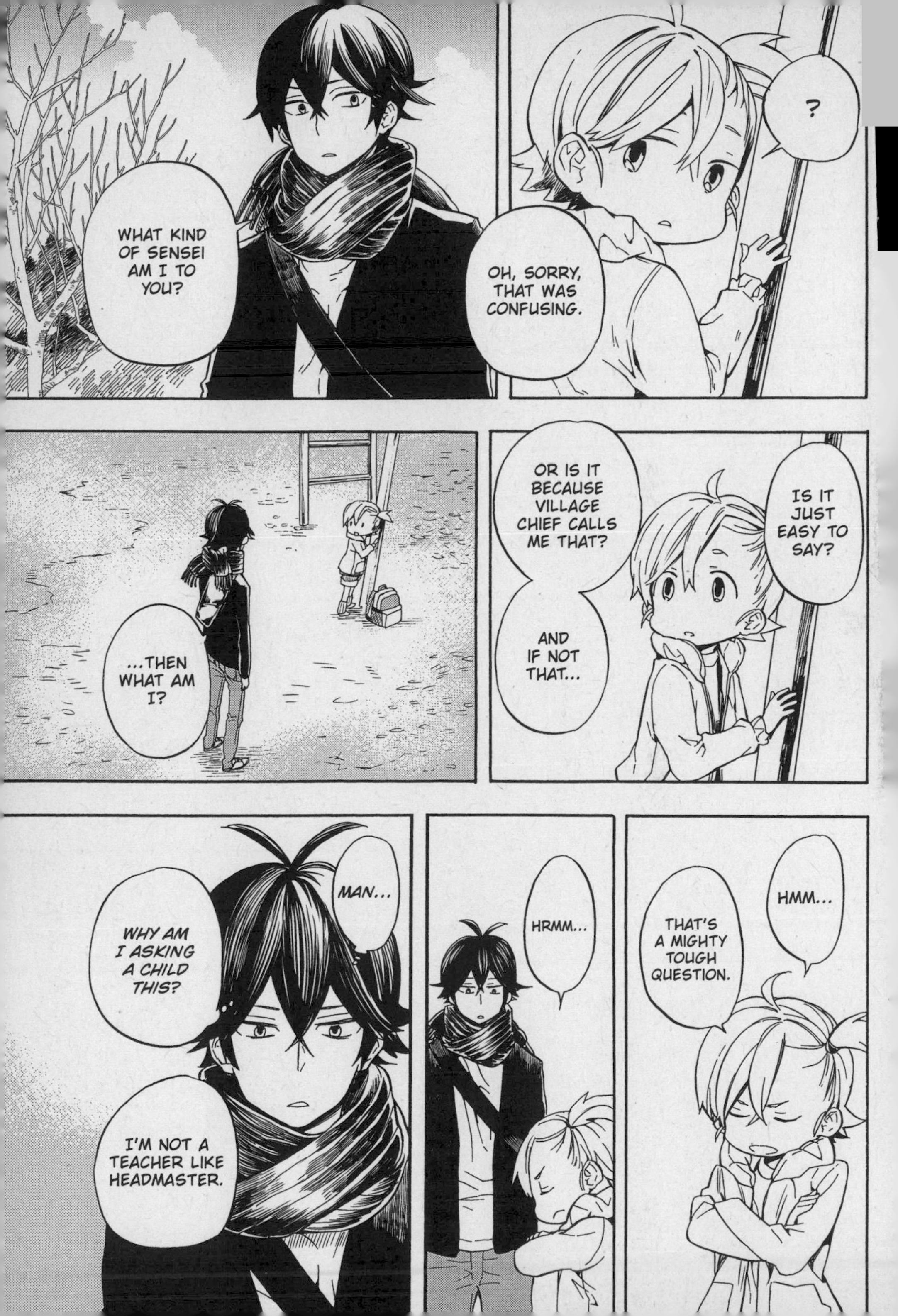
?
OH, SORRY, THAT WAS CONFUSING.
WHAT KIND OF SENSEI AM I TO YOU?
IS IT JUST EASY TO SAY?
OR IS IT BECAUSE VILLAGE CHIEF CALLS ME THAT?
AND IF NOT THAT...
...THEN WHAT AM I?
HMM...
THAT'S A MIGHTY TOUGH QUESTION.
HRMM...
MAN...
WHY AM I ASKING A CHILD THIS?
I'M NOT A TEACHER LIKE HEADMASTER.

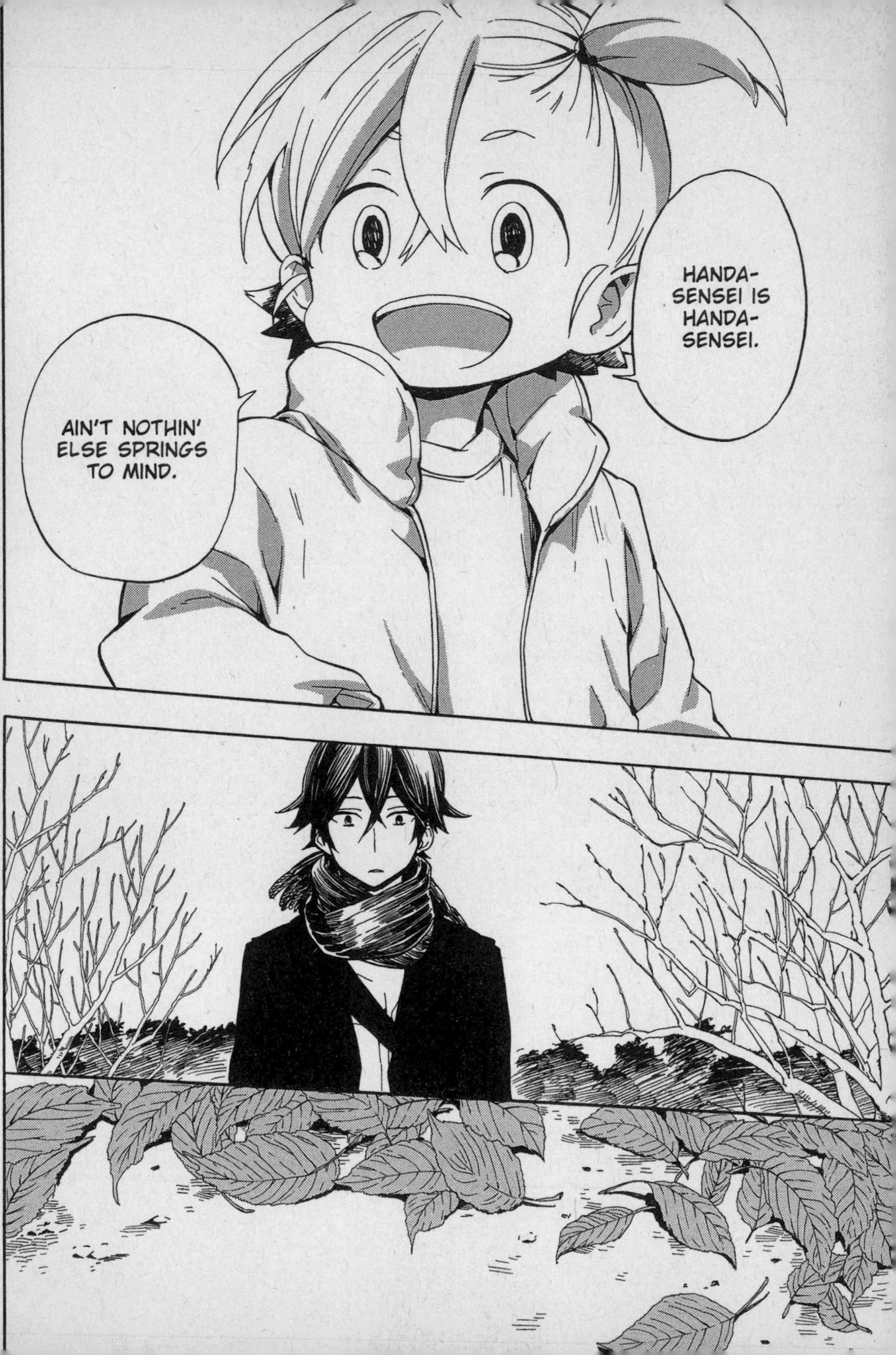
HANDA-SENSEI IS HANDA-SENSEI.
AIN'T NOTHIN' ELSE SPRINGS TO MIND.

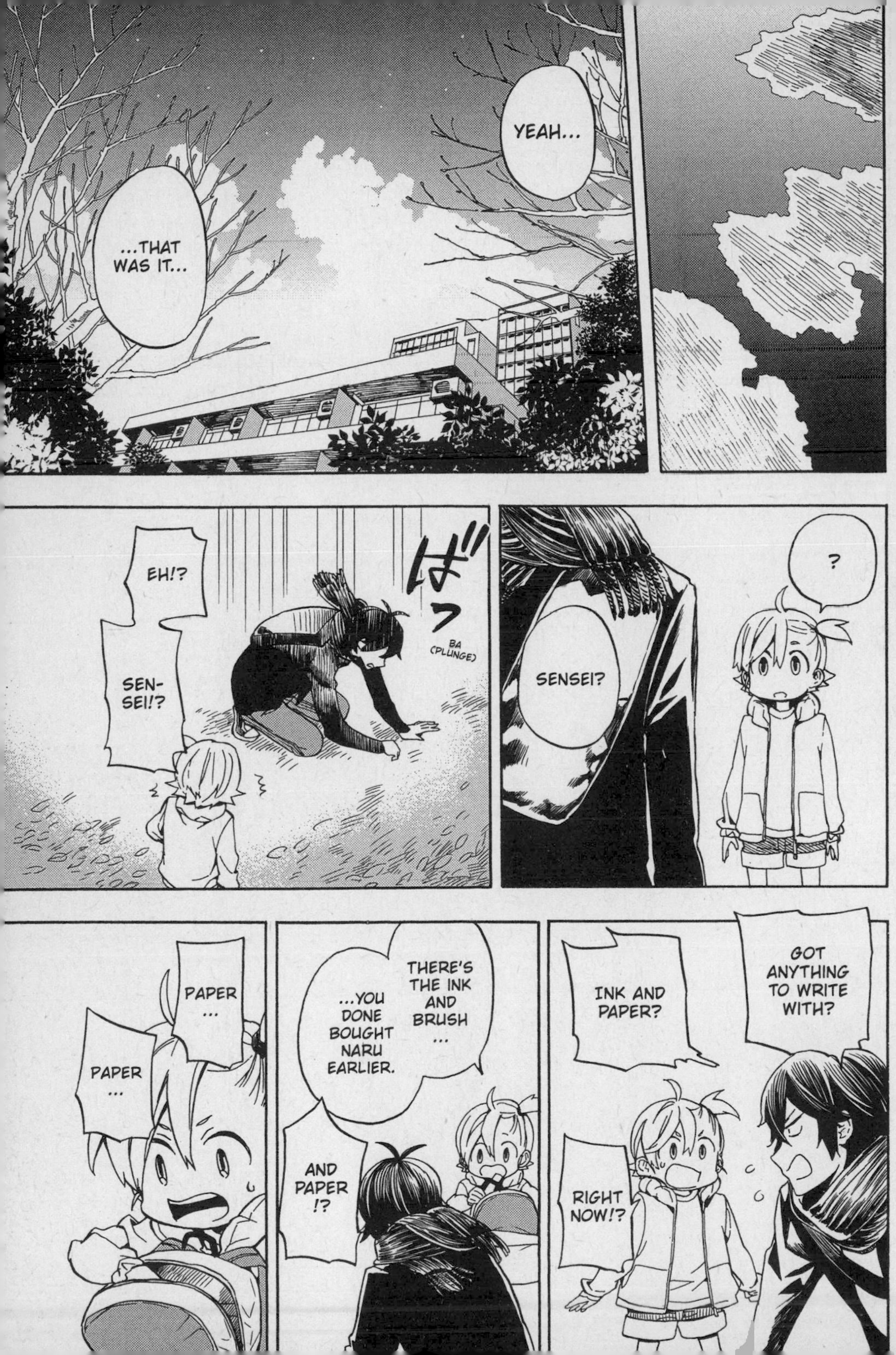
YEAH...
...THAT WAS IT...
?
SENSEI?
ばっ
BA (PLUNGE)
EH!?
SEN-SEI!?
GOT ANYTHING TO WRITE WITH?
INK AND PAPER?
RIGHT NOW!?
THERE'S THE INK AND BRUSH ...
...YOU DONE BOUGHT NARU EARLIER.
AND PAPER !?
PAPER ...
PAPER ...

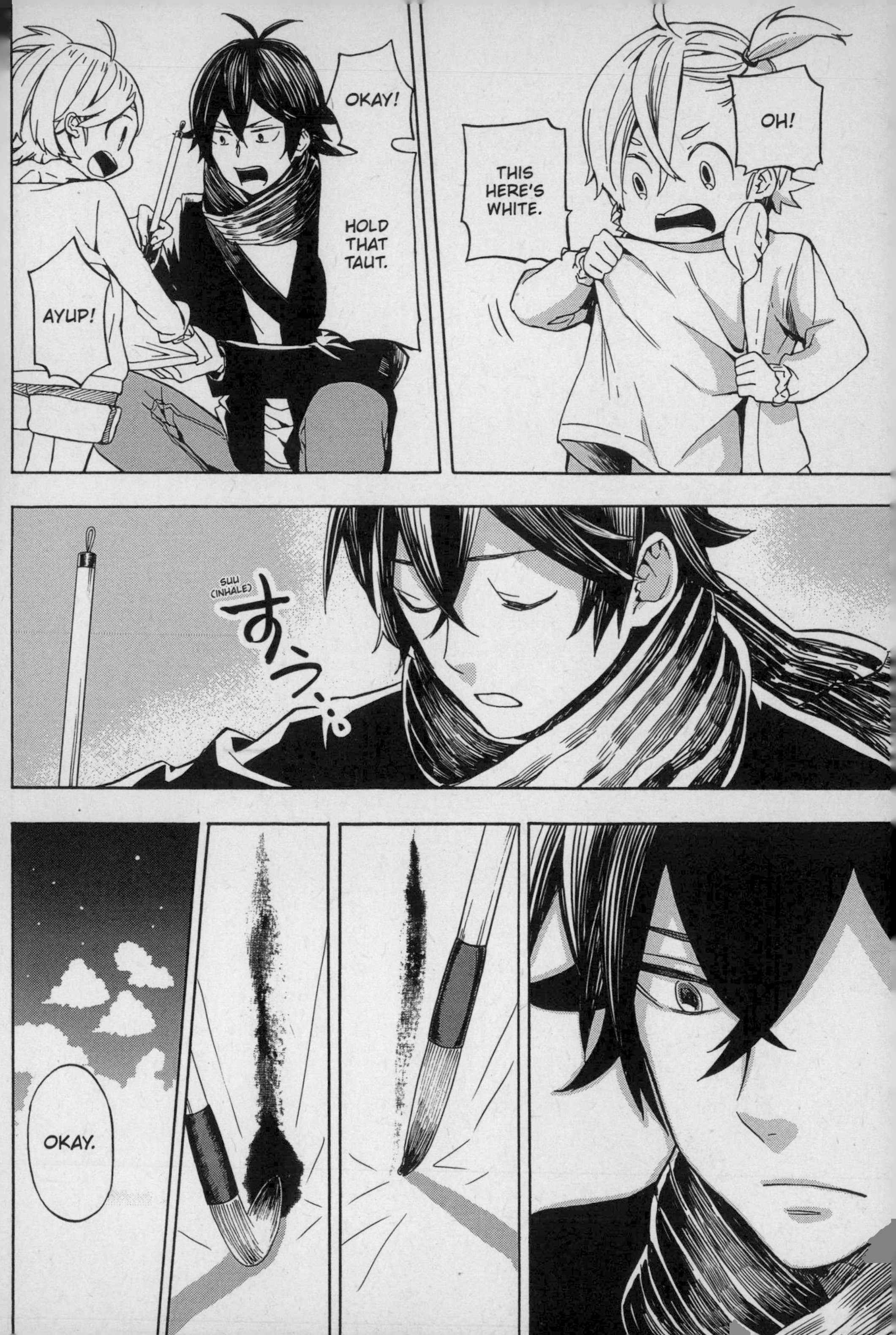
OH!
THIS HERE'S WHITE.
OKAY!
HOLD THAT TAUT.
AYUP!
SUU (INHALE)
すぅ…
OKAY.

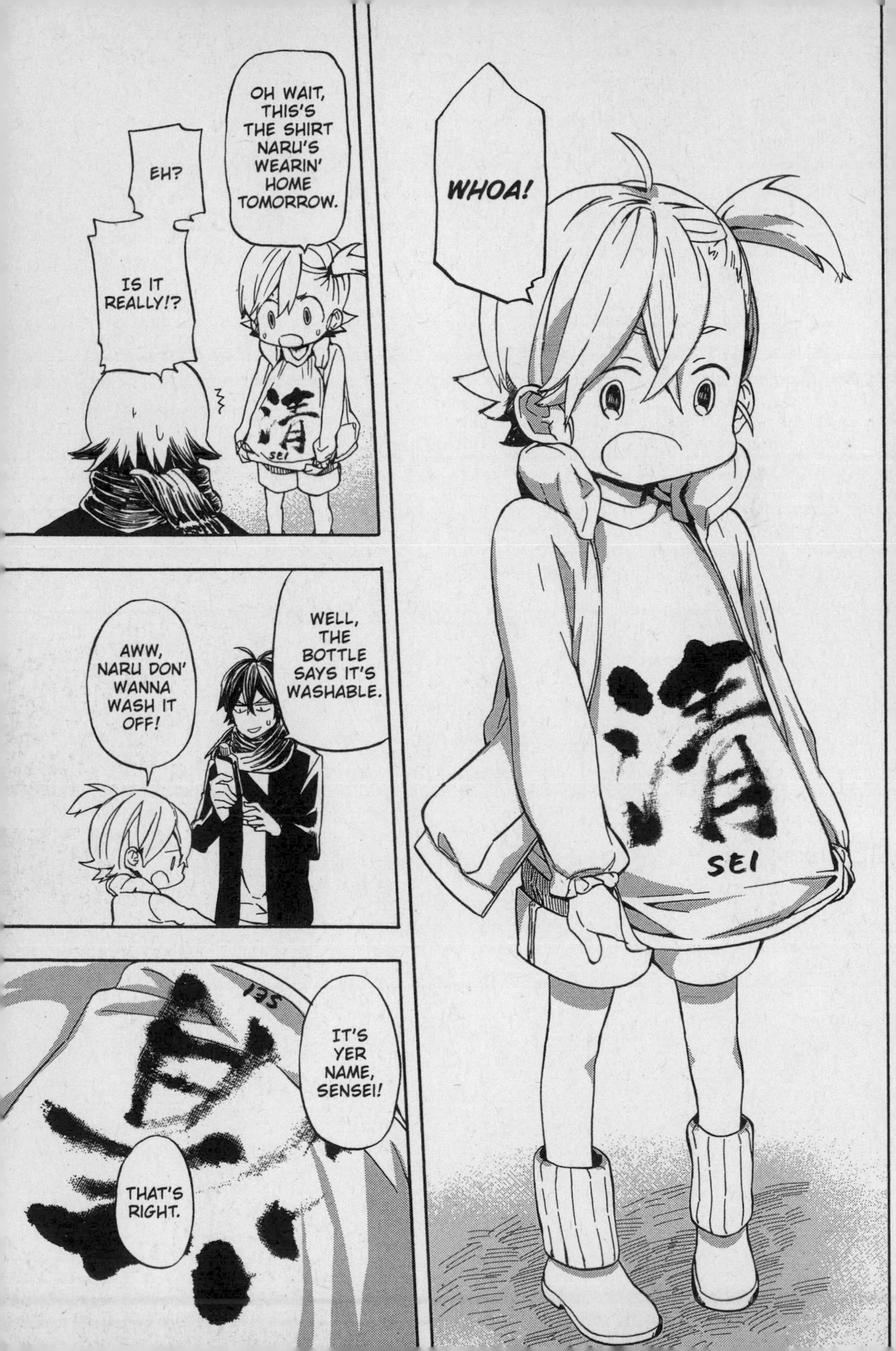
WHOA!
SEI
OH WAIT, THIS'S THE SHIRT NARU'S WEARIN' HOME TOMORROW.
EH?
IS IT REALLY!?
SEI
WELL, THE BOTTLE SAYS IT'S WASHABLE.
AWW, NARU DON' WANNA WASH IT OFF!
SEI
IT'S YER NAME, SENSEI!
THAT'S RIGHT.

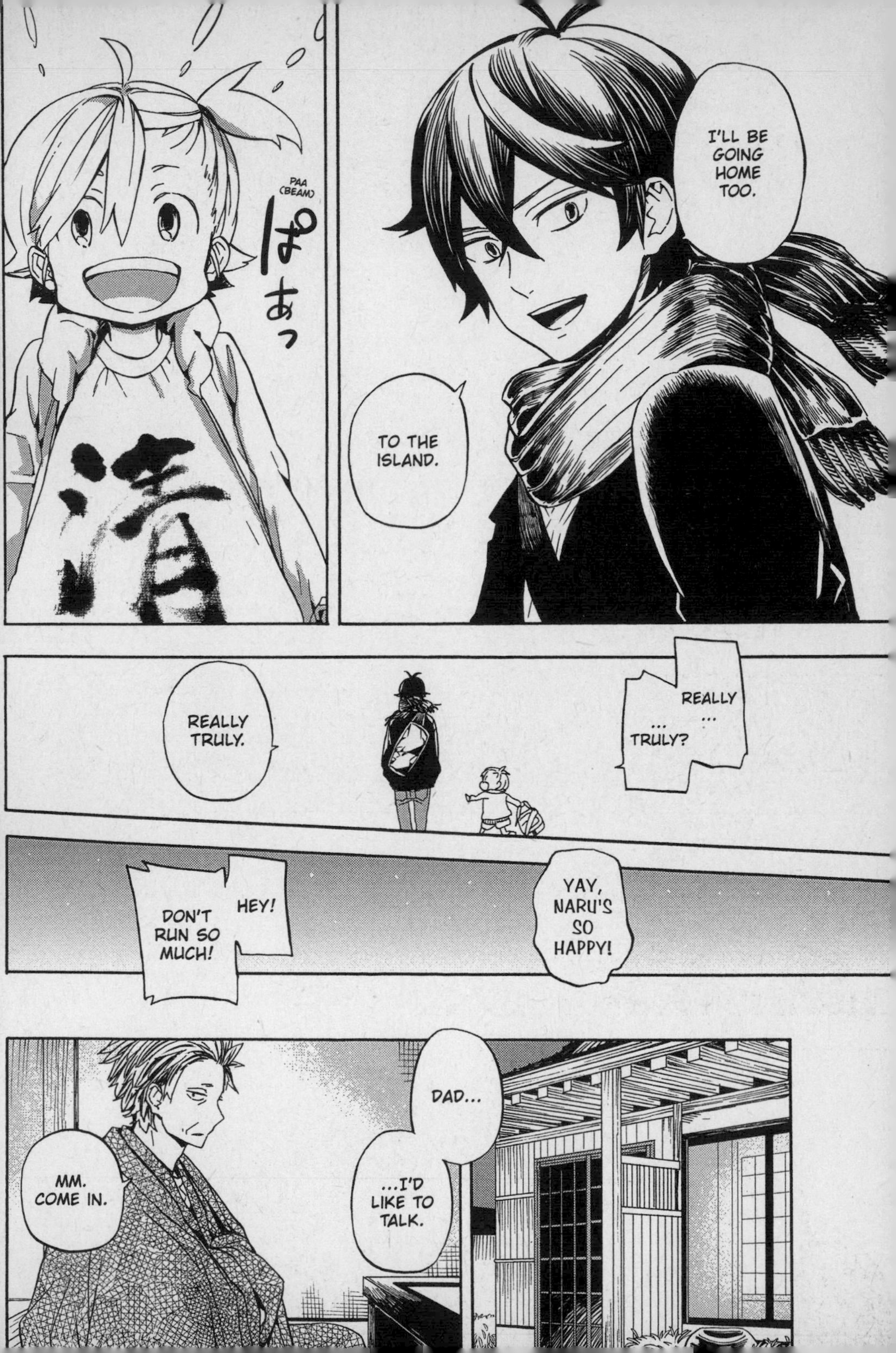
I'LL BE GOING HOME TOO.
TO THE ISLAND.
ぱあっ
PAA (BEAM)
REALLY ... ... TRULY?
REALLY TRULY.
YAY, NARU'S SO HAPPY!
HEY! DON'T RUN SO MUCH!
DAD...
...I'D LIKE TO TALK.
MM. COME IN.

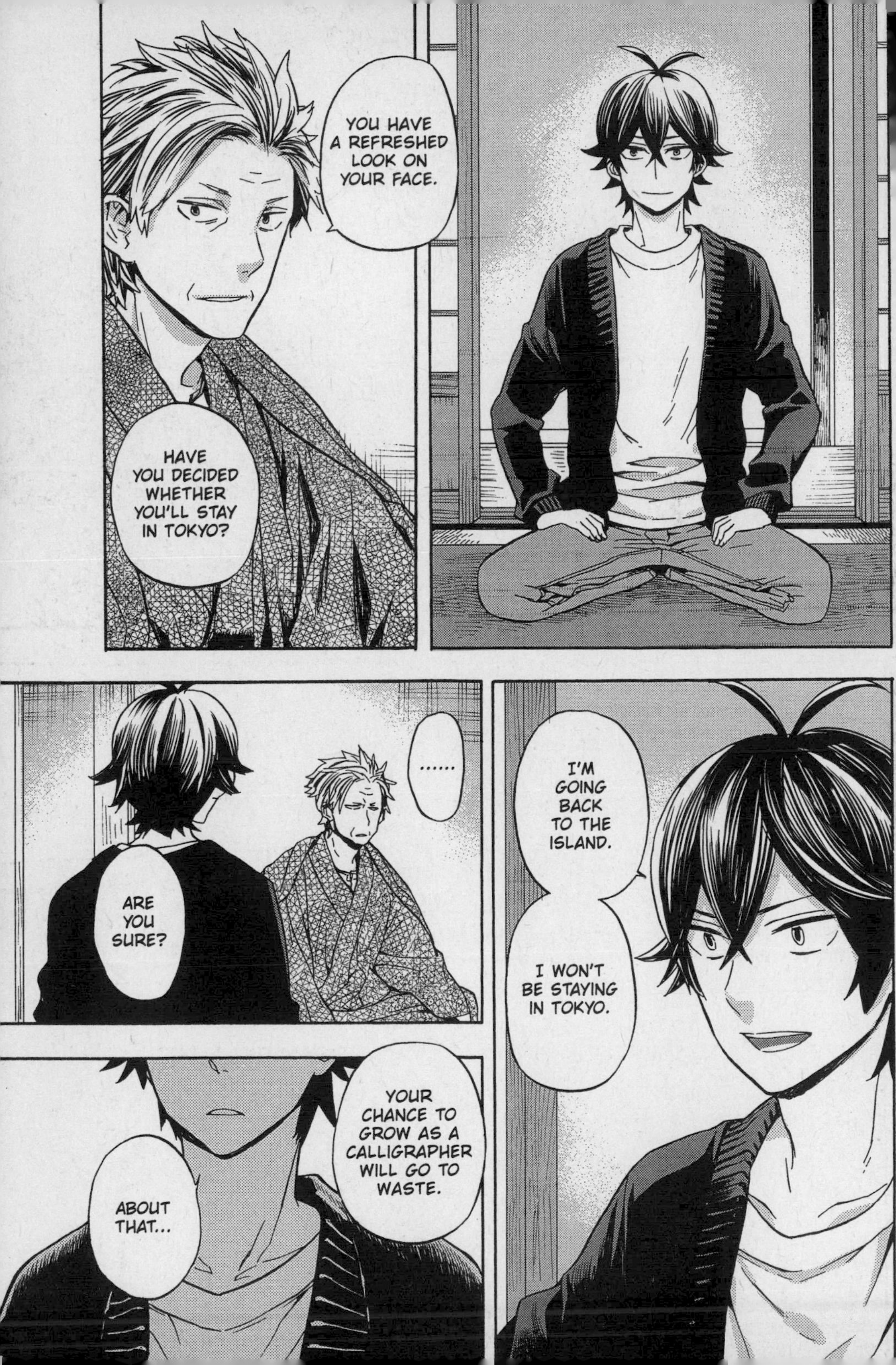
YOU HAVE A REFRESHED LOOK ON YOUR FACE.
HAVE YOU DECIDED WHETHER YOU'LL STAY IN TOKYO?
I'M GOING BACK TO THE ISLAND.
I WON'T BE STAYING IN TOKYO.
......
ARE YOU SURE?
YOUR CHANCE TO GROW AS A CALLIGRAPHER WILL GO TO WASTE.
ABOUT THAT...

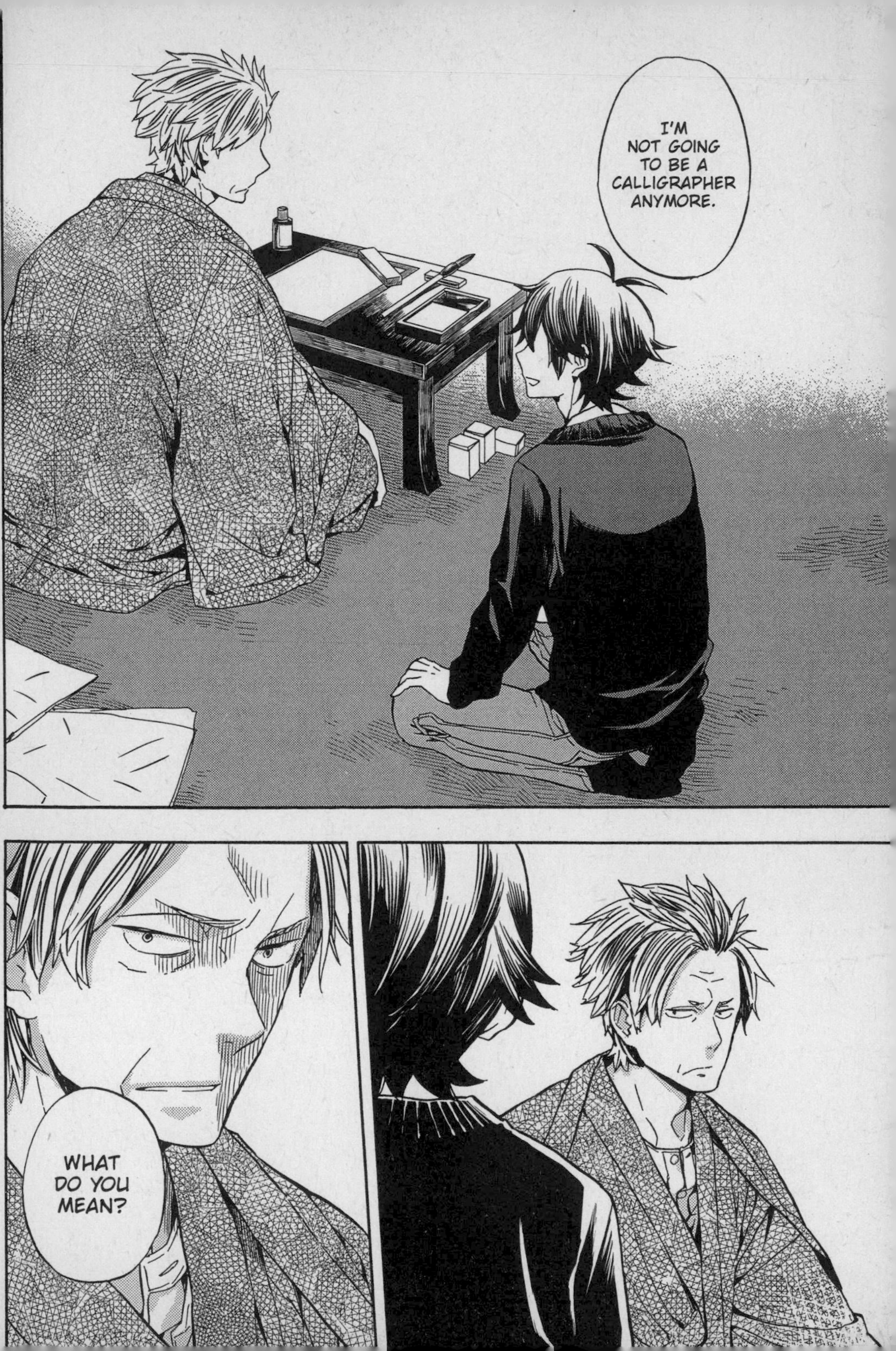
I'M NOT GOING TO BE A CALLIGRAPHER ANYMORE.
WHAT DO YOU MEAN?

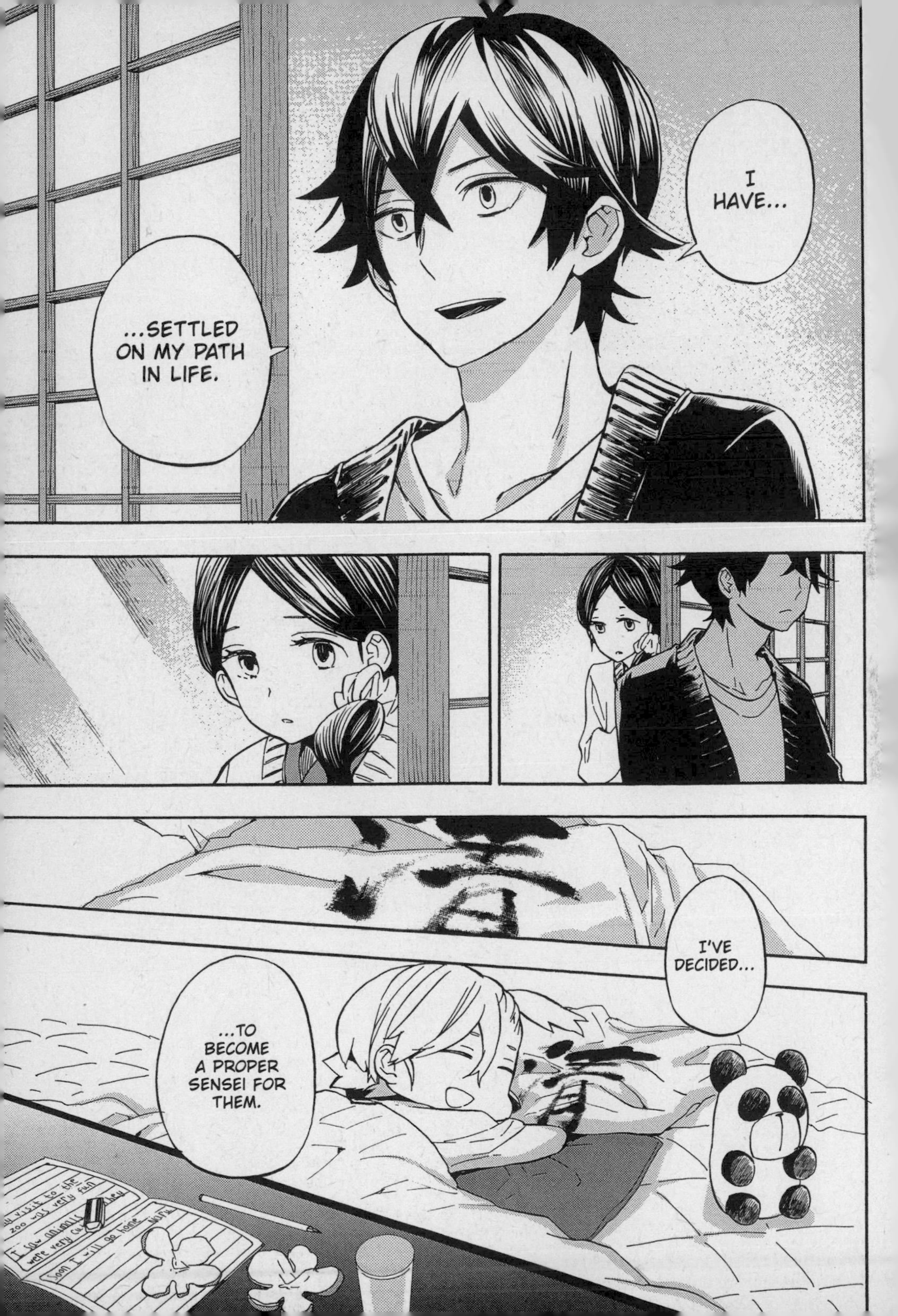
I HAVE...
...SETTLED ON MY PATH IN LIFE.
I'VE DECIDED...
...TO BECOME A PROPER SENSEI FOR THEM.

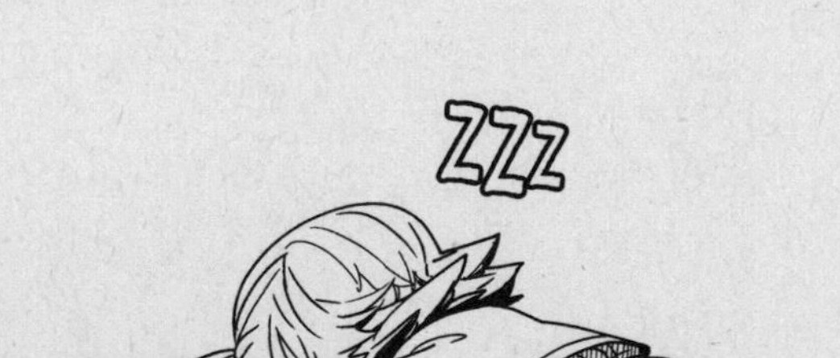
ZZZ

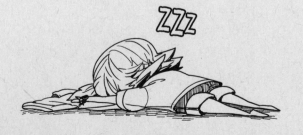

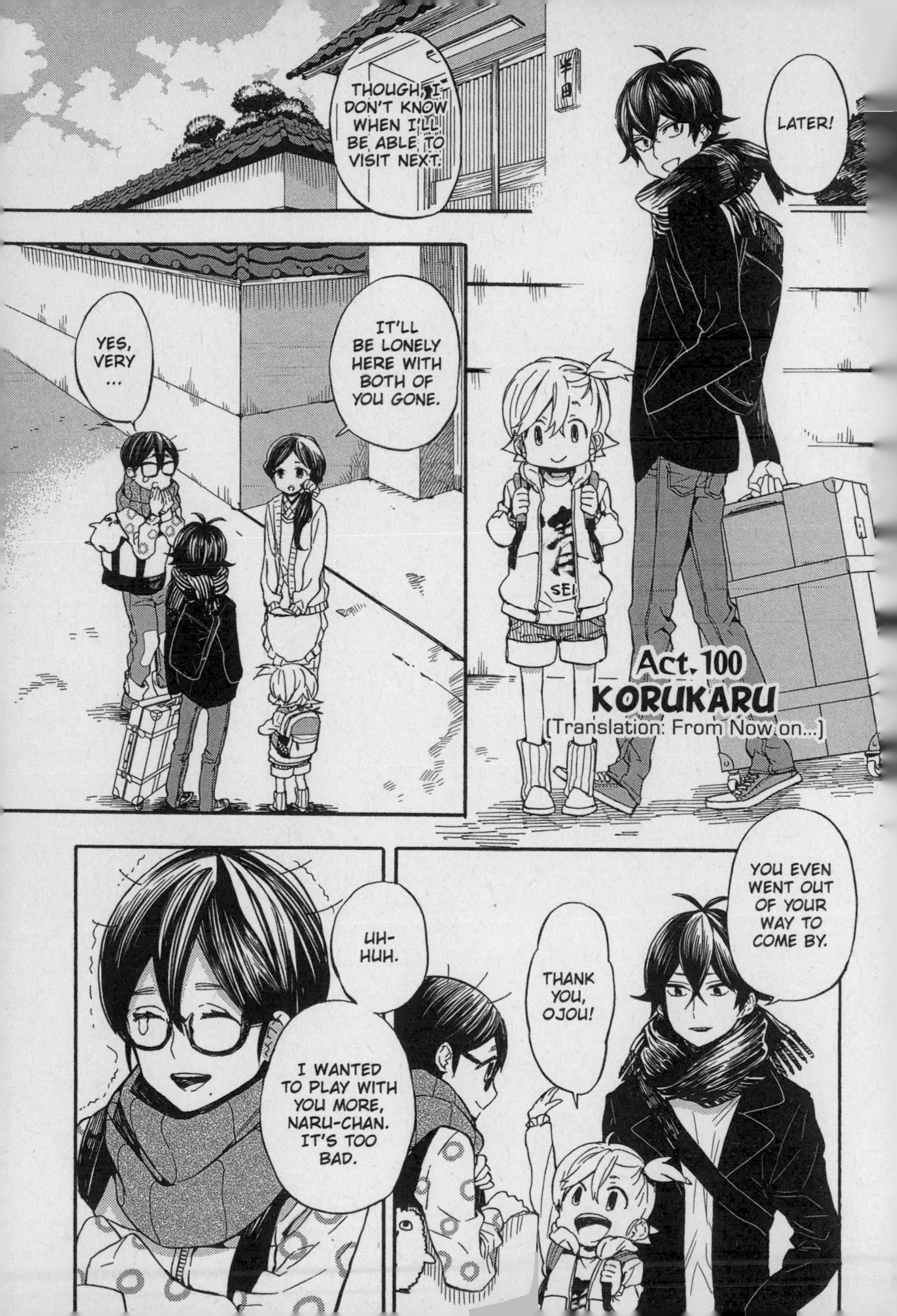
LATER!
Act. 100
KORUKARU
(Translation: From Now on...)
THOUGH, I DON'T KNOW WHEN I'LL BE ABLE TO VISIT NEXT.
半田
IT'LL BE LONELY HERE WITH BOTH OF YOU GONE.
YES, VERY ...
YOU EVEN WENT OUT OF YOUR WAY TO COME BY.
THANK YOU, OJOU!
UH-HUH.
I WANTED TO PLAY WITH YOU MORE, NARU-CHAN. IT'S TOO BAD.

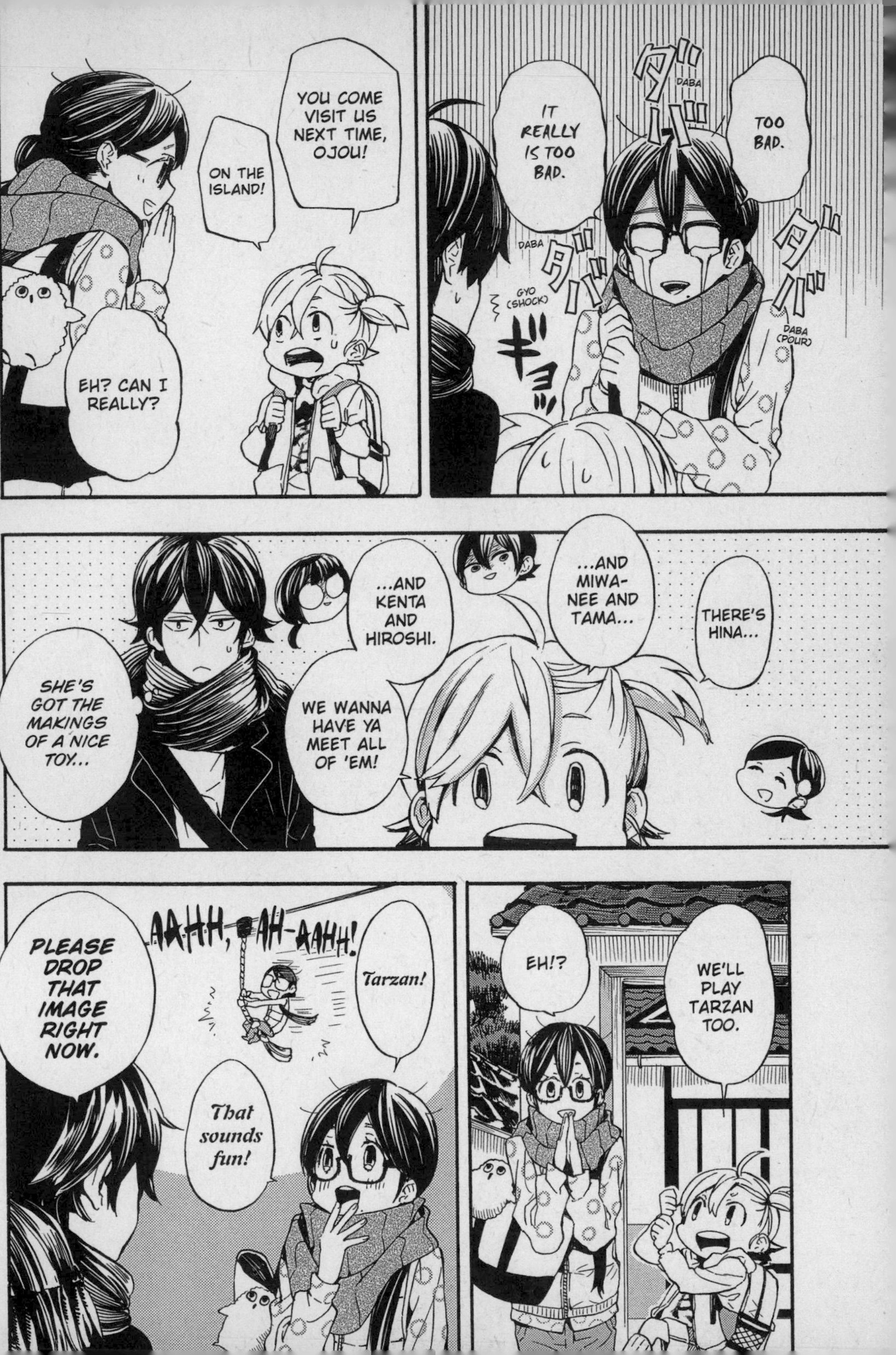
TOO BAD.
DABA
IT REALLY IS TOO BAD.
DABA
GYO (SHOCK)
DABA (POUR)
YOU COME VISIT US NEXT TIME, OJOU!
ON THE ISLAND!
EH? CAN I REALLY?
THERE'S HINA...
...AND MIWA-NEE AND TAMA...
...AND KENTA AND HIROSHI.
WE WANNA HAVE YA MEET ALL OF 'EM!
SHE'S GOT THE MAKINGS OF A NICE TOY...
WE'LL PLAY TARZAN TOO.
EH!?
Tarzan!
AAHH, AH-AAHH!
That sounds fun!
PLEASE DROP THAT IMAGE RIGHT NOW.

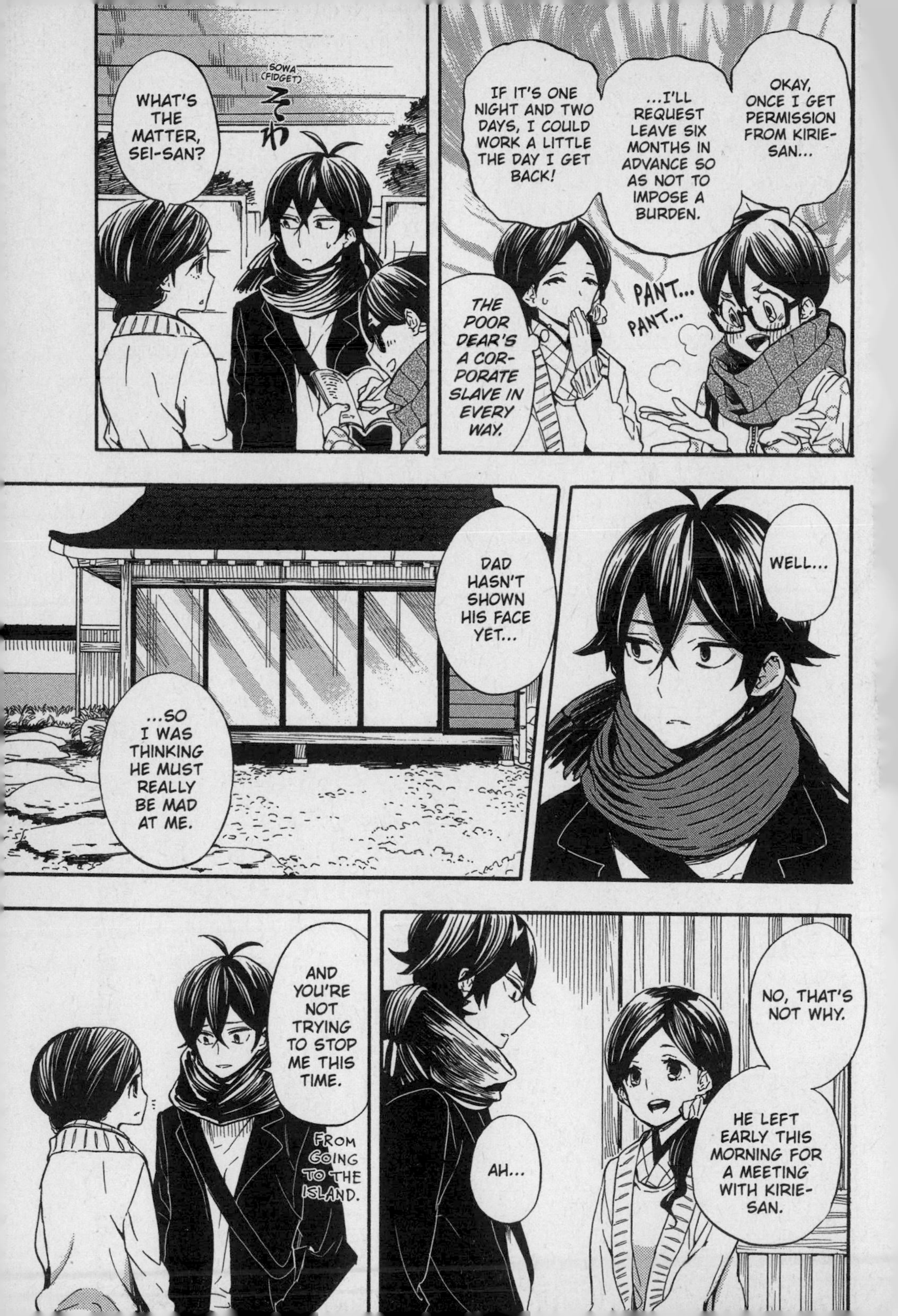
OKAY, ONCE I GET PERMISSION FROM KIRIE-SAN...
...I'LL REQUEST LEAVE SIX MONTHS IN ADVANCE SO AS NOT TO IMPOSE A BURDEN.
IF IT'S ONE NIGHT AND TWO DAYS, I COULD WORK A LITTLE THE DAY I GET BACK!
PANT... PANT...
THE POOR DEAR'S A CORPORATE SLAVE IN EVERY WAY.
SOWA (FIDGET)
WHAT'S THE MATTER, SEI-SAN?
WELL...
DAD HASN'T SHOWN HIS FACE YET...
...SO I WAS THINKING HE MUST REALLY BE MAD AT ME.
NO, THAT'S NOT WHY.
HE LEFT EARLY THIS MORNING FOR A MEETING WITH KIRIE-SAN.
AH...
AND YOU'RE NOT TRYING TO STOP ME THIS TIME.
FROM GOING TO THE ISLAND.

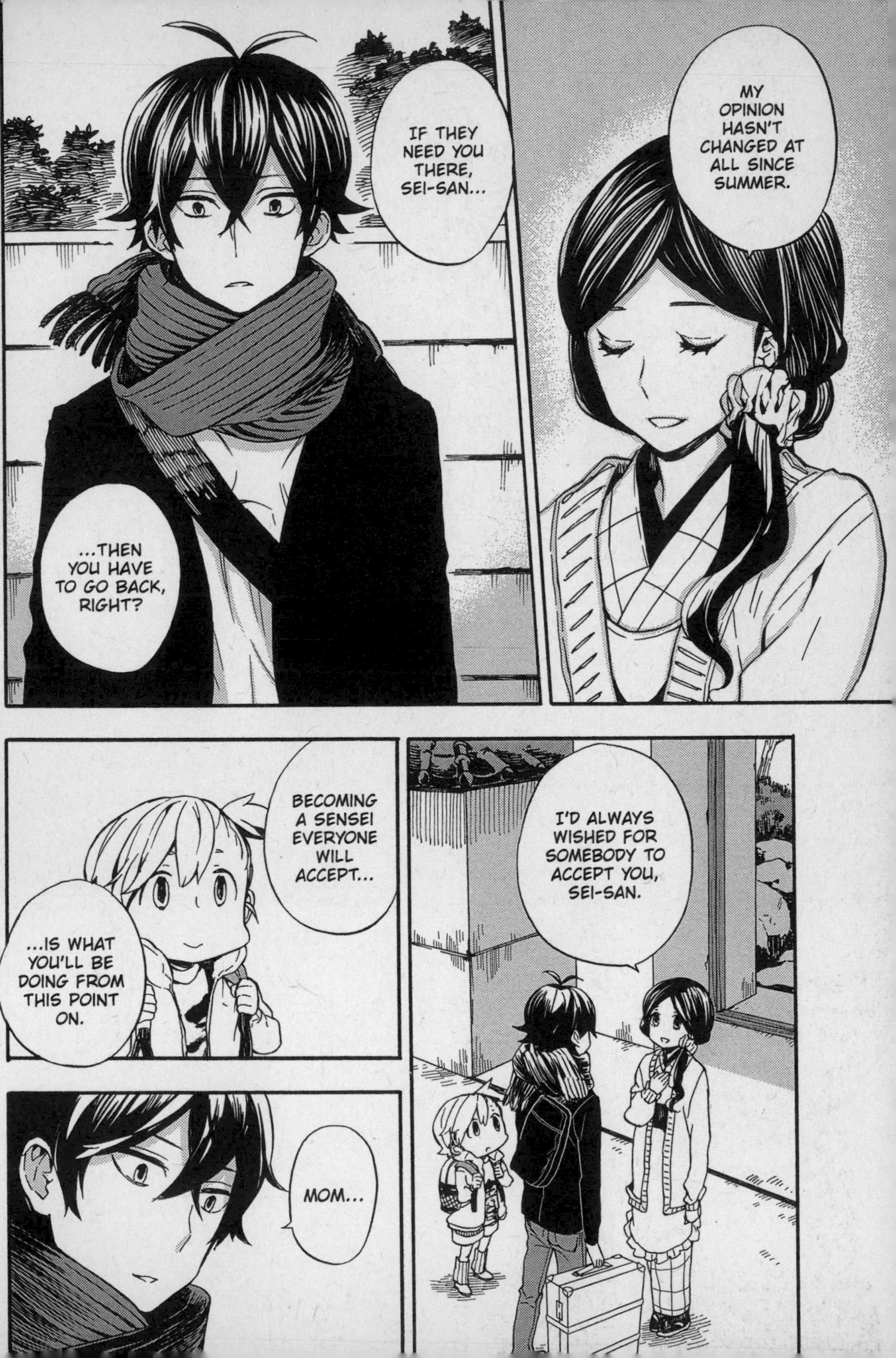
MY OPINION HASN'T CHANGED AT ALL SINCE SUMMER.
IF THEY NEED YOU THERE, SEI-SAN...
...THEN YOU HAVE TO GO BACK, RIGHT?
I'D ALWAYS WISHED FOR SOMEBODY TO ACCEPT YOU, SEI-SAN.
BECOMING A SENSEI EVERYONE WILL ACCEPT...
...IS WHAT YOU'LL BE DOING FROM THIS POINT ON.
MOM...

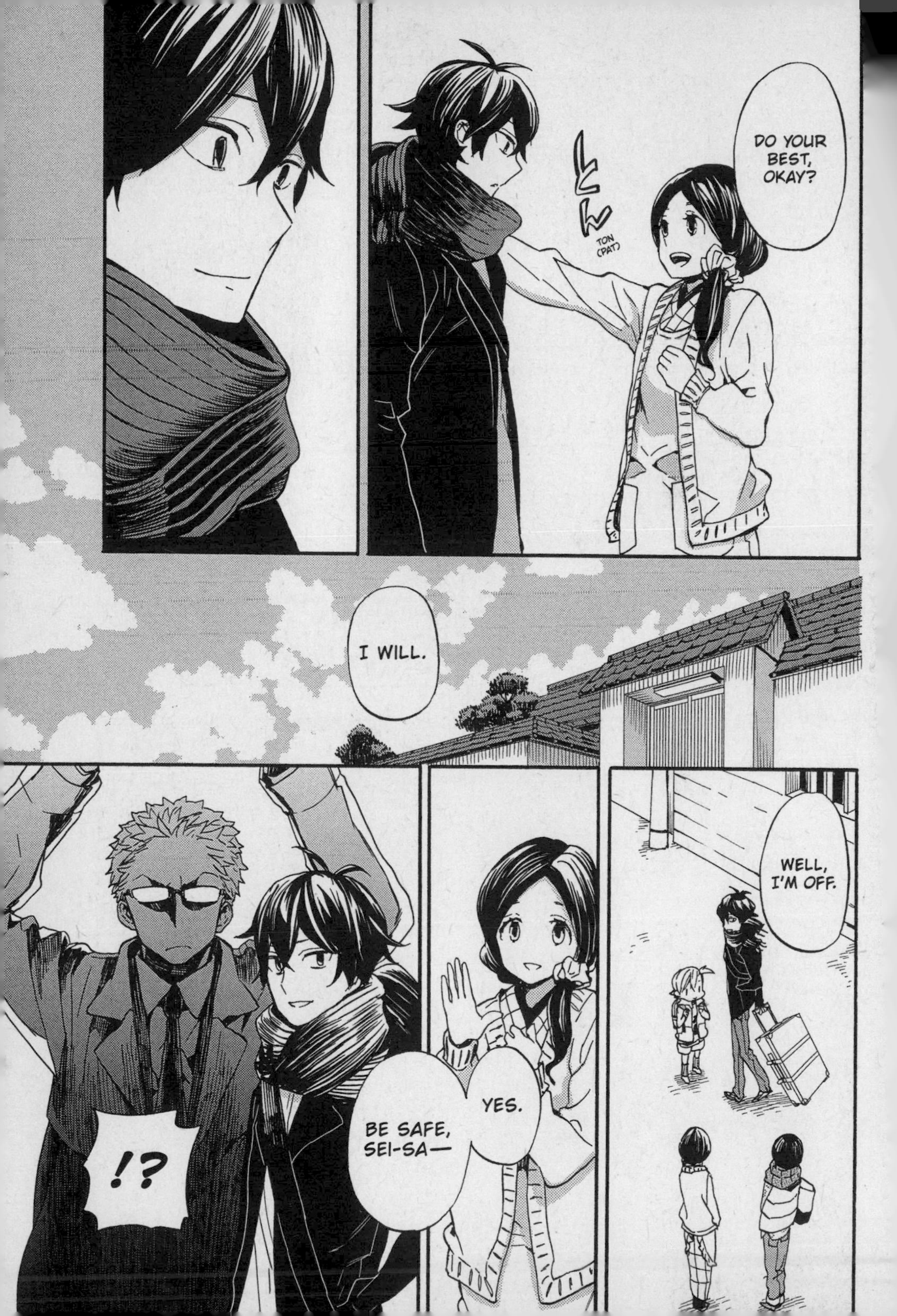
DO YOUR BEST, OKAY?
とん
TON (PAT)
I WILL.
WELL, I'M OFF.
YES.
BE SAFE, SEI-SA—
!?

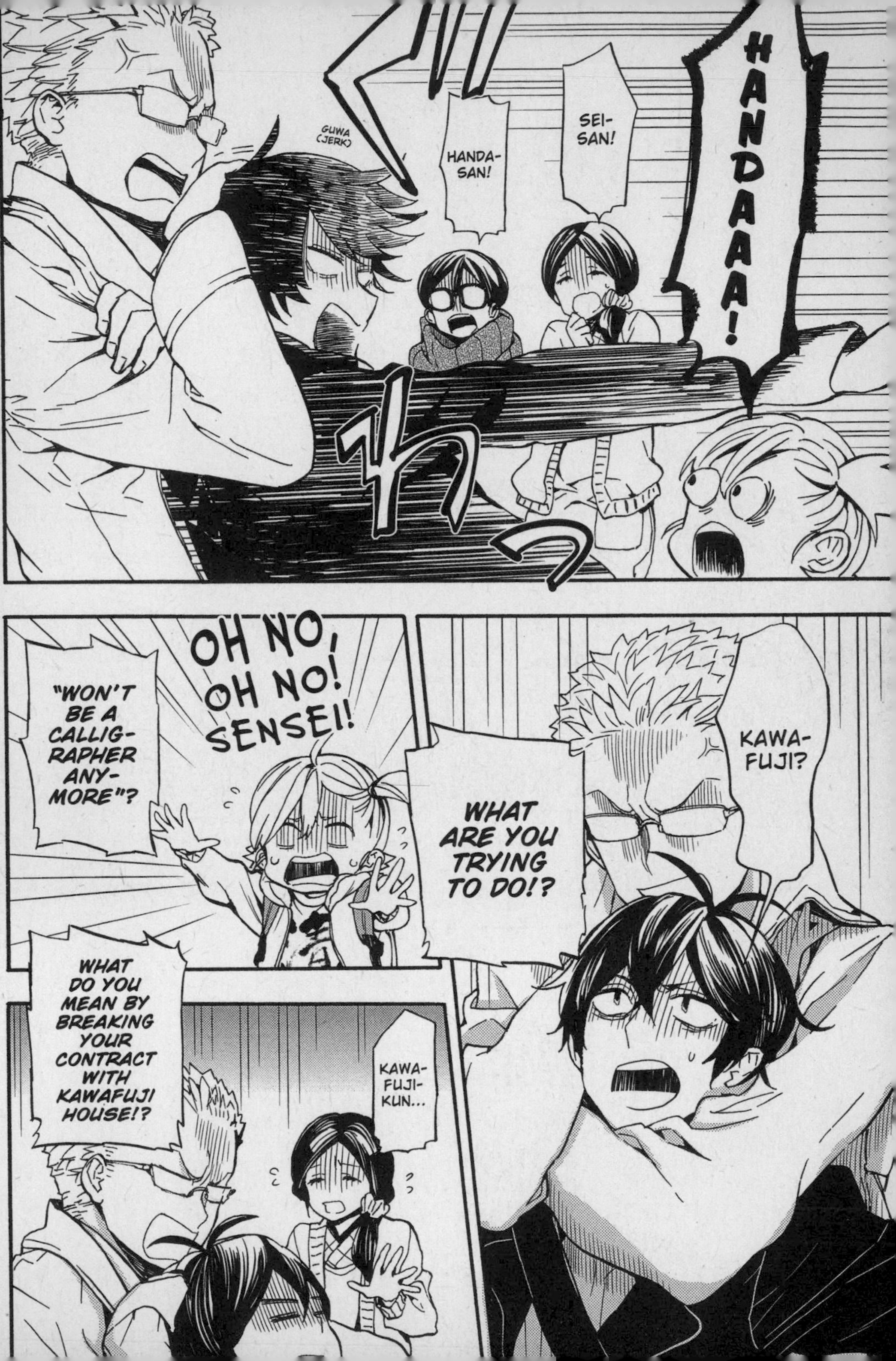
HANDADAAA!
SEI-SAN!
HANDA-SAN!
GUWA (JERK)
KAWA-FUJI?
WHAT ARE YOU TRYING TO DO!?
OH NO, OH NO! SENSEI!
"WON'T BE A CALLIG-RAPHER ANY-MORE"?
KAWA-FUJI-KUN...
WHAT DO YOU MEAN BY BREAKING YOUR CONTRACT WITH KAWAFUJI HOUSE!?

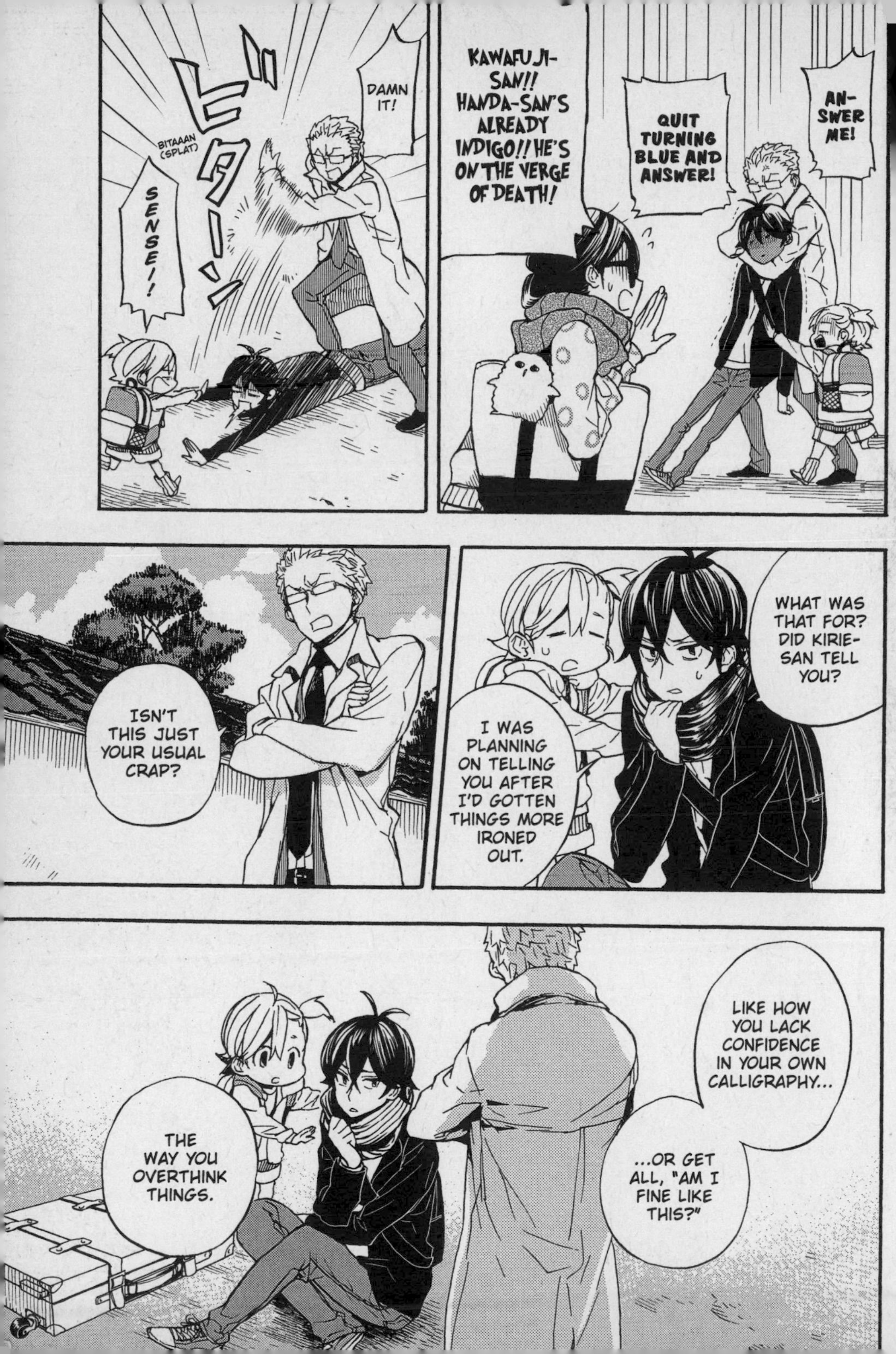
ANSWER ME!
QUIT TURNING BLUE AND ANSWER!
KAWAFUJI-SAN!! HANDA-SAN'S ALREADY INDIGO!! HE'S ON THE VERGE OF DEATH!
DAMN IT!
BITAAAN (SPLAT)
SENSE!!
WHAT WAS THAT FOR? DID KIRIE-SAN TELL YOU?
I WAS PLANNING ON TELLING YOU AFTER I'D GOTTEN THINGS MORE IRONED OUT.
ISN'T THIS JUST YOUR USUAL CRAP?
LIKE HOW YOU LACK CONFIDENCE IN YOUR OWN CALLIGRAPHY...
...OR GET ALL, "AM I FINE LIKE THIS?"
THE WAY YOU OVERTHINK THINGS.

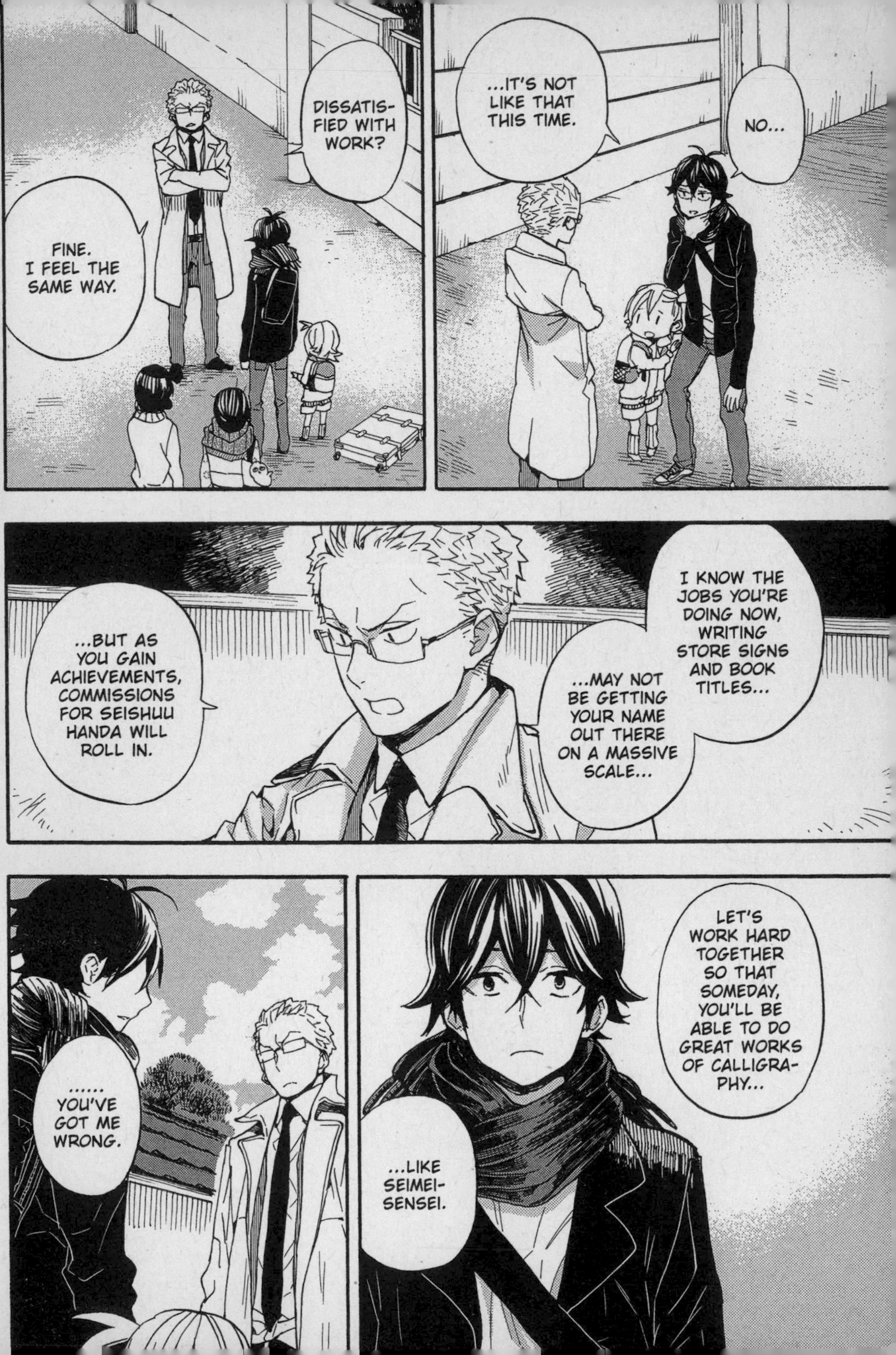
NO...
...IT'S NOT LIKE THAT THIS TIME.
DISSATISFIED WITH WORK?
FINE. I FEEL THE SAME WAY.
I KNOW THE JOBS YOU'RE DOING NOW, WRITING STORE SIGNS AND BOOK TITLES...
...MAY NOT BE GETTING YOUR NAME OUT THERE ON A MASSIVE SCALE...
...BUT AS YOU GAIN ACHIEVEMENTS, COMMISSIONS FOR SEISHUU HANDA WILL ROLL IN.
LET'S WORK HARD TOGETHER SO THAT SOMEDAY, YOU'LL BE ABLE TO DO GREAT WORKS OF CALLIGRAPHY...
...LIKE SEIMEI-SENSEI.
...... YOU'VE GOT ME WRONG.

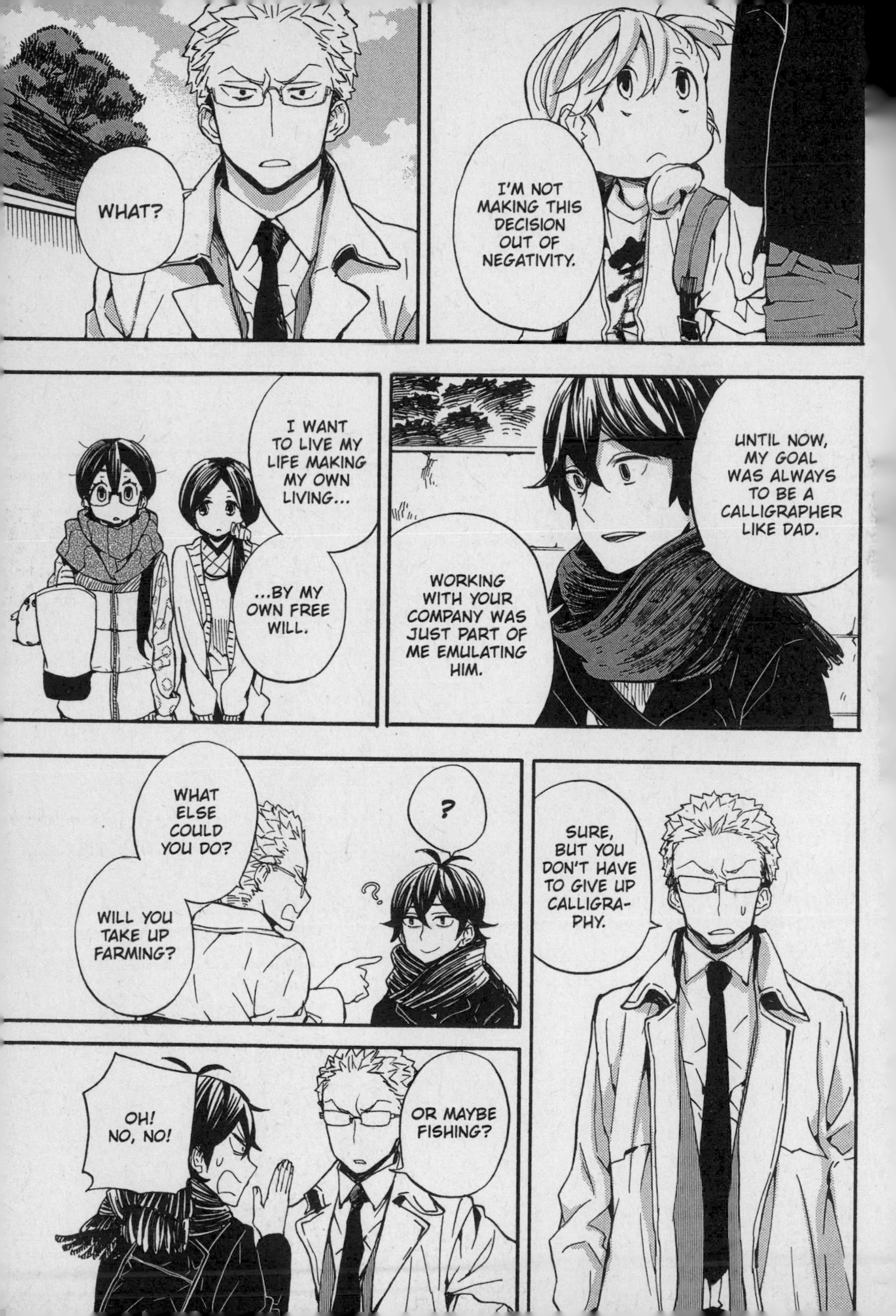
I'M NOT MAKING THIS DECISION OUT OF NEGATIVITY.
WHAT?
UNTIL NOW, MY GOAL WAS ALWAYS TO BE A CALLIGRAPHER LIKE DAD.
WORKING WITH YOUR COMPANY WAS JUST PART OF ME EMULATING HIM.
I WANT TO LIVE MY LIFE MAKING MY OWN LIVING...
...BY MY OWN FREE WILL.
SURE, BUT YOU DON'T HAVE TO GIVE UP CALLIGRA-PHY.
?
WHAT ELSE COULD YOU DO?
WILL YOU TAKE UP FARMING?
?
OR MAYBE FISHING?
OH! NO, NO!

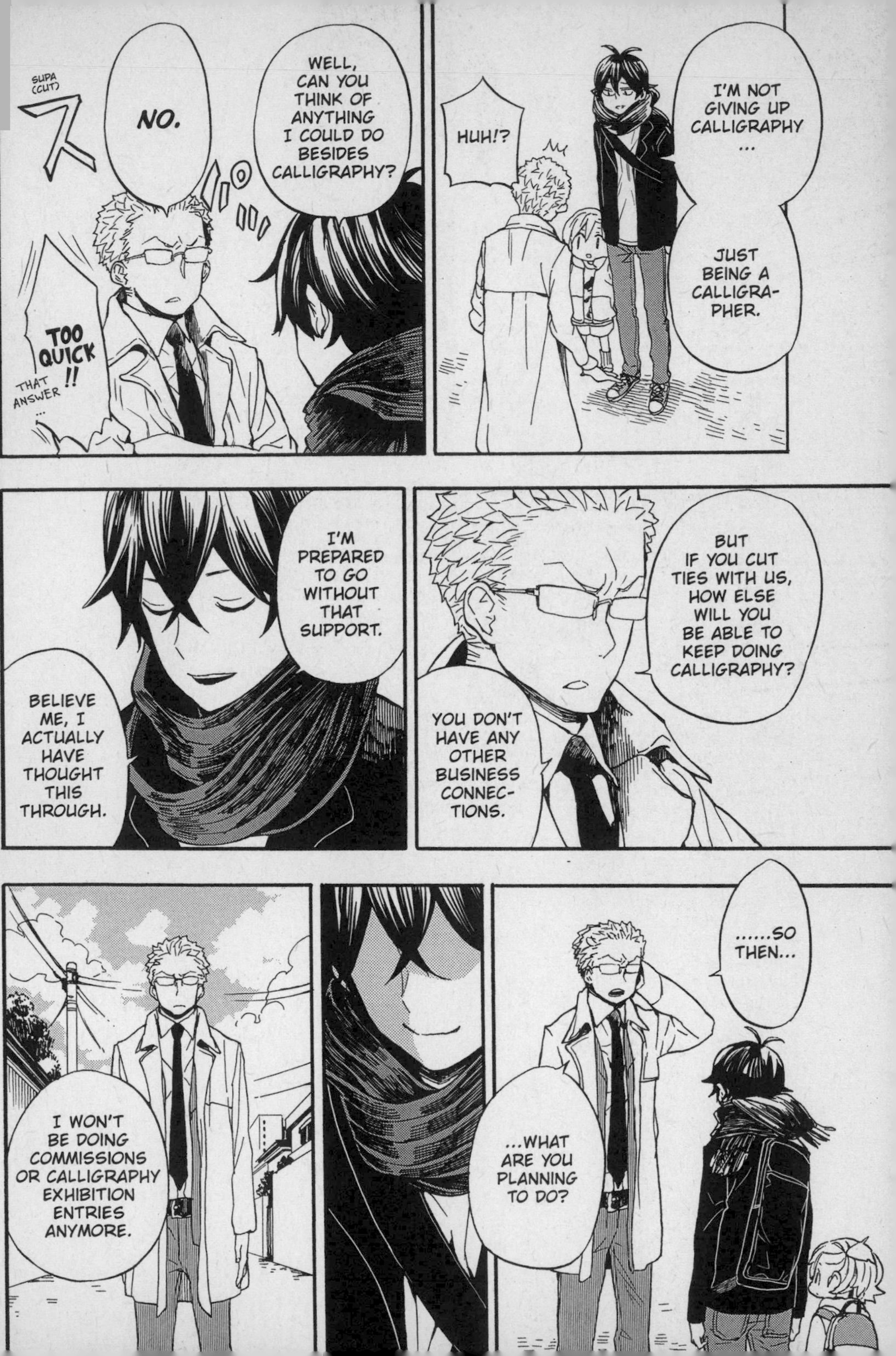
I'M NOT GIVING UP CALLIGRAPHY ...
JUST BEING A CALLIGRAPHER.
HUH!?
WELL, CAN YOU THINK OF ANYTHING I COULD DO BESIDES CALLIGRAPHY?
NO.
SUPA (CUT)
TOO QUICK!!
THAT ANSWER ...
BUT IF YOU CUT TIES WITH US, HOW ELSE WILL YOU BE ABLE TO KEEP DOING CALLIGRAPHY?
YOU DON'T HAVE ANY OTHER BUSINESS CONNECTIONS.
I'M PREPARED TO GO WITHOUT THAT SUPPORT.
BELIEVE ME, I ACTUALLY HAVE THOUGHT THIS THROUGH.
......SO THEN...
...WHAT ARE YOU PLANNING TO DO?
I WON'T BE DOING COMMISSIONS OR CALLIGRAPHY EXHIBITION ENTRIES ANYMORE.

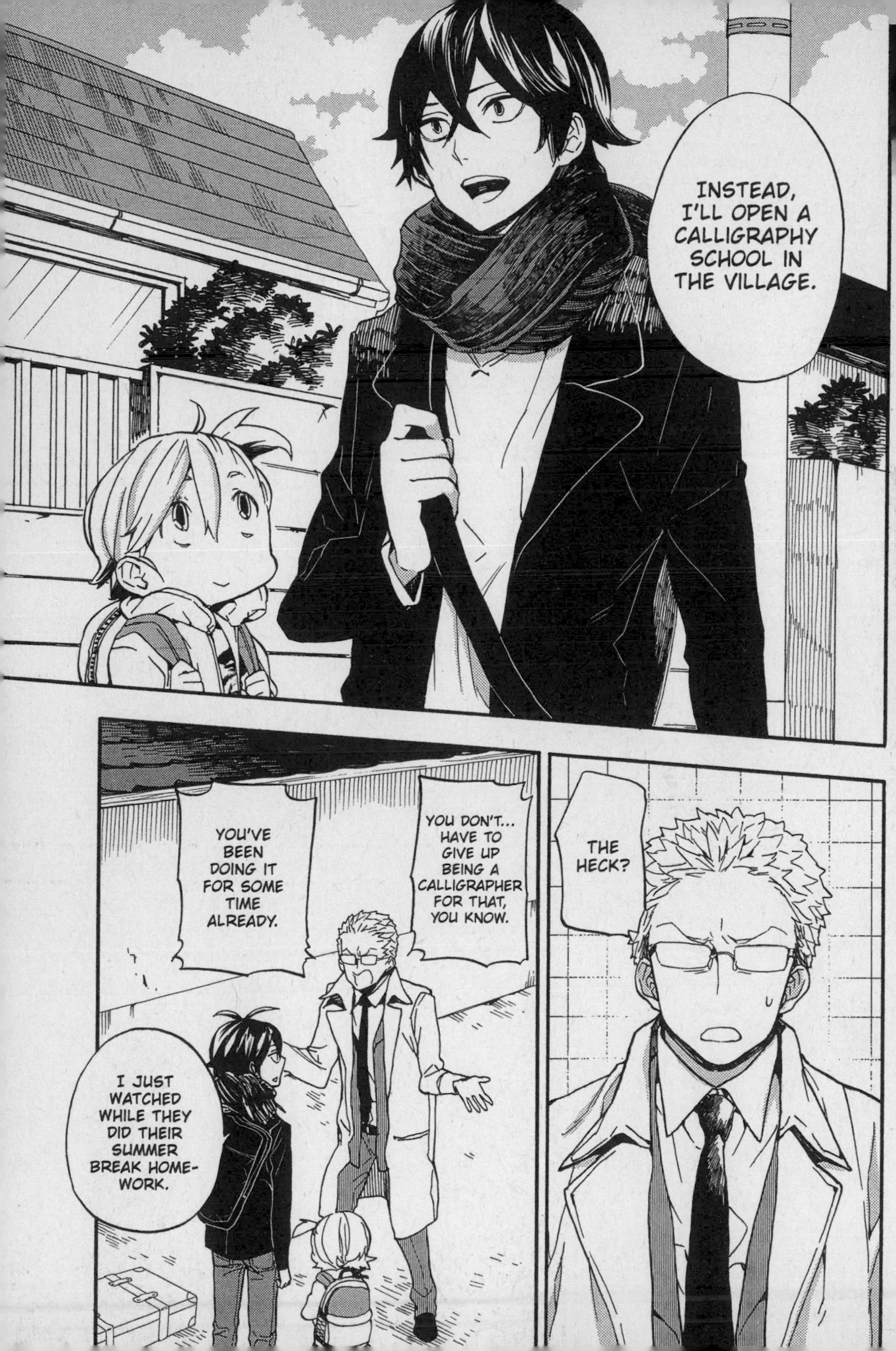
INSTEAD, I'LL OPEN A CALLIGRAPHY SCHOOL IN THE VILLAGE.
THE HECK?
YOU DON'T... HAVE TO GIVE UP BEING A CALLIGRAPHER FOR THAT, YOU KNOW.
YOU'VE BEEN DOING IT FOR SOME TIME ALREADY.
I JUST WATCHED WHILE THEY DID THEIR SUMMER BREAK HOME-WORK.

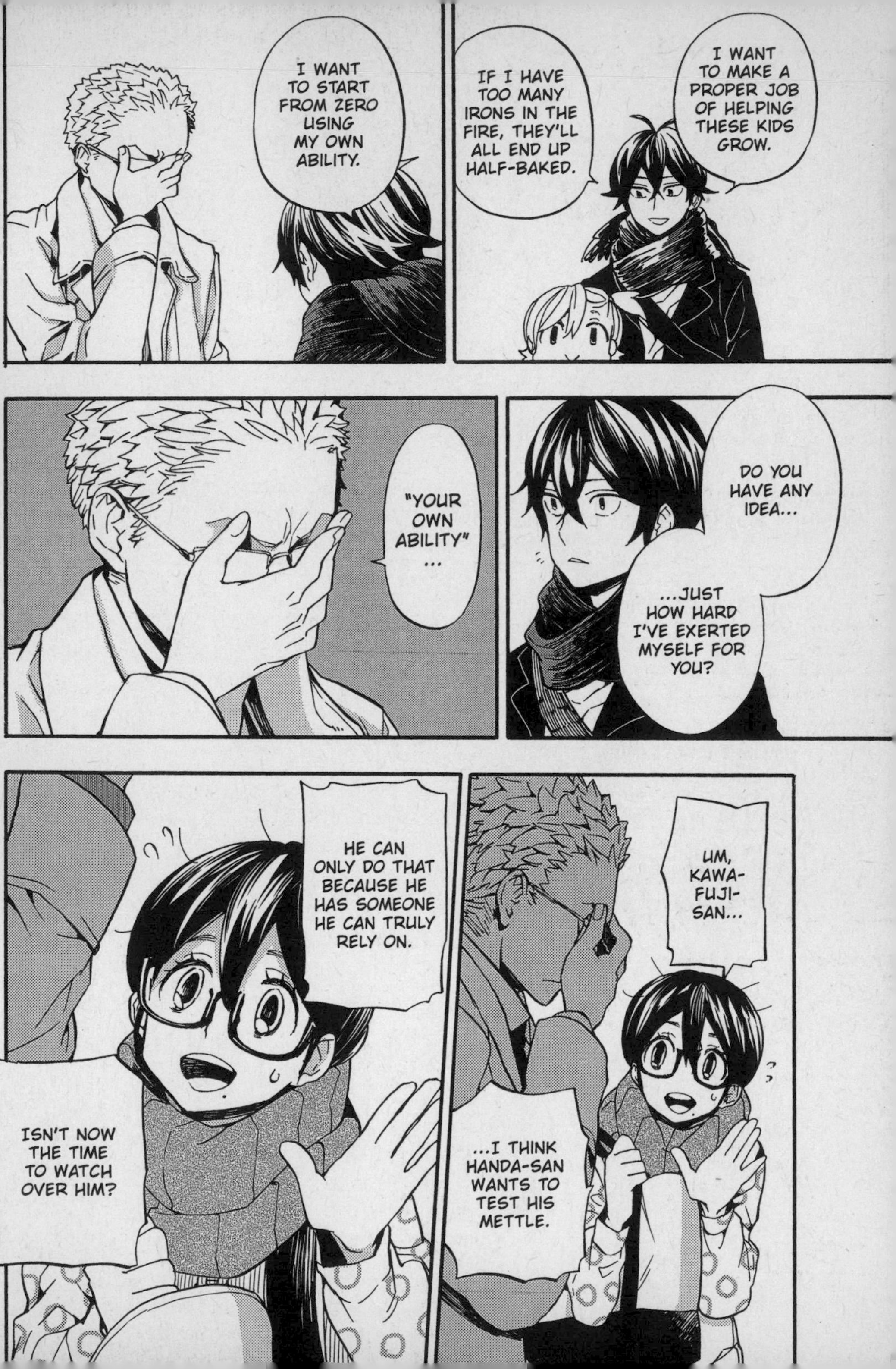
I WANT TO MAKE A PROPER JOB OF HELPING THESE KIDS GROW.
IF I HAVE TOO MANY IRONS IN THE FIRE, THEY'LL ALL END UP HALF-BAKED.
I WANT TO START FROM ZERO USING MY OWN ABILITY.
DO YOU HAVE ANY IDEA...
...JUST HOW HARD I'VE EXERTED MYSELF FOR YOU?
"YOUR OWN ABILITY"...
UM, KAWA-FUJI-SAN...
...I THINK HANDA-SAN WANTS TO TEST HIS METTLE.
HE CAN ONLY DO THAT BECAUSE HE HAS SOMEONE HE CAN TRULY RELY ON.
ISN'T NOW THE TIME TO WATCH OVER HIM?

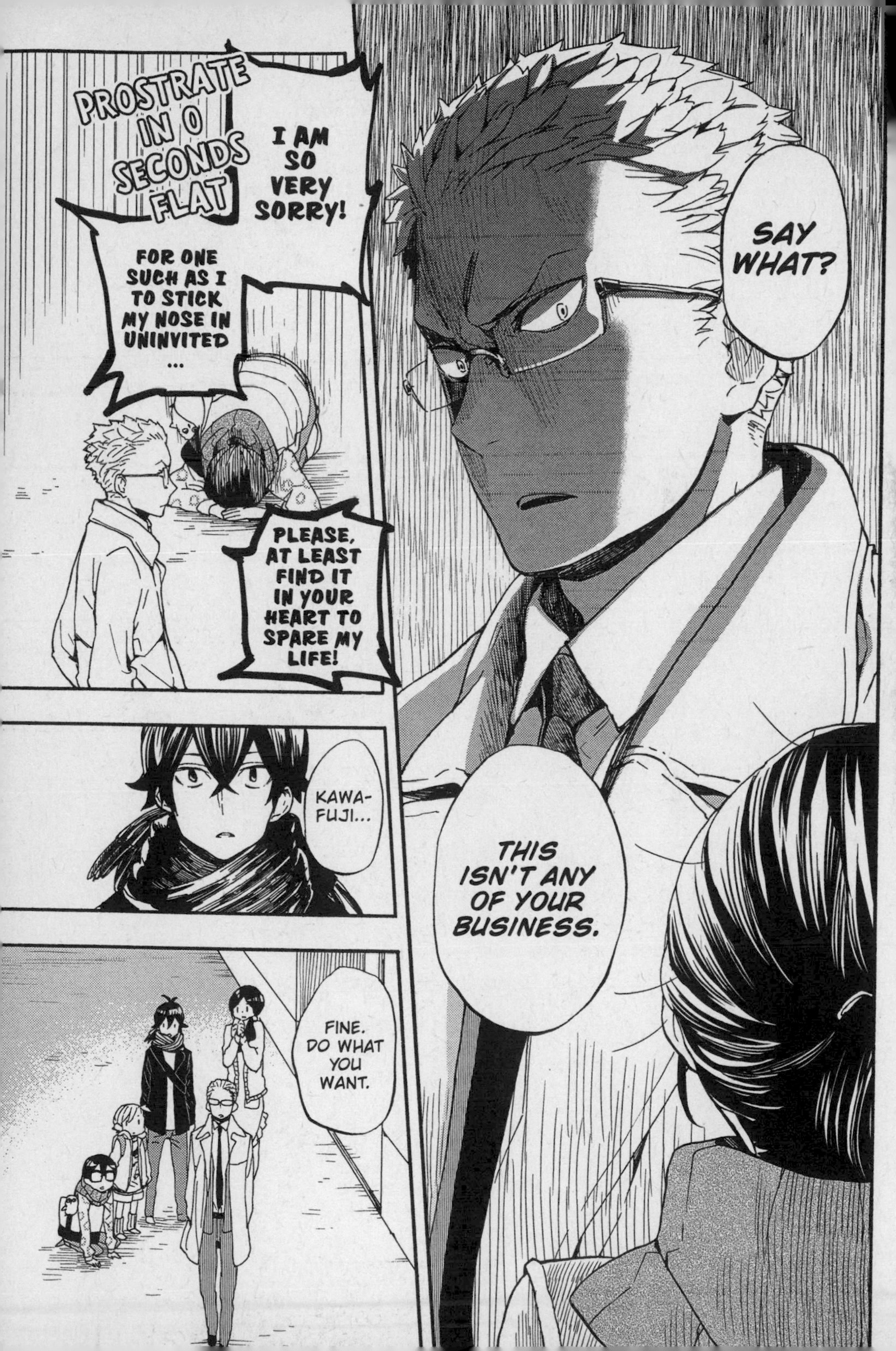
SAY WHAT?
THIS ISN'T ANY OF YOUR BUSINESS.
PROSTRATE IN 0 SECONDS FLAT
I AM SO VERY SORRY!
FOR ONE SUCH AS I TO STICK MY NOSE IN UNINVITED...
PLEASE, AT LEAST FIND IT IN YOUR HEART TO SPARE MY LIFE!
KAWA-FUJI...
FINE. DO WHAT YOU WANT.

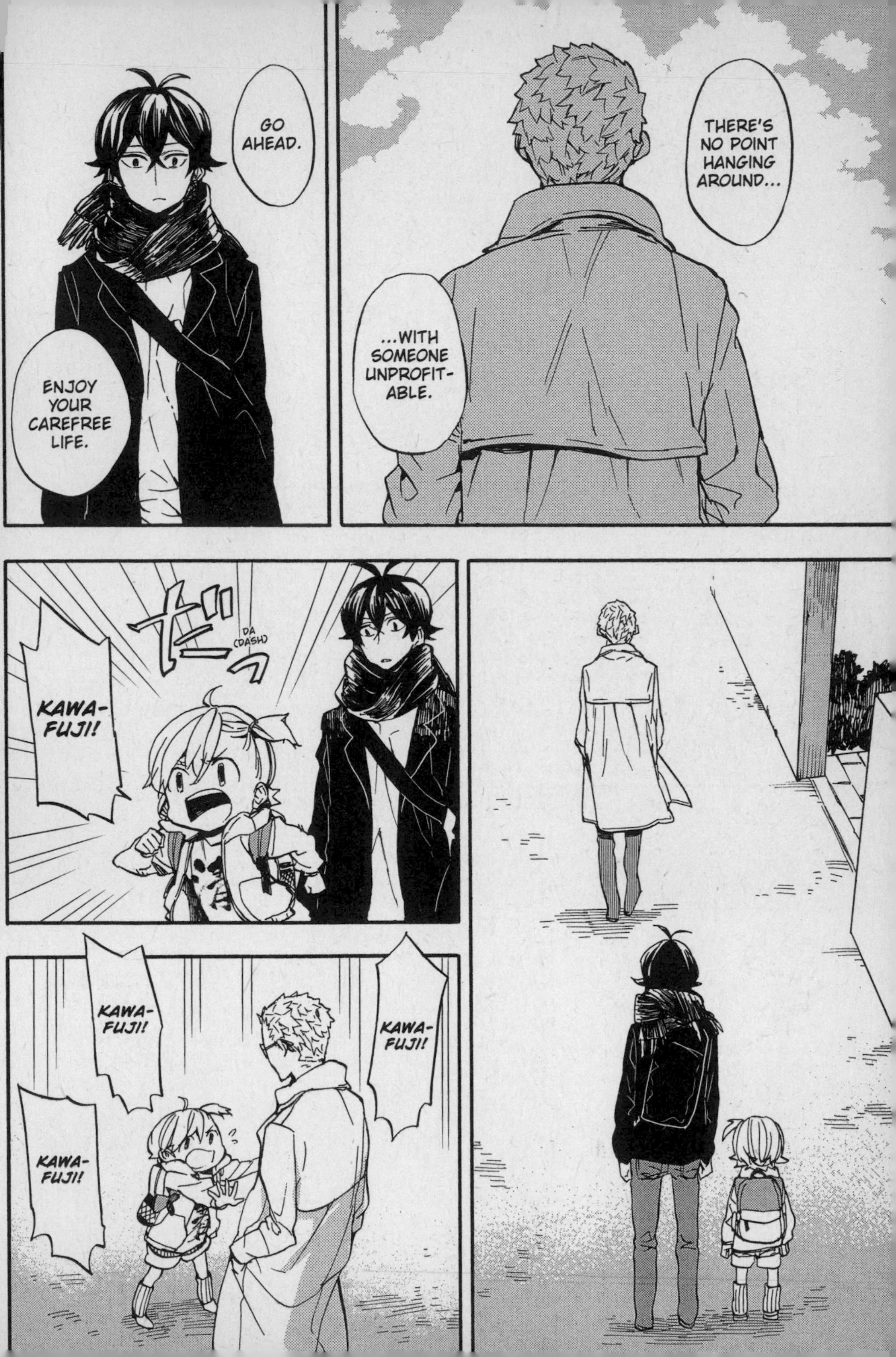
THERE'S NO POINT HANGING AROUND...
...WITH SOMEONE UNPROFIT-ABLE.
GO AHEAD.
ENJOY YOUR CAREFREE LIFE.
DA (DASH)
KAWA-FUJI!
KAWA-FUJI!
KAWA-FUJI!
KAWA-FUJI!

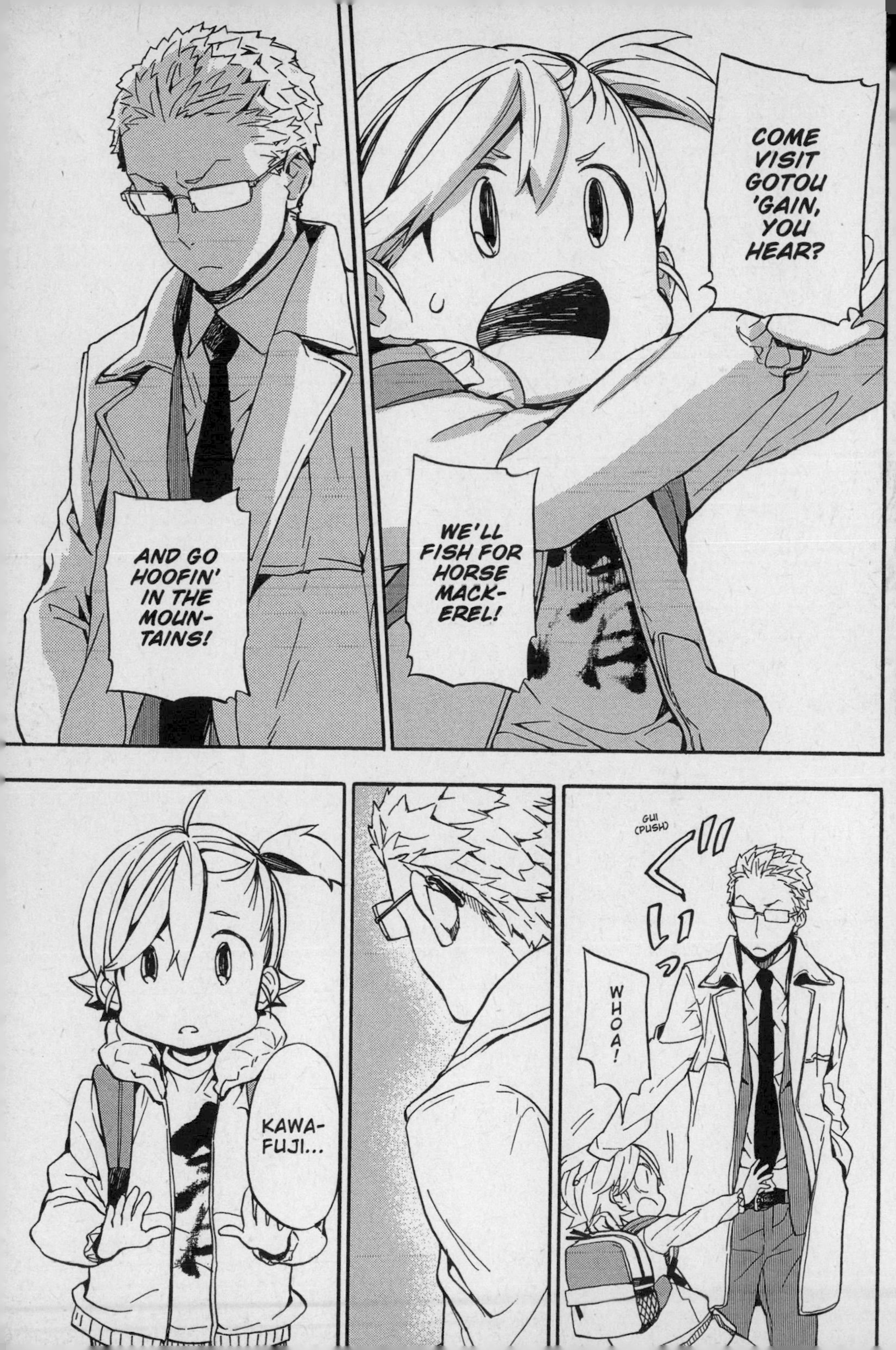
COME VISIT GOTOU 'GAIN, YOU HEAR?
WE'LL FISH FOR HORSE MACK-EREL!
AND GO HOOFIN' IN THE MOUN-TAINS!
GUI (PUSH)
WHOA!
KAWA-FUJI...

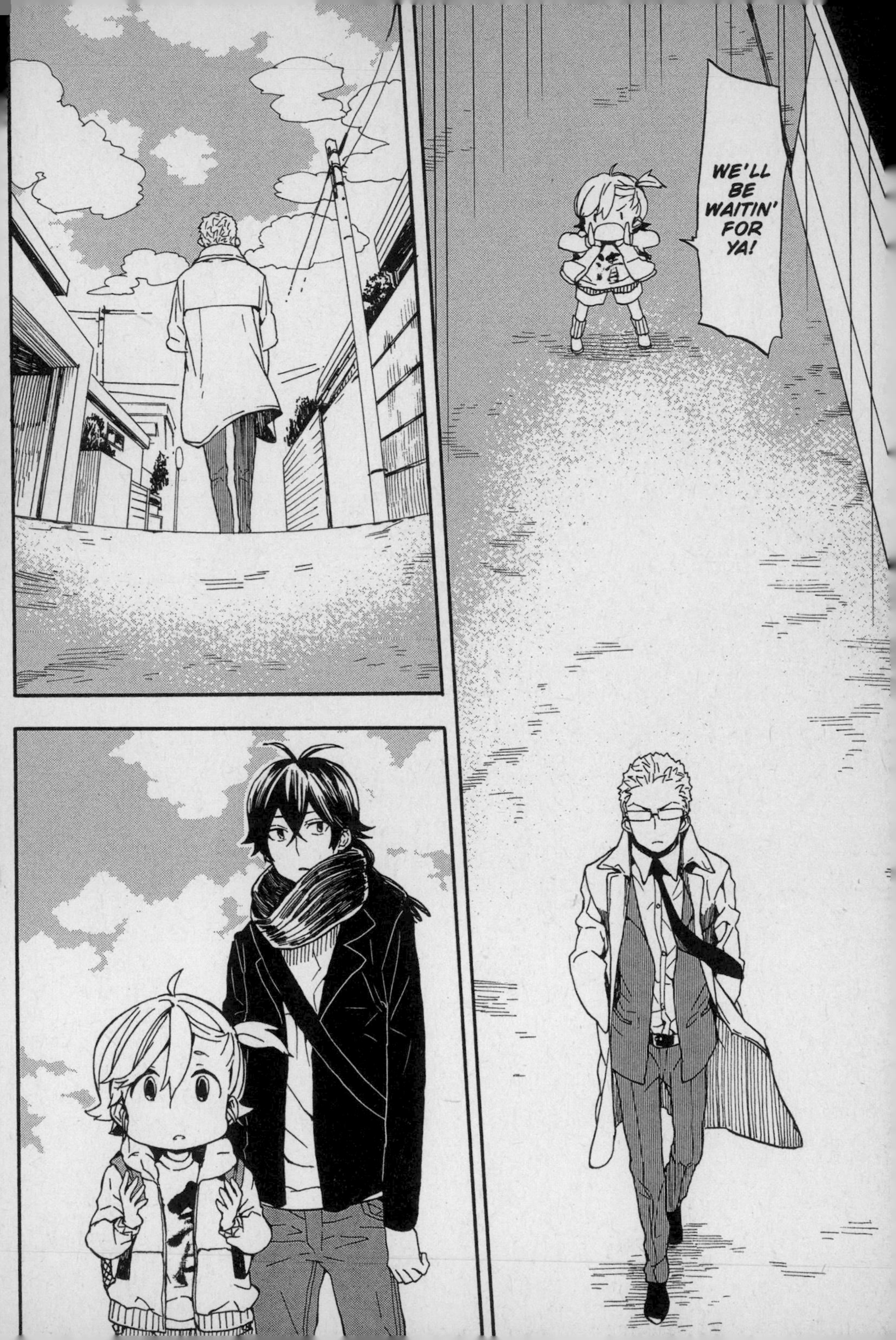
WE'LL BE WAITIN' FOR YA!

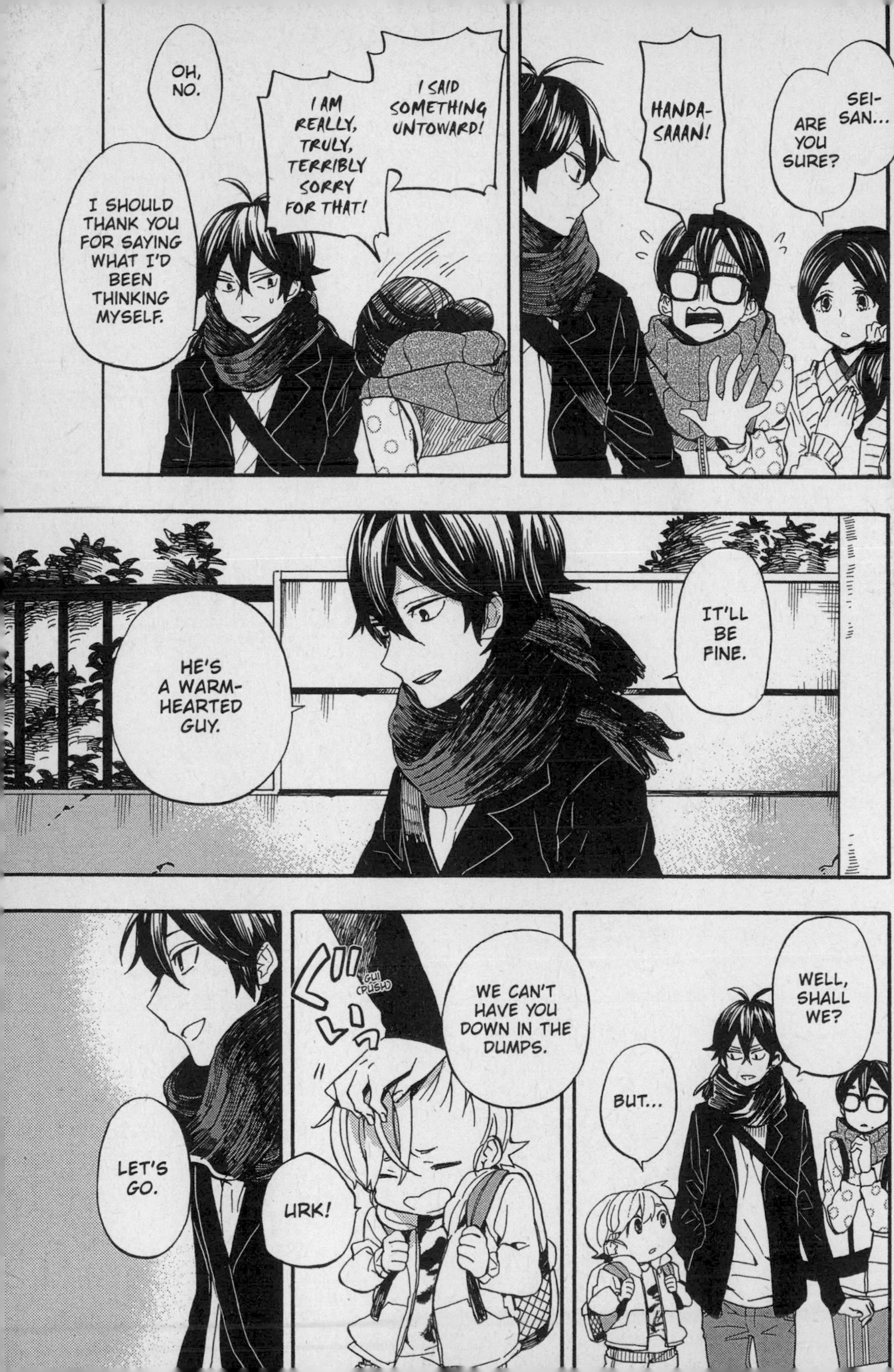
SEI-SAN... ARE YOU SURE?
HANDA-SAAAN!
I SAID SOMETHING UNTOWARD!
I AM REALLY, TRULY, TERRIBLY SORRY FOR THAT!
OH, NO.
I SHOULD THANK YOU FOR SAYING WHAT I'D BEEN THINKING MYSELF.
IT'LL BE FINE.
HE'S A WARM-HEARTED GUY.
WELL, SHALL WE?
BUT...
WE CAN'T HAVE YOU DOWN IN THE DUMPS.
GUI (PUSH)
URK!
LET'S GO.

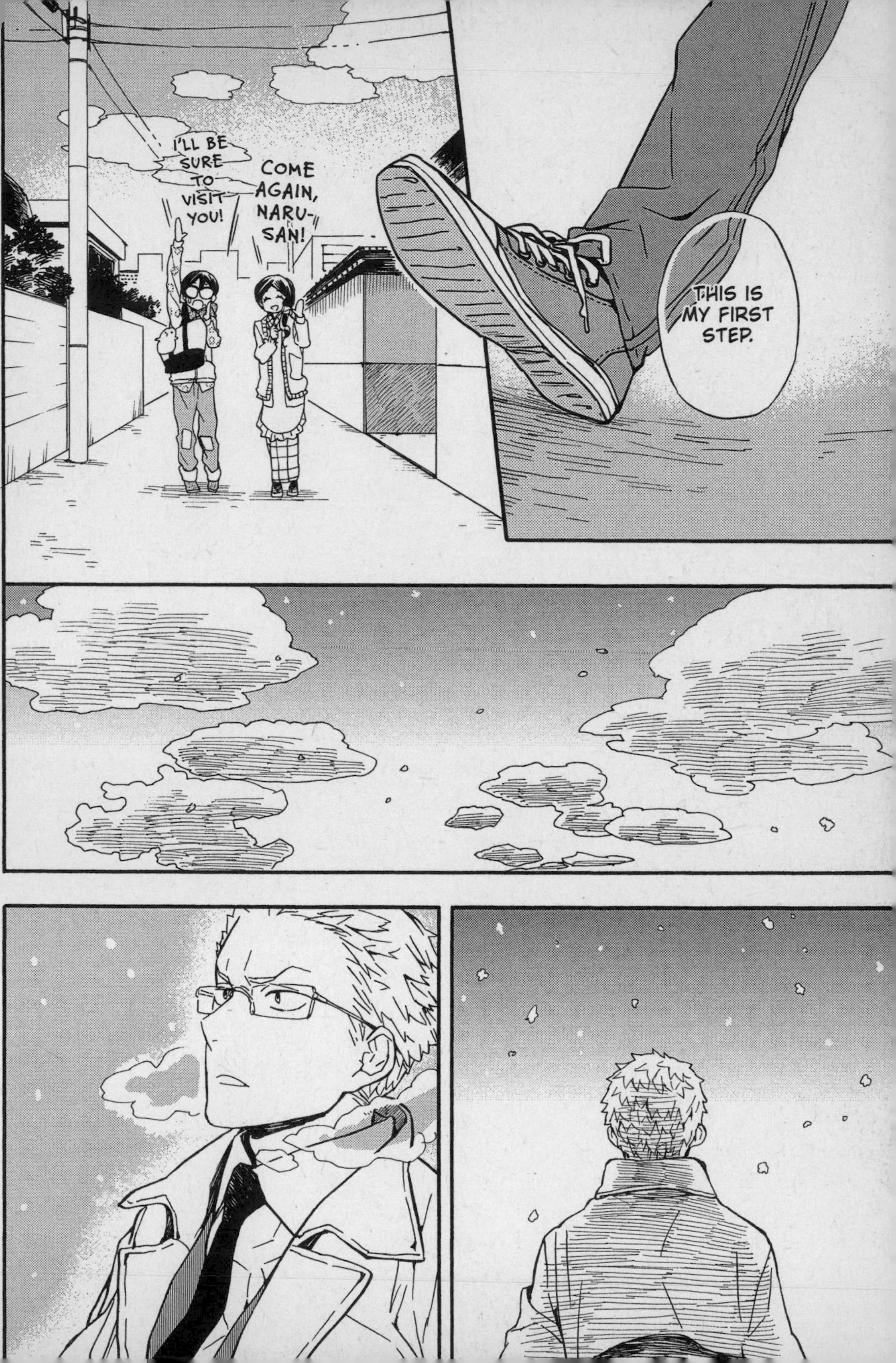
THIS IS MY FIRST STEP.
COME AGAIN, NARU-SAN!
I'LL BE SURE TO VISIT YOU!

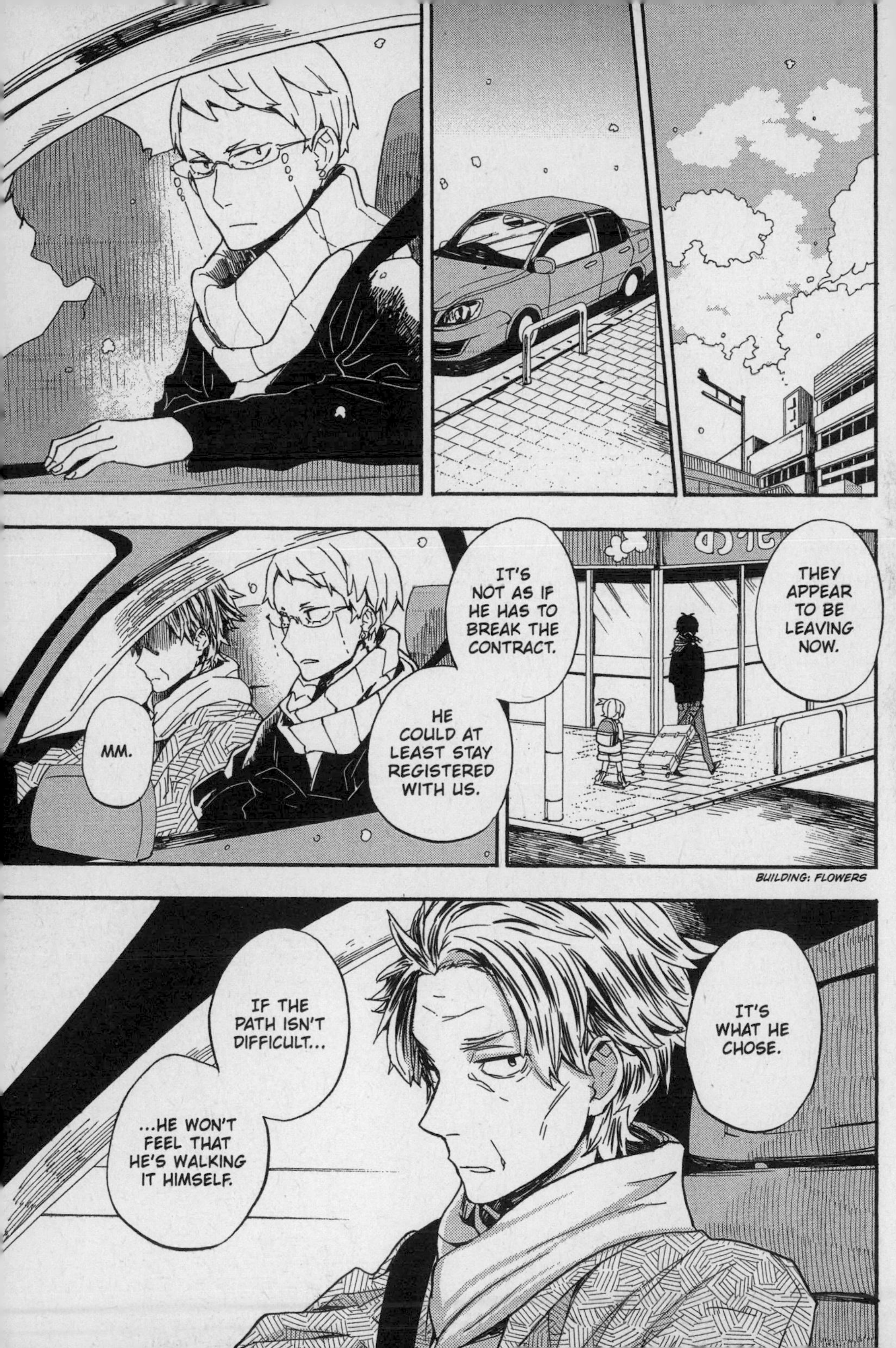
THEY APPEAR TO BE LEAVING NOW.
IT'S NOT AS IF HE HAS TO BREAK THE CONTRACT.
HE COULD AT LEAST STAY REGISTERED WITH US.
MM.
BUILDING: FLOWERS
IT'S WHAT HE CHOSE.
IF THE PATH ISN'T DIFFICULT...
...HE WON'T FEEL THAT HE'S WALKING IT HIMSELF.

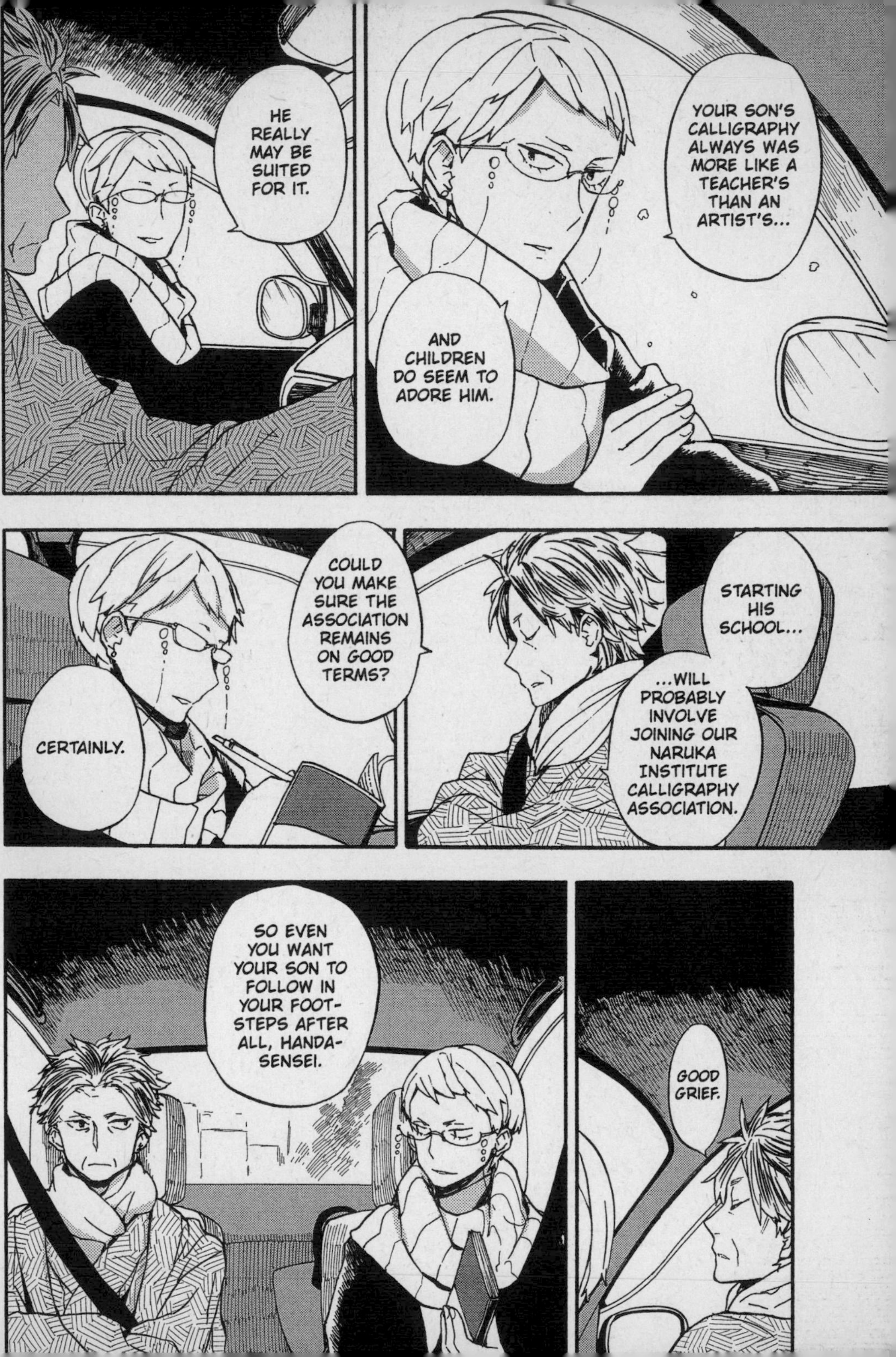
YOUR SON'S CALLIGRAPHY ALWAYS WAS MORE LIKE A TEACHER'S THAN AN ARTIST'S...
AND CHILDREN DO SEEM TO ADORE HIM.
HE REALLY MAY BE SUITED FOR IT.
STARTING HIS SCHOOL...
...WILL PROBABLY INVOLVE JOINING OUR NARUKA INSTITUTE CALLIGRAPHY ASSOCIATION.
COULD YOU MAKE SURE THE ASSOCIATION REMAINS ON GOOD TERMS?
CERTAINLY.
GOOD GRIEF.
SO EVEN YOU WANT YOUR SON TO FOLLOW IN YOUR FOOT-STEPS AFTER ALL, HANDA-SENSEI.

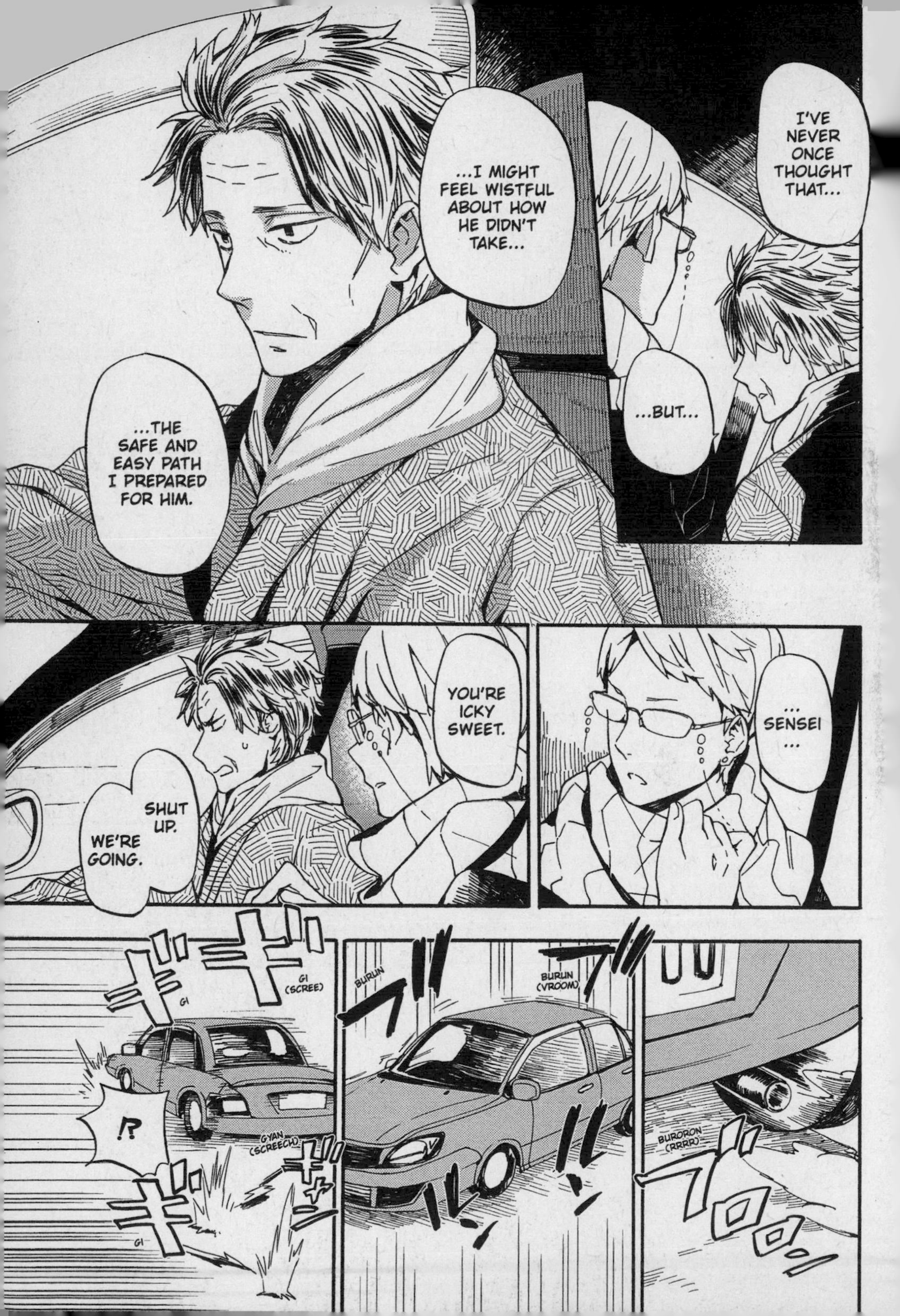
I'VE NEVER ONCE THOUGHT THAT...
...BUT...
...I MIGHT FEEL WISTFUL ABOUT HOW HE DIDN'T TAKE...
...THE SAFE AND EASY PATH I PREPARED FOR HIM.
... SENSEI ...
YOU'RE ICKY SWEET.
SHUT UP.
WE'RE GOING.
BURUN (VROOM)
BURORON (RRRR)
BURUN
GI (SCREE)
GI
!?
GYAN (SCREECH)
GI

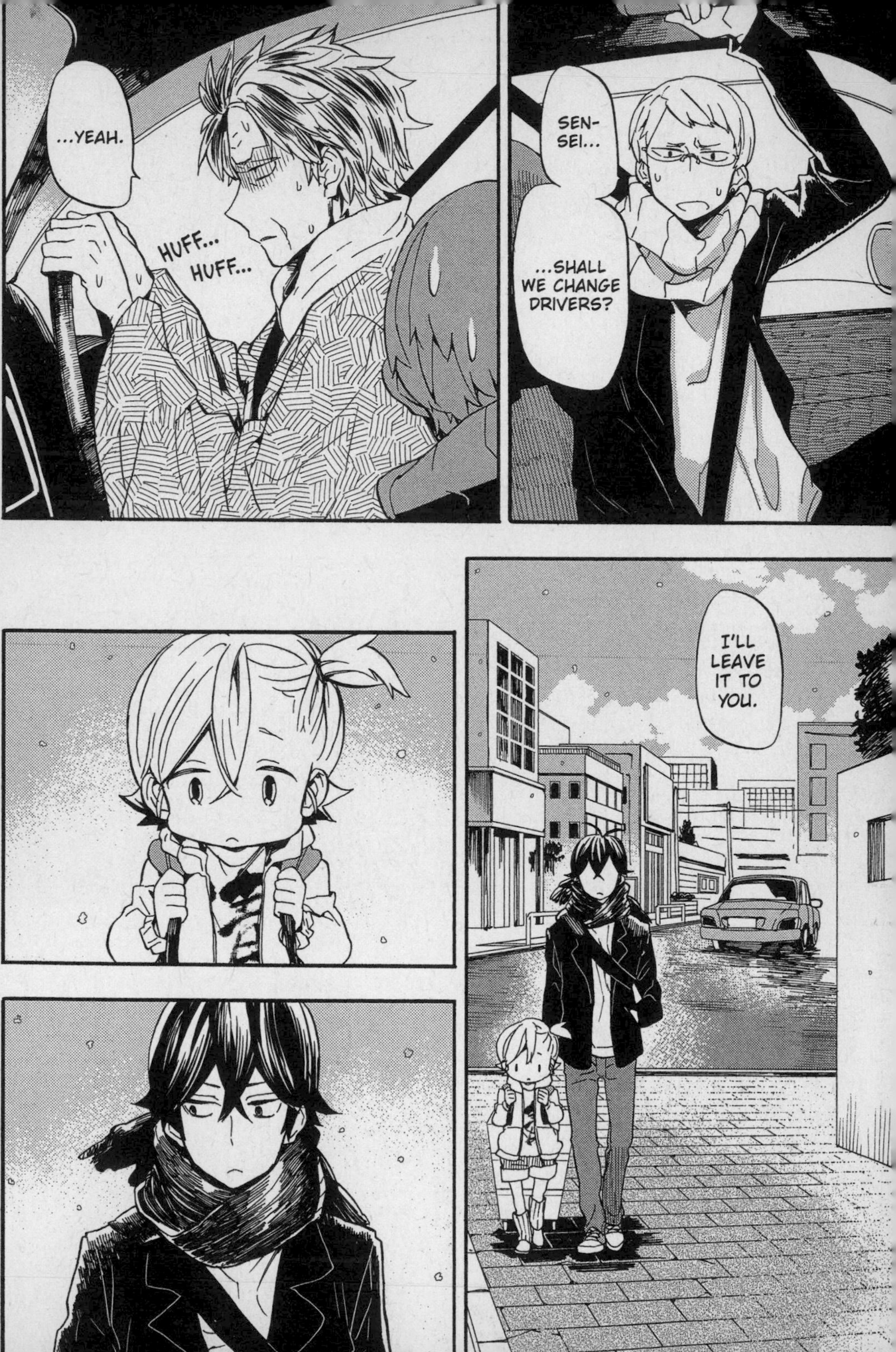
SEN-SEI...
...SHALL WE CHANGE DRIVERS?
...YEAH.
HUFF... HUFF...
I'LL LEAVE IT TO YOU.

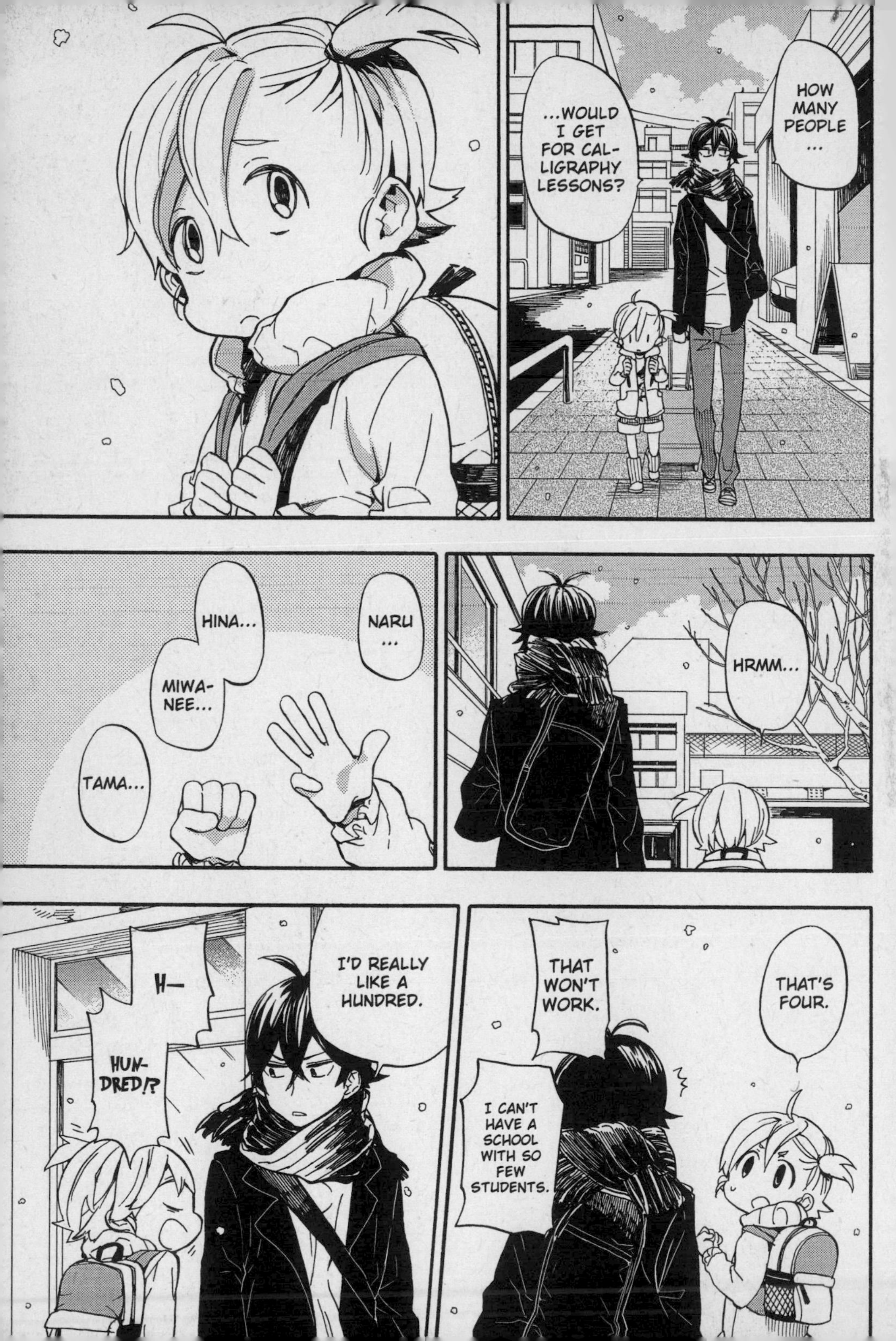
HOW MANY PEOPLE ...
...WOULD I GET FOR CAL-LIGRAPHY LESSONS?
HRMM...
NARU ...
HINA...
MIWA-NEE...
TAMA...
THAT'S FOUR.
THAT WON'T WORK.
I CAN'T HAVE A SCHOOL WITH SO FEW STUDENTS.
I'D REALLY LIKE A HUNDRED.
H—
HUN-DRED!?

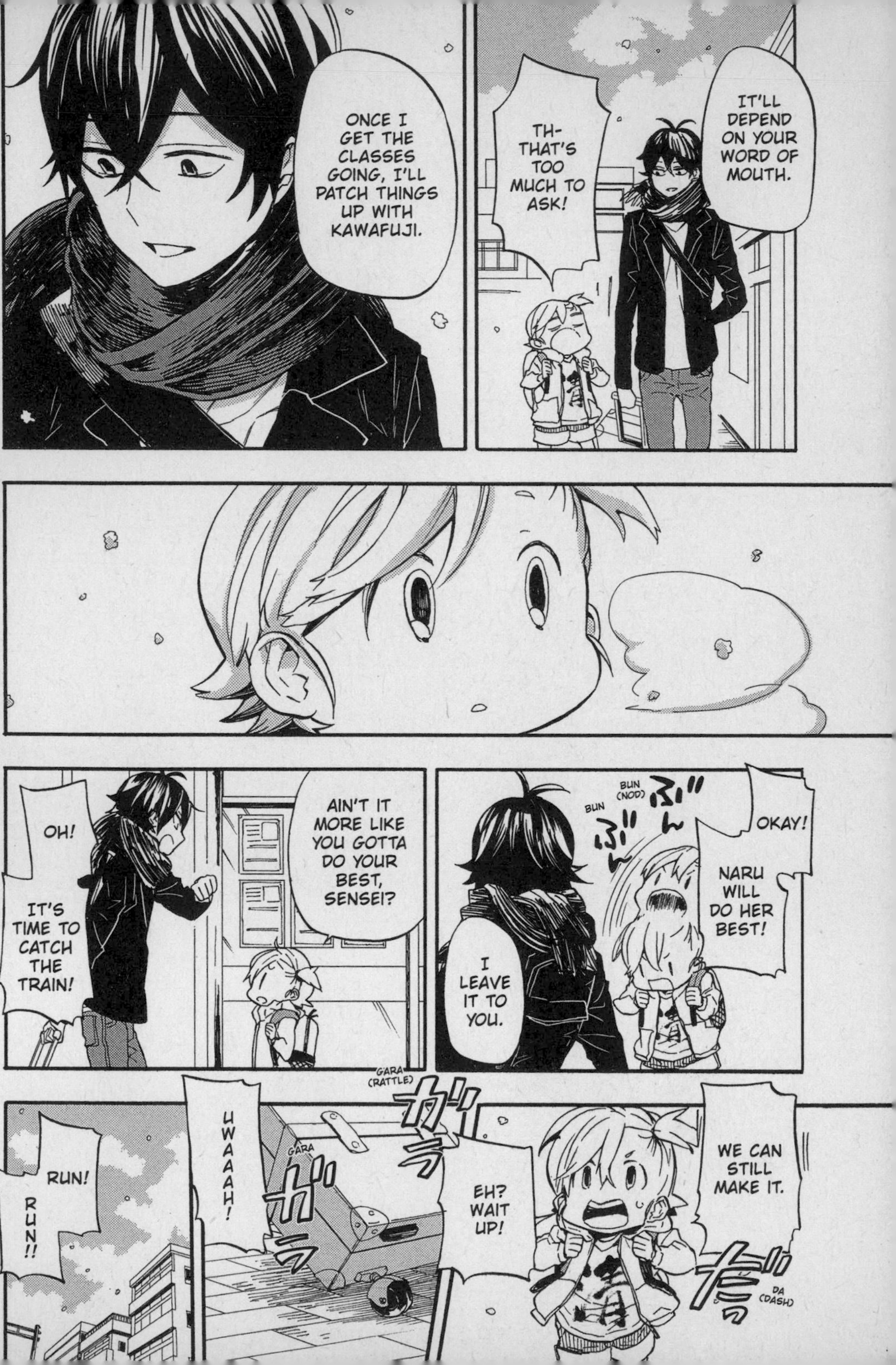
IT'LL DEPEND ON YOUR WORD OF MOUTH.
TH-THAT'S TOO MUCH TO ASK!
ONCE I GET THE CLASSES GOING, I'LL PATCH THINGS UP WITH KAWAFUJI.
BUN (NOD)
BUN
OKAY!
NARU WILL DO HER BEST!
I LEAVE IT TO YOU.
AIN'T IT MORE LIKE YOU GOTTA DO YOUR BEST, SENSEI?
OH!
IT'S TIME TO CATCH THE TRAIN!
WE CAN STILL MAKE IT.
DA (DASH)
EH? WAIT UP!
GARA (RATTLE)
UWAAAAH!
GARA
RUN!
RUN!!

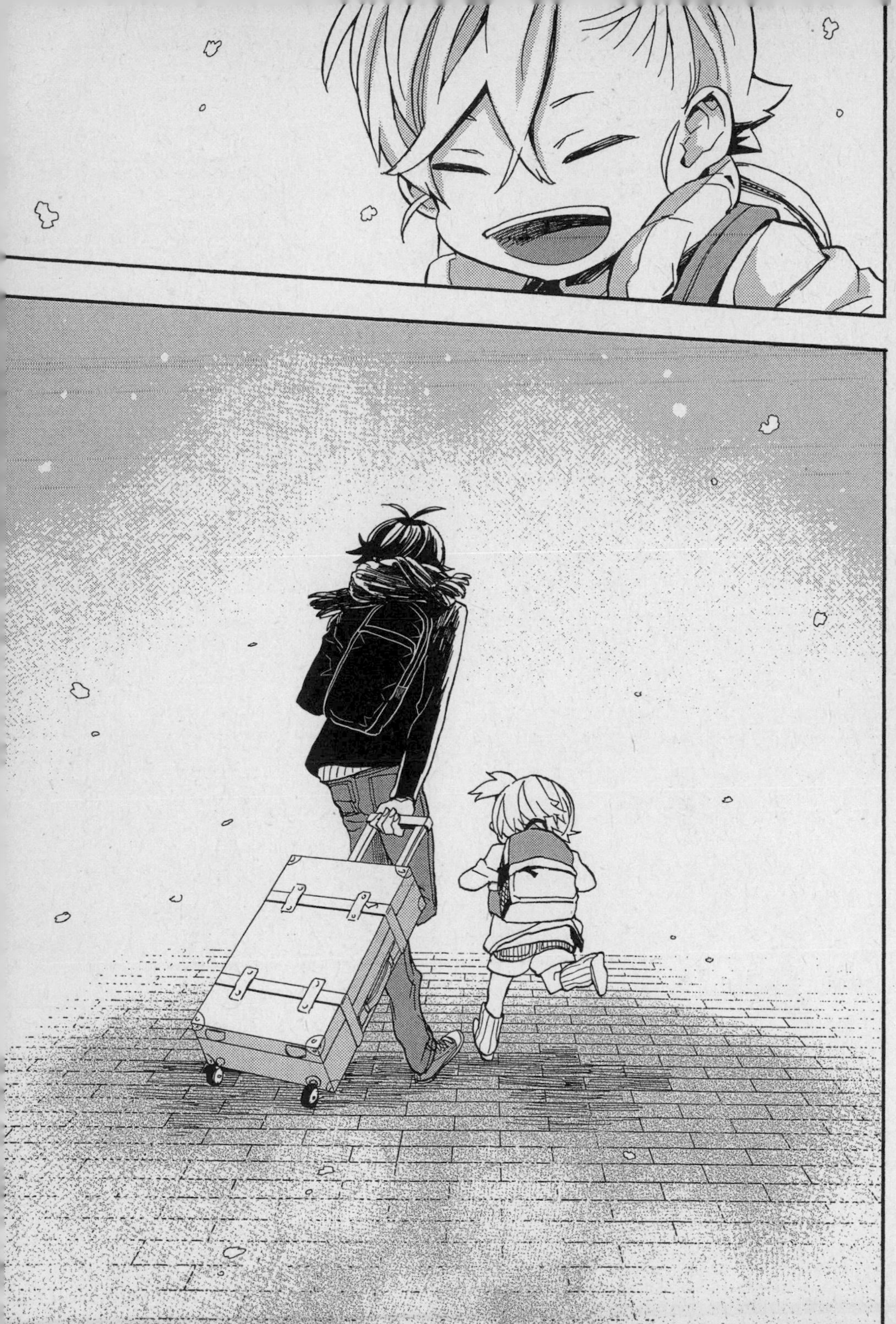

TO BE CONTINUED IN BARAKAMON 14

BARAKAMON

BONUS: DANPO THE 13TH

(Translation: Pond)

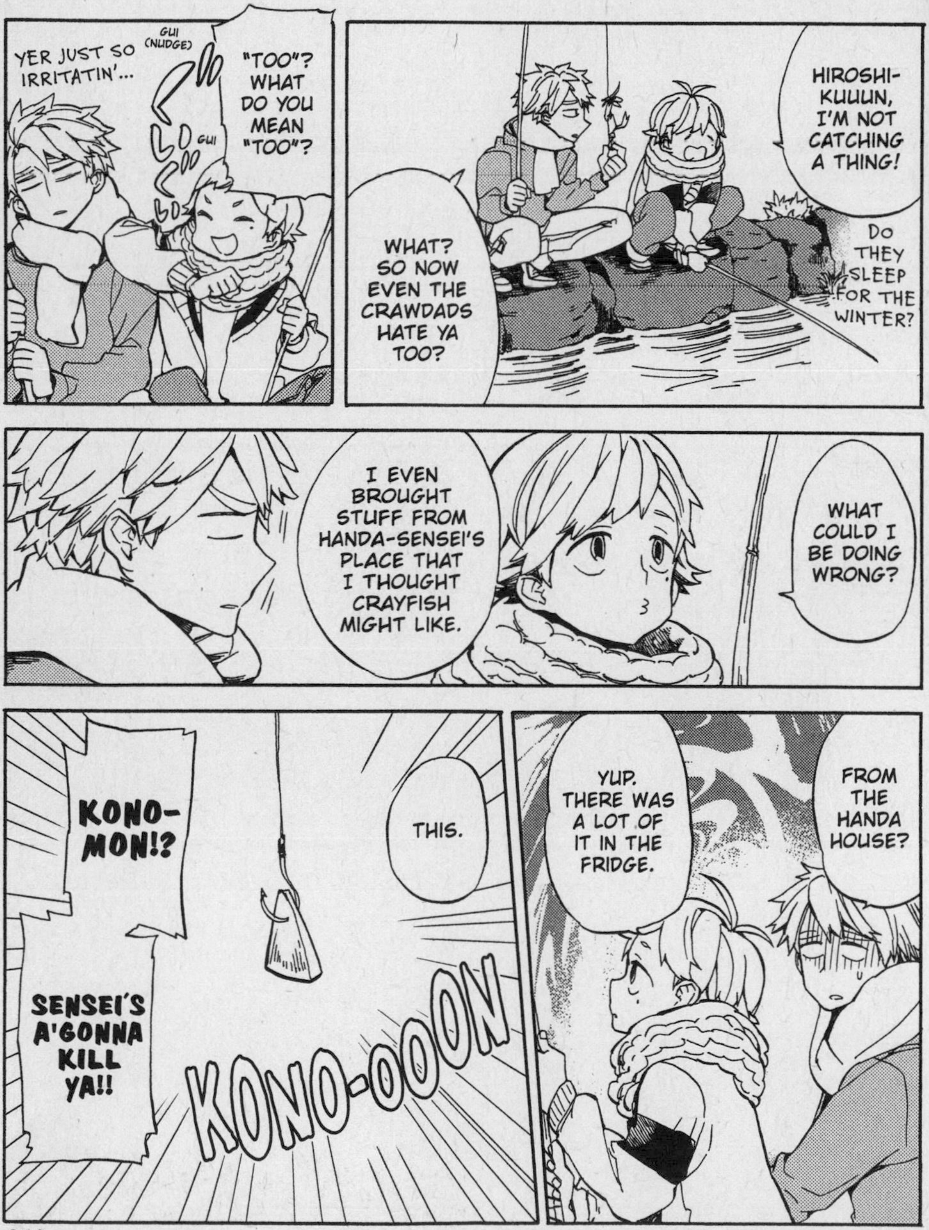

HIROSHI-KUUUN, I'M NOT CATCHING A THING!
DO THEY SLEEP FOR THE WINTER?
WHAT? SO NOW EVEN THE CRAWDADS HATE YA TOO?
"TOO"? WHAT DO YOU MEAN "TOO"?
GUI (NUDGE)
YER JUST SO IRRITATIN'...
GUI
WHAT COULD I BE DOING WRONG?
I EVEN BROUGHT STUFF FROM HANDA-SENSEI'S PLACE THAT I THOUGHT CRAYFISH MIGHT LIKE.
FROM THE HANDA HOUSE?
YUP. THERE WAS A LOT OF IT IN THE FRIDGE.
THIS.
KONO-MON!?
KONO-OOON
SENSEI'S A'GONNA KILL YA!!

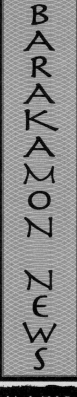

BARAKAMON NEWS

Vol.510

Chapter 100 Thank You! A Huge Gratitude Festival for Barakamon Is Now Underway!!

Everyone, thank you very much for buying Volume 13 of *BARAKAMON*! In this volume, *BARAKAMON* has finally reached chapter 100—my, how time does fly! Again, this was all thanks to your support! For the sake of this day, we began holding a variety of campaigns several months ago—please enjoy our recounting of them!

"I want to see X!" Illustration Campaign

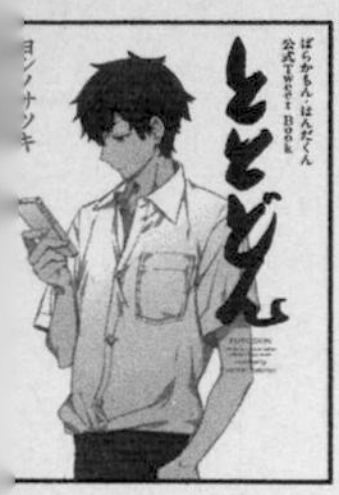
ととどん
ヨシノサツキ

TOTODON
Barakamon & Handa-kun
Official Tweet Book
Size B6/Price: ¥917 (+tax)

From December 21 to 25, 2015, we held a campaign where people could ask Yoshino-sensei via Twitter for particular illustration themes! More than 2,000 different requests came in, ranging from easy to odd! Even Yoshino-sensei winced at "Yasubazooka"!? And how did the 35 chosen requests turn out...? Find out in *TOTODON*, now on sale to popular acclaim! You could also view the event illustrations by checking back through the timeline of the official Twitter account!

Character General Elections and Q&A for Yoshino-sensei!

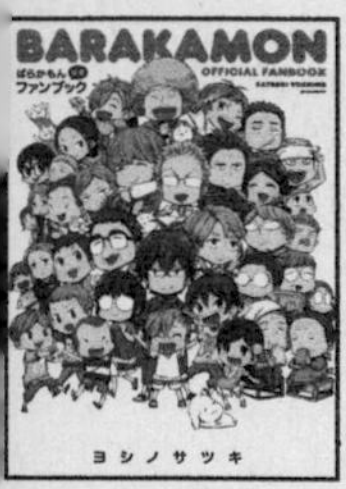
BARAKAMON
OFFICIAL FANBOOK
ばらかもん ファンブック
ヨシノサツキ

BARAKAMON
Official Fanbook
Size B6/Price: ¥857 (+tax)

BARAKAMON's first character popularity poll ran from Dec. 2015 to Jan. 2016! We received an unbelievable 9,421 entries! And how did the rankings turn out...? View the results in the *BARAKAMON Official Fanbook*, now on sale to popular acclaim! You'll also find answers to questions for Yoshino-sensei that were solicited at that same time, as well as a comic specially drawn in connection with the election: "Handa-san - A Convenience-Store Worker's Afternoon"!

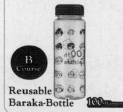

Please note that the items on this page were only available in Japan.

We're Grateful For Your Support! A Gift Lottery, With Love to All the Fans!

In gratitude to all of you who've supported *BARAKAMON* over 100 chapters, we have prepared a gift campaign! A set of no-longer-available merchandise, a reusable bottle specially designed for this campaign, different-color reprints of T-shirts that Yoshino-sensei personally paid to be made for the anime staff—these are all premium goods any fan would drool over! For detailed application instructions and other information, check the obi that came with this volume!

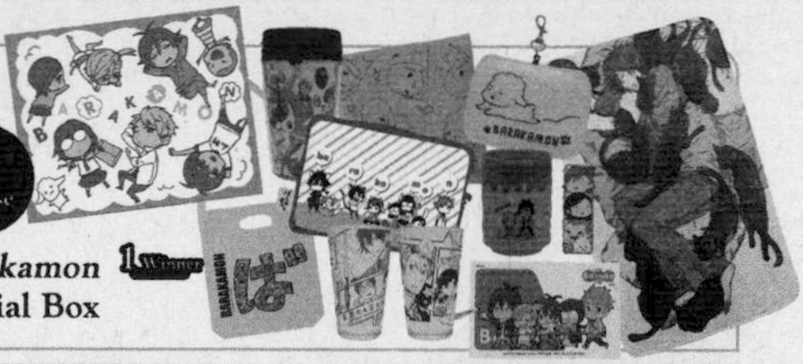

A Course
Barakamon Special Box 1 Winner

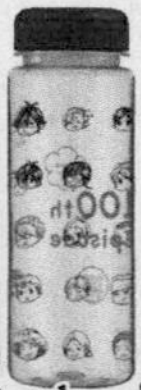

B Course
Reusable Baraka-Bottle 100 Winners

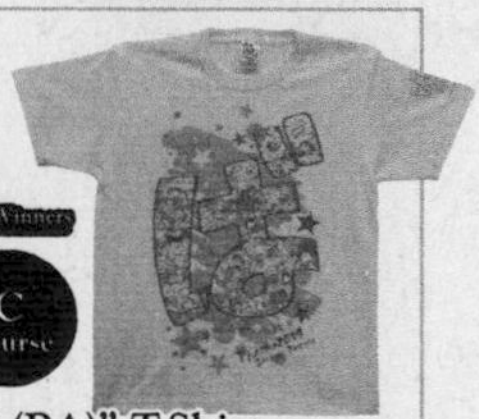

C Course
"ば (BA)" T-Shirt 50 Winners

Application Deadline: valid if postmarked by Tues., April 12th, 2016

BARAKAMON reached a major turning point in chapter 100. We'd be happy if we continue to have your undying support. May we meet again next time, in Volume 14!

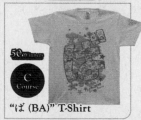

The story heads to a new stage....!

BARAKAMON
Volume 14
by Satsuki Yoshino

Coming in 2017!

COMMON HONORIFICS

no honorific: Indicates familiarity or closeness; if used without permission or reason, addressing someone in this manner would constitute an insult.

-san: The Japanese equivalent of Mr./Mrs./Miss. If a situation calls for politeness, this is the fail-safe honorific.

-sama: Conveys great respect; may also indicate that the social status of the speaker is lower than that of the addressee.

-kun: Used most often when referring to boys, this indicates affection or familiarity. Occasionally used by older men among their peers, but it may also be used by anyone referring to a person of lower standing.

-chan: An affectionate honorific indicating familiarity used mostly in reference to girls; also used in reference to cute persons or animals of either gender.

-sensei: A Japanese term of respect commonly used for teachers, but can also refer to doctors, writers, and artists. Hence, Village Chief is not implying that Handa is a teacher when he calls him "*sensei*."

Calligraphy: Japanese calligraphy has a long history and tradition, with roots stemming from ancient China. One of the traditions carried over was the Chinese expression of the "Four Treasures," which refers to the brush, ink, paper, and inkstone used in calligraphy. Traditionally, an inkstick—solidified ink—is ground against an inkstone filled with water in order to produce ink with which to write. This time-consuming process helped to teach patience, which is important in the art of calligraphy. However, modern advances have developed a bottled liquid ink, commonly used by beginners and within the Japanese school system.

Gotou Dialect: Many of the villagers, especially the elderly ones, are actually speaking the local Gotou dialect in the original Japanese. This dialect is reflected in the English translation with some of the grammar elements of older Southern American English to give it a more rustic, rural coastal feel without making it too hard to read (it's not meant to replicate any particular American accent exactly). This approach is similar to how dialect is made accessible in Japanese media, including *Barakamon*, because a complete dialect with all of its different vocabulary would be practically incomprehensible to most Tokyo residents.

PAGE 8
kidster: The word Kousuke used for Naru was "*gakincho*," a variant of "*gaki*" (kid) that has gained some popularity due to the TV drama series *Gakincho ~Return Kids~*.

PAGE 16
Rotten Sea: This is an actual place! It's a large system of shallow lagoons on the west coast of the Sea of Azov in Crimea.

PAGE 26
suica: A rechargeable RFID smart-card payment system for use on public transportation in the Tokyo and Kanto area, which can also be used to make purchases at some stores and drink machines.

PAGE 32
black rotary phone: As mentioned in volume 4, "*kurodenwa*" (black phone) specifically refers to the standard phone models first provided by the Japanese Communications Ministry during the expansion of telephone access in the 1950s but is often used to refer to rotary-dial phones in general.

PAGE 36
Jou/Ojou: The kanji for Jou's given name, 譲 (deference), looks very similar to the soundalike kanji "*jou*" 嬢 used in "*ojou-sama*," a term of respect for daughters, especially ones from high-class families. Her nickname, Ojou, is a short version of that term of respect, using the kanji that isn't her actual name.

PAGE 39
Jou's color words: We were able to use literal translations of her highly-specific words, with one exception on this page: "cocoa" was originally *momoshiocha*, which roughly means "tea steeped a hundred times." It's a dark reddish-brown that's very close to the color of cocoa, so we used that, especially since both words refer to something you eat or drink.

PAGE 51
Coming of Age Day is an official Japanese holiday on the second Monday of January, when communities hold ceremonies as a rite of passage for young people who've recently turned 20, the age when a person is considered an adult in Japan. Women generally dress up for the ceremony in a very elaborate kimonos, like the one Jou was wearing in her photograph.

PAGE 60
monkeys, wild boars, tanukis: These are animals that can be found living wild in Japan. Another name for tanuki is "raccoon dog," since they resemble raccoons but are more closely related to dogs.

PAGE 61
New Year's money: Naru might not get Christmas presents from her grampa, but she does get a gift of cash for New Year's Day, which is the more traditional family holiday celebrated in Japan.

PAGE 63
"The zoo!": Though the name isn't specified, the zoo they're visiting is Tokyo's Ueno Zoo, which is Japan's oldest zoo and was established in 1882. It's the only place in Tokyo to see giant pandas and one of only three such places in Japan!

PAGE 67
A *tsuchinoko* is a Japanese snakelike cryptid, which people draw pretty much as shown in the panel. Since they don't actually exist, in Japanese, Ojou says the zoo does have a *tsuchibuta*, or aardvark, which we get to see on page 82. Since there aren't any animal names in English that sound similar enough to "*tsuchinoko*," we substituted the large snake anaconda.

PAGE 81
motionless shoebill: Ueno Zoo does have shoebill storks in the West Garden. These birds are known for moving slowly and remaining still for long periods of time, so they're often described as "statue-like"—it's how they can sneak up on prey before making a rapid catch!

PAGE 93
sal-mander, gymnas-um: Naru was dropping syllables in the Japanese words "*sansho[u]uo*" (salamander) and "*tai[i]kukan*" (gymnasium). The English words don't have the repeated vowels that the Japanese do, but at least they're long enough so the joke still works.

PAGE 95
A walking dog (will hit a pole): Japanese proverb meaning that you'll hit upon some opportunity if you get moving, even if you don't have a clear goal or direction in mind or aren't paying attention. The result could be good fortune, or it could be disaster...

PAGE 100
ranklin': The original Japanese word was "*yazeka*," dialect for "annoying."

PAGE 101
Hiroki Matsukata is a Japanese actor born in 1942 who's played tough-guy roles in many historical and gangster films, notably *Battles Without Honor or Humanity*

department store basement: The basement floor of a Japanese department store is like a fancy grocery store, where you'll find a variety of food items for sale, with some of the sellers offering samples.

PAGE 102
dosukoi: A spirited yell used in sumo wrestling.

PAGE 103
Tama's muttering a variety of **Boy's Love terms**. "Reversi,""*riba*" in Japanese, is a male couple that switches up the roles they take during sex, instead of having a consistent "top" and "bottom." An "ultimate bottom" is someone who'll pair with any of the other male characters.

PAGE 119
racing sash: For marathon relay races in Japan, called "*ekiden*," the runners pass a sash to the next team member instead of a baton. This leave the hands free during the bulk of the run.

This race, featuring a certain guy named Higashino, is most likely meant to be the All-Japan Men's Corporate Team Ekiden Championships, also known as the "New Year's Ekiden" since it's held every year on January 1st. It features teams of seven runners covering a total of 100 kilometers in Gunma Prefecture and gets high viewership numbers for its broadcasts on Tokyo Broadcasting System (TBS) Television.

The original Japanese only had the use of a racing sash as a definite clue that this is a long-distance relay race, but that's enough for Japanese readers. That D. Higashino certainly has grown as a person since his high-school sprinting days!

PAGE 123
Katou and Bitou: These somewhat-common Japanese names are used for puns of misunderstanding when describing how much sugar people put in their coffee. "*Katou*" = "adds sugar," while "*bitou*" = "low sugar." ("*Mutou*," a.k.a. "no sugar," must have been on another assignment that day...)

PAGE 131
Beauties of Nature: The four-kanji compound "花鳥風月" (*ka chou fuu getsu*) literally means, "flower bird wind moon" and refers to the Japanese aesthetic of nature themes.

PAGE 167
streaking: "*Kasure*" is a lesser-known calligraphy term for strokes that have streaks of white showing through instead of being solid ink-color, produced by using a relatively dry brush.

SATSUKI YOSHINO

WITHDRAWN

Translation/Adaptation: Krista Shipley, Karie Shipley
Lettering: Lys Blakeslee

Barakamon Vol. 13 © 2016 Satsuki Yoshino SQUARE ENIX CO., LTD. First
published in Japan in 2016 by SQUARE ENIX CO., LTD. English translation
rights arranged with SQUARE ENIX CO., LTD. and Yen Press, LLC through
Tuttle-Mori Agency, Inc.

English translation © 2017 by SQUARE ENIX CO., LTD.

Yen Press
1290 Avenue of the Americas
New York, NY 10104

Visit us at yenpress.com
facebook.com/yenpress
twitter.com/yenpress
yenpress.tumblr.com
instagram.com/yenpress

First Yen Press Edition: March 2017

Yen Press is an imprint of Yen Press, LLC.
The Yen Press name and logo are trademarks of Yen Press, LLC.

Library of Congress Control Number: 2015296448

ISBNs: 978-0-316-55313-1 (paperback)
       978-0-316-43985-5 (ebook)

10 9 8 7 6 5 4 3 2 1

BVG

Printed in the United States of America